The Historical Roots of Human Trafficking

Makini Chisolm-Straker • Katherine Chon
Editors

The Historical Roots of Human Trafficking

Informing Primary Prevention
of Commercialized Violence

Forewords by Joshua M. Sharfstein and Ruth J. Simmons

 Springer

Editors
Makini Chisolm-Straker
Institute for Health Equity Research
Department of Emergency Medicine
Icahn School of Medicine at Mount Sinai
New York, NY
USA

Katherine Chon
Center for the Study of Slavery and Justice
Brown University
Providence, RI
USA

ISBN 978-3-030-70677-7   ISBN 978-3-030-70675-3   (eBook)
https://doi.org/10.1007/978-3-030-70675-3

This Springer imprint is published by the registered company Springer Nature Switzerland AG
The registered company address is: Gewerbestrasse 11, 6330 Cham, Switzerland

Kat:

To the lifelong learners across generations of truth seekers and truth tellers, and to the current moment that challenges us all to confront the lasting legacies of historical injustices. Thank you to Bradley, Kum Hee, Michael, Sandy, Steve, and the community with us on this exploration.

Makini:

This is for Meme, William, Kuhpây, Oliver, Dylan, Matahquhs, Tao-Baby, Miró, Matilda Alev, Tori, Makini Gianna, Ahsun, and all my niblings. Even more so, this is for the seventh generation coming, because I am your ancestor.

Foreword by Joshua M. Sharfstein

Human trafficking is a profound violation of human rights, a reflection of deep prejudice, racism, and inequality, and the source of immense injustice and suffering. Human trafficking is, in a word, so evil that many seek to counter this practice without understanding it, to demand its end without appreciating its origins. It is more challenging to see trafficking as a complex global public health threat that continues to deny millions of people the opportunity, in the words of the World Health Organization, to achieve the "highest attainable standard of health;" WHO defines health as the "state of complete physical, mental and social well-being and not merely the absence of disease or infirmity."[1] Public health challenges must be examined and understood, dissected and demystified. The process is worth the effort. At the core of public health is the principle of primary prevention: Best to keep something terrible from happening in the first place.

Preventing violence reduces suffering and death directly, and spares families and communities from cycles of pain and trauma. A growing body of evidence supports actions, informed by data, at the individual, interpersonal, community, and societal levels. At the individual level, successful prevention programs involve building resilience, countering bias, promoting educational success, and assuring access to health services. An example of individual-level prevention program is the Good Behavior Game, a program implemented in grade school to reduce disruptive behavior in class. This intervention has been associated with lower rates of violence as well as suicidal ideation.[2] At the interpersonal level, prevention strategies include teaching nonviolent resolution of conflict, providing economic and social support for families, and identifying ways to ease longstanding friction between members of different social, racial, ethnic, and religious groups. For example, the anti-violence program Cure Violence uses trusted community messengers to resolve disputes that

---

[1] World Health Organization. Constitution. https://www.who.int/about/who-we-are/constitution. Accessed May 25, 2020.

[2] Kellam SG, Mackenzie AC, Brown CH, et al. The good behavior game and the future of prevention and treatment. *Addict Sci Clin Pract*. 2011;6(1):73–84.

may lead to violence, and has reduced shootings and homicides.[3] At the community level, prevention efforts involve empowering collective action, reducing concentrated poverty, and abating environmental hazards. In Kampala, Uganda, for example, social mobilization efforts have led to dramatically lower social acceptance of intimate partner violence (IPV), as well as much less reported IPV itself.[4] At the societal level, prevention demands undoing violent cultural norms, putting in place laws—backed by evidence—to reduce violence, recognizing and undoing racist policies that reinforce cycles of deprivation, and creating broad opportunities for individuals, families, and communities to thrive. While these efforts remain aspirational in many areas, a growing body of evidence supports the value of specific policies, including responsible gun regulation,[5] alcohol taxes,[6] and restorative justice.[7]

This work does not occur in a vacuum. Ongoing racism and xenophobia can affect perceptions of a problem and limit support for meaningful solutions. When progress stalls, it is common for frustration and fatigue to set in and for attention to shift elsewhere. A poisonous barrier is the attitude that these problems will inevitably persist long into the future.

The antidote is understanding. To counter this ancient and modern public health scourge, we must shine a bright light on the facts about human trafficking. We must study variations of this practice and its evolution from hundreds of years ago until today. We must expose its social and economic origins to develop more fundamental solutions. And we must fully engage government and society to obtain an irreversible commitment to progress.

This textbook is a critical contribution to this effort.

Joshua M. Sharfstein
Vice Dean, Public Health Practice and Community
Engagement, Johns Hopkins University
Baltimore, MD, USA

---

[3] Jeffrey A. Butts, Caterina Gouvis Roman, Lindsay Bostwick, Jeremy R. Porter. Cure Violence: A Public Health Model to Reduce Gun Violence. Annual Review of Public Health. 2015;36:1, 39–53.

[4] Abramsky, T, Devries, K, Kiss, L. Findings from the SASA! Study: a cluster randomized controlled trial to assess the impact of a community mobilization intervention to prevent violence against women and reduce HIV risk in Kampala, Uganda. BMC Med. 2014;12:122.

[5] Crifasi CK, Merrill-Francis M, McCourt A, Vernick JS, Wintemute GJ, Webster DW. Association between Firearm Laws and Homicide in Urban Counties [published correction appears in J Urban Health. 2018 Oct;95(5):773–776]. *J Urban Health*. 2018;95(3):383–390. https://doi.org/10.1007/s11524-018-0273-3

[6] Page N, Sivarajasingam V, Matthews K, Heravi S, Morgan P, Shepherd J. Preventing violence-related injuries in England and Wales: a panel study examining the impact of on-trade and off-trade alcohol prices. *Inj Prev*. 2017;23(1):33–39. https://doi.org/10.1136/injuryprev-2015-041884

[7] Mills LG, Barocas B, Butters RP, Ariel B. A randomized controlled trial of restorative justice-informed treatment for domestic violence crimes [published correction appears in Nat Hum Behav. 2019 Oct 1]. *Nat Hum Behav*. 2019;3(12):1284–1294. https://doi.org/10.1038/s41562-019-0724-1

Foreword by Ruth J. Simmons

The history of human trafficking in all its facets is long, complex, and in many ways, perplexing. In fact, the very term "trafficking," applied to the multifarious aspects of these particular crimes against humanity, is a short-hand representation for an immensely diverse set of activities spread across history, regions, peoples, and purposes. Unifying such a diversity of inhumane activities under one rubric should place in stark relief the reality that as human beings we share an urgent task: that of improving, over time, our understanding of what it means to be human.

The impulse and effort to exploit, abuse, and subjugate others to benefit the wealth and ascendancy of individuals and groups has been chronicled richly across world histories and literature. As more people learn about trafficking, there is an increasing concern about the importance of understanding the types and extent of human trafficking; there is also increased growing in identifying the ways in which trafficking can ultimately be thwarted, and people's agency and full rights established or restored. Thankfully, at this point in the evolution of our understanding of these crimes, we have begun to apprehend the extensive public health consequences of turning a blind eye to the problem.

The public health perspective is especially timely. Modern society's health rests on the willingness and capacity of policymakers, enforcement agencies, nonprofit institutions, and social service agencies to educate the public about labor and sex trafficking; design the proper policies to regulate behavior in this arena; interdict inhumane behavior; and support the survivors of exploitation and abuse. To carry out such tasks and marshal resources to effect equity is an opportunity that must not be squandered. It is easy to be cavalier about and, thus, ineffective in addressing human trafficking, by only ingesting convenient snippets of causes. It is important to act based upon the complete and complex truth.

This textbook is based on the importance of understanding trafficking at its deep roots.

When I began my presidency at Brown University in 2001, I asked officials there whether it was true that founders of the University had been intimately involved in and profited from slavery. The answer I received from some was reassuring and comfortable: "There is no connection between slavery and the founding of the

University." This assertion was made easier by the fact that slavery had been all but erased from official accounts of the University's history. Still, I commissioned a group to examine the history of the founders' activities in this domain. I was struck to learn that many of the Brown Corporation's founding members invested in, trafficked in, and owned slaves. The clarity of the evidence was incontestable and therefore liberating: once we learned the facts of our history, we were able to move beyond speculating about the behavior of colonial forbearers. Knowledge of historical fact empowered the University to ask the supremely relevant question: What are we obligated to do today to cease the perpetuation of similar crimes against humanity?

We quickly realized the importance of understanding and then teaching the more complete history of slavery. The Brown University Center for Slavery and Justice was created for this purpose. Through the support of historical research on trafficking, exhibitions, partnerships around the world, and teaching, the Center plays a role in casting light on the reality and injustice of slavery. Due to the Center's efforts and those of the study that led to the Center's creation, The Brown Project on Slavery and Justice led scores of other institutions to examine their own histories and relationships to slavery as well as their current policies and actions. Uncovering our own history with slavery, Brown leads the global examination of how to use the lessons of history to face and address the persistent threat of human exploitation.

This textbook will be a valuable resource to those who seek a more nuanced and complex view on the issue of human trafficking: beyond a legal definition and description of trafficking's various manifestations, this textbook discusses trafficking's evolution over time, and the economic and social forces that drive its centuries-long persistence and growth. It also reveals the legal framework that now empowers policymakers to track and avert specific practices. The chapter authors emphasize the importance of the historical context in discerning how to address modern forms of trafficking. They also stress socioeconomic factors that suppress the willingness of some to acknowledge the pervasiveness of trafficking and its impact on the lives of ordinary people. That ordinary people (often unwittingly) perpetuate the trafficking of others is also revealed in their analysis.

Challenging the legacy of slavery in all its forms, the chapter authors bring to light the dangers of establishing a hierarchy of victims and crimes. They expose the commonplace aspects of trafficking that go beyond high-profile trafficking such as chattel slavery and sensationalized sex trafficking. In focusing on the fundamental principles of how, in our evolved state as a species, we should treat fellow human beings, the chapter authors offer useful guidance on how to avert a range of exploitative behavior.

At Brown University, we purposefully focused on the larger question of justice. In considering the continuing problem of human trafficking, we can examine this issue in ways that allow us to grasp more fully how to bring justice to bear when anyone is harmed by unfair treatment. In a just society, citizens will care about establishing an ideal and vigorous process of justice that will protect all members from exploitation and abuse. Further, a deep understanding of tarnished and ugly but complete historical truths is essential to advancing these basic human rights.

Ruth J. Simmons
President, Prairie View A&M University
Prairie View, TX, USA

Preface

Since the Trafficking Victims Protection Act was first passed in 2000, increasingly, labor and sex trafficking have been recognized as a travesty, a crime, and a public health problem. Thinking of trafficking as a travesty leaves people shaking their heads, at seemingly isolated cases, and pitying the "victims." Some may be shocked into short-term actions; most do not consider sustainable and revolutionary change as the solution. Treating trafficking as strictly a crime perpetuates the fallacy that prosecution and imprisonment alone will bring justice and prevent further harm. Understanding trafficking as a public health problem offers the opportunity to recognize the complexity of the impacts of trafficking. This lens encourages us to see and address the truth that human trafficking is not an isolated act, but is reinforced by inequitable systems: Both labor and sexual exploitation have been a common occurrence for centuries—normalized and woven into the economic and social fabric of the United States. Recognizing the historical nature of both forms of exploitation in the United States, we have the ability to, in true public health form, meaningfully address and rectify root causes of present-day labor and sex trafficking.

As labor and sex trafficking are being more commonly seen as a public health problem, much of the anti-trafficking work has focused on secondary and tertiary interventions. Secondary interventions occur when trafficking is recognized early and interrupted before there are "major" health, social, or other negative outcomes. Secondary interventions support the separation of a person from the trafficking situation and aim to alleviate short-term ills. Tertiary interventions occur when trafficking is recognized but harms have already occurred. Tertiary interventions aim to remedy the problem at the individual level by, for example, prosecuting the responsible parties and offering relevant support services to those directly wronged. Primary interventions are, admittedly, harder to achieve.

Primary intervention anti-trafficking work thus far has focused on "awareness raising campaigns," prevention education, and efforts to define populations at higher risk for experiencing human trafficking. Stand-alone awareness raising campaigns are largely ineffectual at preventing trafficking. More savvy researchers have also examined protective factors against being trafficked. Unsurprisingly, groups of people who are marginalized and disproportionately experience other ills are suspected to be more vulnerable to being trafficked or are overly represented among those recognized to have a trafficking experience. They are people of color; people living in poverty; people who have survived childhood traumas like sexual or physical abuse, or neglect; lesbians, gays, and bisexuals; people with a transgender life experience or who are gender nonconforming; people who are undereducated or underemployed; people with substance use disorders; people who have been displaced; and so on. Often, people who are trafficked belong to more than one of these groups, with intersecting identities and experiences of oppression and trauma compounding their vulnerability to exploitation.

Still, successful primary prevention does not mean identifying which *types* of people are more likely to be trafficked. Primary prevention means eliminating trafficking altogether. The only way to do that is to remove vulnerability and expand protective factors. This means asking *why* these groups are vulnerable, and asking which systems and cycles create and nurture these vulnerabilities (Chap. 17). This also means investing in equitable resources to build the capacity of individuals, families, and communities to have meaningful social, economic, and political capital. Regardless of intention, who benefits from and contributes to the vulnerability? Primary prevention means answering these questions honestly. In the words of Rabbi Maimonides, we must "accept the truth from whatever source it proceeds" and wherever it leads (Jaraczewski 1912).

Rigorous and reproducible research is an important source of data that can help answer some of these questions. A thorough and honest examination of history offers even more clarity. History illuminates the often convoluted and opaque "systems" that are blamed for trafficking. W.E.B. Dubois said, "A system cannot fail those it was never meant to protect." These systems were purposefully created, supported, and maintained to conserve power and privilege in the hands of a select few. The systems are not failing, they are working. In the now-called United States, such systems were never intended to primarily protect or benefit those we presently recognize as disproportionately impacted by trafficking at the population level.

This textbook was originally intended for an anti-trafficking audience. But trafficking is merely a symptom of the ism-schisms at the core of this nation, so this book is relevant to so many more learners, academicians, and global citizens. Figure 1, "Contextualizing the health impacts of exploitation," is a heuristic, or conceptual framework. It explains the relationship of the systems and ideologies that created and nurture trafficking and related exploitations as we recognize them today. Figure 1, developed with graphic designer Maggie Breslin, helps frame trafficking as a symptom of many interlinked distal and contextual determinants of trafficking. The above-water tip of the proverbial iceberg is what we can see: the morbidity, fertility, and mortality impacts of exploitation across the life course; this is where much of the anti-trafficking public health work has been focused since 2016. But the vast majority of the iceberg is underwater, and has solidified over generations. There is much more that we can and must do.

The factors beneath the surface created and nurture the environment in which human trafficking, by many names, has been thriving for centuries. Where chapter authors refer to "today," "currently," "now," "still," "at the time of this writing," and

Fig. 1 Contextualizing the health impacts of exploitation

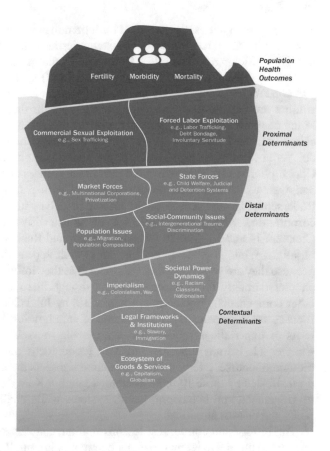

so on, they refer to 2020; the first full year of the COVID-19 pandemic. The chapters' content was not an "escape" for authors; it was more relevant than ever, as precarity of historically vulnerable populations increased. As the facts of COVID-19 morbidity and mortality disparities demonstrate; as the discussions and demands of the 2020 racial justice protestors highlight; as many have said, in some way, for centuries: The distal and contextual determinants of trafficking, such as capitalism, racism, and imperialism, are the strongest "push-pull factors" of trafficking and *all the US inequities* called out during the COVID-19 pandemic. This textbook is intended to help the anti-trafficking movement appreciate that tertiary and secondary prevention alone is insufficient for success.

That is "whack-a-mole" work; trafficking is a symptom of broader societal problems. Primary prevention work will entail anti-racism work, anti-xenophobia work, and anti-sexism work. These are not commonly recognized as anti-trafficking work and they are inadequately funded by anti-trafficking donors and funders, but these kinds of work focus on the structures that undergird and enable labor and sex trafficking. In a society in which race or ethnicity does not predict morbidity and mortality, in a society in which gender identity and expression do not foretell financial security, in a society in which each person has meaningful opportunities to thrive, trafficking need not exist. Historical truth demonstrates that change is possible and how; historical truth offers tools to dismantle the scaffolding that braces up labor and sex trafficking, and rebuild a United States that is just and equitable.

This textbook is a primer: We cannot share and explain all of the relevant history that contributes to present-day inequities like labor and sex trafficking. The chapter authors are experienced and recognized experts in their field and content areas. Many chapters will address multiple, overlapping distal and contextual determinant elements of the conceptual framework; for example, Chapter 2 by Gonzalo Martínez de Vedia discusses capitalism, imperialism, and colonialism. Chapter 5 by Christopher Muller-Tabanera and Beisi Huang focuses on the effects of imperialism and war, which are often deeply entangled with patriarchy. Chapter 7 by Jean Baderschneider and Alison Kiehl Friedman delves into globalism, multinational corporations, and privatization, all of which drive capitalist economies. In Chapters 14 and 15, Makini Chisolm-Straker and Rueben C. Warren, respectively, highlight White supremacy and racism (which appear throughout many chapters because they are so pervasive in US society) as they influence US health care. Other chapters strongly focus on one element, though there are clear intersections with other components. For example, Chapter 10, by John Cheng and Kimberly Chang, focuses on the contextual determinant of immigration policies, recognizing the roots of imperialism, racism, and xenophobia in exclusionary US legislation. In Chapter 11, Erin Williamson and Aria Flood focus on child welfare systems—though, of course, intergenerational trauma transects the experiences of many children affected by these systems. Chapter 13 author Kate Keisel examines the history of US mental and behavioral health systems while challenging their historically racist and classist structures.

The history and consequent lessons that the chapter authors share are meant to encourage the active learner to engage in more digging. Readers should dig into the reference sections and keep reading. Readers should listen to the elders in various communities, who hold story in their memory. Readers must challenge the extant paradigm, often based on incomplete truths at best, and understand the historical events, actions, and efforts that have led to today's trafficking and disparities. Readers must transmit these learnings into active community dialogue to compel transparency and accountability. Truth-telling is a revolution's *beginning*; this book is filled with historical truths.

The Sankofa Adinkra at the beginning of this textbook, drawn by artist Quyên Trương, JD, is a reminder that historical truths can propel us forward. *Sankofa*, from the Ghanaian Twi language, means "go back and get it." It can also refer to the Bono people's Adinkra symbol of the bird facing backward, reaching for the egg; the bird's feet are moving forward. Here, Sankofa is associated with the proverb, "It is not wrong to go back for that which you have forgotten." To move forward, anti-trafficking workers must fully and finally face the ugly, multi-faceted past. Anti-trafficking activists committed to a world free of exploitation must commit to understanding centuries-old, purposefully created structures, institutions, and traumas. Trafficking abolitionists must recognize anti-racism work, anti-poverty work, and anti-patriarchy work as foundational anti-trafficking work.

If US-based anti-trafficking workers are ignorant of history (full history), if anti-trafficking fighters do not conceive of trafficking as a consequence of imperialism, settler-colonialism, White supremacy and institutionalized racism, patriarchy, and capitalist ideals, "anti-trafficking" is merely a title describing actions that will amount to nothing much. If those occupying this field do not understand the centuries of history that created and continue to facilitate trafficking, they will fail to understand trafficking as *a symptom*. Human trafficking is not the full problem; it cannot be "fixed" without fixing the "upstream determinants." The full problems include ignorance of foul truths, unwillingness of those with privilege and power to openly confront national and individual complicity, and a refusal to be disquieted by uncomfortable, sometimes radical change. The continuation of historical and current US hegemony has relied on White supremacy, patriarchy, and other structures of power inequity and injustice. Public health actions rooted in historical knowledge allow apparently ever-present "systems" to be known as deeply and deservedly malleable. Readers of these chapters will be confronted with violent truths. Ida B. Wells said, "The people must know, before they can act…" (Wells 1892). Only after head-on recognition of historical self can anti-trafficking and social justice workers imagine the real possibilities for collective liberation, joy, and love. Now, let us begin, toward revolution.

References

Jaraczewski. (1912). *Die Ethik des Maimonides*. In M. Maimonides, J. I. Gorfinkle, I. Tibbon, & S. ben Judah (Eds.), *The eight chapters of Maimonides on ethics: (Shemonah perakim)*. New York: Columbia University Press. https://archive.org/details/eightchaptersofm00maim/page/36/mode/2up

Wells, I. B. (1892). *Southern horrors: Lynch law in all its phases*. Retrieved on 20 November 2020. From: https://www.gutenberg.org/files/14975/14975-h/14975-h.htm

Notes About the Chapters

Parts: The chapters are organized under two parts. Part I focuses on economic systems whose historical and current market dynamics contribute to human trafficking. Part II focuses on public systems, and the legacies of government laws and policies that disproportionately impact populations at highest risk for human trafficking.

Content: The chapters are written by the chapter authors and do not necessarily reflect the ideas, ideals, values, principles, or beliefs of their employers or organizations, the textbook editors, or the publisher. That said, the chapter authors are experts in their field and the chapters reflect historical facts, however uncomfortable readers may find them.

Language: Unless specifically referencing legislation or law enforcement, the term "victim" is avoided throughout the textbook. This is to respect the agency that some survivors express about their experiences, even while in their trafficking situation; it is also to respect the survivorship it takes to live through trauma. Moreover, this reinforces the truth that the trafficking experience can be complex, and requires a more nuanced, public health framework. That said, when survivors speak about their situations, their language choices are respected.

Gender is commonly discussed within a Western framework that perpetuates a binary understanding. Gender is and always has been a spectrum of social experience. Chapter authors use gender-inclusive language when appropriate, and sometimes forgo traditional gendered pronoun use (e.g., using "they" instead of "s/he") to do so.

New York, NY, USA   Makini Chisolm-Straker
Providence, RI, USA   Katherine Chon

Acknowledgments

The generosity and ferocity of all the chapter authors is sincerely appreciated and admired. These chapters were all written during the COVID-19 pandemic, and the co-occurring national uprising around racial and ethnic disparities that people of color in the United States have faced, suffered, fought, and survived for centuries. This text is an impressive feat of all the authors working through complicated, complex, and profoundly painful circumstances. Some authors got sick, some had kin who died. This book is a labor of deep-seated love and the work produced is relevant to more than anti-trafficking scholars and workers. While each chapter can stand on its own, the chapters together illustrate the patterns and depth of how historical injustices have shaped nearly every market and system in which we participate. The chapter authors wrote this textbook to our fellow public health workers and all justice fighters, for the communities we serve and the seventh generation.

We are so grateful for a forgiving and a torchlight of a publishing editor, Janet Kim, MPH: thank you for knowing that public health needs historical context to succeed.

We thank our foreword authors Drs. Ruth Simmons and Joshua Sharfstein for their encouraging support and visions for a more equitable world through study, dialogue, and accountability.

We are indebted to artist Quyên Trương, JD and designer Maggie Breslin for sharing their gifts and time with patience and charity. Your works convey a story through a single image and organize complexity into understanding.

Kat:

Thank you to Tony Bogues, Shana Weinberg, Spencer Crew, and the faculty and external advisory board members at the Brown University Center for the Study of Slavery and Justice. My twenty-year journey in anti-trafficking work started at Brown, inspired by the leadership of President Ruth Simmons who called for a full and open exploration into the institution's history with slavery and the rigorous implementation led by Professor Jim Campbell. Thank you to Joshua Sharfstein, Faria Zaman, Michele Decker, and staff, faculty, and fellows at the Bloomberg American Health Initiative. Your personal and institutional support informed how we addressed contemporary public health priorities in the context of historical and multi-generational injustices.

Thank you to Frances Ashe-Goins, Rod Ashton, Minh Dang, Derek Ellerman, Latecia Engram, Kenya Fairley, Tina Frundt, Naomi Goldstein, Mark Greenberg, Carolyn Hightower, Ruth Leemis, Jim Macrae, Rochelle Rollins, Michelle Sauve, Jane Segebrecht, Adrienne Smith, and Carlis Williams. I carry forward what I have learned from you. Thank you to my life partner Brad and my family for providing bunker space, uninterrupted time, and encouragement in its many forms. And thank you to Makini, for your diligence, energy, inspiration, positivity, and multiple rounds of grace and patience as you experienced me amidst COVID-19 personal challenges. You rallied us all to overcome the multiple obstacles that came with living and working through unprecedented times.

Makini:

Thank you to Mommy (Tambra E. Chisolm, MSW, MA) and Daddy (Howard O. Straker, EdD, PA, MPH), for obvious reasons. Cynthia W. Pong, JD, thank you for your edits and your real-life heroism. Thank you to Dr. Lynne D. Richardson for having my back and moving me forward, and to Dr. Robert Dittus for fighting for me. Thanks to Kat, for inviting me to help tell this story; it's one I've been trying to tell for years.

Thank you to Nancy Anderson, Iris Chung, Ula Hwang, Renee James, Ania Kubin, Kevin W. Lee, David Li, Michelle P. Lin, Rosa Gimson, Brad Myles, Mika Nagasaki, KaMing Gordon Ngai, Jammie Patton, Kristin Potterbusch, Camille Elise Powe; Elizabeth Shittu, Lia Sifuentes Davis, Craig Spencer, Noemi Velasquez, and Ling Zhang; thank you all for your connections, advice, and/or translations. Thank you to my Amos fam. Thank you to all my kinfolk; I'm glad the universe chose you for me, and that we are bound together.

Contents

About the Editors

Makini Chisolm-Straker, MD, MPH has served in the anti-trafficking field for over 15 years. She conducts original public health research about human trafficking; for example, Dr. Chisolm-Straker collaborated with Covenant House New Jersey to develop the first validated, labor and sex trafficking screening tool (for use among young adults experiencing homelessness). Dr. Chisolm-Straker educates clinicians on how to serve this patient population and advises and collaborates with policy-makers on ethical, inclusive, person-centered anti-trafficking prevention and intervention efforts. She served on the SOAR initiative of the US Department of Health and Human Services to develop a comprehensive, introductory educational program for healthcare practitioners serving patients with trafficking experience. Dr. Chisolm-Straker is interested in how primary prevention rooted in history and understanding of systems and intersectionality of experiences lead to effective anti-trafficking action. Dr. Chisolm-Straker earned her Medical Doctorate and Bachelor of Arts in Religious Studies from Brown University in Providence, Rhode Island, and her Master of Public Health with a Certificate in Public Health and Humanitarian Aid from Columbia University in New York City.

Katherine Chon, MPA is a Bloomberg American Health Initiative Fellow at the Johns Hopkins School of Public Health, in Baltimore, Maryland, focused on violence prevention based on 18 years of experience developing organizations and shaping strategies to combat human trafficking. Ms. Chon is the founding director of the Office on Trafficking in Persons at the US Department of Health and Human Services (HHS), strengthening the nation's public health response to human trafficking through data-driven policies, programs, and primary prevention. She is the federal executive officer of the National Advisory Committee on the Sex Trafficking of Children and Youth in the United States and serves on numerous federal interagency working groups, including the Senior Policy Operating Group of the President's Interagency Task Force to Monitor and Combat Trafficking in Persons. Prior to government service, Ms. Chon was the co-founder and president of Polaris, establishing the global organization's innovative programs to assist survivors of trafficking, expand anti-trafficking policies, and fundamentally change the way local communities respond to human trafficking. Ms. Chon is an advisor to Brown University's Center for the Study of Slavery and Justice and a member of the National Academies of Sciences, Engineering, and Medicine's Committee on Approaches to Estimating the Prevalence of Human Trafficking in the United States. She received her Master in Public Administration from Harvard University Kennedy School of Government in Cambridge, Massachusetts, and Bachelor of Science in Psychology from Brown University in Providence, Rhode Island. Any views expressed within this textbook are solely those of the respective authors and editors and do not necessarily represent the views of HHS or the United States.

Contributors

Jean Baderschneider, PhD, MA is an accomplished business executive and a global leader in the fight against human trafficking. With over 35 years of international experience, including procurement, strategic sourcing, and supply chain management, she has a deep understanding of high-risk operations/locations and complex partnerships.

She retired as Vice President of Global Procurement from ExxonMobil in 2013. During her career she was responsible for operations all over the world, including Africa, the Americas, the Middle East and Asia. Dr. Baderschneider has 13 years of experience working on anti-trafficking efforts globally. She has served as a Director of Polaris, Made in a Free World, and Verité. She has a global network of government and business leaders.

Dr. Baderschneider is a past Director of the Institute for Supply Management and the Executive Board of the National Minority Supplier Development Council. She was a Presidential appointee to the Department of Commerce's National Advisory Council of Minority Business Enterprises. She is a past board member of The Center of Advanced Purchasing Studies and the Procurement Council of both The Conference Board and the Corporate Executive Board.

Dr. Baderschneider is Director or Advisor for a number of companies. In addition, she is on the Board of Directors of the Nizami Ganjavi International Center. She participates in the Santa Marta Group and is a member of the UK Expert Advisory Panel on Modern Slavery and the Liechtenstein Initiative for a Financial Sector Commission on Modern Slavery.

Dr. Baderschneider has a master's degree from University of Michigan in Ann Arbor and a PhD from Cornell University in Ithaca, New York. She is the recipient of Cornell's Jerome Alpern Award and Nomi Network's Corporate Social Responsibility Award.

Griffin Thomas Black, MPhil is a PhD candidate in history at the University of Cambridge, UK, where he is a Paul Mellon Fellow at Clare College. He researches the historical intersections of abolitionist actors in the United Kingdom and the

United States. Formerly a research assistant at the Gilder Lehrman Center (GLC) for the Study of Slavery, Resistance, and Abolition of the MacMillan Center at Yale University, in New Haven, Connecticut, he assisted with GLC Director David Blight's Pulitzer-prize-winning book *Frederick Douglass: Prophet of Freedom*. With Blight, he has written on Douglass's time lecturing in the United Kingdom. His dissertation will focus on nineteenth-century transatlantic reform networks and how organized abolitionism served as a catalyst for activists focusing on a range of human rights issues in both the United States and the United Kingdom. Mr. Black also is currently researching the recent history of the development of the British Modern Slavery Act of 2015.

Kimberly S. G. Chang, MD, MPH is a family physician at Asian Health Services (AHS) in Oakland, California. In 2015, Dr. Chang completed the Commonwealth Fund Minority Health Policy Fellowship at Harvard University, examining the role of federally qualified health centers in addressing human trafficking. Previously, Dr. Chang was the inaugural Clinic Director at AHS's Frank Kiang Medical Center, and provided care for many commercially sexually exploited children. She trained thousands of front-line multidisciplinary professionals on the human trafficking healthcare intersection, provided invited expert testimony to the US Helsinki Commission on "Best Practices in Rescuing Trafficking Victims," serves on the National Advisory Committee on the Sex Trafficking of Children and Youth in the United States, and co-founded HEAL Trafficking. She was elected as Vice Speaker of the House on the Executive Board of Directors for the National Association of Community Health Centers in 2018, and was appointed to the American Public Health Association Committee on Women's Rights. She was nationally recognized with a Physician Advocacy Merit Award from the Institute on Medicine as a Profession, and featured in *The New York Times, U.S. News and World Report, PBS NewsHour, The Sacramento Bee*, and several podcasts.

Dr. Chang received her BA from Columbia University in New York City; her MD from the University of Hawaii in Honolulu; specialized in family medicine at the University of California, San Francisco; and earned her MPH from the Harvard T.H. Chan School of Public Health in Boston, Massachusetts, where she was recognized with the 2015 Dr. Fang-Ching Sun Memorial Award for commitment to promoting the health of vulnerable people, and the 2020 Emerging Public Health Professional Award.

John Cheng, PhD is Associate Professor in the Department of Asian and Asian American Studies at Binghamton University in New York and an historian of the nineteenth- and twentieth-century United States with transdisciplinary interests in racial formation, popular culture, and the history of science and technology. He is the author of *Astounding Wonder: Imagining Science and Science Fiction in Interwar America* and was an advisor and contributor to California Newsreel's documentary series, *Race: The Power of an Illusion*. His current book project, *Precarity and Persistence*, examines Asian American racial citizenship in twentieth-century

United States through the lens of denaturalization and expatriation, processes to cancel and remove citizenship. Recounting the efforts of Asian migrants and their families, first, to resist losing their citizenship on the basis of racial ineligibility, then, to regain that lost citizenship, the book reveals the racial precarity present within US notions of citizenship historically. For many years, John was a volunteer and board member for the Asian/Pacific Islander Domestic Violence Resource Project (DVRP) in Washington, DC, and he is currently part of local community efforts to assist victims of anti-Asian racism, spurred by racialization of the COVID-19 pandemic, in upstate New York.

Katherine Chin, BA is a program assistant at the US Department of State and a former research assistant at Brown University's Center for the Study of Slavery and Justice in Providence, Rhode Island, where she wrote and edited pieces on migrant labor, human trafficking, and decarceral alliances in the fight for sex workers' and migrant workers' rights. Her research foci include migration studies, racial capitalism, labor rights, and the carceral state. Ms. Chin has a BA from Brown University in International Relations. She speaks and reads Chinese and French.

Minh Dang, MSW is the Executive Director of Survivor Alliance, an international NGO that empowers survivors of slavery and human trafficking to be leaders in their own communities. She is also a Research Fellow at the University of Nottingham's Rights Lab, studying the well-being of survivors of slavery and human trafficking. Ms. Dang has been a scholar-activist in the anti-slavery movement for over 10 years, promoting survivor leadership, lived-experience expertise, and community-based participatory research. She is a trainer, educator, and love warrior. Ms. Dang was appointed by President Barack Obama to the US Advisory Council on Human Trafficking and served on the Board of the Human Trafficking Legal Center. She is a proud two-time UC Berkeley alum, with a BA in Sociology and Masters in Social Welfare, with an emphasis on Community Mental Health.

Luis C.deBaca, JD coordinated US government activities in the global fight against contemporary forms of slavery as head of the State Department's Office to Monitor and Combat Trafficking in Persons during the Obama Administration. As Involuntary Servitude & Slavery Coordinator in the Justice Department's Civil Rights Division, he was one of the United States' most decorated federal prosecutors, investigating and prosecuting dozens of human trafficking cases involving over 600 victims. He developed the "victim-centered approach" that has become the global standard, was the principal Department of Justice drafter of the Trafficking Victims Protection Act, and contributed to the United Nations "Palermo Protocol." He is currently the Robina Fellow in Modern Slavery at the Gilder Lehrman Center for the Study of Slavery, Resistance, and Abolition of the MacMillan Center at Yale University in New Haven, Connecticut, where he teaches in the Law School, the School of Architecture, and the Department of History. He advises governments, businesses, and civil society on compliance, enforcement, and transparency.

Anna Mae Duane, PhD is associate professor of English and American Studies at the University of Connecticut in Storrs. She has written or edited six books on the history of childhood, including *Suffering Childhood in Early America: Violence, Race, and the Making of the Child Victim*; *Slavery Before and After Emancipation: An Argument for Child-Centered Slavery Studies;* and, most recently, *Educated for Freedom: The Incredible Story of Two Fugitive Schoolboys Who Grew Up to Change a Nation*. From 2016 to 2018, she was a member of the Modern Slavery Working Group at Yale Gilder Lehrman Center for Slavery, Resistance and Abolition in New Haven, Connecticut. Her work has been supported by the Fulbright Foundation and the National Endowment for the Humanities.

Aria Flood, MPH has over 10 years of experience in youth program planning, implementation, and management, with an emphasis on school-based public health programming. As the Director of US Prevention at Love146, Ms. Flood is responsible for developing, promoting, and evaluating trafficking prevention programs to effect systemic change. Ms. Flood co-authored the Not a Number prevention education curriculum, and travels domestically, presenting at conferences and providing training on human trafficking for professionals who work with youth. She leads a team that advises schools, government agencies, and nonprofit organizations on the implementation of effective trafficking prevention education strategies for diverse populations of youth. Ms. Flood has a BS from the University of Florida in Gainesville and an MPH from the University of Texas School of Public Health in Houston.

Alison Kiehl Friedman, MBA has over two decades of experience working at the intersection of social justice and corporate accountability. Over the course of her career, Alison helped direct policy for People for the American Way, where she focused on protecting an independent judiciary and advancing voting rights, led the Alliance to Stop Slavery and End Trafficking in crafting California's consumer transparency bill and helped lead the State Department's Office to Monitor and Combat Trafficking in Persons. She recently ran for Congress in Virginia and currently directs the International Corporate Accountability Roundtable, a group of over 40 human rights organizations that coordinate advocacy and communications around corporate accountability. Alison is a graduate of Stanford University in Palo Alto, California, and Saïd Business School at Oxford University in the United Kingdom.

Aaron Halegua, JD is the Founding Member of Aaron Halegua, PLLC and a research fellow at both NYU School of Law's Center for Labor and Employment Law and US-Asia Law Institute. Mr. Halegua recently assisted over 2400 Chinese construction workers trafficked to Saipan to recover $14 million in backpay, and he is currently litigating a case in a US federal court to recover compensation for workers injured on that project. Mr. Halegua also has consulted for Apple, Asia Society, International Labor Rights Forum, Ford Foundation, Service Employees International Union, International Labor Organization, and Brown University on labor issues in China, Thailand, Myanmar, and Mexico, including human trafficking. He is the author of numerous book chapters, articles, and op-eds about labor issues, including the report *Who Will Represent China's Workers: Lawyers, Legal Aid, and the Enforcement of Labor Rights* (2016). Mr. Halegua has an AB from Brown University in Providence, Rhode Island, and JD from Harvard Law School in Cambridge, Massachusetts. He was a Fulbright Scholar at Peking University Law School in Beijing, China, after college. He speaks, reads, and writes Mandarin Chinese.

Sharon Hawkins Leyden, MSW, LCSW has more than 35 years of experience working with transitional age youth, adults, and seniors with significant vulnerabilities. She has worked predominantly with issues pertaining to sexual exploitation, eviction from the foster care system, isolation, poverty, systemic racism, and chronic homelessness. Throughout her career, her work has focused on three primary issues: raising people out of poverty, helping people re-author stories of trauma, and working for equality of access through social justice practices.

As part of her work, Consultant Hawkins-Leyden founded a transition-age youth homeless agency offering shelter and mental health programming designed to increase wellness and combat the effects of trauma. She has designed and implemented a coordinated entry system for homeless adults providing efficient access to services, and she is currently designing and implementing programming for homeless seniors that provides seniors with the ability to leave a legacy of how to survive against great hardship.

Additionally, Consultant Hawkins-Leyden has worked internationally with survivors of human trafficking and modern slavery. She continues to design and implement programs, as well as to teach emerging social work students about the intersectionality of poverty, trauma, and survival in the United States and overseas.

Nitana Hicks Greendeer, PhD a citizen of the Mashpee Wampanoag Tribe, has worked for the past 15 years with the Wôpanâak Language Reclamation Project as a teacher, researcher, language and curriculum developer, and as the Head of School for the Wôpanâak Language immersion school, Weetumuw Katnuhtôhtakamuq. She has served her tribal community as the Director of the Education Department for the Mashpee Wampanoag Tribe.

Dr. Hicks Greendeer teaches in the Native American and Indigenous Studies program at Brown University in Providence, Rhode, Island, previously as a presidential postdoc and now as an adjunct professor. Her broader interests include culture-based education and culturally appropriate curricular models, language education, and Indian education.

Through her education, language, and academic work, Dr. Hicks Greendeer works to give Wampanoag children positive, culturally relevant educational experiences as a means of decolonization and to increase personal and community wellness.

Beisi Huang, LMSW is a counselor, case manager, and court advocate for survivors of trafficking with a focus on Mandarin-speaking Chinese women. Since

October 2016, she has worked with nearly 200 survivor clients. She is a specialist in victim identification, particularly for Chinese women trafficked in the illicit massage industry. With her experiences in direct work with the women, she has trained and provided technical assistance to over 30 partnerships across the United States, including law enforcement, attorneys, service providers, and community organizers. Ms. Huang has a Master of Social Work from New York University and a BA in English from Shanghai Normal University in China.

Kate Keisel, LMSW is the Co-Founder and Chief Executive Officer of the Sanar Institute, a leading organization that addresses the impacts of complex trauma. Ms. Keisel has over a decade of experience working with individuals and communities impacted by human trafficking in the United States, Latin America, West Africa, and South Asia. She has worked to build and prioritize person-centered approaches that holistically address the vulnerabilities created though violence perpetration and other traumatic events. She serves as an expert consultant in complex trauma for a diverse range of stakeholders, including the US National Human Trafficking Training and Technical Assistance Center and Office for Victims of Crime Training and Technical Assistance Center. Ms. Keisel holds a Bachelor's Degree in International Studies with a focus on human rights in Latin America and a Master's Degree in Clinical Social Work with a focus on complex trauma. She utilizes postgraduate training in Eye Movement Desensitization and Reprocessing, Trauma-Sensitive Yoga, and other evidence-based modalities to provide bilingual support to individuals and communities. Ms. Keisel's work is informed by her lived experience with complex trauma healing, clinical training, and work with thousands of individuals on their own journey to build empowered lives in the aftermath of trauma.

Gonzalo Martínez de Vedia, MA has over 10 years of experience advocating for the rights of low-wage workers, with a special focus on labor trafficking. He currently is a senior program manager at Verite, where his work focuses on ethical recruitment in the Americas. Previously, he designed and implemented interventions against forced and coerced labor in the Texas agricultural sector as a program manager with the Combatting Human Trafficking team at the McCain Institute at Arizona State University in Tempe. Martínez has also served as a senior policy associate at Humanity United, where he helped manage the Alliance to End Slavery and Trafficking, and as a human trafficking specialist for the Worker Justice Center of New York, where he led targeted outreach to high-risk workplaces and led several multiagency anti-trafficking task forces. Martínez has also served as a human rights commissioner for the County of Ulster, New York, and policy co-chair for Freedom Network USA. He has informed rights-related coverage for Univision, *This American Life*, and *The New York Times*, among many other outlets. Martínez was born and raised in Buenos Aires, Argentina. He holds a master's in Criminal Justice from Arizona State University and a BA cum laude from Cornell University in Ithaca, New York.

Chris Muller-Tabanera, MDiv is the National Director of Heyrick Research. Heyrick Research is a counter-trafficking organization that provides data, intelligence, and strategy to support collaborative efforts to combat the illicit massage industry. Over the course of his career, Mr. Muller-Tabanera has created and delivered trainings across the United States on the unique characteristics of the illicit massage industry and best practices in identifying and responding to exploited workers. He is frequently consulted by law enforcement on investigations and has been featured in numerous news articles about the illicit massage industry, including *The New York Times*. Prior to joining Heyrick Research, Mr. Muller-Tabanera was the Director of Training and External Affairs at Restore NYC. He has an MDiv from Gordon-Conwell Theological Seminary in Hamilton, Massachusetts, and a BA in Communication and Media Studies from the University of San Diego in California.

Ai-jen Poo, BA is an award-winning organizer, social innovator, author, and a leading voice in the women's movement. She is the Executive Director of the National Domestic Workers Alliance, Director of Caring Across Generations, Co-Founder of SuperMajority, and Trustee of the Ford Foundation. Ms. Poo is a nationally recognized expert on elder and family care, the future of work, gender equality, immigration, narrative change, and grassroots organizing. She is the author of the celebrated book *The Age of Dignity: Preparing for the Elder Boom in a Changing America*.

In 12 short years, with the help of more than 70 local affiliate organizations and chapters and over 200,000 members, the National Domestic Workers Alliance has passed Domestic Worker Bills of Rights in nine states and the city of Seattle, and brought over 2 million home care workers under minimum wage protections. In 2011, Ms. Poo launched Caring Across Generations to unite American families in a campaign to achieve bold solutions to the nation's crumbling care infrastructure. The campaign has catalyzed groundbreaking policy change in states, including the nation's first family caregiver benefit in Hawaii, and the first long-term care social insurance fund in Washington State.

Joshua M. Sharfstein, MD is Vice Dean for Public Health Practice and Community Engagement and Professor of the Practice in Health Policy and Management at the Johns Hopkins Bloomberg School of Public Health in Baltimore, Maryland. He is also the Director of the Bloomberg American Health Initiative. Previously, Dr. Sharfstein served as Secretary of the Maryland Department of Health and Mental Hygiene, as the Principal Deputy Commissioner of the US Food and Drug Administration, as Health Commissioner for Baltimore City, and as minority professional staff for the Committee on Government Reform of the US House of Representatives.

Dr. Sharfstein trained as a pediatrician and is a member of the National Academy of Medicine and a fellow of the National Academy of Public Administration. He is the author of *The Public Health Crisis Survival Guide: Leadership and Management in Trying Times* and co-author of *The Opioid Epidemic: What Everyone Needs to Know*.

Ruth J. Simmons, PhD is President of Prairie View A&M University in Prairie View, Texas. Prior to joining Prairie View, she was President of Brown University in Providence, Rhode Island, from 2001–2012. Before serving as president of Brown, she was President of Smith College, the largest women's college in the United States, in Northampton, Massachusetts.

A graduate of Dillard University in New Orleans, Louisiana, Simmons completed her PhD in Romance Languages and Literatures at Harvard University in Cambridge, Massachusetts. Before her appointment as president, she served in various faculty and administrative roles at the University of Southern California, Princeton University, and Spelman College.

Simmons has served on numerous non-profit boards, including the boards of trustees of Dillard University, Howard University, Princeton University, and Rice University. She serves on the Council of the Smithsonian National Museum of African American History and Culture, the Board of Trustees of the Museum of Fine Arts of Houston, and the Board of the Houston Branch of the Federal Reserve Bank of Dallas. In addition, she chairs the Governing Board of the Holdsworth Center, which supports public school leadership in Texas.

She has been awarded over 40 honorary degrees. Simmons is a member of the National Academy of Arts and Sciences, the American Philosophical Society, and the Council on Foreign Relations. In 2012, she was named a 'chevalier' of the French Legion of Honour by the President of France.

Natalicia Tracy, PhD is Afro-Brazilian and the first one in her family to earn a PhD (Sociology) from Boston University in 2016. She writes and teaches about race, power, and immigration in the United States in courses in Sociology, Labor Studies, and Human Services at the University of Massachusetts Boston. She also has been Executive Director of Boston's Brazilian Worker Center since 2010, where she has worked on educating members of the immigrant community on the racial divides that immigrants carry with them from Latin America to Boston. Dr. Tracy is a co-founder of the Massachusetts Coalition for Domestic Workers, and helped lead the campaign to pass the state's 2014 Domestic Worker Bill of Rights, and in 2015 won rights for domestic workers in the state of Connecticut. She is the co-author of *Invisible No More: Organizing Domestic Workers in Massachusetts and Beyond* (2014), and other publications on immigration issues.

Among many awards received, Dr. Tracy received the 2014 Greater Boston Labor Council, AFL-CIO, Leadership Award for her advocacy for domestic workers and the passing of landmark legislation. In addition, she has been appointed by Boston mayor Marty Walsh to serve on the city's Living Wage Advisory Committee. Dr. Tracy is also a member of the Advisory Board of the Mayor's Office of Immigrant Advancement, and a board member at the Women's Institute for Leadership Development, as well as Jobs with Justice. She sits on the Greater Boston Labor Council, representing the Brazilian Worker Center.

Rueben C. Warren, DDS, MPH, DrPH, MDiv is Professor of Bioethics and Director of the National Center for Bioethics in Research and Health Care at

Tuskegee University in Alabama. Among Dr. Warren's adjunct appointments are: Professor, Schools of Dentistry and Graduate Studies and Research, Meharry Medical College in Nashville, Tennessee, and Clinical Professor, Department of Community Health/Preventive Medicine, Morehouse School of Medicine in Atlanta, Georgia. His Former adjunct appointments: Professor of Public Health, Medicine and Ethics, Interdenominational Theological Center (ITC) in Atlanta, and Professor, Department of Behavioral Sciences and Health Education, Rollins School of Public Health at Emory University in Atlanta. Dr. Warren was Associate Director of Minority Health at the Centers for Disease Control and Prevention (CDC) in Atlanta. He also was Director of Infrastructure Development, National Institute on Minority Health and Health Disparities, National Institutes of Health (NIH), in Bethesda, Maryland. Dr. Warren earned a BA degree from San Francisco State University in California and earned an MPH and a DrPH and completed a Teaching Fellowship at Harvard School of Public Health in Boston, Massachusetts. He completed a Dental Public Health Residency at Harvard School of Dental Medicine, and earned an MDiv from ITC. Dr. Warren is board-certified in Dental Public Health. He has more than 40 years of health care and public health experience in addressing health challenges in people of color. Human trafficking provides a unique chance to synergize the intersectionality of health, public health, health care, and various sphere of ethics and social justice.

Jennifer Weston, BA (Hunkpapa Lakota, Standing Rock Sioux Tribe) is a writer and producer who has worked for the past 25 years with Tribal community programs focused on environmental justice, Indigenous education, and language revitalization. Currently she directs the Wôpanâak Language Reclamation Project (WLRP). Prior to joining WLRP in 2012, Weston managed Cultural Survival's endangered languages program in Cambridge, Massachusetts, building a network among 350+ Indigenous communities, serving as researcher and producer for the 2011 documentary WE STILL LIVE HERE: Âs Nutayuneân, and the film's companion website, OurMotherTongues.org. Jennifer is an active learner of Lakotiyapi and Wôpanâôt8âôk.

Erin Williamson, LCSW, MPA has over 15 years of direct service, program management, and applied research experience in the fields of social service and criminal justice, with particular expertise in the areas of human trafficking and child sexual exploitation. Ms. Williamson has authored several peer-reviewed publications, presented nationally, and served on national advisory committees, including the US Department of Health and Human Services National Advisory Committee on the Sex Trafficking of Children & Youth in the United States. In her current role as Vice President of Global Programs at Love146, Ms. Williamson is responsible for leading the organization's global programs strategy and implementation. Ms. Williamson has an MPA from American University and an MSW from The Catholic University of America, both located in Washington, DC.

Part I
Market Dynamics of Human Trafficking

Chapter 1
Market Dynamics of Human Trafficking: Part I Introduction

Makini Chisolm-Straker and Katherine Chon

To truly understand labor and sex trafficking, the anti-trafficking worker must have, at least, a basic historical comprehension of markets that have been impacted by exploitation including trafficking. In this section of the textbook, chapter authors offer in-depth examples of industries, both legal and illicit, in which human trafficking has been and can be found. These chapters do not represent all the markets impacted by trafficking, but the authors discuss the historical depth and contemporary continuation of institutionalized and systemic exploitation. This is meant to help the reader conceptualize how foundational exploitation is to the US and global economies. With a deeper and specific understanding of market forces, the reader can clearly see the ways in which industry-specific workers are exploited. Chapter authors offer concrete actions for market disruption and reshaping, such that exploitation is not needed, desired, or used.

1.1 Historical Market Examples

A dominant US historical example of human trafficking is in agriculture. White plantation owners used African and African-descendant enslavement and forced labor for cultivation of agriculture. Raw materials (e.g., cotton, tobacco, and rice) were sold in legal markets, for the profit of the plantation owners, who owned not only the plantation land but also the workers and equipment. Items produced from the agricultural work of African and African-descended people were used by consumers living across the colonies, territories, and, later, the United States. Slavery

M. Chisolm-Straker (✉)
Institute for Health Equity Research, Department of Emergency Medicine,
Icahn School of Medicine at Mount Sinai, New York, NY, USA
e-mail: Makini.Chisolm-Straker@mountsinai.org

K. Chon
Center for the Study of Slavery and Justice, Brown University, Providence, RI, USA

© Springer Nature Switzerland AG 2021
M. Chisolm-Straker, K. Chon (eds.), *The Historical Roots of Human Trafficking*,
https://doi.org/10.1007/978-3-030-70675-3_1

was embedded in the lives of all who lived on the land, even if they did not own slaves themselves and even if they were enslaved or free but poor (Chernos Lin 2002). It tainted the clothes they wore, the food they ate, and the tools they used. Even after the abolition of slavery, similar deceptive recruitment and control schemes to enslave people in agriculture historically exist through policies and practices (Chap. 9) contributing to exploitative agricultural labor in contemporary times (Barrick et al. 2013; Palacios 2017).

Another historical market, often overlooked, is the slave market itself. Most slave owners did not travel to the African continent to procure their own slaves. Rather, they went to local slave markets, where Africans and their progeny were sold—as commodities—at the auction block. And while the historical North is often cast as the "free" portion of the United States, White people owned slaves here too. It is important to note that northern colonies were slower to adopt the use of Africans for slavery not necessarily because of a more progressive morality. Rather, they did not have the land space that the southern colonies had for large plantations and crop cultivation, and there were others who were still forced to be available for sale and exploitation: Native Americans.[1] Native slavery was pervasive throughout North America (including the Caribbean), but this history is less commonly known or meaningfully acknowledged (Chap. 16).

In addition to the forced labor of Indigenous and Black people, more than half of the White population of the northern colonies were indentured servants (though they at least had a chance at future freedom). Although Northern states began to make slave importation illegal before Southern states did, slavery itself was not outlawed in all of New England until 1840. In 1810, after the 1808 abolition of US engagement in slave importation, 30,000 slaves were still counted in the US census of Northern states where they were likely to work as domestic help (Chap. 4) in a household or small business (including small farms, churches, and medical services) (Strochlic n.d.). Enslaved people were also used in the construction of buildings, including prestigious universities, and the wealth of slave traders funded institutions (Brown University 2007). During the time of legal slavery, the main risk factor for being enslaved, in any market, was being born Native or Black.

1.2   Contemporary Market Examples

Even after the abolition of slavery in 1865, markets continued to rely on forced or coerced laborers. The long-reach of exploitation-based products and service endures in contemporary forms of exploitation recognized in the twenty-first century. In 2017, Polaris – a non-governmental organization founded out of Brown University - released a typology report detailing the different industries in which human

---

[1] Native people were also used in Southern slavery, including prior to the forced mass importation of Africans for plantation work.

trafficking was reported between 2007 and 2016. Reliant on calls into a national hotline on human trafficking, the data is limited: only those who know about trafficking and the hotline number, and were able to call in, reported concerns of trafficking. Moreover, some forms of trafficking are more commonly recognized by the public (usually sex trafficking), and some people or communities are less likely to call in trafficking reports or concerns. Despite the limitations, at the time of this writing, these are the only national level data available on human trafficking in the United States. Polaris grouped the types of trafficking into 25 market or industry categories[2]; most of the categories fall under labor trafficking though sex trafficking accounted for more reports (4,340 labor trafficking v. 8,683 sex trafficking). Of note, there were 3,928 cases that involved both labor *and* sex trafficking.

In considering the typology of contemporary forms of human trafficking, readers might consider how they interact with each market and how that market affects the country as a whole: escort services; illicit massage, health and beauty; outdoor solicitation; residential sex trafficking; domestic work; bars, strip clubs, and cantinas; pornography; traveling sales crews; restaurants and food service; peddling and begging; agriculture and animal husbandry; personal sexual servitude; health and beauty services; construction; hotels, hospitality; landscaping; illicit activities; arts and entertainment; commercial cleaning services; factories and manufacturing; remote interactive sexual acts; carnivals; forestry and logging; health care; and recreational facilities (Polaris 2017). Every person living in the US engages with more than one of these markets. This does not mean that all workers in these industries are being trafficked, but these are examples of the diverse ways in which people are trafficked in the US.

The Polaris data do not include how people are exploited outside of the country for the creation of products sold in the US (Chap. 7). For example, many US-based stores sell clothing that was made outside of the US and with materials sourced from outside the country (Benedit-Begley 2020). In 2020, a US government report listed 155 goods from 77 countries on its list of goods produced by child labor or forced labor, newly adding gloves, rubber gloves, hair products, pome and stone fruits, sandstone, and tomato products to the list (US Department of Labor 2020).

Exploited labor also fuels the healthcare industry and its supply chains. For example, surgical instruments for elective and emergency operations and personal protective equipment (PPE) for healthcare workers are produced outside the US (Bhutta 2017; Nadvi and Halder 2002; Bhutta and Santhakumar 2016). Most notably during the response to COVID-19, more than 41 million gloves produced under allegations of forced labor entered the US market for distribution to medical professionals and first responders. Pre-pandemic migrant workers in Malaysia each had daily production targets to package 15,000 gloves, a quota that increased by 400% over a year. They worked at least 12 hours a day, with only 1 day off a month, and experienced penalties for missing quotas, poor environmental conditions, and debt bondage (SCB 2020). During the COVID pandemic, the demand for PPE greatly

---

[2] Polaris also identified 10 other types of trafficking not yet defined/categorized.

increased. For example, the shares of one of the top glove manufacturers in the world increased by 417% in 2020 compared to the previous year due to pandemic-related demand, and despite a 6.5% decrease in their sales volume due to importation bans in the US from forced labor allegations (Huang 2020; Lim 2020).

The US has prohibited trade in goods and products mined, produced, and manufactured by forced labor or indentured servitude (in whole or in part) since the Tariff Act of 1930. Prior to 2015, exceptions were made for goods produced by forced labor if they were needed to meet the "consumptive demands" of the country. While there are several laws prohibiting the use of federal funds to procure goods and services produced by forced labor, the response to COVID-19 spotlights gaps in public health emergency preparedness plans, which must go beyond building stockpiles and disseminating PPE to also being conscious of responsible sourcing and including protections against forced labor.

1.3   Context-Based Interventions Are Essential

An understanding of domestic and global markets is crucial for sustainable and effective trafficking prevention action. Market dynamics are unique, and unique interventions are warranted. For example, measures against forced labor in construction (Chap. 6) may not be as relevant or impactful in anti-exploitation measures in the US-based residential sex trafficking industry. Today's trafficked persons may have different vulnerabilities depending upon the industry in which they are exploited, and traffickers in different industries use different recruiting and control techniques. Application of a singular exploitation abolition method will be unsuccessful at scale, as "one size" cannot fit all. For example, in 2017, it was reported that 71% of child labor occurs in the agriculture industry and 42% of that work occurs in informal and family businesses that rely on child labor (IV Global Conference on the Sustained Eradication of Child Labour 2017). While some market dynamics may overlap, appropriate anti-trafficking measures must be specific to geography, commodity, labor or service, and at-risk populations.

Furthermore, child and forced labor is aggravated by conflict and climate disasters. Human-made, natural, and public health emergencies can lead to physical dislocation, social disconnection, disruption to essential life services (e.g., food, education, and health), and increased financial insecurity. Baseline socioeconomic disparities contribute to higher risks for human trafficking preceding a disaster. They are then further exacerbated by the conditions of a disaster, especially when combined with market forces of high demand for quickly produced, low cost goods or services. Risks continue to compound the longer the socioeconomic conditions are destabilized. Hence, diplomacy, climate justice work, global trade, and market reforms are important anti-exploitation measures to decrease the use and occurrence of human trafficking (those efforts are also important in their own right).

An anti-trafficking approach based on public health principles rests on the understanding that markets, communities, laws, policies, social norms, and oppressions are all deeply intertwined. They work together to create and nurture the circumstances that allow trafficking and other forms of exploitation to flourish. In farming, it may be enough to cut off the supply of one nutrient for the plant to fail; that is not so for the eradication of trafficking. A restructuring of multiple systems, accounting for the context of history, is necessary. A core principle of public health calls for a comprehensive grasp of complicated, complex, and sometimes nuanced strategies. This section's chapters highlight some important ways in which some markets are at higher risk for human trafficking. For example, in Chap. 2, Martínez de Vedia uses the agricultural market to deconstruct how contemporary incentives of capitalism continues to use force and coercion of the workforce. This is a product of the historical legacies of legislation, racism, classism, and xenophobia in this industry. How are such things overcome? Legislation is important yet insufficient: Crimes are committed daily; the risk of punishment is not deterrent enough to positively impact safety, health, and well-being at population levels. A collective reshaping of values is required. Various governmental agencies (e.g., Department of Education and Department of Agriculture) and community organizations must develop policies and offer programming to support humane, respectful, and responsible ways of considering and employing laborers and of reducing risk for commercial sexual exploitation. This contributes to the *primary prevention* of exploitation.

In a top-down approach, legislators write laws and expect society to comply. But history illustrates via the failures of reconstruction, desegregation, and other major systemic change that such attempts require long-term vigilance and bottom-up approaches too. The chapters in this section demonstrate how a change in law does not immediately lead to changes in behavior, just as legal integration of races has not prevented the practice and persistence of racial segregation (Chaps. 14 and 15). Grassroots and individual efforts need meaningful support via funding, laws, and new anti-exploitation norms sustained over time. A public health anti-trafficking approach is a holistic one that requires the contribution of all relevant sectors and actors. An effective public health approach calls for and works in historical and cultural context.

References

IV Global Conference on the Sustained Eradication of Child Labour. (2017, November 16). *Buenos aires declaration on child labour, forced labour and youth employment.*

Barrick, K., Lattimore, P. K., Pitts, W., & Zhang, S. (2013). *Indicators of labor trafficking among North Carolina migrant farmworkers.* Retrieved 15 October 2020 from https://notrafficking. org/wp-content/uploads/2020/01/CoHT-NCJRS-.pdf.

Benedit-Begley, S. (2020). At 14, I Worked in a Sweatshop. Here's What I Think of Fashion Week. *Zora.* Retrieved 23 October 2020 from https://zora.medium.com/ at-14-i-worked-in-a-sweatshop-heres-what-i-think-of-fashion-week-97757ea403c1.

Bhutta, M. (2017). Time for a global response to labour rights violations in the manufacture of health-care goods. *Bull World Health Organization, 95,* 314.

Bhutta, M., & Santhakumar, A. (2016). *In good hands. Tackling labour rights concerns in the manufacture of medical gloves [report].* British Medical Association Fair and Ethical Trade Group.

Available at: https://www.bma.org.uk/collective-voice/influence/international/global-justice/
fair-medical-trade/medical-glovesreport.

Brown University Steering Committee on Slavery and Justice. (2007). *Slavery and justice*.
Providence: Brown University.

Chernos Lin, R. (2002). The Rhode Island slave traders: Butchers, bakers and candlestick makers.
Slavery and Abolition, 23(3), 21–38.

Huang, E. (2020). World's largest medical glove maker sees strong growth ahead as pandemic
sparks global surge in demand. *CNBC*. Retrieved 15 October 2020 from https://www.cnbc.
com/2020/09/18/top-glove-sees-strong-growth-ahead-covid-19-sparks-global-demand-
surge.html.

Lim, J. (2020). Top Glove expects to resolve US import ban issue by year end. *The Edge
Markets*. Retrieved 15 October 2020 from https://www.theedgemarkets.com/article/
top-glove-expects-resolve-us-import-ban-issue-year-end.

Nadvi, K., & Halder, G. (2002). *Local clusters in global value chains: Exploring dynamic linkages
between Germany and Pakistan [Report]*. Sussex: Institute of Development Studies, University
of Sussex Brighton. Available at: https://www.ids.ac.uk/files/Wp152.pdf.

Palacios, S. P. I. (2017). Trafficking in US Agriculture. *Antipode*. Retrieved 15 October 2020 from
https://onlinelibrary.wiley.com/doi/abs/10.1111/anti.12330.

Polaris. (2017). *The typology of modern slavery*. Retrieved 19 October 2020 from https://polar-
isproject.org/resources/the-typology-of-modern-slavery-defining-sex-and-labor-trafficking-in-
the-united-states/.

SCB Economic Intelligence Center. (2020). *COVID-19 increased global demand for medical
glove. EIC indicates that Malaysia gains more from export than Thailand*. Retrieved 15 October
2020 from https://www.scbeic.com/en/detail/file/product/6857/fnyoncnigx/EIC-Note_rubber-
glove_EN_20200601.pdf.

Strochlic, N. (n.d.). How slavery flourished in the United States. *National Geographic*.
Retrieved 19 October 2020 from https://www.nationalgeographic.com/culture/2019/08/
how-slavery-flourished-united-states-chart-maps/#close.

U.S. Department of Labor. (2020). *List of goods produced by child labor and forced labor*.
Retrieved 15 October 2020 from https://www.dol.gov/sites/dolgov/files/ILAB/child_labor_
reports/tda2019/2020_TVPRA_List_Online_Final.pdf.

Chapter 2
Capitalism, Colonialism, and Imperialism: Roots for Present-Day Trafficking

Gonzalo Martínez de Vedia

2.1 Introduction

Although mass-scale, institutionalized slavery has been a defining part of the history of the United States, this practice neither originated nor ended within this one nation's borders. Virtually, all chapters of world history contain elements – often major elements – of unfree labor including chattel-type slavery. To better understand what makes the history and current state of unfree labor in the US unique warrants knowledge of how these practices have manifested in other contexts, including before the formation of modern US society and government.

Modern practitioners in the anti-trafficking field who choose to bypass historical analysis will nonetheless, knowingly or not, confront the living legacies of past forms of trafficking. Take the example of the crime data analyst tasked with providing a regional task force information about the human trafficking risk profile in its particular jurisdiction: With a wide and recent body of research on the scope and character of human trafficking at their disposal, the analyst would quickly determine that several unique sectors of the economy, both formal and informal, are known to contain higher-than-average incidences of forced and coerced labor. From among a list of sectors that include domestic work, commercial sex, and extractive industries, the analyst might focus on the agricultural sector as a particularly trafficking-prone industry (Barrick et al. 2013; Owens et al. 2014; Kepes et al. 2010).

In order to translate that general finding into specific insights about the farm labor workforce in their jurisdiction, the analyst might navigate to the latest Agricultural Census database (USDA 2020). From among metrics about acreage, import/export values, and market trends, the analyst would at first seem to dead end in their search for information about the farmworkers who so often appear as victims in labor trafficking indictments. The Census data portal, under the category

G. Martínez de Vedia (✉)
Verité, Amherst, MA, USA

© Springer Nature Switzerland AG 2021
M. Chisolm-Straker, K. Chon (eds.), *The Historical Roots of Human Trafficking*,
https://doi.org/10.1007/978-3-030-70675-3_2

Demographics, only lists information about farm operators. Has the US Department of Agriculture (USDA) neglected to include the milkers, hand-harvesters, and produce packers who power this multi-billion-dollar sector?

After trial and error through the data dashboard, the analyst makes a discovery. Data about farmworkers are indeed to be found, but set apart from the farm owners, in another section: "Expenses." There, alphabetically sublisted as a "Commodity" after "Feed" and "Fertilizers," is "Labor." The USDA dashboard further allows the analyst, through that menu, to display measures of this "labor" in one of two ways: dollar cost or headcount. Unlike with farm owners, no information about race, gender, or age is offered about this "commodity" in the US Agricultural Census.

At this juncture, the anti-trafficking analyst, having made their find, might filter data to their geographical jurisdiction, collate a few "Quick Stats" (see Fig. 2.1), such as total number of seasonal farmworkers, and bundle them into a report. Another analyst might choose to both get these statistics *and* interrogate why the US Department of Agriculture lists the two to three million people who earn wages on US farms as a "commodity."

The former task meets the short-term needs of the anti-trafficking field. This chapter argues that the ability of the anti-trafficking field to grapple with the latter type of question – about the past and present of human commodification (Chap. 7) – might determine the lasting success of its efforts at large. Through an analysis of the history of unfree labor as it manifested before the formation of the United States, as well as throughout several chapters of US history, this chapter will identify that certain recurring dynamics have served to power every iteration of forced and coerced labor: Namely, the skill of traffickers and their enablers to other, commodify, and subsequently profit from subsectors of society has proven to be as adaptable as it is entrenched. A comprehensive anti-trafficking response does well to identify how ideologies aimed against non-White, non-European, and/or non-Christian people have time and again served to facilitate a pervasive enough othering that it permits the coercing and forcing of labor for a profit at scale.

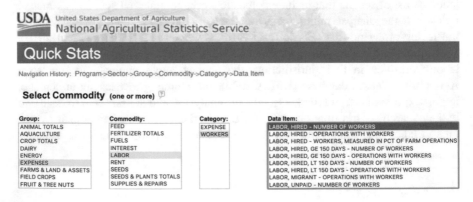

Fig. 2.1 Quick stats – a service of the US Agricultural Census (USDA 2020)

2.2 Discussion

2.2.1 Unfree Labor in the Americas Before and Beyond the 13 Colonies

The Native peoples of the American continents, including many in the areas now called the United States, have left record of intra- and intertribal forms of unfree labor across a varying geography, several cultural contexts, and from well before the arrival of Spanish expeditions in 1492. As opposed to later, European-propelled chapters in the history of the Americas, these forms of unfree labor were often limited to specific cultural contexts and temporal frames and not practiced ubiquitously or uniformly across all sectors of the preColumbian Americas (Reséndez 2016).

The launch, first by Spain and later by many other European powers, of imperialist ventures in the American continents opened way to an unprecedented homogenization, expansion, and eventual institutionalization of unfree labor. One historian estimates that between the arrival of Christopher Columbus in Hispaniola and the end of the seventeenth century – that is, before the first successful colonial efforts by British settlers in North America – between 892,000 and 1,800,000 Native people had already been enslaved by European colonizers in the Americas (Reséndez 2016). The highest prevalence of enslaved Natives was at first in the areas that today form the Caribbean, Mexico, and Central America, although South America eventually outpaced all other regions on this front.

The specific practice of Spanish and subsequent Portuguese enslavement of Native Americans introduced certain unique traits that outlasted that particular period. For one, the enslavement took place under pressure to further the economic and imperial interests of European powers. Furthermore, slavery in this historical chapter was often administered under the pretenses of religious evangelization and with the explicit purpose of converting Native peoples to Christianity (Bowden 1981; Kendi 2016; Treuer 2019). Indeed, the pretense that European invaders were helping Indigenous people by providing them entrance to European religious ideology served to both embolden and rationalize campaigns to capture and compel labor. These religious imperialist and, in particular, European-serving motives are present in subsequent stages of the development of unfree labor systems in the Americas.

In other words, elements of the above formula proved to have a longer history than the specific practice of Spanish-led enslavement of Native peoples nearest to the equatorial latitudes of the Americas. By the time the Spanish crown moved to banish the practice of "Indian Slavery" within its colonies starting in 1542 – which nonetheless proved largely unenforceable (Reséndez 2016) – Portuguese colonists had already opened way to another source of unfree labor in the Americas with the first shipments of Africans across the Atlantic.

The enduring practice of enslaving and trading people native to the American continents, coupled with the transatlantic slave trade of Africans, would go on to become the primary forms of unfree labor in the Americas for over three centuries.

Throughout their respective and overlapping histories, the former practice is estimated to have ensnared an estimated 2.5–5 million Native Americans (Reséndez 2016), while the latter shipped about 12.5 million Africans to the American continents (Hugh 1997). At minimum, this amounted to a combined 15-million-person slave economy, which necessarily involved greater numbers of unfree laborers when including those who were assigned legal slave status upon birth to enslaved parents.

The remaining sections of this chapter focus on how these two forms of unfree labor, along with a few others, manifested and evolved in the area now called the United States and how those manifestations inform modern conceptions of and responses to forced and coerced labor in the US.

2.2.2 Evolving Forms of Unfree Labor in Early North American Colonial Period

The first European forays into the areas now called the US largely focused on fishing and other financial pursuits. In their effort to prove value to their financial backers, these early European arrivals extended the practice (which started decades before in lower latitudes) of capturing Indigenous peoples both for the purpose of coercion into work locally and for showcasing, sale, and/or servitude in Europe (Reséndez 2016). In 1501, for example, a Portuguese expedition is recorded to have taken 57 Native people captive in or near modern-day Maine for sale in Europe (National Humanities Center 2006).

By 1584, the British made their first attempt at gaining a permanent foothold on the North American continent, with Sir Walter Raleigh's creation of the Roanoke Colony (modern-day North Carolina). Having experienced anti-protestant persecution in Europe, this particular group self-conceived as different from previous European ventures in the Americas in that they sought to create refuge from tyranny, for themselves and for the unfree laborers of the Iberian colonies (Morgan 1975). By the time Roanoke was found abandoned in 1590, however, and despite their stated ideals "That no Indian be forced to labor [unwillingly]" (Quinn 1955, as cited in Morgan 1975), these settlers had veered in the same direction as their Spanish and Portuguese counterparts. This was in part due to the capitalistic motives of the Roanoke colonizers. In their brief few years on North American soil, they prioritized experimentation with exportable agricultural goods and searches for minable deposits rather than focus on farming or fishing for their own subsistence. For basic food staples such as corn, they relied on a Native population that at first aided their "guests" willingly but ultimately found themselves struggling to meet the scale of the demands (Morgan 1975). This false start of a settlement developed the use of unfree labor in the region insofar as the colonists coerced help from Native peoples through the threat and actual use of violence, including kidnapings and lethal acts.

The first lasting British colony in the Americas began in Jamestown, in modern-day Virginia, in 1607. By the time a second colonial settlement was established up the Atlantic Coast in Plymouth, Massachusetts, in 1620, the Virginia settlement had already received, 1 year prior, a shipment of 20 Angolan "captives of war." They were put to work in early colonial enterprises and primarily tasked with agricultural and domestic work. Records from that first forced arrival of Africans to the North American British colonies, as well as subsequent disembarkments, mark the countries of origin of the unfree laborers, as well as their status as "servants." It was not until decades later that colonial governments first began to define the terms of North American colonial slavery legally and explicitly introduced race as a core determinant of slave status (Morris 1996; Kendi 2016).

This relatively short-lived period between the first disembarkment of Africans on British colonial soil (1619, Virginia) and the first formalization of racialized slavery in colonial law (1641, Massachusetts) provides a partial contrast to later periods. What started in the mid-seventeenth century as less formal and less racially specific forms of unfree labor evolved into the legal and economic institution of chattel slavery, which primarily focused on the subjugation of African and African-descended peoples. Eventually, all British colonies in North America would adopt racial definitions of slavery into their legal codes (Morris 1996).

In part, these codifications of race-based slavery served to differentiate that form of unfree labor from another that was a mainstay of the economic life of the colonies: indentured servants who were mostly White. Throughout the colonial period, tens of thousands of Europeans served terms of indenture – commonly 7 years – before they were granted certain rights and often also property (Kendi 2016; Morgan 1975). Before slavery laws, some persons of African origin were afforded this type of an arrangement upon the completion of which they were able to own land and even manage unfree labor of their own.

2.2.3 Rise, Boom, and Fall of US Chattel Slavery

Once informal cultural norms and practices of slavery found their way into colonial legal codes and eventually the US Constitution as well as individual states' laws, unfree labor arrangements became state-sanctioned and legally enforceable. These legal codes tied race (non-White), place of origin (non-European), and often religion (non-Christian) to slave status. As opposed to other forms of unfree labor in earlier colonial history, legalized slavery assigned slave status for life and specified that this designation was inheritable, from slave mothers to their children (Morris 1996).

In this new "peculiar institution," colonists-turned-revolutionaries found a solution to some of their largest logistical concerns, including the ability to compete with adversarial world powers and to gain more economic independence. Slavery also fueled their capitalist and imperialist ambitions: private industrial development, territorial expansion, and financial underwriting for religious campaigns and institutions of higher learning (Baptist 2014; Wilder 2013). A society that was once primarily concerned with subsistence pivoted to the lucrative harvesting of cotton, tobacco, indigo, and other "cash crops" on land expropriated, often violently, from

Native peoples. Indeed, expansion from the first of the colonies to new ground often had this capitalist motive at its core.

Eli Whitney's invention of the cotton gin shortly after the United States gained its independence gave this newly sovereign nation the ability to scale production of what became its most profitable export to record levels. Previously, it was the spinning of harvested cotton that bottlenecked production. After the gin revolutionized that rung of the production chain, it was most often a farmer's ability to import and manage labor that set its production potential. This created unprecedented demand for slave labor. Eventually, fueled by record numbers of Africans sold into the US slave market, the aggressive monocultural use of colonized lands often led to land exhaustion. This pushed early US capitalists into new territory, where the cycle would begin anew: Land was expropriated through force and fraudulent treaties with Native peoples (Treuer 2019), and legal slaves alongside other types of unfree laborers were forced to this new ground to generate wealth (Beckert 2014).

This path of US-imperialist expansion, dispossession, and exploitation shaped the contours of modern US geography and institutions: States were formed and accepted into the Union, institutions of higher learning were established and financed on slave labor, complex systems of trade, banking, and financial speculation were born of this slave-driven economy (Baptist 2014; Beckert 2014; Wilder 2013).

Modern observers might ponder how the rise and boom of a slave economy – from the first disembarkment of 20 deported Africans in Virginia in 1619 to the 3.9 million slaves counted by the US Census in 1860 – could have transpired in the same period that saw the US gain independence and define its identity around ideals of liberty, freedom, "inalienable rights," and even some (gendered) conceptions of equality. A complex tapestry of intellectual, economic (Chap. 14), and political fights over this dissonance famously culminated in the US Civil War and eventual dismantling of state-sanctioned chattel slavery. Until that juncture, however, and despite the efforts of spirited abolitionists, escaped-slaves-turned-activists, and political and religious leaders of conscience, the prevailing political forces of early US history allowed the slave trade room to grow decades past when other nations abolished this practice. In fact, the internal market for people born enslaved within the institution of US chattel slavery was so strong that the time period when the greatest number of legally enslaved people lived in the US was *after* the 1807 Act Prohibiting Importation of Slaves (Manson et al. 2019).

The way in which political coalitions, backed by economic interests, gave uninterrupted legal cover to their "peculiar institution" from the first colonial slave codes through 1865 holds lessons about what makes other manifestations of unfree labor after chattel slavery as lasting, adaptable, and seemingly intractable as they are – especially in the US context. At its heart, the institution of chattel slavery rested on the conception that certain others stand, inherently, apart from the self-selected core of society, government, and industry. As such, they were relegated to subservient identities and roles, such as three-fifths personhood and compelled labor (Morrison 2017).

This conception served as a means to an end. The proponents of this system of othering remained focused, often obsessively, on how to maximize economic gain from the labor of the subjugated class. In other words, the controlling interests of US industry, backed by the state, developed methods both brutal and often intricate of commodifying human beings (Rosenthal 2018; Schermerhorn 2015; Baptist 2014; Beckert 2014; Kendi 2016).

> *Tracing the historical, overt role of capitalism in trafficking to the modern context*
> Although the basic formula of commodifying labor through force and coercion remains embedded in modern capitalist systems, present-day corporations (Chap. 7) have largely found ways to claim roles only as unknowing or "passive" participants of crimes against workers while allowing outsourced actors to shoulder legal risk as the primary "active participants" in human rights abuses (De Vries 2019; Kepes et al. 2010). By acting as reputational risk shields and legal liability buffers, outsourced intermediaries, contractors, and field-level managers permit the resource-controlling heirs of the coercive capitalism of ages past to benefit financially from systemic violence against socially othered groups without taking on as obvious or seemingly intentional a role.

Throughout early US history and beyond, the othering and commodification of certain sectors of the US population did not only serve to create exploitable, unfree labor on grounds of race. It was also effective at disenfranchising women based on gender, dispossessing Native peoples of land based on religion (as well as lack of European descendance), and excluding alternating sets of new immigrant arrivals based on place of origin (Chap. 10). As such, othering proved to be a versatile tool of self-selected "inside" classes (Morrison 2017). Understood in this way, it is predictable that this method of subjugation went on to outlast the particular institution of race-based, legalized chattel slavery.

2.2.4 Late 19th to Early Twentieth Century: Slavery by Other Means

To understand present forms of compelled labor in the US, no chapter in history may hold as many insights as that immediately following the fall of the legal institution of slavery. It was in this period, during Reconstruction, that many sectors of the US economy which depended on chattel slavery set about the task of crafting new ways to secure other forms of unfree labor (Chap. 9). Former Confederate states in particular became a wide and varied testing ground for new ways to coerce labor from othered populations (Blackmon 2008). The methods employed in that era closely match techniques detailed in modern-day criminal indictments against labor traffickers.

Whereas race once served as a categorical way to relegate an entire sector of the population to forced labor, new criteria had to be developed. Former slaveholders quickly leveraged the economic disadvantages of newly "freed" people against them. "Vagrants" were apprehended and legally put to work powering the same industries slaves once did, in part taking advantage of the 13th Amendment's exception for compelled convict labor (Foner 2015). California, having recently joined the US as a "free soil" state, codified the use of these practices specifically *against* Native peoples with the duplicitously named Act for the Government and Protection of Indians[1] (passed in 1850 and finally repealed in 1937) (Johnston-Dodds 2002; Reséndez 2016). In these workplaces, employers happened upon a method that is still proving effective for labor traffickers in present day: by becoming not just the employer but also the purveyor of other basic necessities such as housing, transportation, supplies, and food, employers leveraged such control over their "employees" they could often take back with one hand the wages they paid workers with the other. In present legal terms, this practice is known as debt bondage.[2] When victims of these ploys would question them or attempt to exert the freedom that had purportedly been assigned to them by the 13th Amendment, Reconstruction-era labor traffickers, much like their modern counterparts, simply resorted back to brute force including lethal force (Foner 2015). This private use of coercion and violence by employers to secure unfree labor took place against the backdrop of a generally violent and discriminatory environment for othered groups in what came to be called the Jim Crow era.

In this period, pretenses for compelling labor shifted from explicit racial terms to terms focused on economic status that targeted certain racial groups (e.g., Blacks and Natives). Despite this adaptation, the core formula of unfree labor remained the same during Reconstruction and beyond: subsectors of the population were othered and subsequently commodified for economic gain by White business owners. This era held a dangerous lesson for those seeking to gain advantage by compelling the labor of others: slavery could be achieved, as one historian framed it, "by another name" (Blackmon 2008).

Commodification and Trafficking.
By definition, human trafficking involves some degree of "commodification" of a person. Not all the ways that people are commodified constitute human trafficking, but all human trafficking does in some way to extract economic profit or services out of a person. It is the fact that a person is commodified *and* that they are commodified through force, fraud, and/ or coercion that defines human trafficking. In order to understand how specific people in specific contexts – such as schools or hospitals – present as trafficked and commodified persons, it helps to understand the forces that drive human commodification generally.

---

[1] The act additionally facilitated the removal of California Natives from their lands, separated at least one generation of children from adults, families, languages, and cultures, and indentured Native children and adults to Whites.

[2] 22 USC § 7102(5): "The term 'debt bondage' means the status or condition of a debtor arising from a pledge by the debtor of [their] personal services or of those of a person under [their] control as a security for debt, if the value of those services as reasonably assessed is not applied toward the liquidation of the debt or the length and nature of those services are not, respectively, limited and defined."

2.2.5 Twentieth Century: Myopic Rise and Eventual Broadening of Anti-trafficking Frame

Present-day campaigns against human trafficking have often cast themselves as heirs to the abolitionist campaigns of past chapters in history. However, the terminology of "trafficking in persons" links back to a highly specific concern that gained prominence in the early twentieth century: the forcing or coercing of White women into commercial sex (Chap. 9) (Cyrus 2015). Official action such as the International Agreement for the Suppression of the White Slave Traffic of 1904 and the US White-Slave Traffic Act of 1910, also known as the Mann Act, gave rise to a unique conception of "abolitionism." In this iteration of "abolitionism," those to be "freed" were of one gender (women), one race (White), and exploited for one purpose (commercial sex). Far from the roots of traditional abolitionism, this twentieth century, anti-trafficking "abolitionism" reserved, if not in law, in rhetoric, victimhood status for a single racial group. Once implemented, this "abolitionism" was often leveraged to criminalize consensual interracial sexual relations. Official acknowledgement of this misuse recently led to the presidential pardon of a professional boxer whose conviction under this Act is widely seen as having been motivated by racism (Eligon and Shear 2018).

Tellingly, the "abolitionists" of the early twentieth century did not weigh in on public policy matters wherein the legacy of unfree, othered labor was concerned. In 1935, for example, proponents of the National Labor Relations Act (NLRA) made a concession to Southern Democrats to secure its passage: the bill would exclude from its landmark labor protections domestic and agricultural workers, so as not to give the predominantly African-descended workers in those sectors equal footing with the White working class (Gilmore 2008). The repercussions of this racially motivated concession are felt to this day. US farm workers, now transformed to a majority immigrant workforce, still lack the rights enshrined in this bill such as collective bargaining protections (Brennan 2014). Not coincidentally, domestic and agricultural workplaces rank among the most common sources of modern-day labor trafficking cases (Feehs and Currier 2020; Owens et al. 2014).

Indeed, it would be nearly a century before the early 1900s, "abolitionism" would intersect with labor trafficking and its related drivers of racism, xenophobia, and othering. As a first step in that direction, a series of US and international redrafts of the "trafficking in persons" frame slowly and incrementally broadened the term to include, at least on paper, a concern for people of all ages, gender identities, racial backgrounds, and venues of exploitation. In its 1921 International Convention for the Suppression of the Traffic in Women and Children, the League of Nations removed the explicit racial emphasis of earlier conventions. By 1949, the United Nation's Convention for the Suppression of the Traffic in Persons included men as well as women.[3] It would not be until the U.N.'s fourth world conference in 1994, however, that the trafficking frame first included definitions beyond the realm of commercial sex (Bonilla and Mo 2019).

---

[3] Here, "men and women" (rather than "people of all genders") is used as a phrase. This implies inclusion but still excludes (by not considering or ignoring) transgender, nonbinary, and intersex folks.

2.3   Conclusion

At the turn of the twenty-first century, the United Nations and the US enacted, correspondingly, a Protocol and an Act that each defined in similar terms the general frame that is in use, to date, to criminalize the forcing or coercing of labor. Whereas past legislation had defined unfree labor in whichever common terms were used for it in their eras – slavery, peonage, and indentured servitude – these modern conventions describe with great variety and specificity the actions, means, and purposes involved in the making of unfree labor. Furthermore, these modern legal definitions do not attempt to specify identities of neither victims nor perpetrators by race, gender, or any other such criterion. Spain's 1542 New Laws of the Indies for the Good Treatment and Preservation of the Indians specifically set out to ban the enslavement of people native to the Americas. When the US Congress enacted the 1807 law "to prohibit the importation of slaves," the authors specified they were referring to "any negro, mulatto, or person of color" (Slave Trade Prohibition Act 1807). As recently as the twentieth century, as discussed above, "anti-trafficking" acts specified a concern for White victims in particular. Against that historical backdrop, the current definitions of the Trafficking Victims Protection Act could be called the most adaptable and universal definitions of unfree labor since the start of official action against it.

This blank slate, however, comes with a distinct risk. As this chapter has demonstrated, the trajectory of unfree labor in the United States and beyond *is* deeply intertwined with race, geographical origin, and religion. Indeed, both state-backed and illicit forms of labor trafficking throughout history have consistently relied on the othering of varying subsets of the population as defined by those categories in order to commodify them for profit. Although it is prudent for lawmakers to create definitions of trafficking broad enough to capture all present and future forms of this form of abuse, it would be misguided for current anti-trafficking campaigns to turn a rightfully identity-blind definition into naively identity-blind plans of action. Those who force or coerce labor have historically targeted groups that are otherable along any avenue of discrimination (often along many at once), and continue to do so in present times.

History-informed responses to human trafficking must take this reality into account, by both allowing for the fact that, as one US federal enforcement agency states, this type of abuse "can happen in any community and victims can be any age, race, gender, or nationality" (USDHS 2020) and adjusting for the reality that the process of othering and commodifying people was never an equal opportunity enterprise nor is it today. Non-White persons remain overrepresented among US populations with a trafficking experience relative to their share of the general population, as are foreign nationals (Bouche 2018; Bouche 2020; Feehs and Currier 2020). Racist and xenophobic ideologies manifested in present politics and policy (Chap. 12) directly sustain this pattern.

Insofar as human trafficking serves to create wealth for its perpetrators, this racism, xenophobia, and related forms of othering are not ends in themselves, but means to an ages-old end of human commodification. In the example of the agricultural sector analysis set forth in the introduction, this implies that anti-trafficking work must involve both addressing individual cases of human trafficking and correcting the ideological structures that allow an official government census to survey demographics of predominantly White farm owners – a humanizing treatment – while only counting mostly foreign-born, non-White farm workers by headcount and cost in the same category of other farm "commodities" – a markedly dehumanizing categorization (USDA 2020). The example serves as a reminder that racist, xenophobic, and related ideologies of human othering and commodification still transit in barely disguised plain language even when not coded into hard law.

To combat human trafficking means to challenge that language at every manifestation. Before British colonies in North America first codified the practice of unfree labor into race-based slave laws, *and also after these slave laws were abolished,* the kidnappers, transporters, brokers, managers, and owners of unfree labor have found subtler ways to engrain their choice to dehumanize people for profit into systems of rationalization. Before the slave codes, a ship disembarked in 1619 carrying African "servants" (Blackmon 2008); before state-enforced chattel slavery, an early British colonist in modern-day Virginia recorded in a 1627 willed the transfer to his heirs of "debts chattles servants negars cattle or any other thynge" (Kendi 2016); after the 13th Amendment, Antebellum land owners were soon found employing "vagrants" turned compelled workers (Blackmon 2008). Today, when any public or private actor, and especially one as standard-setting as a federal census, chooses to categorize, as in the aforementioned 1627 will, human labor next to cattle, anti-trafficking practitioners must take notice. History suggests dehumanizing language precedes and sustains dehumanizing acts of exploitation, which include the hundreds of cases of human trafficking identified by service providers and/or indicted by prosecutors each year.[4]

2.4 Recommendations

1. *Rehistoricize training and educational materials on human trafficking.* Practitioners of all professions are often introduced to the issue of human trafficking through case studies that begin and end within the confines of single instances of modern unfree labor, usually described through the case's course through the criminal justice system. While instructive, these case studies must be paired with context about which demographic groups are most often victimized in this way, which sectors of the economy are most often host to such cases, and

---

[4] Farm workers accounted for 17.7% of all such cases in the US in 2019, tied for second with restaurant workers after domestic workers (Feehs and Currier 2020).

which actors most often facilitate and/or perpetrate the use of force, fraud, and coercion.[5]

2. *Pair statistics about the prevailing forms of contemporary unfree labor with the factors that have proved to determine manifestations of unfree labor in the past as well.* That contextualization will necessarily involve detailing of how capitalism, colonialism, and imperialism have and continue to build unfree labor into value chains.

3. *Resurface how racism, nativism, and/or religious ideology can create permission structures around the aforesaid systems of oppression today, as they have in the past.* By naming the dynamics at play behind systemic trends in unfree labor, anti-trafficking professionals will be best equipped to address them.

4. *Identify and amend legislation that still serves to legitimize the othering of selected groups by economic interests for the purpose of commodification, including trafficking.* Domestic and farm workers, for example, have had to rely on individual states to bridge still-existing Jim Crow-era exemptions from basic labor protections (Brennan 2014).

References

Baptist, E. (2014). *The half has never been told: Slavery and the making of American capitalism.* New York: Basic Books.

Barrick, K., Lattimore, P. K., Pitts, W. J., & Zhang, S. X. (2013). *Indicators of labor trafficking among North Carolina Migrant Farmworkers.* Retrieved from https://www.ncjrs.gov/pdffiles1/nij/grants/244204.pdf.

Beckert, S. (2014). *Empire of cotton: A global history.* New York: Vintage Books.

Blackmon, D. (2008). *Slavery by another name: The re-enslavement of Black people in America from the Civil War to World War II.* New York: Anchor.

Bonilla, T., & Mo, C. (2019). The evolution of human trafficking messaging in the United States and its effect on public opinion. *Journal of Public Policy, 39*(2), 201–234.

Bouche, V. (2018). Survivor insights: The role of technology in domestic minor sex trafficking. *Thorn.* Retrieved from https://www.thorn.org/wp-content/uploads/2018/01/Thorn_Survivor_Insights_DMST_Executive_Summary.pdf.

Bouche, V. (2020). *Human trafficking data* [Database]. Retrieved from http://www.humantraffickingdata.org/.

Bouche, V., & Daku, M. (2019). Who's disproportionately prosecuted for human trafficking? Young Black men. *The Washington Post.* Retrieved from https://www.washingtonpost.com/news/monkey-cage/wp/2019/01/11/young-black-men-are-disproportionately-likely-to-be-prosecuted-for-human-trafficking-this-explains-why/.

Bowden, H. (1981). *American Indians and Christian missions: Studies in cultural conflict.* Chicago: University of Chicago Press.

---

[5] This analysis must also account for the fact that the US criminal justice system tends to overpolice and overprosecute non-White persons relative to their share of the offender population, a general trend that has been specifically observed in the present enforcement of laws against human trafficking (Bouche and Daku 2019).

Brennan, D. (2014). *Life interrupted: Trafficking into forced labor in the United States*. Durham: Duke University Press.

Cyrus, N. (2015). *The concept of demand in relation to trafficking in human beings: A review of debates since the late 19th century*. Demand AT Working Paper No 1. Vienna: ICMPD. Retrieved from http://www.demandat.eu/publications.

De Vries, I. (2019). Connected to crime: An exploration of the nesting of labor trafficking and exploitation in legitimate markets. *British Journal of Criminology, 59*, 209–230. https://doi. org/10.1093/bjc/azy019.

Eligon, J., & Shear, M. (2018, May). Trump Pardons Jack Johnson, Heavyweight Boxing Champion. *The New York Times*. Retrieved from https://www.nytimes.com/2018/05/24/sports/jack-johnson-pardon-trump.html.

Feehs, K., & Currier, A. (2020). *2019 Federal Human Trafficking Report*. Human Trafficking Institute. Retrieved from https://www.traffickinginstitute.org/wp-content/uploads/2020/05/2019-Federal-Human-Trafficking-Report_Low-Res.pdf.

Foner, E. (2015). *Reconstruction: America's unfinished revolution* (pp. 1863–1877). New York: Harper Perennial.

Gilmore, G. (2008). *Defying Dixie: The radical roots of civil rights* (pp. 1919–1950). New York: Norton.

Hugh, T. (1997). *The slave trade: The story of the Atlantic slave trade, 1440–1870*. New York: Simon & Schuster.

Johnston-Dodds, K. (2002). *Early California laws and policies related to California Indians*. California Research Bureau. Retrieved from https://www.library.ca.gov/Content/pdf/crb/reports/02-014.pdf.

Kendi, I. (2016). *Stamped from the beginning: The definitive history of racist ideas in America*. New York: Nation Books.

Kepes, Q., Kepes, N., & Viederman, D. (2010). *Immigrant workers in US agriculture: The role of labor brokers in vulnerability to forced labor*. Retrieved from https://www.verite.org/wp-content/uploads/2017/03/HELP-WANTED_A-Verite%CC%81-Report_Migrant-Workers-in-the-United-States.pdf.

Manson, S., Schroeder, J., Van Riper, D., & Ruggles, S. (2019). *IPUMS national historical geographic information system: Version 14.0* [Database]. Minneapolis: IPUMS. Retrieved from https://doi.org/10.18128/D050.V14.0.

Morgan, E. (1975). *American slavery, American freedom*. New York: W. W. Norton & Company.

Morris, T. (1996). *Southern slavery and the law, 1619–1860*. Chapel Hill: University of North Carolina Press.

Morrison, T. (2017). *The origin of others*. Cambridge, MA: Harvard University Press.

National Humanities Center. (2006). *On the arrival of two ships in Lisbon, Portugal, from the expedition of Gaspar Corte Real to the North Atlantic Ocean* [Letter]. Retrieved from http://nationalhumanitiescenter.org/pds/amerbegin/contact/text1/gcreal.pdf.

Owens, C., Dank, M., Breaux, J., Banuelos, I., Farrell, A., Pfeffer, R., Bright, K., Heitsmith, R., & McDevitt, J. (2014). *Understanding the organization, operation, and victimization process of labor trafficking in the United States*. Retrieved from https://www.urban.org/sites/default/files/publication/33821/413249-Understanding-the-Organization-Operation-and-Victimization-Process-of-Labor-Trafficking-in-the-United-States.PDF.

Quinn, D. (Ed.). (1955). *The Roanoke voyages: 1584–1590*. London: Cambridge University Press.

Reséndez, A. (2016). *The other slavery: The uncovered story of Indian enslavement in America*. New York: Mariner Books.

Rosenthal, C. (2018). *Accounting for slavery: Masters and management*. Cambridge: Harvard University Press.

Schermerhorn, C. (2015). *The business of slavery and the rise of American capitalism, 1815–1860*. New Haven: Yale University Press.

Slave Trade Prohibition Act. (1807). 2 Stat. 426 Chapter 22, 9 Congress, Session 2.

Treuer, D. (2019). *The heartbeat of wounded knee: Native America from 1890 to the present*. New York: Riverhead Books.

U.S. Department of Agriculture: National Agricultural Statistics Service. (2020). Quick stats [Online query tool]. Retrieved from https://quickstats.nass.usda.gov/#07763A9B-1C14-3BE9-8075-C1FAEC61889B.

U.S. Department of Homeland Security. (2020). *What is human trafficking?* Retrieved from https://www.dhs.gov/blue-campaign/what-human-trafficking.

Wilder, C. (2013). *Ebony and Ivy: Race, slavery, and the troubled history of American universities*. New York: Bloomsbury Press.

Chapter 3
Manufacturing Freedom

Luis C.deBaca

3.1 Introduction

3.1.1 The Women at the Factory Gate

Peering through the factory fence, the Vietnamese women strained to see if any cars were coming down the isolated road. Perhaps they would be able to wave someone down who might help them. Factory guards, armed with truncheons, appeared. The garment factory owner, who seemed to have absolute power over them, came and started taking photos of them as they clustered at the gates. Afraid and dejected, they returned to the cramped barracks where they were housed on-site. In the morning, they would return to their sewing machines. But the food was restricted, their passports had been taken, and they owed debts for their recruiting and transportation to the job. Anyone who spoke up risked arrest and political consequences with the Vietnamese secret police. Slowly, the women began to think about how to seek help, pooling the few words in English they could think of so that the interpreter in their group could write a note. She smuggled the note, with the universal emergency word "SOS" written across the top, out of the factory into the hands of a sailor who eventually got it to the authorities. But before she or the others could be rescued, the interpreter and others were arrested and deported at the owner's direction. The remaining workers were threatened, starved, and eventually beaten behind the

L. C.deBaca (✉)
The Gilder Lehrman Center for the Study of Slavery, Resistance, and Abolition, Yale University, New Haven, CT, USA
e-mail: amb@chamberslopez.com

© Springer Nature Switzerland AG 2021
M. Chisolm-Straker, K. Chon (eds.), *The Historical Roots of Human Trafficking*,
https://doi.org/10.1007/978-3-030-70675-3_3

factory fence. Their enslavement[1] did not take place in a developing country, but in the United States. It was the year 2000.

The resulting prosecution served as a test case for the new countertrafficking approach emerging in US and international law. With social services, immigration options, and government support, the hundreds of Vietnamese and Chinese workers did not just see factory owner Kil Soo Lee brought to justice under the involuntary servitude and slavery statutes. They were able to reunify with family and carve out a life of freedom in the United States.

3.1.2 The Little Match Girls

The Match Girls were finished. The factories in which they worked were dirty and dangerous, and they were on their feet for 12–14 hours at a time. The machinery could catch their skirts and hair, and the managers had made it clear that the machines and matches were the first priority, not the safety of the workers. Beatings, fines, and food restrictions were all too common, and if a woman or girl was injured by one of the machines or by the racks of matches blowing up, they were unceremoniously fired without any medical care or social support. They got word to a woman known as a social reformer—an upper-class woman with political and literary contacts—who began to tell their story, characterizing their plight as "White slavery" (Besant 1888). Almost immediately, the factory bosses started an internal investigation to identify the whistleblowers. Three were singled out. For a week, the bosses gave them bad assignments or rejected their work as flawed so that they only earned a pittance and then turned them out onto the street penniless. With nothing left to lose, the Match Girls walked off the job.

Their strength changed the world. In the first major international strikes of the late 1800s, the first factory workers to rise up were the teenaged girls of London's East End. These young women's activism was the "match to fire the Thames," and they were credited with triggering the start of a labor movement—including the enormous London Dockworkers' Strike of 1889. This was the seminal moment in the formal labor movement, resulting in standards and practices that continue in the factory setting to this day such as the right to organize, the minimum wage, and maximum hours (Stafford 1961).

---

[1] A note on terminology. With an emphasis on the US context, one of the slaveries to be considered in this chapter is the racist legal system of chattel slavery of African-Americans in the United States. Other slaveries with differing legal names take place after Emancipation (slavery, involuntary servitude, peonage, debt bondage, convict leasing, forced labor, labor trafficking, etc). In the last 20 years, "human trafficking" or "trafficking in persons" have become dominant, with a recent resurgence of "slavery" led by the Commonwealth Countries. For this chapter, the many names of slaveries will be used interchangeably as roughly synonymous. "Slaveries" is not a typo, but a conscious attempt to put the many forms of compelled service across time and space in context, "invok[ing] pluralities of perceptions, of exploitation forms, and of meanings of the term" (Bravo 2017).

These two cases, over a century apart, are examples of how factory settings are often the sites of worker abuse and exploitation; it is often of women and children who are made vulnerable by immigration, poverty, or social exclusion. The cases are also examples of how workers, even in the direst of straits, can turn their sweatshops into sites of resistance. And such resistance can drive the development of labor protections and worker-friendly policies.

But, while factories (especially garment and electronics) are commonly mentioned sites of exploitation in today's modern slavery and human rights transparency discussions, enforcement of antislavery or anti-trafficking statutes has been rare in factory settings. This chapter will explore this conundrum, identify common and competing approaches to combat abuse in factories, ground current cases and practices in historical context, and make recommendations both for improvement in the manufacturing sector and for how lessons learned in factories can inform interventions in other common sites of exploitation.

3.2   Discussion

3.2.1   Factory Cases at the Dawn of the Twenty-First Century Antislavery Movement

The garment factory case set forth in the Introduction, *United States v. Kil Soo Lee*, was one of the first prosecutions brought after the passage of the United States Trafficking Victims Protection Act of 2000 (TVPA). Because so much of the offense conduct predated the passage of the new law, the prosecution was brought under the postCivil War slavery statutes; the TVPA's main impact on the case was in victim protection, allowing for resettlement, integration, and both short- and long-term immigration benefits for the survivors. While some of the workers chose to return home, the majority chose to resettle in the United States. The TVPA's victim services and immigration provisions would not be tested over time in small matters, but suddenly and by what was at the time the largest slavery prosecution in US history, with approximately 300 victims.

That the TVPA existed at all and that the immigration services and other victim protection provisions were available to the Daewoosa victims (and the agents, prosecutors, victim/witness staff, churches, refugee organizations, legal aid lawyers, social workers, and others who came to their aid) was in many ways the legacy of political processes kickstarted by the discovery of another major garment factory slavery case a few years earlier in the Los Angeles area: *United States v. Manasurangkun* (the "El Monte" case; see Fig. 3.1).

In the summer of 1995, a group of more than 70 Thai garment workers were found in a garment factory guarded with walls and razor wire in El Monte, California, just outside of Los Angeles. Some of the workers had been there as long as 6 years and held under threats of violence and deportation, after being recruited to come to

Fig. 3.1 Cases and law/enforcement timeline

the United States with promises of a better life. This shocking story broke just weeks after CBS News had aired a high-profile report on a large farmworker case in Florida, *United States v. Flores*. The public and political response to the discovery of the El Monte sweatshop was a shock to a Department of Justice enforcement effort that had seen its once-robust Involuntary Servitude and Slavery program (Chap. 9) shrink to just a case or two a year in the wake of the 1988 adverse Supreme Court decision, *United States v. Kozminski*. As a result, the Justice Department's Civil Rights Division sought to produce an internal Manual for the Investigation and Prosecution of Worker Exploitation and Abuse, so that critical lessons of the El Monte and *Flores* cases would not be lost.

This internal manual blossomed into the National Worker Exploitation Task Force (WETF), an interagency effort chaired by the Civil Rights Division and the Office of the Solicitor of Labor. Boosted by the energy of President Bill Clinton's 1998 Memorandum on Steps to Combat Violence Against Women and Trafficking of Women and Girls, the Task Force's legislative recommendations were to become the TVPA. While containing victim protections such as new visa programs and ensuring access to public benefits, the TVPA was an enforcement-driven law. It reflected the experiences of law enforcement as well as social service providers in meeting the needs of victims in the El Monte case and other high-profile prosecutions.

3.2.2 An Alternative Response to Worker Exploitation in Factories

Enforcement was not the only policy approach coming out of the Clinton White House relevant to worker abuse in factories in the late 1990s. A separate effort, seemingly uncoordinated with the WETF or anti-trafficking mandate, arose in response to a broad-based antisweatshop movement. In 1996, just as the El Monte case was ending in Los Angeles, high profile sweatshop cases in overseas supply chains came to light. White-hot scandals in the supply chains of Nike and television host Kathie Lee Gifford's clothing line for Walmart combined with a student-led movement based on concerns about university-branded apparel (Schrempf-Stirling and Palazzo 2016).

The solutions of the antisweatshop movement, facilitated by the Department of Labor and the Clinton White House, were less about enforcement and more about corporate social responsibility (CSR) and self-auditing.[2] In the field of social auditing, codes of conduct and standards are set by the brands or retailers (or groups representing their interests), imposed upon suppliers (and ideally, their subcontractors) and monitored by auditing firms who typically concentrate on issues such as safety, wages, and workers' rights. One of the best known of the Multi-Stakeholder Initiatives (MSIs) that emerged from the antisweatshop movement is the Fair Labor Association (FLA). The FLA was founded to ensure safety and decent work conditions along the university-branded garment supply chain and has built upon its experience to work in related industries. The tools and approaches of the MSIs have become dominant in the field of Business and Human Rights (BHR), which has seen great growth since the promulgation of the United Nations Guiding Principles on Business and Human Rights (the "Ruggie Principles") in 2011.

The two approaches to forced labor that emerged from factory abuses in the 1990s reflect two different assumptions about worker exploitation. Optimally, these approaches can work in tandem to cover all aspects of the issue. One approach (the BHR approach) assumes the companies as key stakeholders and seeks to improve their compliance with labor standards while continuing factory operations so as not to disrupt the industries. The other approach (antislavery/trafficking) responds to the human rights crime committed by the factory owner or managers and is likely to result in the closing of the business and seizure of its assets to provide restitution to the victims. It does not focus on all of the parties as stakeholders, but on the workers as rights holders. It is this second, carceral, response that is seen as antislavery/trafficking enforcement.

In factory cases, however, law enforcement responses are almost unheard of, whether in the United States or elsewhere. There may be many disincentives for labor inspectors or other enforcement arms to classify a factory case as slavery/trafficking as opposed to wage theft or other labor violation. Corruption aside (though it has a dramatic impact on some countries' manufacturing sectors), it could be as simple as performance measures: labor inspectors often do not have a way to get credit for criminal enforcement activities, even if a successful case happens as a result of their work. It may be an issue of training: labor inspectors are typically trained on "their" mandates as opposed to the human rights violation of slavery/trafficking and as a result are so focused on wage or safety issues that they might miss the indicators of forced labor.

In the Daewoosa case, labor inspectors had been in the factory and had assessed back wages against Kil Soo Lee on behalf of the workers. Indeed, one of the counts he was convicted of in addition to the slavery charges included his theft of the

---

[2] The recommendations and actions of the Administration were criticized by antisweatshop activists and Labor as being too corporate-friendly (Hapke 2004).

worker's government-ordered back pay: as the workers received their settlement, they were loaded onto a bus to a local bank, where they were forced to sign the checks back over to him. The officials in that case were literally in the middle of a slavery situation, but did not recognize it due to their "lens." Tragically, to the seam-stresses, the ineffectualness of the initial federal response proved Mr. Lee's power over not just them but also the federal government.

The strengths of the BHR lens might also, counterintuitively, shield abuse from view. If a supplier, under pressure from more powerful companies up the supply chain, publicly announces that they will undertake workers' rights activities – even if they are ineffectual or even intentionally misleading – it slows the scandal and creates an impression that they are therefore a "clean" factory. Manufacturers, gov-ernments, and international organizations announce public/private partnerships, the success of which becomes more of a goal than uncovering abuses that might call the agreements into question (Ibrahim 2020). Governmental labor inspectorates shift their attention to other worksites, and abuses thereafter occur quietly, out of sight of infrequent auditing visits from brand representatives. The effectiveness of such audits, and the certification schemes they support, has been questioned by research-ers and activists (LeBaron 2018, MSI Integrity 2020).

So, too, social auditors and government officials used to inspect for safety and health violations in unsafe settings may simply overlook slavery in factories that appear safe and clean. Many allegations of worker abuse in Asia have taken place in the electronics industry that requires sterile environments – but looks can be deceiv-ing. Auditors and others, used to seeing unsafe piles of cloth in a garment factory or witnessing illegal dumping of harmful chemicals in other factories, can be blinded by the cleanliness of a modern electronics factory.[3] But the esthetics of clean suits and well-lit workrooms do not give insight into the mental condition of the workers or any structural, financial, or physical coercion they may be facing. Recruiting debts and other coercion are common in these sectors as well. Factory managers claim to be holding workers' passports for safekeeping, and workers indeed often initially give over their documents willingly. Recruiting and transportation fees – and the resulting debts – are cast as reasonable costs and have only recently been recognized as coercive, whether through regulations such as President Barack Obama's Executive Order 13627 or by companies themselves in their contracts with suppliers.

Another form of enforcement bias might be taking place, with the dramatic emphasis placed on sex trafficking (especially of US-born children) in the wake of the enactment of local anti-trafficking statutes by US states. The rhetorical and political focus on child sex trafficking has resulted in enforcement teams led by vice investigators familiar with the commercial sex industry but unfamiliar with more legitimate businesses like manufacturing. Even at the federal level, larger cases of

---

[3] Former FLA executives, called in by Apple to inspect factories operated by Foxconn, were pil-loried for publicly complimenting the working conditions and cleanliness of the plants upon their initial visits.

labor trafficking have been handled through administrative or private action rather than as criminal cases.[4]

To be fair, another reason why there may not be as many prosecuted cases in the factory setting is that more formal or industrial factories are indeed monitored more than other worksites. A factory with an imperfect auditing scheme (one that concentrates on safety rather than workers' human rights or economic power or that is part of an MSI that exists more for "greenwashing"[5] than to uncover and remediate abuse) is still a factory that is more monitored than a fishing fleet, private homes, brothels, or many agricultural worksites. The strong nature of industrial labor unions, and the comparatively formal setting of factories, may make abuses in factories less prevalent in some countries. Perhaps it actually is easier to categorize abuses in a dirty garment factory with locked stairwells and exposed wiring than in a sleek modern electronics factory. The challenge, however, is to look beneath the surface, at the lived experience of the workers.

3.2.3 What Are Factories?

Factories often call to mind the huge industrial buildings of early twentieth century, populated by thousands of strong men performing heavy industrial labor. These fictional factory men are protected by powerful unions and capable of supporting an entire family just on their salary. The reality, however, is much less glamorous, much dirtier, and more dangerous and likely to involve women workers. According to the US Trafficking in Persons (TIP) Report and NGO human rights actors, factories with forced labor problems produce not only garments and electronics but also rubber gloves and other medical supplies, leather goods, sports equipment, and processed food (TIP Report 2018). A factory can be clean and new, or cramped and dangerous; it might have walls and barracks and defined spaces, or it might be a cluster of sheds and pavilions. Factories can be seen as places where dispossessed agrarian workers are exploited or can be seen (as by the International Monetary Fund and World Bank) as threshold opportunities of development. While labor unions see themselves as protectors of factory workers, they have come to represent fewer and fewer workers and, even in countries where labor organizing is legal, unions are often not present in some of the more abusive manufacturing or processing sectors or are unable to provide adequate voice to the workers (Josserand and Kaine 2016).

---

[4]Two of the largest such cases are *David v. Signal* (2012), in which high-skilled Indian welders who were held on an Alabama shipyard brought suit against the company, and *EEOC v. Hill Country Farms*, in which the government brought disability discrimination action against those who abused developmentally disabled US citizen adults in a poultry processing operation in Iowa.

[5]"Greenwashing" is a commonly used term to characterize how companies use marketing to make themselves and their products as environmentally friendly rather than changing their business practices. Until a similar term specific to modern slavery ("free-washing?") comes into common use, "greenwashing" is being borrowed for social as well as environmental hypocrisy.

3.2.4 Where Have the Factory Cases Gone?

Occurring relatively back-to-back and given their prominence in the TVPA formulation and implementation, the El Monte and Daewoosa garment factory cases seemed to indicate that the United States had a major problem with slavery in factory settings, rather than in agriculture, domestic service, the commercial sex trade, or the other settings. Although most cases since have emerged in nonfactory settings, these major cases simultaneously presented attributes as varied as emergent victim care needs of very large populations, money laundering and banking, and the need for international investigation and diplomatic engagement. As a result, these cases, with several other complex cases in the 1990s (*US v. Flores*, *US v. Cadena*, and the "Deaf Mexican" trinket peddling case *US v. Paoletti*) were the testing grounds for techniques that became applicable to slavery/trafficking in all of its forms – the model that became known as the multiagency "victim-centered approach" to combatting trafficking.

The hallmark of the victim-centered approach was to assemble a multiagency team from the inception of the case, combining government investigators, labor inspectors, victim/witness specialists, immigration specialists, social service providers, legal aid, medical professionals, and even religious charities as appropriate, in order to address the needs of the victims concomitant to the needs of the prosecution. This approach, so necessary when dealing with dozens or even hundreds of victims in a factory setting, turned out to be equally effective in small cases as well.

The cases fueled reforms: the El Monte case led to the internal working group that became the interagency WETF and led to the TVPA. The Daewoosa prosecution was the proving ground for the Continued Presence and T-visa immigration programs and the victim care ethos of the new law. Both involved dozens or hundreds of victims, requiring a victim-centered approach by prosecutors and investigators partnering closely with community-based organizations, many of whom are still leaders in the anti-trafficking response. Some of those leaders are the Coalition to Abolish Slavery and Trafficking (CAST), Heartland Alliance, MOSAIC Family Services, and the Thai Community Development Center. Prosecutors from the El Monte and Daewoosa cases not only went on to establish a more robust anti-trafficking enforcement effort, making the multiagency victim-centered approach the gold standard for investigations and prosecutions, but also have played key roles in legislative and diplomatic efforts against trafficking and slavery.

But for all of the importance of the sweatshop prosecutions of the 1990s and the recognition of manufacturing-sector abuses in the law and politics of trafficking, further labor trafficking prosecutions in the United States have typically not occurred in factories. Rather, such cases are prosecuted more commonly in cleaning, restaurants, agriculture, domestic service, and home healthcare industries. And most trafficking prosecutions in the United States are now not for labor abuse but for commercial sexual exploitation, primarily of children. This mirrors international trends as well and begs some troubling questions: Are all factories in the US actually "clean?" Are factories in the other countries only "semi–dirty" rather than rising to the level of a provable forced labor case? How can law enforcement's gaze be turned to encompass forced labor as well as child sex trafficking? If there *are* abuses in factories, but law enforcement persists in not being aware of or not responding to them, what are other alternatives to confronting forced labor in this setting through noncarceral responses?

3.2.5   *Garment Manufacturing Shifted Overseas, so the Abuses Likely Did as Well*

The El Monte case drew the nation's attention, and the following year saw the scandals involving Nike and Kathy Lee Gifford. Revelations that campus athletic wear was tainted by forced labor started a student-driven antisweatshop movement. Spurred to action by the El Monte case, the Department of Labor and the US Immigration and Naturalization Service brought high-profile action against New York factories, raiding dozens of them in 1996 alone (Dugger 1996).

These enforcement actions, aimed at "cleaning up" the garment industry, focused on assessing wage/hour penalties or enforcing immigration laws, rather than uncovering additional slavery cases. This perfect storm of enforcement and consumer interest, combined with the postCold War explosion of globalization to drastically reduce the size and scope of the US domestic garment industry. Garment manufacturing in the United States is now a shadow of its former self. Much of it has been moved overseas, and the big industry players started selecting the sites of their factories in order to minimize costs and regulatory interference (Chap. 7), while still retaining access to the US and European markets.

Still, manufacturers wanted the "Made in the USA" label not just for the nativist appeal but also for the lack of tariffs. US insular possessions became one way to have the benefit of low costs and lax regulations while still being on US soil. One such manufacturing operation took place in the Commonwealth of the Northern Mariana Islands (CNMI). About a 4-hour flight from Japan, the Marianas island chain (the Territory of Guam and the CNMI) is the westernmost part of the United States. The largest island, Saipan, is famous for its beaches and the horrible battle fought there during World War II. In the 1980s, Saipan became known as a garment manufacturing hub when Korean manufacturers seized the opportunity to access the US market. During this time, the CNMI maintained its own immigration system through its local Department of Labor and Immigration. Suddenly, almost half of the population of 60,000 on a 12-mile-long island situated nearly 6000 miles from the US mainland were guest workers from Asian countries.[6] By 1996, the

---

[6] Guest-worker systems in many countries, while allowing entry and work in the more formal sectors of factory and manufacturing jobs (as well as construction, domestic service, and a host of other sectors), typically link the immigration status of the foreign worker to the continued employment by their employer sponsor. Implicit or explicit threats of being sent home before they have earned enough to pay off recruitment fees are an effective means of coercion, tamping down labor activism in all but the most extreme cases.

factories were sending up to $600 million in garments to the mainland United States tariff-free.

The workers in the Saipan garment factories made up almost half of the 30,000 guest workers on the island. Whether working in the factories, in restaurants, hotels, brothels, or as guards, a common refrain among victims in the CNMI was that they had been told that they were immigrating to the United States (Global Survivor Network 1999).[7] While technically true, the Commonwealth at that time did not have an immigration regime that squared with the rest of the United States and the workers were therefore neither able to travel onward to other parts of the country nor make the kind of wages necessary to pay off the recruitment loans they had taken out in order to acquire the opportunity. Adding to their invisibility, initial complaints about the CNMI situation were not on behalf of the misled and mistreated workers, but from mainland garment and textile concerns who did not want competition from factories in the territories.

Human rights reporting, media interest, civil lawsuits, and labor activism drew the attention of the Clinton Administration, which convened an interagency working group to address immigration, labor, and law enforcement issues in the Commonwealth. The island became a political flashpoint as high-ranking Republican Congressmen[8] touted the CNMI as a capitalist success story and blocked reform legislation. Once funding for increased law enforcement personnel was finally in place, investigations were started, but by that time, the factory owners had had time to change their ways. The unsuccessful enforcement activities against the garment factories had an unintended consequence, however. As part of the increased federal presence, the Department of Labor ran public service announcements in Mandarin to inform the garment workers that they could not be held against their will and urging them to report abuse if they were being held in servitude. This outreach did not result in the liberation of any of the women from the factories or the prosecution of any garment factory owners or managers, but it did trigger the escape of women who had been brought in for a secondary purpose related to the garment factories.

As is often the case, forced labor in one sector in the CNMI led to involuntary servitude in another sector. The managers and executives visiting their holdings on the island needed to be entertained, and a booming hospitality industry (Chap. 5) followed on the heels of the factories. A group of women who had been enslaved as "bargirls" in a karaoke establishment, and subjected to forced labor and forced prostitution, escaped after seeing the PSA that the Department of Labor aired. The case of *United States v. Kwon Soon Oh* resulted in a greater federal law enforcement presence on Saipan and the formation of anti-trafficking task forces in the Commonwealth. But the real changes were structural. Legislation closed the

---

[7] Abused workers' accounts repeatedly indicated that they had been lured with promises of an US experience that did not differentiate from the mainland, even to the point of being told that Saipan was within driving distance of San Francisco.

[8] In this case, it was specifically male Congresspersons.

immigration loophole, brought up the minimum wage to that of the US mainland, and required that in order to access the US market duty-free, at least 50% of the labor had to be US workers. As a result, garment factories are no longer a booming industry in the Commonwealth.

The financial success of the Saipan factories did not go unnoticed by Korean businessman Kil Soo Lee, who used the CNMI example to pitch his garment enterprise to the government of another US Insular Possession: the Territory of American Samoa, 2500 miles south of Hawaii. As often happens when local governments see the possibility of securing a manufacturing facility, the government of American Samoa gave Lee tax breaks and access to land and infrastructure so that he could build the Daewoosa (Sect. 3.1.1) garment factory. But when the time came to staff the factory, instead of the hundreds of jobs for American Samoans that the government was promised, Lee brought in Chinese and Korean workers, confining them in fenced-in barracks and starting the cycle of exploitation.

The abuses at Lee's Daewoosa factory were possible in part because American Samoa was a zone of impunity. In contrast to Saipan, which had a small Federal Bureau of Investigation (FBI) office, a federal District Court, and Department of Labor (DOL) coverage from nearby Guam, American Samoa did not have any federal law enforcement presence. When the Department of Labor attempted to respond to initial complaints in the Daewoosa factory, they had to run the case out of their San Francisco office, over 11 hours away by jet. The DOL was dependent upon reciprocity from the American Samoa Attorney General's office for assistance with the case, and the government of American Samoa was still trying to make Lee's operation successful. As mentioned above, the apparent success of the investigation (obtaining back-pay for the workers) was immediately undercut through extortionate threats and the workers remained enslaved in the factory despite the federal administrative response. It was not until a subsequent, carceral, response by the FBI and federal prosecutors that Lee's factory was seized and the workers were released from involuntary servitude. When the FBI intervened, the average weight of the women in the factory was 34 kilograms.

3.2.6 Offshoring Need Not Mean Off-Loading Liability and Responsibility

From this review, it appears that exploitation in factories in the United States has more recently occurred in geographically remote locations with jurisdictionally questionable coverage of labor and immigration laws. Such sites seem to have been identified and exploited quickly by foreign factory owners eager to gain tariff-free access to the US market. US manufacturing of all forms has gone overseas, but especially in sectors long-recognized as sites of abuse, such as garment and seafood processing.[9] And now, whether because of the interventions discussed in this chapter or changes in the global apparel market, US territorial possessions (while still experiencing labor abuses in construction, sexual servitude, and child sex trafficking) are no longer laboratories in the garment industry's quest for the perfect balance of labor exploitation and market access.

It is not just manufacturing *jobs and factories* that have been sent overseas, but the *externalities*[10] of forced labor have been exported to foreign workers in the same way that externalities of pollution and environmental degradation have been shifted to foreign communities (and vulnerable and socially excluded communities in the United States). Multinational corporations do not just seek out wage differentials but also lax regulatory schemes or enforcement regimes as well. The US Foreign Corrupt Practices Act is limited in its application, focusing mainly on bribery: accordingly, so long as a firm does not engage in financial corruption, they can profit from unscrupulous labor and environmental practices (Chap. 7); furthermore, the Supreme Court's narrowing of the scope of the Alien Tort Claims Act seems to have cut off a cause of action that public interest litigators had used successfully in the 1980s and 1990s to challenge human rights violations in other countries.

On the other hand, a variety of efforts seek to hold companies accountable for extraterritorial human rights abuses, including forced labor and violations of broader human rights due to diligence reporting requirements. In 2012, President Obama issued Executive Order 13627, mandating that federal procurement practices prevent human trafficking in government contracts for goods or services, banning the type of recruitment fees that helped to enslave the El Monte and Daewoosa victims (US Executive Office of the President 2012). Implementing regulations, spelling out the definition of recruiting fees, were issued during the Trump Administration (US Federal Register 2018).

Moreover, through the 2016 Trade Facilitation and Trade Enforcement Act, the United States has closed a decades-old loophole in its ability to block goods made with forced labor from entering the country. In 2019, US customs officials began to issue "stop orders" against certain goods, one example of which is medical supplies, specifically rubber gloves from certain large factories in Malaysia (Syam and Roggensack 2020). Shocked by the prospect of real enforcement as opposed to light-touch regulations that could be absorbed as a normal cost of doing business, in early 2020, the rubber glove manufacturers fired their local management, vowed transparency, issued back-pay to workers and retained ethical trade consultants to set up new systems in the factories (Aziz 2020).

---

[9] The dramatic changes in the garment industry due to globalization and offshoring are perhaps not the only structural reasons that factory cases are not the norm in the United States. New immigration laws and programs, and enforcement sweeps based on paperwork auditing, have rendered more formal factory settings (as opposed to meat processing or nursery operations) less likely to be staffed by vulnerable nonskilled immigrant workers who are most susceptible to forced labor.

[10] "Externality" is an economic term that "refers to situations when the effect of production or consumption of goods and services imposes costs or benefits on others, which are not reflected in the prices charged for the goods and services being provided." (Khemani and Shapiro 1993).

Given the modern supply chain, abuses in a factory in the Jordanian Qualifying Industrial Zones, the Malaysian medical supply business, Chinese factories of all varieties, and garment factory sweatshops such as Rana Plaza in Bangladesh) are as much US factory exploitation as if the factory was located on the mainland or one of the insular possessions of the United States itself. These are now the dominant sites of forced labor for the United States market, rather than the sweatshops of New York or the garment factories of Los Angeles. The focus of enforcement and regulation must necessarily shift to the supply chain, lest the US merely outsource its slavery along with its manufacturing sector. The extraterritorial provisions of the Trafficking Victims Protection Act will become increasingly important, especially in civil litigation or customs enforcement, as tools to reach factory-based slaveries; these provisions can be used to prevent manufactured goods tainted by exploitative practices from reaching US consumers.

3.2.7 State Sponsored Slaveries in Factories

Not every instance of involuntary servitude in a factory setting exists solely in the private sector. There are several ways in which factory owners get to access nation-state power for labor force control. The most common method is through the use of guest worker programs, which can create vulnerabilities and even systemic coercion as employers' ability to discipline workers carries the threat of arrest or deportation by withdrawing legal immigration status at will. In some situations, guest worker programs have direct state involvement. In the Daewoosa case, the two labor brokerage companies that provided the workers to Lee were competing arms of two powerful government ministries. As such, it was reasonable for the workers to assume that the penalty for worker activism would draw not just financial penalties in the contract and the inability to repay their recruiting debts but also the attention of the state's security apparatus. Indeed, deported workers who were sent home were visited by Vietnamese security officials, who let them know that they would be under close observation for any further troublemaking. Vietnamese garment workers in Russian factories have faced similar threats (Vozhdaeva 2012). Even more obviously coercive is the common practice in North Korean labor export schemes (e.g., in construction, factory labor, and seafood processing) of sending members of the national security force with the workers, both as managers and infiltrated in with the other migrants as spies (Sullivan et al. 2017).

Migrant and otherwise exploitable labor in factories are not only recruited migrants. In China, in addition to the results of massive rural to urban internal migration, factory labor is being performed at scale by political prisoners and disfavored ethnic minorities, especially Muslim Uighurs (Xu 2020). Large prison labor camps aside, because state-sponsored forced labor relies on a pervasive structural threat of official punishment, there may be less overt beating or abuse in such a setting, but the overarching threat of what happens to dissidents in an authoritarian country permeates the jobsite as much as it does the village.

3.2.8 Globalized Manufacturing and its Discontents[11]

In the classic 1960 documentary about peonage in the mid-Century United States, *"Harvest of Shame,"* the pioneering US broadcaster Edward R. Murrow shockingly started the program with footage of poverty-stricken African Americans, some appearing drunk, or mentally ill, jockeying for position on the open-bed trucks that would take them out to the produce fields around Immokalee, Florida. Over the disturbing scene, Murrow recounts a conversation: "[a] farmer told me, we used to own our slaves; now we just rent them." (CBS News 1960). This insight landed explosively on a US-based viewing public in the midst of a Civil Rights awakening. Murrow consciously chose to air his expose over the Thanksgiving holiday to make US audiences enjoy the bounty of the harvest aware of just how their food was being produced, but the reality of race and poverty in their country. The award-winning documentary had a dramatic effect, calling attention to the plight of the farmworkers and leading to reform legislation that is used to this day in anti-trafficking investigations and prosecutions. The tragedy of the globalized manufacturing economy in the year 2020 is that US businesses and consumers have even less of a connection to the abuse that is done in their name than did the television viewers of 1960.

Sadly, in examining the history of factories since El Monte, it appears that media attention and federal interventions—whether through slavery prosecutions (e.g., El Monte, Daewoosa), labor enforcement (e.g., the New York factory cases), or structural changes (e.g., the closing of Saipan wage and immigration loopholes and the imposition of a 50% US citizen workforce requirement)—were not followed by improved conditions for workers in garment factories in the way that Murrow's documentary occasioned change in the fields. Rather the result was the closing of the factories and the near-shuttering of the US garment industry. How then can reforms in this sector take place without merely driving multinational garment suppliers to the next lenient country? What kind of pressure can brands put on suppliers in order to improve conditions, but not shut them down entirely? (Chap. 7)

3.2.9 Historical Antecedents: Early US Factories as Sites of Enslavement

Slavery in US factories is not new and cannot be attributed solely to globalization. A case in point is found at the dawn of industrialization and the first years of the United States, in Thomas Jefferson's nail factory at his plantation Monticello. Jefferson used the labor of enslaved African-American children while they were small and nimble, with the manual dexterity to make nails. This, not the agrarian ideal that he romanticized, was one of the most profitable aspects of Jefferson's plantation operation. Jefferson's trade in the casks of nails that were used in

---

[11] Apologies to Stiglitz.

rvitude were not present in the North and thus not directly incorporated into the
strial operations or labor-management systems that developed in a modernizing
ed States.[13] Similarly, the British industrial heartland was not directly a slave
omy and society as was the British Caribbean. While there were grave labor
es, they were not predicated on a chattel enslaved workforce, but rather on the
l-to-urban flow as smallholders and tenants were driven off their land through
osure, transition to a cash economy, and the efficiency of the new machines.

ccordingly, the industrial model commonly thought of today as "the factory"
not built with a legally enslaved workforce in mind. As a result, conditions in
factory were often contested, leading to the growth of labor actions (aka
ikes") and the creation of labor unions to organize and speak for the workers. At
r most effective, unions became not just the representatives of the employees of
factory, but of all workers in an industry, equalizing the power dynamic and
ercutting the ability of unscrupulous employers to ride out a labor action confi-
t that they could outlast or divide poor workers.

While conditions in nineteenth century factories were not perfect and were
ost always contested by management and workers, the US manufacturing econ-
y appears to have been built on the ideology of free labor, as opposed to sustain-
; and profiting from the legal economic and political system of slavery – a basis
t grew into working class abolitionist sentiment in the North (Foner 1995). This
ds a kernel of truth to the oft-repeated canard about the Civil War: the Southern
rarian defenders of slavery could not compete in the long term with the industrial
ght of the North. There were some manufacturing, distilling, milling, and pro-
ssing operations in the South before the war, but they were not of the scale in the
dustrial North (Vedder and Lowell 1980).

The ideas that people in the United States typically hold about historical chattel
avery conceives of it as having been in nonindustrial settings, often on large rural
antations. That vision of slavery, combined with the growth of an urban industrial
bor movement in the post–Civil War era, means that exploitation, certainly a fact
f life in factories, either did not directly take the form of involuntary servitude or
as not seen as such. White working men in northern factories, no matter how
xploited, did not see themselves as people who could be enslaved.

Dominance of "White Slave Trafficking" Frame Erases Women's Factory Experiences and Their Resistance

The factory experiences of women, on the other hand—and immigrant women in
particular—stand apart from these understandings of who was, or could be,
impacted by slavery. This, when juxtaposed with common tropes of the time about
immigrant women in the sex industry, led to some strange outcomes. It was broadly

---

[13] After Emancipation, Southern employers without a frame of reference for how to manage a non-
enslaved labor force sought to replicate that level of power with newly freed African Americans,
even in industrial settings such as the postwar Birmingham steel mills. This echoes today as "right
to work" laws that allow management mechanisms that prevent unionization – laws that have now
spread out of the South.

buildings in and around Virginia was sufficient to insulate
farming operations at Monticello from the vagaries of th
(Weincek 2012).

Accounts of conditions in the small factory are shocking,
posed against the founder's ideals of freedom and the dor
popular culture. Historians and biographers have tended eith
ings in which he is ambivalent or even opposed to the institu
ents him as presiding over a beautiful mountain plantation th
World architectural vernacular. That heroic vision of Jefferso
forge in the purpose-built factory that he designed. The laudi
ens the ring of the anvils upon which the enslaved children dr
fles the sound of their cries as they were beaten on his orders
quota of nails. And it masks any vision of leading US slaveho
anything other than gentlemen farmers. Erasing the reality of
tory and similar manufacturing efforts across the South hel
industrialists as the sole exploiters of factory labor, while inve
paternalism for Southern slavers.

This historic, romantic tendency is bigger than Jefferson. A
roots the site of slavery in US lore as a memory-misted field,
house of the master. It elides the varied truth of the nail factory
cooperage, and the sailmaker's shed. It erases the exploitation
tions – of Black bodies on construction sites of buildings, roads
ways (Littlefield 2010). It silences sexual violence and the
reproductive, and nursing choice, much less the resilience and res
people in maintaining sexual autonomy (Berry and Harris 201
cultural blinders that lead to a misdiagnosis by logical fallacy: I
not in a factory, so if it is in a factory, it is not slavery.

The Formal, Industrial Factory of the Nineteenth Century

The growth of factories in the Northeast resulted in much more tha
turing or the production of agricultural processing machinery such a
Fabric mills (fed by cotton produced by enslaved African-America
begin to grow in number and complexity, hastening the transition
northeast into urban and semiurban areas. Jobs in fabric mills and ga
provided – for the first time – large-scale year-round work outside o
women (Thomas 1979). From the beginning, these factories' indust
were not set up on the basis of chattel slavery or even the less perm
of indentured servitude or debt peonage.[12] Employers' use of racia
ability to control the lives of their workers through flat-out ownership

[12] The industrialization of the Northeast happened after most of the Northern state
slavery. While Northern institutions thereafter profited in many ways from South
region's social, economic, and political systems were not overtly based on ownersh
control of a large captive Black population.

known that young women from Eastern Europe were often recruited by labor brokers for various jobs in US cities, only to be exploited in sweatshop factories or in prostitution, but the solutions to each of these abuses were not the protections of the 13th Amendment even it was used to protect immigrant men enslaved on Southern railroad projects (e.g., *United States v. Sabbia)* and immigrant children from being held as street musicians (e.g., *United States v. Arancola).* Rather, for women, the dominant frame was focused not on their freedom, but on their morality and purity.

Immigrant women and girls engaged in prostitution – whether forced or voluntary – saw themselves cast as victims under the misnamed "White Slave Trafficking Act" (Chap. 9), an approach that despite the title and rhetoric provided them few remedies under the law. For the many immigrant women and girls abused in the garment factory sweatshops of the Northeast, because they were not in prostitution, they were not seen as potentially having been enslaved or subjected to sexual predation, but as suffering conditions that could be solved by unionization. Especially after the tragedy of the Triangle Shirtwaist Factory fire in 1911, the labor lens was so strong that it eclipsed the new federal slavery statute, which had recently removed any limitations as to victims' race or the economic sector in which they worked (Chap. 9). This does not mean that the labor lens in the wake of that tragedy was inappropriate. The International Ladies' Garment Workers' Union (ILGWU) and other unions that resulted changed not just US society, but the labor movement and even women's suffrage, as working-class women began to organize and become part of the right to vote movement (Stein 1977). Nevertheless, the recasting of the 1911 fire as leading to a labor movement that "helped make American working conditions the finest in the world" (as a commemorative plaque on the site claims) is troubling. Such triumphalist discourse on the part of both the labor movement and US government diverts focus from the trafficking and servitude in the Triangle Shirtwaist Factory and contemporary sweatshops (Hapke 2004).

There is evidence that Progressive Era women themselves saw the interconnectivity of the various political and social reform movements. One of the most fascinating images of the time is of an unnamed 14-year-old garment worker, progressive campaigner and leading suffragette Fola La Follette, and anti-trafficking activist Rose Livingston[14] walking a picket line on a strike in 1913 (Fig. 3.2) (Bain News Service 1913). The overlapping social reform movements and the willingness of the upper-class "mink brigade" to stand in solidarity with garment workers and "fallen women" is a reminder that the artificial divide between sex and labor trafficking often is belied by the relationships among the affected communities.

---

[14]Livingston was *a* survivor who not only led daring rescues of girls and women from sex trafficking in Chinatown, New York, but also toured on the prosuffrage speaking circuit with the daughter of Elizabeth Cady Stanton.

Fig. 3.2 Fola La Follette and Rose Livingston. (Photo credit: Library of Congress, Prints & Photographs Division, LC-DIG-ggbain-12,397)

The Racialized Counter-Reality: Convict Leasing

This idea of the factory as being a place where brave, empowered, White male workers stood up to business interests (as opposed to being enslaved and unable to access power) is the dominant narrative of the factory in the United States. But there was a very different type of labor practice in the nascent manufacturing sector in the Jim Crow South. Heavy industries[15] such as the steel foundries that sprung up in post-Civil War Alabama depended on the widespread use of unfree Black labor. African-Americans were leased from state prisons and county jails and in addition to agriculture were used in various stages of steel production: in coal mining to supply fuel, in the initial production of pig iron, and in other harsh settings (Worger 2004). The steel industry consumed workers who were all the more disposable under convict leasing schemes; these workers did not have to be accounted for on an accounting schedule as property, as they previously would have been under chattel slavery. If convict laborers were injured or died from harsh conditions or punishments, Southern steel bosses – typically former slaveholders – would simply get more prisoners from the state.

The same was true of building materials such as bricks. The brick manufacturing process in the South did not automate or embrace new technology. This was in no

---

[15] The manufacturing of large and heavy products, large equipment and facilities, or complex or numerous processes.

small part because the owners of firms such as the Chattahoochee brick company (Samuel 2020) could simply send convicts into the still-dangerously hot kilns to stack and unstack the bricks. If convicts were irreparably injured or killed, the company could simply send for more under their contract with the prisons and jails.[16]

These manufacturing settings became so abusive that they occasioned legislative inquiries into the "great cruelty" that was happening ("Georgia Lease System Fosters Great Cruelty" 1908). Unlike debt bondage on farms, the level of abuse in the manufacturing/industrial sector was impossible to ignore, especially as major Northern finance and business interests balked at such practices. Such abuse was politically difficult to square with the image of "the New South" that boosters and politicians wanted to project. Cities such as Atlanta stopped buying bricks made with convict labor, and states ended their leasing schemes. And so, the practice of convict leasing in industrial and mining settings in the US South technically died out in the early twentieth Century (Blackmon 2008).[17]

The Racialized Counter-Reality: "Naval Stores"

Another major US manufacturing industry was built upon – and sustained by – both chattel slavery and subsequent forms of involuntary servitude. For centuries, one of the most dangerous and abusive industries in the country was the "naval stores" industry of the Southern pine forests, which supplied first the Royal Navy and thereafter the US Navy with turpentine and pitch. These products, needed for treating ropes on sailing vessels, waterproofing wooden ships, and painting iron ships, started as rosin harvested from pine trees much as rubber sap is harvested from rubber trees. In the time before fossil fuels, pine distillation operations were the backbone of the US chemical industry (Outland 2004).

A critical industry both for economic and strategic interests, the distilling operations were isolated and dangerous, with the prospect of explosions, fires, and spillovers of burning pitch akin to napalm. Much as with brick kilns, the abuses in the naval stores sector became impossible to ignore in the Progressive Era. Federal prosecutions were brought (*United States v. Clyatt, United States v. Venters*) and Congressional hearings were held on the issue. The industry fought back, spending enormous legal fees to try to ward off federal jurisdiction (Daniel 1990). In the *Venters* case, as with the situation in Saipan generations later, investigators found

---

[16] Brick kilns continue to be a site of enslavement, with the TIP Report and human rights advocates reporting endemic abuse in Indian and Pakistani kilns, including multigenerational debt bondage. Even more harrowing abuses have been reported in China, where men with intellectual development disorder are often flat-out kidnapped to work in the kilns.

[17] While convict leasing schemes have died out in the United States, forms of prison labor survive within the penitentiary walls, such as furniture making and call centers. Such programs are often characterized as voluntary, but come with an extremely low prison minimum wage and the lack of applicability to postincarceration careers. Recent lawsuits have challenged involuntary labor in immigration detention settings, specifically custodial services in for-profit detention centers (Levy 2018).

not only the abused workers in the distilling operations but also women who were being held in sexual servitude in the work camps (Chap. 5). Then, as now, the lines between labor trafficking and sex trafficking were more blurred than many would believe.

Again, it does not seem to have been enforcement that put an end to the abuses in the naval stores industry. And with a Southern Black workforce that was neither the focus of the industrial unions nor in a legal stetting where they could flourish, it was also not union activity that changed the employers' ways. Rather, the transition to truly free labor in the naval stores industry in the piney woods of the South in the 1940s and 1950s may have come as much from technological and business change in the United States as it did from civil rights or labor enforcement.

For instance, it was Southern storekeepers who kept the records of sharecropping and peonage debts for the farmers and naval stores distillers, creating "company store" situations where the workers became increasingly indebted to their bosses through high-priced groceries. The new "cash and carry" grocery stores of the 1930s allowed workers to buy their own food, rather than through such a closed system. Erection of transmission poles during New Deal rural electrification efforts yielded the widespread adoption of individual telephones that ended the storekeepers' monopoly on communication. This enabled Black workers to contact their families, attorneys, and even the National Association for the Advancement of Colored People (NAACP) for help. And, the market penetration of automobiles allowed avenues for escape faster than the employers, and their dogs could track fleeing workers down on foot (Outland 2004).

But it was also broad industrial technological change that ended centuries of abuse in naval stores industry. Increased use of petrochemicals replaced some pine-based products, and new distillation techniques allowed for the extraction of rosin by grinding smaller trees into shreds, rather than tapping trees by hand in a mature forest (Outland 2004). Distillation was removed from the racialized setting of the rural South and became just another industrial process, performed in more regulated and formal settings. Today, while it echoes in the abuses of the palm oil and rubber industries, many anti-trafficking activists do not know of the naval stores industry. But these chemical factories were once one of the most abusive sites of trafficking and slavery in the United States.

3.2.10 An Opportunity for Improvement – Worker-Led Social Responsibility

While the El Monte and Daewoosa cases were extremely important in the development of modern anti-trafficking tools in the United States, these types of trafficking occurrences do not appear to be the norm. Traditional factory settings typically come with a baseline of labor protections, however, imperfectly enforced. This represents an opportunity: it could be that even relatively ineffectual labor standards in factory settings would have enough of a salutary effect to empower workers to report abuses or otherwise advocate for themselves.

In recent years, especially after the Rana Plaza disaster in Bangladesh, multinational companies engaging in Corporate Social Responsibility (Chap. 7) efforts around worker exploitation, fair recruiting, and slavery/trafficking have turned to the concept of "worker voice" in diverse factory settings (Donaghey and Reinecke 2018). Those companies have the wherewithal to have put extensive auditing and worker contact programs into place or to insist that audit teams have access to the workers as a condition of their contracts with suppliers. However, as with Multi-Stakeholder Initiatives generally, widespread problems have been identified in auditing practice, exposing the inherent conflict of interest of companies and brands' involvement in workplace monitoring (LeBaron 2018).

To be blunt, too many actors have a built-in bias toward keeping the product flowing. Corporate Social Responsibility experts who are responsible for implementing Business and Human Rights guarantees are weak compared to their colleagues in business operations and purchasing. Companies, and the MSIs in which they participate, typically opt for nonpunitive amelioration, as opposed to forceful interventions that would convince suppliers that corporate demands for worker safety and health are not just window dressing. Moreover, some of these "worker voice" initiatives are being put in place in countries where neither the government nor the companies are willing to undertake systemic changes to ensure workers' rights to meaningfully organize nor are those actors willing to contribute to workers' welfare or the well-being of the factory.

Worker-driven Social Responsibility (WSR) is a different model, which has made a major difference in the agricultural sector in the southeast United States. WSR is being considered in other sectors as well and in late 2019, was adopted for the first time in manufacturing (Business & H.R. Resource Center 2019). This approach, pioneered by the Coalition of Immokalee Workers (CIW) and enforced through the Fair Food Program, embeds worker protection standards in the procurement contracts between the brands and their suppliers. The Fair Food Standards Council, not the brands, has the power to suspend purchasing from a grower found to be using forced labor, tolerating sexual harassment, or allowing safety and health violations in their operations. The CIW dates back to the *Flores* case – discussed above (Sect. 3.2.1) as the immediate precursor to the El Monte prosecution – and many of their members are survivors of the many modern slavery cases that have been brought to court in southwest Florida in the last 25 years.

While their success has come from perseverance, inspired lawyering, and brilliant negotiating (Marquis 2017), the Coalition's ability to mobilize federal law enforcement to vindicate workers' rights through criminal prosecution had a major effect on brands and growers alike. Popular consumer brands were no longer able to tolerate abuses in their supply chain as being low-level nuisances. And in the wake of the 2008 amendments to the TVPA (which extended liability to those who knowingly or in reckless disregard profit from trafficking), growers were faced with a legal exposure far greater than the Department of Labor civil monetary penalties they had traditionally absorbed as a matter of doing business.

The fields around Immokalee and along the east coast are finally a different place from when the grower so easily dismissed his African American workers to CBS News in 1961. Because of worker-led education programs, participation in safety and health efforts, and the work of an effective and trusted independent auditing team that harnesses the power of the workers, labor abuses – not just involuntary servitude but also sexual harassment and sexual abuse – are a dimming memory in a place that had recently been known as "ground zero for modern slavery" (Bowe 2003).

In 2019, the Immokalee WSR approach crossed from the agricultural sector to the factory setting with the adoption of the program by garment workers in Lesotho. There, the CIW and Fair Food experts consulted with coalition of unions and women's organizations on how to obtain enforceable agreements from brands and suppliers that involve an independent complaint mechanism with the power to dismiss grievances. This cross-pollination of empowered African factory workers joining with US agricultural workers is the future of Worker-driven Social Responsibility.

The Immokalee model not only harnesses market consequences, binding agreements, and honest auditing but also represents the successful interplay between the competing approaches of carceral antislavery solutions, corporate-involved labor, and administrative solutions. While much of the modern anti-trafficking movement is predicated on enforcement as a solution, there is a need for more than carceral interventions; structural responses are needed as well. Successfully investigating allegations of forced labor, raiding a factory, aiding victimized workers, and even vindicating their right not to be enslaved is only part of the modern anti-trafficking solution. While criminal law has a focusing power, it has never been able to make the systemic changes needed in the manufacturing sector.

At the same time, systemic and root cause changes (primary prevention) do not negate the necessity of stopping the crime, removing the perpetrator from an opportunity to offend again, and punishing the violation against the individual and society (tertiary prevention). Both approaches have to be carried out in parallel, as in the CIW model. The prospect of consumer stigma and continuous federal criminal investigations became as untenable for companies like Walmart and Whole Foods (Marquis 2017) as did the cruelty of the convict labor system to the Atlanta city government or US Steel a century before (Blackmon 2008). Driven by these government interventions and corresponding changes in buyers' risk calculus, market forces put pressure on growers to join the Fair Food Program. Civil society should insist on robust enforcement in manufacturing settings as well; by so doing, it can harness the state's power on behalf of workers.

3.3   Conclusion

3.3.1   So, What Are Factories?

Factories, and more informal manufacturing operations, have long been sites of trafficking and slavery. Institutional, jurisdictional, and cultural obstacles have prevented effective anti-trafficking, and antiexploitation enforcement and globalization have allowed companies to offshore jobs in order to seek out cheaper and less-regulated alternatives. But factories have also often been sites of resistance and worker power. This is visible in the growth of the labor movement, the enshrining of minimum labor standards and norms, and the creation of regulatory institutions.

Factories are focal points. Because of the human cost, exposed abuses in factories capture the consumer and regulatory interest far more effectively than the small, anonymous majority of trafficking cases. This is demonstrated in horrible tragedies such as the Triangle Fire or the Rana Plaza collapse; these are the known names.

Factories are sites of innovation. Monitoring/auditing schemes and attempts to provide workers a voice are a model that can be applied to other sectors vulnerable to modern slavery. As workers and trafficking survivors unite across sectors, factories are a proven testing ground for Worker-driven (rather than Corporate) Social Responsibility.

Factories are sites of opportunity. When labor rights are observed and the recruiting is not fraudulent, factories can help lift people and their communities out of poverty. A manufacturing job can have a transformative effect on workers and their families.

Factories are part of US history. They are part of both the "American Dream" and of the nightmares of slavery and exploitation. From Thomas Jefferson's nail factory to the turpentine distilleries, from the brick kilns of the South to the El Monte sweatshop, various forms of slavery persist. US consumers must recognize this, despite every incentive and teaching aimed at diverting the collective memory from the truth and toward conceptualizing slavery only as a romanticized agrarian past. To remain prey to these fallacies would be to dishonor the memory of all who suffered in slavery in the rise of the modern world and built the United States.

3.3.2 Sites of Memory, Sites of People, and Sites of Hope

Because slavery happens to people, first and foremost the people who have survived this crime so monstrous must be recognized (Skinner 2009). Taking the time to honor their memory is especially important because "forays into biography add flesh-and-blood urgency to...legal reasoning, much as Frederick Douglass' *Narrative* infused urgency into the original abolitionists' appeals" (Swanson and Stewart 2018).

So, remember the Match Girls of London and their bravery standing up to their abusive employers. Those teenagers were the impetus for even larger action in England and across the world. Their example not only influenced politicians and businessmen but forced cultural and religious actors to stand with workers – leading to the Papal Encyclical that recognized the value of work and the need for unionization (Leo XIII 1891). They showed that factories can be not just sites of suffering but also *sites of power*.

And remember the women at the Daewoosa factory gate and their courage in resisting their enslaver. Despite ineffectual administrative responses and Kil Soo Lee's abuses of power, their bravery launched a test case for the law that modernized the 13th Amendment's promise of emancipation. As the women of Daewoosa wrote their SOS note to be smuggled out of the factory, they ended their missive "we hope in your help."[18] Their journey to freedom – and the resulting spread of the antislavery ethos of the TVPA and Palermo Protocol – proves that factories can also be *sites of hope*.

3.4   Recommendations

1. *Recruitment fees should be banned* through regulation, government procurement rules, and contract language.
2. *Passports of foreign workers should not be confiscated*, nor kept in a central location controlled by the factory; workers should be provided with safe and locked alternatives so that their identification documents are under their control.
3. *Guest worker systems should be reformed to allow job mobility*, ending the practice of tying the worker to their sponsoring employer under threat of deportation.
4. *Businesses should track their supply chains* through to the manufacturing site and those of key inputs, using independent, unannounced auditing programs that are not performative paper compliance charades.
5. *Workers in manufacturing and other industrial settings should have access to complaint mechanisms* – preferably independent of management – with required company feedback and prompt remediation.
6. *Workers' right to organize should be recognized by governments and facilitated by manufacturing companies*. Retaliation against workers for organizing or participating in union activity should be treated as evidence satisfying the elements of forced labor.
7. *Labor inspections and regulation of the manufacturing industry should be robust*, with consequences that cannot simply be absorbed periodically as the price of doing business.
8. *Anti-trafficking actors should learn from and develop prevention and intervention efforts based on the unique historical features of industrial manufacturing*, including the protections achieved by workers and their supporters over more than a century.
9. *Investigators and private auditors should recognize that*, regardless of apparent labor protections and a veneer of formality, *trafficking and slavery can indeed happen in factory settings*.

---

[18] Due to the workers' unfamiliarity with English, the note read "We hope in your HEPL."

10. *Performance measures for agencies and inspectors should include their participation in investigations under trafficking and slavery statutes* as well as labor codes. Trainings for inspectors and local police should include modules on recognizing the signs of labor and sex trafficking alike, rather than simply focusing on one form of abuse.

11. *Industrial disasters* should not simply be responded to as tragic safety violations, but *should be investigated to ascertain whether workers were being held in forced labor conditions*; post-tragedy responses should seek to improve conditions, empower workers, and prevent future such occurrences.

12. *The limitations of business-friendly interventions should be recognized.* While multistakeholder initiatives have put compliance structures around manufacturing, those processes are often flawed; they are difficult to monitor, inefficient, corrupt, and subject to regulatory capture or are merely "greenwashing" in actuality. MSIs and business-focused approaches should not take the place of worker empowerment and government regulation.

13. Law enforcement responses should not be taken off the table in favor of addressing "root causes" such as poverty and systematic social exclusion. Rather, *enforcement-based responses, in parallel with root-cause anti-trafficking action*, can serve as a goad, incentivizing companies to cooperate in Worker-driven Social Responsibility programs.

References

Aziz, A. (2020, August 10). Top Glove still resolving US ban, remediation fee now at RM53m. *The Edge Markets*.

Bain News Service, P. (1913). *14-yr. old striker, Fola La Follette, and Rose Livingston*. Retrieved from the Library of Congress. https://www.loc.gov/item/2014692415/.

Berry, D., & Harris, L. (Eds.). (2018). *Sexuality and slavery: Reclaiming intimate histories in the Americas*. Athens: University of Georgia Press.

Besant, A. (1888, Saturday, June 23). White slavery in London. *The Link: A journal for the servants of man*.

Blackmon, D. (2008). *Slavery by another name: The re-enslavement of Black people in America from the Civil War to World War II*. New York: Anchor.

Bowe, J. (2003, April 21). Nobodies. *The New Yorker* Available online at https://www.newyorker.com/magazine/2003/04/21/nobodies.

Bravo, K. E. (2017). Interrogating everypersons' role in today's slaveries. *Temple International and Comparative Law Journal, 31*, 25–43.

Business & Human Rights Resource Center. (2019, August 16). *Lesotho: Unions & women's groups sign binding agreements with Levi's, Wrangler, Children's Place & others to combat gender-based violence in factories*.

CBS Productions. (1960). *CBS Reports. Harvest of shame*. United States: CBS Television.

Daniel, P. (1990). *The shadow of slavery: Peonage in the south, 1901–1969*. Urbana: University of Illinois Press.

David v. Signal. (2012). U.S. Dist. LEXIS 114247 (E.D. LA, 2020).

Donaghey, J., & Reinecke, J. (2018). When industrial democracy meets corporate social responsibility – A comparison of the Bangladesh accord and alliance as responses to the Rana Plaza Disaster. *British Journal of Industrial Relations, 56*, 14–42.

Dugger, C. W. (1996, June 3). A tattered crackdown on illegal workers. *New York Times*.

EEOC v. Hill Country Farms (d/b/a Henry's Service Corp.) (S.D. Iowa 2013).

Foner, E. (1995). *Free soil, free labor, free men: The ideology of the republican party before the civil war*. Oxford/New York: Oxford University Press.

Georgia Lease System Fosters Great Cruelty. (1908, July 25). *The Tennessean*.

Global Survival Network. (1999). *Trapped: Human trafficking for forced labor in the Commonwealth of the Northern Mariana Islands (a U.S. Territory)*. Washington, DC: Global Survival Network.

Hapke, L. (2004). *Sweatshop: The history of an American idea*. New Brunswick: Rutgers.

Ibrahim, N. (2020, August 29). Sexual assault, forced labor, wage theft: Garment workers in Jordan suffer for US brands. *The Guardian*.

Josserand, E., & Kaine, S. (2016). Labour standards in global value chains: Disentangling workers' voice, vicarious voice, power relations, and regulation. *Relations Industrielles/Industrial Relations, 71*(4), 741–767.

Khemani, R., & Shapiro, D. (1993). *Glossary of industrial organisation economics and competition law*. Directorate for Financial, Fiscal and Enterprise Affairs, OECD.

LeBaron, G. (2018). *The global business of forced labor*. Sheffield.

Leo XIII, P. (1891). *Rerum Novarum* – Encyclical Letter of Pope Leo XIII on the Conditions of Labor.

Levy, A. (2018). *Fact sheet: Human trafficking & forced labor in for-profit detention facilities*. The Human Trafficking Legal Center.

Littlefield, D. (2010). *The varieties of slave labor*. Freedom's Story, National Humanities Center. Available online at http://nationalhumanitiescenter.org/tserve/freedom/1609-1865/essays/slavelabor.htm.

Marquis, S. (2017). *I am not a tractor: How Florida farmworkers took on the fast food giants and won*. Ithaca: Cornell University Press.

MSI Integrity. (2020, July). *Not fit-for-purpose: The grand experiment of multi-stakeholder initiatives in corporate accountability, human rights and global governance*.

Outland, R. (2004). *Tapping the Pines: The Naval Stores Industry in the American South*. Baton Rouge: Louisiana State University Press.

Samuel, M. (2020, August 21). Amid Debates About Memorials, Advocates Push to Remember Atlanta's Forced Laborers. *National Public Radio*.

Schrempf-Stirling, J., & Palazzo, G. (2016). Upstream corporate social responsibility: The evolution from contract responsibility to full producer responsibility. *Business & Society, 55*(4), 491–527.

Skinner, E. B. (2009). *A crime so monstrous: Face to face with modern slavery*. New York: Free Press.

Stafford, A. (1961) *A Match to Fire the Thames*. London: Hodder and Stoughton.

Stein, L. (Ed.). (1977). *Out of the sweatshop: The struggle for industrial democracy*. New York: Quadrangle/New York Times Book Company.

Sullivan, T., Kim, H., & Mendoza, M. (2017, October 5). *Nuclear-armed North Korea profits from US, EU seafood sales*. Associated Press.

Swanson, E., & Stewart, J. (Eds.). (2018). *Human bondage and abolition: New histories of past and present slaveries*. Cambridge: Cambridge University Press.

Syam, A., & Roggensack, M. (2020). *Importing freedom: Using the U.S. Tariff Act to combat forced labor in supply chains*. The Human Trafficking Legal Center.

Thomas, D. (1979). *Women at work: The transformation of work and community in Lowell, Massachusetts, 1826–1860*. New York: Columbia University Press.

Trafficking Victims Protection Act of 2000, Pub. L. No. 106–386 §2A, 114 Stat.1464 (2000), codified at 22 U.S.C. § 7101.

United States, Executive Office of the President. (2012, September 25). *Executive order 13627, strengthening protections against trafficking in persons in federal contracts*.

United States Federal Register. (2018, December 20). *Federal Acquisition Regulation: Combating Trafficking in Persons—Definition of "Recruitment Fees"*. 83 Fed. Reg. 65,466.

Vedder, R. K., & Lowell, E. (1980). The profitability of antebellum manufacturing: Some new estimates. *The Business History Review, 54*(1), 92–103.

Vozhdaeva, O. (2012, August 10). Vietnam workers kept like slaves at factory in Russia. *BBC*.

Wiencek, H. (2012). *Master of the Mountain: Thomas Jefferson and his slaves*. New York: Farrar Straus.

Worger, W. (2004). Convict labour, industrialists and the state in the US South and South Africa 1870-1930. *Journal of Southern African Studies, 30*(1), 63–86.

Xu, V. X. (2020, March 1). *Policy brief: Uyghurs for sale: 'Re-education', forced labour and surveillance beyond Xinjiang*. Report No. 26/2020. Australian Strategic Policy Institute Ltd.

Chapter 4
Invisibility, Forced Labor, and Domestic Work

Ai-jen Poo and Natalicia Tracy

4.1 Introduction

4.1.1 Judith's Story

Judith was 38 years old when she left her husband and four children in the Philippines, to work in the United States (Daluz 2018). She found a job in New York as a domestic worker for the family of a Japanese diplomat; she was promised $1800 each month, paid holidays, and other benefits, and a path to US citizenship. Judith accepted the job and planned to send money home for her children; however, her employer quickly changed the terms of their agreement, and her "employment" quickly became forced labor.

Judith's wages were cut by more than two-thirds such that she only received $500 each month and had no paid holidays. She was required to work up to 18-hour days, providing full-time childcare while also being responsible for all the cooking and cleaning of the home. Often, she did not have enough food: once, her employer left for 3 weeks and only gave her $20 to stock up on food; she had strict instructions not to eat anything in the pantry as that food was too expensive. Her employers—her traffickers—held her passport and threatened to have her deported if she told anyone about her working conditions. Judith did not have family or community in New York that she could turn to for support, and her family in the

---

With contributions by Fiona Ramsey, Roberta Capobianco, and Jennifer Dillon.

A.-j. Poo
National Domestic Workers Alliance, New York, NY, USA
e-mail: aijen@domesticworkers.org

N. Tracy (✉)
Brazilian Workers Center, Allston, MA, USA
e-mail: Ntracy@braziliancenter.org

© Springer Nature Switzerland AG 2021
M. Chisolm-Straker, K. Chon (eds.), *The Historical Roots of Human Trafficking*,
https://doi.org/10.1007/978-3-030-70675-3_4

Philippines was relying on her to send money home. She was isolated, threatened, and trapped.

Over time, Judith became friends with two women who worked across the street from her, and when she told them a little about her situation, one of them would bring her food and leave it with the doorman. Her friend encouraged her to leave, assuring her she would not be deported or sent to jail. A year after Judith came to the United States she connected with a local domestic workers' cooperative, Damayan, and received the support she needed to escape. Today, Judith is a leader in local and national efforts to prevent domestic worker trafficking and establish stronger workplace protections for domestic workers everywhere.

4.1.2 Forced Labor and Domestic Work

Judith's story is all too common. Domestic work is one of several work sectors in which traffickers exploit worker conditions, using intimidation, isolation, threats, and even assault. The International Labour Organization (ILO) estimates that nearly 24.9 million people are in forced labor at any given time, and of these 16 million are exploited in the private sector for labor such as domestic work, construction, or agriculture (International Labour Office, 2017). While the methods are consistent across industries—abuse of vulnerability, deception, restriction of movement, isolation, physical and sexual violence, intimidation and threats, retention of identity documents, withholding of wages (Chap. 6), debt bondage, abusive working and living conditions, and excessive overtime (International Labour Office, 2012)—forced labor in domestic work exploits the unique nature of this kind of work. The industry's connection to chattel slavery, and social and cultural norms enable forced domestic laborers to remain invisible as they live and work in US neighborhoods.

Forced labor in domestic work challenge pre-conceived ideas of what "modern slavery" or "human trafficking" looks like. Commonly, the perpetrators are well-respected professionals and members of the community, such as doctors and executives (Chap. 5). In the case of Judith, the perpetrators were diplomats living in lavish homes in expensive neighborhoods. In another example, two physicians trafficked Natalicia (chapter co-author) to Boston from Brazil as a teenage nanny. Despite her abusive treatment from her employers, Natalicia could not just leave because she had become very attached to the children, especially the oldest boy who would make drawings for her and comfort her when she cried; "I did feel a very real connection with the children. People don't understand that you can't just walk out" (Tracy, 2018).

In the case of domestic workers, the tools that employers use to bind workers are invisible—intimidation, threats, manipulation—enabling the crime to take place in full view of, and yet unrecognized by the public. In 2017, Pulitzer prize-winner Alex Tizon shared the story of Lola, his nanny, who came to the United States from the Philippines with his parents, who were her traffickers. Her enslavement took place in a suburban Los Angeles neighborhood and she was with the family for

56 years. Alex shared her story—and his, as one of the family's children she raised—in his article "My Family's Slave" for *The Atlantic*, revealing the complexity and intimacy of his relationship with her, and the exploitation that enabled her enslavement to continue in the contemporary United States for decades. The story changed the way people conceptualize and look for forced labor (Tizon, 2017).

As the current structure of the global economy positions and entrenches many workers in exploitative situations (Chap. 7), never before has it been more important to learn from the experiences of workers that have survived labor exploitation and human trafficking. Survivors like Judith are the movement's most powerful leaders who shine a light in the shadows where forced labor thrives. By developing the leadership of domestic workers and centering their experiences in policy and movement strategies, anti-trafficking actors can end the conditions that allow forced labor to exist and ensure that every domestic worker has the dignity and respect they deserve in the workplace.

4.2   Discussion

4.2.1   Who are Domestic Workers?

There are 2.2 million domestic workers in the United States (Wolfe et al., 2020). They are the nannies who care for the nation's children, the housecleaners who bring order to homes, and the homecare workers that enable elderly or disabled loved ones to live independently. They work behind the closed doors of private residences, doing the work of the home so that others can work outside the home; they do the work that makes all other work possible.

The gender and racial demographics of the domestic workforce social norms and historical conditions that have contributed to contemporary domestic work being undervalued and underpaid. The domestic workforce today is disproportionately female (Chap. 14): in the United States, 91.5% of domestic workers are women, compared to 46.3% of other workers (Wolfe et al., 2020). As US domestic work has historically been the work of the women[1] of the household—caring for the home, children, and family members—it is seen as "women's work" and not considered "real" or "professional" work, regardless of whether it is performed by an unpaid family member or a paid domestic worker. The gender-based discrimination common to domestic work contributes to the continued devaluation of this work and its relegation to the informal workforce rather than recognizing it for what it is: skilled, professional work.

Many of the first domestic workers were enslaved Indigenous (Chap. 16) and Black women; they worked as nannies or housekeepers for White slave-owners. With the sanction of the 1850 Act for the Government and Protection of Indians,

---

[1] This may be true in other countries as well but the focus of this chapter is the US experience.

White settlers kidnapped women and children for domestic labor (Johnston-Dodds 2002); between 1852 and 1867, an estimated 3000–4000 Indigenous children were kidnapped in California and forced to work as domestic servants (Magliari, 2012). Today, 21.7% of the domestic workforce is Black (Black workers comprise 11.9% of other occupations) and domestic workers are more than twice as likely to be a naturalized US citizen or non-naturalized immigrant than other workers (Wolfe et al., 2020). Specifically, the contemporary domestic workforce predominately includes native-born Black women and foreign-born immigrant women from Central and South America, Asia, the Caribbean, and Africa. Many of these immigrant women today, in a "Chain of Pare" (Parreñas, 2001), are leaving an impoverished Global South to fill care work needs in the Global North. Contemporary children also continue (Chap. 8) to participate in the domestic workforce across the Americas and many experience forced labor. For instance, in Haiti, *restavek* children are sent to work for wealthier families as a result of cultural myths surrounding the perceived benefits and opportunities that come from this form of employment. Some Haitian families in the United States have carried this tradition with them; in 2008, one South Florida mother and her adult daughter were convicted of keeping a teenager in domestic servitude (Loney, 2010).

4.2.2 The Unique Nature of Domestic Work

Domestic work's unique conditions are exploited by traffickers for forced labor. As work, it is uniquely private: domestic work takes place behind the closed doors of private residences, in families' most intimate spaces. This professional work is tucked out of public view. It blurs the line between private and public, work and home; people often say "she's part of the family" as praise for domestic workers, blurring the line between family and professional relationships.

These conditions create an environment where abuse and exploitation can take place unchecked. Domestic workers typically work in isolation—most employers require no more than one nanny, housekeeper, or caregiver—so interactions between employers and workers are not usually witnessed by another party. Abusive employers can use the isolation of this work to control workers. Without knowledge of standard working conditions, workers may be unaware of their rights and available recourse.

In addition, many employers do not consider their home to be a workplace—an extension of considering domestic work to be "informal" or "not professional" work—and are resistant to addressing a domestic worker's workplace rights and protections. Without any centralized registration or regulation of domestic workplaces, a "wild West" environment is created. This leaves workers feeling unsafe in their place of work, without witnesses to their treatment, and without any formal body to turn to when they are mistreated.

4.2.3 Social Invisibility and Stigma

The hiddenness of domestic work is both logistical—it takes place in private homes—and due to the social invisibility related to stigma and the sector's history. In patriarchal society, where men hold primary power, authority, and social privilege, the value of women's work is directly connected to the power women hold in the structuring of society. Simultaneously, domestic work is devalued because it is performed by women. This creates social pressure to further make invisible the professional domestic workforce. And when women participate in the labor force outside the home, the pressure to manage domestic affairs does not ease correspondingly (Glynn, 2018). In fact, outsourcing this work is often seen as a failure, rather than a solution. Many working mothers feel "nanny guilt" (Thomas, 2018) and feel pressured to hide or downplay their nanny's importance in their family. Many employers of housecleaners never even see the domestic workers who clean their homes while the employer works outside the home. While there is a positive association attached to other services women utilize, such as "my hairstylist" or "my trainer," there is often shame attached to admitting that a nanny made the baby's food, or that the woman of the house does not do the home's cleaning and upkeep. This stigma can be publicly seen in online discussions around celebrities' use of, and openness to hiring, domestic workers. In 2019, actress Charlize Theron controversially said she did not hire a nanny for her two children, sparking debate over whether she was implying that women should be able to "do it all" (Cordoza, 2019). Alternatively, others make an effort to include their engaging domestic staff in their public image: also in 2019, Chrissy Teigen publicly thanked her personal chef and nannies on Instagram for their contributions to her household (Teigen, 2019). Still, she was criticized for hiring domestic workers even as she recognized their contributions.

The invisibilizing[2] of this workforce—both intentional and unintentional—enables traffickers to exploit this work condition: it is more difficult to identify forced labor when community members are trained by society and history not to notice the laborers. So even as the visibility of human trafficking, as a concept, has become more widespread, most public awareness and policy change has come to focus on sex trafficking. This form of trafficking can feel more aligned with general expectations of what "trafficking" and "traffickers" look like (Chap. 9). Meanwhile, according to the National Human Trafficking Hotline which maintains one of the most extensive data sets on human trafficking in the United States, domestic work continues to be the industry with the highest number of labor trafficking cases reported (National Human Trafficking Hotline, 2019).

---

[2] Neologism: to make invisible.

4.2.4 Historical Factors: Forced Labor and Colonialism in the United States

When White settlers attacked Yana communities in northern California in the early 1860s, killing most of the adults and capturing the children to use as forced labor, Nellie's life changed forever. As a young child, she was given to a White household and forced to work as an unpaid domestic worker. Her servitude finally ended when she died of tuberculosis as a teenager. Other children from the same raid suffered similar fates, forced to work without pay for White families until they turned 21. A 7-year-old child, Lena, was given to a wealthy store owner. Three-year-old Ella labored for a former judge (Magliari, 2012). This practice of capturing Indigenous children and forcing them to perform domestic labor was common at the time and is a direct result of the history of North American colonialism and chattel slavery.

Chattel slavery is the most commonly recognized form of slavery referenced in relation to the history of the United States. The first enslaved Africans were brought to US colonies in 1619, and by the 1860 census, the number of enslaved people in the United States had reached four million. This forced labor fueled the early domestic workforce: in the late seventeenth century about 10% of (and more in the eighteenth century) enslaved African women and their descendants worked in the United States as baby nurses (or "wet-nurses"), cooks, housekeepers, and other domestic servants on plantations in the South (Clark Hine et al. 2018). At its most violent and depraved, forced domestic labor not only denied workers of the humanity and dignity they deserved, it also robbed them of their human rights, agency, and safety. The legal enslavement of people (largely Black Africans and their descendants) subjected them to sexual assault and torture even as they were forced to care for the families and homes of their enslavers and traffickers.

Even after emancipation, many "free" Black laborers found they had limited legal rights in relation to their labor. While slavery had ended in name, state-enacted Black codes emerged to create and control a stable workforce of former slaves. Faced with few options, many Black people signed contracts to work a year or more for low wages, and laws like the peonage system (Chap. 9) in Alabama prevented workers from leaving: employers applied charges to workers which resulted in the worker being indebted to the employer, and peonage laws prohibited the worker from leaving while there was outstanding debt (Martin 1993). These practices were not only exploitative, but, as a form of peonage,[3] would be illegal today.

Colonialism and the violent acquisition of Mexican land (Chap. 2) into the US territory (present-day Texas, Nevada, Utah, western New Mexico and Colorado, southwest Wyoming, and most of Arizona (1821–1848)) fostered conditions for forced labor. When Mexico won independence from Spain in 1821, the Mexican

---

[3] Also called "bonded labor," peonage is when a person's services are used to repay a debt. Freedom is achieved when the debt is paid. When the terms are vague, the person holding the debt has control over the worker; services can be demanded indefinitely. Debt bondage can be passed through generations.

government confiscated land once owned by Spanish Catholic missions and sold or gave it to hundreds of elite Spanish-Mexican families, known as *Californios (Guglielmo and Joffroy, 2021)*. Without access to their own ancestral land, most Indigenous Mexican women had to work for *Californio* families for food and shelter, and many labored as indentured servants with contracts that required their lifelong labor. Similar dynamics occurred more widely throughout the Southwest, in other territories formerly Mexican, as in Texas with the *Tejanos* and New Mexico with *Hispanos*. The servants' dependency on employers for survival meant that it was difficult—if not impossible—to leave exploitative and violent conditions, and they too became enslaved domestic workers. As the demand for domestic labor grew, US Whites adapted forms of involuntary labor from Spanish colonial practices. The kidnapping of Indigenous women and children further enabled White settlers to establish economic and political power in the West. By the late nineteenth century, employers turned increasingly to Chinese immigrant men (Chap. 10), European immigrant women, and Mexican-American women as a source of domestic labor (Guglielmo and Joffroy, 2021).

4.2.5 Policy Factors: Invisibility by Design and by Default

Forced labor in domestic work has been both enabled by policy explicitly legalizing its practices, (e.g., the "work-or-fight" order of 1918 that forced Black women back into low wage domestic work (National Archives n.d.)), as well as by intentional legislative exclusions that facilitate forced labor conditions. In the 1930s, the US Congress developed labor rights as part of the New Deal, to formalize workers' basic rights and protections. During the development of this legislation, Southern Congressmen insisted on the specific exclusion of domestic workers (and agricultural workers) from Social Security, the minimum wage and overtime payment rules afforded by the 1938 Fair Labor Standards Act, (FLSA), and the collective bargaining laws of the 1935 National Labor Relations Act (NLRA) (Farhang and Katnelson, 2005). These two workforces were disproportionately Black and, given the history of race-based slave labor in the US, were routinely abused in the workplace. Rather than protect these workers, these laws continued to disempower domestic workers and allowed employers to maintain disproportionate amounts of control and dominance.

In the face of a deep history of institutionalized worker disempowerment, the path to legally supported workplace power for domestic workers has been long and difficult. In 1974, more domestic workers were included in minimum wage and overtime protections due to the organizing and leadership of Black domestic workers (US Department of Labor). In 2015, under the Obama Administration, the Department of Labor issued the Home Care Final Rule, to explicitly extend minimum wage and overtime protections to home care workers, who had previously been excluded by the Companionship Exemption of the FLSA (US Department of Labor).

While great gains have been made, domestic workers are still excluded from the *Occupational Safety and Health (OSH) Act*, which assures safe and healthful working conditions for working people. In addition, laws like the 1964 Civil Rights Act (US Equal Employment Opportunity Commission, 1964) and the 1993 Family and Medical Leave Act (FMLA) (US Department of Labor, 1993) also exclude many domestic workers, as these laws include numeric employee thresholds. That is to say, at least 15 employees for the Civil Rights Act and 50 for the Family and Medical Leave Act are needed for the protections to be required. Due to the unique nature of domestic work and most employers not having use for more than one nanny, housecleaner, or homecare worker, most domestic workers are automatically excluded from these landmark pieces of worker protection legislation.

From forced labor of Native Americans and the forced migration of Africans for enslavement, to the forced labor of trafficked immigrants, the connection between historical domestic work and immigration is intricately tied to the present-day exploitation of workers who are isolated and disconnected from their families and communities of support. Every year, thousands of domestic workers enter the United States on temporary visas to provide essential care work (Chap. 14) for US-based families. These visas are tied to the employer, creating a power dynamic (Chap. 6) in which the employer has control over the worker's ability to legally stay in the United States. These visas include the A-3 visa extended to diplomats, the G-5 visa of employees of international organizations, B-1 visas extended to specific categories of employers (Chap. 9), and the J-1 visas for live-in au-pairs (Human Rights Watch, 2001). There are also a large number of undocumented domestic workers whose visa status is exploited by unscrupulous employers, who use isolation, fear of deportation, language barriers, and separation from community support networks as a ready-made weapon of control to facilitate trafficking. These, often undocumented, workers are also discriminated against in pay and benefits. As the National Domestic Workers Alliance of 2012 *Home Economics* study points out, these workers "pay a substantial wage penalty and face additional constraints on their capacity to resist wage violations and abusive working conditions" (Burnham and Theodore 2012).

4.2.6   The Growing Care Economy

Despite efforts to keep domestic workers in the shadows of the national economy and society, the changing demographics of US society are greatly growing the need for a robust, thriving care economy. "Baby boomers" are living longer than previous generations, and at the time of this writing, there are 10,000 people turning 65 every day in the United States (Heimlich 2010). The growing preference of seniors is to age in place, as opposed to moving into a residential facility. Thus, there is an increasing need for caregivers in the home and other domestic workers. These workers help people stay at home safely and comfortably; they perform or support activities of daily living, such as cooking and cleaning, and help people with bathing and dressing. Moreover, the number of people in the United States with health conditions such as Alzheimer's disease and other dementias will nearly triple between 2015 and 2060, further adding strain to US society's need for care services (Matthews et al., 2018). These demographic shifts are reflected in the Bureau of Labor Statistics' employment projections: jobs for home health aides and personal care aides will increase by 34% between 2019 and 2029, while all other occupations will increase by an average of 7% (US Bureau of Labor Statistics, 2020).

Simultaneously, family structures have changed as women increasingly participate in the workforce outside the home, (US Bureau of Labor Statistics, 2020), and more families now have two working parents, rather than one working outside the home and one staying home (Pew Research Center, 2015). This shift creates an increased need to outsource the responsibilities that were previously held by the women in the home, including caring for children, senior care, and house cleaning. The reliance of the US economy on a stable and thriving care economy cannot be understated. Every worker with family members in need of care relies on domestic workers so that the rest of the workforce can go to their jobs outside the home. And yet domestic workers are more than three times more likely to be living below the poverty line than other workers and earn on average less than half the median wage of other workers (Wolfe et al., 2020). This is a key factor that drives many domestic workers and their families into poverty, especially for the many who are the sole or main breadwinner in their households.

The COVID-19 pandemic further reveals the vulnerability of domestic workers in various ways: thousands were laid off without any right to benefits, and others who were identified as "essential" workers have had to work with limited protection or training, risking their health and the well-being of themselves and loved ones (Gonzalez and Anderson 2020).

4.2.7   The Path Forward

The legacy of explicit and implicit decisions of US policymakers to keep domestic workers in positions of vulnerability and exploitation is long, deep, and broad. It has leveraged and deepened racial divisions, helped shape labor legislation and immigration law, and it has hidden behind sexist, racist, and xenophobic cultural norms that invisibilize a workforce of almost 2.5 million. But the movement for the respect and dignity of domestic workers has been growing, building over the generations.

In the 1960s, Dorothy Bolden organized domestic workers on buses in Atlanta and helped start the National Domestic Workers Union of America. The now-called National Domestic Workers Alliance has united over 70 organizing and advocacy affiliates and chapters in more than 30 cities across the nation. The exploitation and importance of domestic workers are gaining more visibility. The 2018 Oscar-winning film *Roma* centered an Indigenous domestic worker as the central character in the film, which was based on director Alfonso Cuarón's family in 1970s Mexico City. The feature-length film showed her life as full of the complexity that every domestic worker experiences: she is both part of the family and not, her relationship with her employer is both intimate and distant, and she is both vulnerable and powerful. And a movement is building to bring more awareness about the US's urgent need for a robust care economy with good jobs for workers: in 2019 Caring Across Generations and the Women's Alzheimer's Movement partnered to draw attention to the US's lack of preparedness for the increase of caregiving that will be required to support the growing population with Alzheimer's disease.

At the center of every successful anti-trafficking effort is the development of strong networks of educated and organized trafficking survivors. Their leadership sheds light on the reality of and the conditions that enable trafficking; such awareness makes it easier for community members to identify when trafficking is occurring. Labor trafficking thrives in the shadows and exploits conditions where workers are invisibilized. By centering survivors, and following their leadership in survivor-led solutions and preventive strategies (Chap. 17), the United States can better counter the conditions that traffickers exploit. In addition, investing in trusted local community-based organizations—which are rooted in domestic worker communities and are best positioned to identify domestic workers in trafficking situations—helps create the support networks necessary for domestic workers to escape abuse. Finally, educating the public at large is key to shifting social perceptions and cultural norms that have created the conditions that enable forced labor to continue; education is an important part of teaching what it means to be a good employer.

4.2.8 Beyond Survival

Beyond Survival is a campaign launched in 2013 by the National Domestic Workers Alliance, in partnership with nine anchor groups that organize nannies, house cleaners, and homecare workers: Adhikaar based in New York; CASA in the DC and Baltimore metro areas; Damayan in New York City and New Jersey; the Labor Justice Committee based in El Paso, Texas; The MataHari Women's Worker Center of Greater Boston in Massachusetts; and Mujeres Unidas y Activas in San Francisco, California. Beyond Survival focuses on lifting up the experience and vision of trafficked domestic workers to tell stories of leadership and policy change led by workers themselves. Through survivor work and expertise, the anchor organizations have collectively supported over 110 domestic worker trafficking cases and demonstrated that survivor-led strategies, rather than law enforcement-led strategies, are the key to prevent and ultimately end trafficking. These trusted groups are also well positioned to support survivors in gaining education and training opportunities (e.g., public speaking and writing, understanding legislative processes, critical policy literacy, media skills) that equip them for civic leadership and calling attention to the problem of trafficking and to its necessary solutions. At its core, forced labor removes workers' power and agency, so Beyond Survival organizes to build worker power and enable survivors to shine a light on the exploitation they faced. Survivors are leading the way with changes on the policy, cultural, and economic levels.

4.2.9   National Domestic Workers Bill of Rights

Domestic workers experience a spectrum of labor abuses, from disrespect in the workplace, to wage theft, to harassment and assault, and labor trafficking in the extreme. Raising workplace standards is a powerful way to curtail abuse across the sector, including educating domestic workers about their rights, providing support for domestic workers experiencing abuse, and reducing the conditions that labor traffickers can exploit. In 2019, Senator Kamala Harris and Representative Pramila Jayapal introduced a *National Domestic Workers Bill of Rights*, which would create a new nationwide standard for domestic work jobs, in every state. It would strengthen worker rights laws that currently exist to finally include domestic workers and create new ones that meet the demands and needs of the domestic work sector. The legislation would give domestic workers common workplace protections such as the right to overtime pay for live-in domestic workers, paid sick days, meal and rest breaks, the right to a safe workplace, and protection against harassment and discrimination. In addition, it includes rights and protections that address the unique challenges of domestic work, such as:

- Establishing privacy and autonomy for domestic workers, so that live-in domestic workers are guaranteed privacy and have access to a phone and the internet. This combats isolation and makes it more feasible that workers can reach out for help if needed.
- Establishing a hotline that domestic workers can call if they are worried about their safety.
- Providing resources for community organizations to educate domestic workers about their rights, and the enforcement of these new rights and benefits. This reinforces the Department of Labor's role in overseeing workplace protections for J-1 visa recipients.
- Written agreements and fair scheduling practices, and a wages and standards board to set industry-wide standards.

When enacted, the National Domestic Worker Bill of Rights will be the first ever nationwide rights and protections legislation for domestic workers. The bill shines a light on the nation's growing need for care workers and preserves the basic rights to the labor dignity every domestic worker deserves.

4.3   Conclusion

Domestic work has always been at the heart of US homes, families, and the national economy. Domestic workers do the work that makes all other work possible, and yet this workforce has been exploited throughout history and their work continues to provide critical support to the economy and society without the wages and protections they deserve. But what is not seen cannot be fixed, and the invisibility of domestic workers—visually, culturally, legally—has created an environment where forced labor can take place hidden and unrecognized.

The history of forced labor and domestic work sets the stage for abuse within the sector today, but the domestic worker movement is making new history under the leadership of domestic workers themselves. Fighting for respect and dignity, domestic workers are demanding their rights be recognized under the law and their contributions be recognized in society. Domestic workers are lifting up each other's voices so that fellow industry-workers across the nation will know they are not alone. Domestic workers support one another through strong community organizations and networks that counter the isolation that their work can bring. By centering domestic workers, exploring the legacy of exploitation that has devalued domestic work, and investing in trafficking survivor leaders, the United States can re-imagine not only how to intervene on labor trafficking but also prevent it altogether.

4.4   Recommendations

1. *Center and support trafficking survivor leadership*, building strong networks of educated and organized survivors who can raise awareness around the conditions that enable trafficking and exploitation and bring domestic worker trafficking out of the shadows.
2. *Pass the National Domestic Workers Bill of Rights*, to legislate nationwide standards for domestic work. This will give domestic workers both common workplace protections as well as rights and protections that address the unique challenges of domestic work.
3. *Educate the public on the social perceptions and accepted norms that enable trafficking to continue*, and enable members of the public to identify forced labor if they come in contact with it.
4. *Pass federal legislation to create a path to legalization and citizenship for undocumented immigrants in the United States.* Undocumented immigrants are particularly vulnerable to exploitation by traffickers and unethical employers.

References

Burnham, L., & Theodore, N. (2012). *Home economics: The invisible and unregulated world of domestic work*. National Domestic Workers Alliance.
Clark Hine, D., Hine, W. C., & Harrold, S. (2018). *The African-American Odyssey* (Vol. 1, 7th ed.). New York: Pearson.
Cordoza, R. (2019, October 15). Charlize Theron shares biggest lessons she teaches her kids Jackson and August. *US Magazine*.
Daluz, J. (2018, March 12). I am a survivor of human trafficking: Judith's story. *The Atlantic*.
Farhang, S., & Katnelson, I. (2005). The southern imposition: Congress and labor in the new deal and fair deal. *Studies in American Political Development, 19*, 1.

Glynn, S. J. (2018, May 18). *An Unequal Division of Labor*. Center for American Progress.

Gonzalez, P. L., & Anderson, T. (2020). *6 months in crisis: The impact of COVID-19 on domestic workers*. NDWA Labs.

Guglielmo, J., & Joffroy, M. (2021). *A history of domestic work and organizing*. Smith College.

Harris, S. K. (2019, July). Bill S.2112. Domestic Workers Bill of Rights Act.

Heimlich, R. (2010, December 29). *Baby boomers retire*. Pew Research Center Fact Tank.

Human Rights Watch. (2001). Hidden in the home: Abuse of domestic workers with special visas in the United States. *Human Rights Watch, 13*(2).

International Labour Office. (2017). *Global estimates of modern slavery: Forced labour and forced marraige*. ILO.

International Labor Organization. (2012). ILO Indicators of Forced Labour. ILO.

Johnston-Dodds, K. (2002). *Early California laws and policies related to California Indians*. California Research Bureau. Retrieved from https://www.library.ca.gov/Content/pdf/crb/reports/02-014.pdf.

Loney, J. (2010, February 18). Haiti "restavek" tradition called child slavery. Reuters.

Magliari, M. (2012). Free state slavery: Bound Indian labor and slave trafficking in California's Sacramento Valley, 1850-1864. *Pacific Historical Review, 81*(2), 183.

Martin, D. (1993). The birth of Jim Crow in Alabama 1865-1896. *National Black Law Journal, 13*(1), 184.

Matthews, K., et al. (2018, September 19). Racial and ethnic estimates of Alzheimer's disease and related dementias in the United States (2015–2060) in adults aged ≥65 years. Alzheimer's & Dementia: The Journal of the Alzheimer's Association

National Archives. (n.d.). Work or fight 1918. *Records of Rights*. Retrieved 30 October 2020 from http://recordsofrights.org/events/127/work-or-fight.

National Human Trafficking Hotline. (2019). *Hotline statistics*. Retrieved 30 October from https://humantraffickinghotline.org/states.

Parreñas, R. (2001). *Servants of globalization: Women, migration and domestic work* (2nd ed.). Stanford: Stanford University Press.

Pew Research Center. (2015, December 17). Parenting in America.

Teigen, C. (2019, November 29). Instagram.

Thomas, N. (2018, February). The nanny guilt is real: Why I hesitated hiring help. *The Bump*.

Tizon, A. (2017, June). My family's slave. *The Atlantic*.

Tracy, N. (2018, March 12). I am a survivor of human trafficking: Natalicia's story: I was a fixture in the house; a robot there to do things for them. I felt invisible, dispensable, and alone. *The Atlantic*.

U.S. Bureau of Labor Statistics. (2020, September 1). Fastest growing occupations. *Occupational Outlook Handbook*.

U.S. Bureau of Labor Statistics. (2020, September 1). Home health aides and personal care aides. *Occupational Outlook Handbook*.

US Department of Labor. (1993). *The family and medical leave act of 1993*.

US Department of Labor. *Domestic service final rule frequently asked questions*.

US Equal Employment Opportunity Commission. (1964). *Title VII of the civil rights act of 1964*.

Wolfe, J., et al. (2020, May 14). *Domestic workers chartbook*. Economic Policy Institute.

Chapter 5
Modern-Day Comfort Stations: Human Trafficking in the US Illicit Massage Industry

Chris Muller-Tabanera and Beisi Huang

5.1 Introduction

5.1.1 Historical Roots

The historical roots of trafficking in the illicit massage industry (IMI) in the United States today are multifaceted, and there are a multitude of socio-political determinants. These include lack of job opportunities for Asian immigrants (Chap. 10), transnational organized crime, and shame and stigma connected to exploitation to name a few. For the purposes of this chapter, focus is paid to exploring the legacies of wartime and post-conflict policies and practices normalizing the commercialized sexual exploitation of East Asian women. This chapter is not meant to be a comprehensive address of the IMI, but a framing of institutional and structural issues to help readers historically situate the illicit massage industry and trafficking in modern-day United States. Learners can mine the reference list for more on the issue.

From the beginning of the twentieth century to beyond World War II, two key drivers of large-scale sexual exploitation, specifically of East Asian women and girls, were the aggressive agenda of the Imperial Japanese Army and the proliferation of US military presence throughout the region of East Asia. Throughout the early 1900s, Japan engaged in multiple wars across Asia and the Pacific (Min, 2003). At the time, Japan had a longstanding history of legal prostitution (Min, 2003). To support the extensive war effort, the Japanese government began the mass mobilization of women for military sexual slavery (Min 2003; Tanaka 2002). Government-controlled "comfort stations" were instated as early as 1904 during the Russo-Japanese War (Min

C. Muller-Tabanera (✉)
Heyrick Research, Arlington, VA, USA
e-mail: chris@heyrickresearch.org

B. Huang
New York, NY, USA

© Springer Nature Switzerland AG 2021
M. Chisolm-Straker, K. Chon (eds.), *The Historical Roots of Human Trafficking*,
https://doi.org/10.1007/978-3-030-70675-3_5

2003; Soh 2008). A "comfort station" was a euphemism for a military brothel, where young women and girls were forced or coerced into prostitution (Min 2003; Soh 2008; Yoshiaki 1998).

These institutional practices were arguably built on ideological foundations in Neo-Confucianism that valued patriarchy and were developed over two centuries during the Edo period (Min 2003; Soh 2008). Patriarchal values were paramount in Japanese culture, and women and girls were expected to comply with the hierarchy of male dominance in relationships at home and in the community (Min 2003). But during the Meiji period that followed (1867–1912), this relational dynamic took a critical turn. Emperor Meiji put a more extreme emphasis on the family's subordination to the nation state, and in turn, the individual's subordination to the emperor (Min 2003). Taking advantage of patriarchal ideology already imbedded within the social and economic fabric, Emperor Meiji created the ultimate justification for using women to serve the nation's imperial agenda. For the following decades and successive emperors, this would be the rationale for using women's bodies to satisfy the sexual appetites of male soldiers at war (Tanaka 2002; Yoshiaki 1998).

After the Russo-Japanese war, Russia conceded Korea to Japan, and in 1910, Korea became an official colony of the Japanese Empire (Min 2003). During the Pacific War and spanning into the theater of World War II, Korea and other occupied territories throughout Asia became the epicenter for the sexual exploitation that contributed to the development of a large-scale sex trafficking industry (Min 2003; Tanaka 2002). Estimates ranging between 20,000 and 400,000 young women and girls (Min 2003; Soh 2008; Tanaka 2002) from Japan, Korea, China, Taiwan, and the Philippines were induced into sexual servitude in military brothels in occupied territories throughout Asia by the Japanese government (Min 2003; Tanaka 2002). But the overwhelming majority of women forced into military sexual exploitation and servitude were Korean, mostly unmarried and between the ages of 18 and 22 (Min 2003).

The Japanese government recruited Korean women who came from rural, poor, or jobless migrant families (Min 2003). This subgroup of the population drastically increased after Japan's appropriation of vast amounts of land following colonial takeover. For women who were not coerced or abducted by force, they were often deceived through false offers of employment in other cities or neighboring countries (Min 2003; Tanaka 2002). Many families were defrauded with an advance payment in order to ensure that their daughter would be given "priority placement" (Min 2003; Tanaka 2002).

As these young women were exploited in the military brothels, they endured incredible suffering. Survivors report being systematically raped and beaten by Japanese soldiers, as often as 40 times a day (Min 2003; Tanaka 2002). Testimonies of rape, torture, confinement, malnutrition, humiliation, and forced abortions were the norm (Min 2003; Tongsuthi 1994). A theme throughout Korean survivor testimonies is the distinct prejudice and inhumane treatment they received because they were Japan's colonial subjects (Min 2003). In 1945, when Japan lost the war, reports estimate that between 75% and 90% of "comfort women" died by the end of World

War II (Levy and Sidel, 2007). For the women who survived, their suffering continued after returning home, due to extreme trauma, shame, and stigma (Min 2003). But there were many women whose sexual enslavement continued within the "comfort" system even after Japan's defeat (Hughes et al 2007; Vine 2015).

Despite being enemies on the battlefield, the US and Japanese governments were figurative allies in the subjugation of Asian women and girls (Tanaka 2002). After WWII, the United States continued Japan's prior practice of sexual exploitation in Korea (Vine 2015). With the rapid increase of US military presence in Korea, the demand for commercial sex noticeably increased. Official agreements were made between the United States and Korean governments which resulted in the creation of camp towns surrounding US military bases (Moon 1997; Vine 2015). These districts were designated to provide entertainment and boost morale for US troops stationed abroad, and only US citizens and those who worked in these areas were allowed entry (Hughes et al 2007; Moon 1997). Former Japanese "comfort stations" were soon known as "rest and relaxation" centers, and "comfort women" were then referred to as "entertainers," among a host of other euphemisms. Although prostitution was and still is illegal in South Korea, the commercial sex industry was rampant in these camp towns (Hughes et al 2007; Moon 1997). Women and girls, predominantly from Korea, the Philippines, and China, were brought into these camp towns to meet the sexual demands of US military men (Hughes et al 2007; Min 2003). Although different than the "comfort stations" in notable ways, these women and girls experienced similar legacies of exploitation by members of the military. In basic economic terms, the bodies of vulnerable Asian women were (still) the "product" being sold, but now the US military filled the role of the customer, with the South Korean and US governments securing the market (Vine 2015). The official government treaties favored and protected the United States and its servicemen, and soldiers committed sex crimes against women without penalty, in effect receiving total impunity for their actions (Hughes et al 2007). Despite "zero tolerance policies" of the US government, military servicemen rarely receive any legal consequence for crimes committed while stationed abroad (Demick 2002; Fukushima & Kirk 2013; Tabassum & Cornwell 2012; US Department of Defense 2019).

This period produced a trend in US military policy (Moon 1997; Vine 2015). As in South Korea, the United States went on to sign official agreements with South Vietnam, Thailand, Hong Kong, and the Philippines during the Vietnam War (Truong 1990). These Asian governments agreed to provide areas for "Rest and Recreation" or "Rest and Recuperation" for the US military (Vine 2015; Woan 2008). These stations were commonly referred to as "intoxication and intercourse" centers among military personnel, better reflecting what regularly took place in the bars, nightclubs, and massage parlors that densely populated these districts (Vine 2015). A consistent characteristic of these camp towns throughout Asia were the backgrounds of the women who were recruited and exploited. Women and girls with limited education and very few job options, often coming from communities with weakened economies fractured by war, as well as those who had run away from home to escape abuse (Hughes et al 2007; Min 2003; Moon 1997). False offers of meaningful employment were one recruitment scheme for women and girls who were experiencing desperate financial hardship (Hughes et al 2007; Min 2003). Time and again it was a combination of inequities that made women vulnerable to being taken advantage of by traffickers. Even as US military presence in Asia has decreased over time and bases have closed, cities like Bangkok and Manila have booming sex tourism industries to this day as legacies of former markets catering to military personnel (Moon 1997; Fukushima 2013; The Red Light Guide n.d.). Along with these infamous red-light districts is the sex trafficking of young women and girls in an attempt to meet the demands of predominantly foreign male sex buyers (ECPAT 2020; Redfern 2019; Tabassum and Cornwell 2012).

As these US military bases ignited nearby commercial sex markets, they also ignited a dehumanizing, racist stereotype of Asian women and girls among those from Western cultures. Since the early twentieth century, one of the primary influences of how the United States viewed Asia was through experiences during and after war (Nemoto 2009). Western interactions with Asian women who were subjected to military sexual exploitation and servitude produced a distorted and demeaning stereotype (Woan 2008; Lee 2018). The representation of the hypersexualized Asian woman (or girl) was a direct outcome of US military encounters in East Asia (Nemoto 2009; Woan 2008). Asian women are portrayed as submissive, demure, and delicate, and this caricature is often utilized to serve as a complement to a central White male character with an exaggerated heterosexual masculinity (Lee 2018; Nemoto 2009; Woan 2008). This Asian archetype infantilizes Asian adult women, presenting them as simple objects to be dominated and consumed (Lee 2018; Woan 2008). Over time, this racist and sexist portrayal has been popularized and perpetuated by the dominant US media (Kubrick 1987; Schönberg &Boublil 1989; Ratner 2001). As a result, the hypersexualized stereotype of Asian women further feeds the demand of predominantly White male sex buyers in the marketplace. The two together continue to fuel each other in the present-day trafficking industries in the United States, but none more notable than the illicit massage industry.

During World War II, Korea was already an epicenter of the Japanese government's large-scale sex trafficking of women and girls in military brothels. After the war, official treaties signed between the United States and South Korea created camp towns surrounding military bases, often in the same locations of previous "comfort stations." Camp towns established a flourishing sex market that was ripe to be exploited by criminal actors. Traffickers transported women from throughout the Asia Pacific region to meet the rising demand for commercial sex by US servicemen (Hughes et al 2007; Moon 1997). Transnational organized crime networks began trafficking women to the United States to be used in the nation's growing illicit massage industry, replicating the illicit business model outside Korea (Hughes et al 2007).

At the turn of the twenty-first century, Korean organized crime networks with ties between South Korea and the United States dominated the industry (Hughes et al 2007). These networks facilitated IMB operations and the transport of women nationwide (Hughes et al 2007). Traffickers used debt bondage as the primary method to exert control over exploited workers, who were primarily younger Korean women (Hughes et al 2007). According to numerous reports from law enforcement agents and service providers, US military personnel played a role in bringing Korean women to the United States (Hughes et al 2007). For example, "sham marriages" between Korean women and US military servicemen were heavily used to get women into the country and quickly handed over to Korean American gangs operating IMBs (Hughes et al 2007). Some marriages with US military personnel were sincere but ended in divorce, leaving Korean women isolated and forced to survive on their own (Hughes et al 2007). Korean IMB recruiters would target and entice these women with false job offers (Hughes et al 2007). Over the last 20 years, the industry has evolved and shifted primary recruitment in other countries, but Asian women continue to be trafficked and systematically exploited to meet the demand for commercial sex in the United States.

5.2 Discussion

5.2.1 IMI Today

The Business

According to analysis from online sex buyer review sites, the IMI in the United States is comprised of over 10,000 businesses.[1] These establishments put on the façade of a legitimate massage business in order to facilitate commercial sex operations (Kulish 2019). These storefront brothels are organized into an unknown number of cells or networks, typically organized along ethnic lines, such as Chinese, Korean, or Thai (Polaris 2018). This industry thrives on the anonymity and easy access for both the sellers (business owners, facilitators) and the sex buyers, facilitated by online advertising and IMB review websites (Polaris 2018).

The industry has shifted greatly in its sources of recruitment, business model structure, and coercive tactics. Structurally, the broad network of Chinese-run businesses appears diffused throughout the country (Odenath 2020; Polaris 2018).[2] What was once a more traditional, hierarchical pyramid structure, often more reflected in the Thai and Korean networks, is now a more decentralized model, with smaller, regional networks often competing or coexisting in the same communities (Kulish et al 2019; Odenath 2020; Hughes et al 2007; Doucette 2002).[3]

---

[1] According to Heyrick Research's (primary author's professional knowledge; unpublished data) analysis of Rubmaps.ch data, as of September 2020 there were 10,422 suspected IMBs marked as "open" and "erotic" in all 50 states. California had the largest number of suspected IMBs (2499), followed by Texas (1117) and Florida (885), while South Dakota has the smallest number of suspected IMBs (2).

[2] Odenath (2020); See also Polaris, 35–38.

[3] See Hughes et al. (2007) for interviews and news articles referencing the dominant theme of Korean organized crime behind IMBs across the US, for example, this 2002 article referencing the

There are IMBs active in all 50 states, but most roads lead back to either Flushing, New York, or the San Gabriel Valley near Los Angeles in California (Kulish et al 2019). These two areas serve as hubs for the industry, where traffickers receive, recruit, and transport women to different locations all across the nation (Polaris 2018).

Illicit massage businesses are usually staffed by one female manager and an average of two workers.[4] In areas like Brooklyn or Queens, New York, where there is a high density of IMBs, there are often four to six workers in one location.[5] In states with licensing requirements, businesses will almost always display valid massage therapist licenses.[6] But these credentials are often for therapists who are not on-site or are likely procured fraudulently.[7] Another common pattern is for storefronts to be opened by individuals, with addresses in New York or southern California, who can be called "establishers" (Kulish et al 2019; Odenath 2020). These individuals quickly transfer ownership and oversight to a local facilitator or franchisee of a larger criminal network (Odenath 2020).

On average, a single IMB will have 8–12 customers per day, who are predominantly or exclusively male (Bouche and Crotty 2017; Solutions to End Exploitation 2009). IMB house service fees range from $50 to $100, with sex services costing an additional $50 to $300 tip for the exploited worker. A 2017 study found the average IMB can gross more than $465,000 in revenue every year.[8] For the industry as a whole, that could be as high as $3.8 billion in annual revenue.[9] While exploited workers may keep some of their tips as income, it is common for managers to charge them excessive fees for room and board, luggage storage, phone cards, lingerie, condoms, or other business supplies (Kulish et al 2019; Polaris 2018).

Research about the US commercial sex market shows that sex buyer demographics generally reflect the demographics of their surrounding communities (Demand Abolition 2018; Polaris 2018; Martin 2017). A 2018 report classifies "high-frequency" buyers as individuals who purchase sex weekly or monthly, and this group makes up about 25% of active sex buyers (Demand Abolition 2018). However, these high-frequency buyers account for nearly 75% of the transactions in the marketplace, and this particular group lists IMBs as a favorite venue to purchase

---

industry's primarily Korean distinction, Doucette (2002). According to Heyrick Research's 2019 analysis of Rubmaps.ch data, 84% of suspected IMBs are marked as "Chinese."

[4] This manager-to-worker breakdown is commonly reported to service providers, and is consistent with Heyrick Research and Restore NYC's experience working with women from IMBs.

[5] This knowledge is consistent with Heyrick Research and Restore NYC's experience working with women from IMBs.

[6] Heyrick Research has seen this common practice to display licenses inside IMBs, although the licenses almost always do not represent any person on-site working at the location. Other attempts to pose as legitimate massage businesses include displaying esthetician or cosmetology licenses.

[7] Ibid.

[8] This estimate for an average IMB is based on Bouche and Crotty (2017).

[9] This estimate is based on Bouche and Crotty (2017). As the study notes, it is important to keep in mind that this estimate is only using one city to deduce the national profit of the IMI and thus is slightly flawed. While similar demand research in Dallas, TX, Grand Rapids, MI, and Denver, CO found similar revenue estimates, the national estimate is still limited.

sex (Demand Abolition 2018). This group is predominantly White, and while sex buyers are generally found across the income spectrum, one important exception is that high-frequency buyers are more likely to earn $100,000 or more annually (Demand Abolition 2018). Polaris analyzed activity on RubMaps, a popular IMB sex buyer review website, and also found those participating on the site were more likely to be White, wealthy, and older than the general internet population (Polaris 2018). Qualitatively, these findings are consistent with Heyrick Research's knowledge of IMB customers, based on years of survivor accounts of their experiences in IMBs and from working with law enforcement entities across the country (Nash 2020).

The Workers

At the time of this writing, the vast majority of workers in US IMBs where trafficking takes place are from mainland China, but women also come from Taiwan, South Korea, Thailand, and Vietnam (Polaris 2018; Kulish et al 2019; Odenath 2020; Hughes et al 2007; Doucette 2002).[10] The average worker is 30–50 years old (Polaris 2018; Restore NYC 2017). Many women lack economic opportunities or need to pay off large debts (Polaris 2018). Restore NYC reported that Chinese survivors of trafficking have an average debt of $45,000 (Restore NYC 2017). This cause of debt is varied, but include property loans, family medical expenses, small business debt, a son's wedding expenses, or travel debt (Huang & Woo 2017; Polaris 2018). Women from IMBs also often report fleeing difficult personal situations, like spouses with alcoholism, domestic violence, or divorce (Polaris 2018). Due to extreme gender inequality in their home country, a sub-set of Chinese women have minimal education, low levels of literacy, and speak little to no English, contributing to risk factors for trafficking recruitment schemes to the United States (Huang & Woo 2017).

Women from China are most commonly recruited in one of two ways. Some are recruited directly from China, with full-service travel agencies offering visa-application assistance, flights, and airport pickup upon arrival (Polaris 2018). Some agencies promise work authorization and jobs at Chinese-run businesses (Polaris 2018). These visa services can range widely in cost, but it is common for women to borrow money from loan sharks, family members, or the travel agency itself (Polaris 2018). Workers will obtain valid visitor B1 or B2 visas and then typically travel from Beijing, Guangzhou, or Shanghai to either LAX or JFK (Polaris 2018).[11] In

---

[10] See Hughes et al. (2007) for interviews and news articles referencing the dominant theme of Korean organized crime behind IMBs across the US, for example, this 2002 article referencing the industry's primarily Korean distinction, Doucette (2002). According to Heyrick Research's 2019 analysis of Rubmaps.ch data, 84% of suspected IMBs are marked as "Chinese."

[11] These common travel arrangements are regularly described by Chinese clients at Restore NYC.

some cases, clients served at Restore have reported being smuggled into the United States across the Canadian or Mexican border.[12]

Women with pre-arranged jobs (unbeknownst to them are in an IMB) usually begin work upon arrival. For women who are already present in the United States, the other primary way they find work in IMBs is by word-of-mouth or social media (Polaris 2018). They will hear about working in massage parlors from other women while temporarily residing at family-style hostels in Chinatowns, or by responding to fraudulent recruitment ads on social media platforms like WeChat or job postings in the World Journal (Kulish et al 2019; Polaris 2018).

The authors and contributors have served hundreds of immigrant women who have been exploited and trafficked in the illicit massage industry.[13] A consistent theme embedded in women's stories is their financial responsibility to family. Survivors share that their family is counting on them and that they cannot let their family down. Traffickers, who often share the same ethnic background of individuals they exploit, understand and manipulate positive values for fealty and exploit it in subtle methods of coercion. It is common for survivors to disclose that they had not previously worked in the massage industry.[14] In China, massage work is often viewed as an undesirable job and may be associated with prostitution in certain districts. Women report staying away from the industry because of its reputation and the potential stigma associated with taking a job in a US massage parlor. But after arriving in the United States, many of these women soon realize that the economic opportunities they hoped for are not available to them. Due to language barriers, they are mostly limited to living and working in Chinese communities. Factors like their age, minimal education, limited job experience, not having work authorization, recent migration, and having little to no social network further limit their options for work.

Worker Manipulation and Experiences

It is within this context that women are recruited to work in the illicit massage industry. IMB job recruiters and bosses offer women jobs at IMBs, and women are told they can do the job without having to learn English. They are assured that they can earn good money, do not need work authorization, no prior education or professional massage experience is required, and that they will receive training on the job.

---

[12] Chinese clients served at Restore NYC have reported this, but it is understood to be extremely rare compared to the more common travel methods described above.

[13] The remainder of the discussion depicting the experiences of exploited workers in the IMI is based upon the authors' and contributors' years of direct service with this distinct population of individuals, along with our shared knowledge of working with other subject matter experts across the country. At the time of this writing, the majority of women being exploited in the IMI are Chinese, so the following will highlight in depth the common experiences of Chinese exploited workers.

[14] Based on author(s) experience in direct service provision.

On top of this, the bosses and IMB managers will provide housing and food on-site, or that travel to and from the business will be coordinated for them. For a 40-year-old Chinese woman, who speaks limited to no English, who came to the United States with the primary aspiration to financially provide for her family members back home, and with very limited job opportunities, it is this type of job offer that she is eager to receive. Where trafficking takes place, the promised benefits are later used by IMB traffickers and store managers as a means to exert power and control over workers.

Some women ask the recruiters if the business is "legitimate" (*dàlìdiàn*), and recruiters emphasize that it is a "green parlor" (*lùdiàn*), implying there will be no sexual activity. Women are told no "yellow" (*huángsè*), slang terminology for prostitution, and "that" (*nàgè*) does not happen here. They are assured they will be safe and that there will be other workers with them at the location. Other recruiters deflect questions about illicit activity and confrontationally ask whether or not the woman wants a job. At this point, survivors often report they felt like they had no other choices and they could not afford to turn down the offer. With all the barriers they faced upon US arrival, they take the job, despite apprehension about doing massage work. Survivors often speak about a sense of urgency while they are in the United States, and that every day they are not working is distressing. Women express that they feel they do not have the luxury to wait longer or keep searching for another job. Traffickers exploit the economic pressures with false promises to provide what the women are seeking—a job, money to send home, and community.

After women take a job at an IMB, depending on its location, they may be asked to arrive independently, or be picked up and transported directly to the IMB. It is common for women to be transported for multiple hours without knowing where they are going. Upon arrival, it is a tactic for some managers to form an emotional bond with the new worker. This is referred to as having "sister talks" or "mothering;" managers serve as a generous host and caretaker. This bonding is subtle but powerful and can happen rather quickly. Managers often speak about the challenges of being a Chinese woman and migrating to the United States, or the difficulties of being so far from their loved ones. They may bond with the workers over the hardships they may have survived. By acknowledging shared experience, workers report that managers make them feel immediately welcomed and understood, even when disoriented in a new environment.

Once a woman starts working, she soon finds that the job is not what she was told. This is an experience with deception and fraud. For instance, she may be skipped over when it is her turn to provide massage because the customer is a "frequent customer" (*shúkè*). She may not make the amount of money promised or may not receive any tips for just doing massage. It is only a matter of time until she encounters a customer who gets upset or physically violent if there is no "extra service." Survivors often express a sense of shock and fear when these first violent interactions with customers occur because the customer was denied a sex act.[15]

---

[15] Ibid.

When a worker first speaks up about this, their concerns may be minimized or downplayed by a manager. The manager may instruct the worker to make the customer happy. If she continues to resist, a manager may question her, "Do you want to make money or not? Isn't that why you came to the US?" Or the manager may say, "You are hurting our business and giving us a bad reputation. Don't make it harder for the rest of us here." Some managers say, "I gave you a job and a place to stay. And this is how you repay me? Are you not grateful?"

These common questions and statements above are examples of how bosses and managers exploit cultural norms like indebtedness (*rénqíng*), social harmony (*guānxi*), and saving face (*miànzi*) (Huang & Woo 2017). For example, it is culturally implied that favors must be returned and debt repaid (*rénqíng*) (Huang & Woo 2017). To not do so would likely be dishonorable, cause the loss of face (*miànzi*), and potentially disrupt the harmony of the group (*guānxi*). Invoking gratitude, favors, and maintaining a positive reputation for the group are ways that bosses subtly but effectively add pressure. Many women end up feeling like the only way to pay back their debt is to engage in work they do not want to do.

There are trafficking cases at IMBs where women experience a more overt and explicit form of coercion. For example, survivors have reported being verbally threatened that if they do not comply and provide sex services, managers will report them to the police and have them deported. Other workers report having their identification documents taken from them and used as a means to restrict their movement. Or, they are threatened that if they do not perform sex acts on or with customers, IMB bosses will tell their family back home they are "prostitutes"; this would bring shame on the worker. While this more explicit form of coercion does occur, within the IMI it is more common for managers to use subtle and implicit methods with great compliance effect. Some managers simply give "the look" (*yǎnshén*). It is subtle but extremely communicative: If she does not get in line, there will be consequences.

At some point in the experience, IMB workers consider the choice, "Do I stay or do I go?" The answer to this is often another question, "Where would I go?" For women who have traveled to a more suburban, predominantly White area to live and work at an IMB, they are far removed from a Chinese community; there is an even greater feeling of isolation and powerlessness. In considering how to respond to social and financial pressures, women are often coerced into continued engagement in commercial sex since the IMI business model generally limits payment to women through tips earned from customers; while the base pay for massage services go to the IMB owners and managers, tips are associated with the provision of sex services. Women grapple with concepts of "choice" in a system designed to limit their options, often sacrificing their own well-being, enduring shame, and coping with trauma from repeated sexual violence in exchange for protecting the hopes of their loved ones.

Women who have experienced trafficking in IMBs describe routine feelings of "numbness" (*mámù*). Dissociation is also common, and some women have described feeling like robots or lifeless machines in order to perform commercial sex services day after day. Many survivors regularly disclose feelings of shame and "heaviness" as a result of their sexual exploitation, and that having to do "that" (*nàgè*) is a stain or "dirty dot" (*wūdiǎn*) in their life that will never go away.[16] Often, the longer a worker has been in the industry, the more difficult it is for her to leave. The violence, labor, and sexual exploitation in the workplace become normalized, and over time and through incredible resiliency (Chap. 13), this reality becomes accepted by the individual. Many women speak of their suffering in IMBs as the temporary sacrifice they make for the ultimate benefit to each of their families.

Collective Trauma to Build Community

Even more than the localized IMB experience, IMI workers have shared in a collective compound trauma. They share vulnerabilities that brought them to the United States, they share the burden of life responsibilities in their middle years, and they share the displacement of being immigrants. They share the sorrow of being away from children and family. They share in often unspoken experiences of exploitation in the commercial sex industry, and the shame associated with this work. They share the "choiceless choice" of staying in the IMI. For women who have been trafficked in IMBs, it is their shared experiences of trauma, over a lifetime, that provides a deep sense of identity and belonging. The sense of community has become their protection and a collective coping mechanism (Chap. 17); this community provides a sense of belonging and understanding. Professionals in the anti-trafficking space often speak of the trauma-bonds formed between the exploiter and the exploited. Although this is evidenced with IMB managers and exploited workers, the primary bond in the industry exists as a strong bond between the workers.

5.2.2 Barriers to Solutions

Meaningful contemporary anti-trafficking response to the illicit massage industry has been rife with obstacles. In particular, the commonly accepted viewpoint from community members, select law enforcement, and even many anti-trafficking providers is that the businesses are harmless and that trafficking does not take place in this industry (Polaris 2018). Moreover, IMBs have become the source of humor, as serving "happy endings" (Polaris 2018). These businesses often operate in plain sight and the veil of legitimacy has provided an effective cover against legitimate claims of human trafficking or commercial sexual exploitation. Sex buyers who frequent these establishments have the plausible defense of just "getting a massage" (Polaris 2018).

The majority of anti-trafficking service providers in the field lack the ethnic, cultural, and linguistic capacity to effectively connect with and serve exploited

---

[16] Based on author(s) experience in direct service provision.

industry workers, who are primarily Chinese. Historically, service provider or law enforcement attempts to bridge this cultural, ethnic, and citizenship power gap dynamic have yielded poor results and caused more harm than good. In a traditional law enforcement approach, developing human trafficking cases have been over-whelmingly dependent on a victim coming forward and self-identifying. But women in IMBs often have little to no interaction with the actual IMB owners or others higher within the criminal network. There may be some minor contact during recruitment or after an initial incident at an IMB. On-site managers are often the main point of contact for exploited workers, and these managers were often once sexually exploited themselves. But despite the manager's position of authority and role in exploiting lower level workers, they are viewed as a worker within the worker community too. In effect, all of this creates an incredible level of protection for traf-fickers and sex buyers. For exploited workers in IMBs, sharing openly with anyone outside the worker community is arguably an extreme act. For a worker to transpar-ently share about their needs to a service provider, tell names and phone numbers to law enforcement, or detail their forced sexual encounters with an immigration attor-ney—directly pushes against strong values of "saving face" (*miànzi*), "returning the favor" (*rénqíng*), and "maintaining the social harmony" of the group (*guānxi*). Speaking out would stray from being one of the group and cause an individual to stand out. But more so, it would risk betraying the trust within their unique com-munity, even those exploited by IMI traffickers who share a similar cultural back-ground as the workers. Hence it is not uncommon that an exploited worker does not engage services, does not identify as a "victim," nor cooperates with law enforce-ment; and exploited workers that do not fit a stereotype of victimhood are classi-cally dismissed. The declination to claim victimization is incorrectly interpreted (particularly by non-Asian law enforcement officers) as definitive evidence that there is no victimization or forced labor; consequently, law enforcement incorrectly interprets that trafficking does not exist in this space (Chap. 13). The industry has some major differences with other forms of trafficking in the United States and requires cultural and linguistic competencies to identify the unique ways trafficking presents in the IMI.

A common tactic of local vice units has been to conduct prostitution "stings" or sweeps of IMBs, arresting workers once a solicitation for sex services is made at the establishment (Chin et al 2019). But this tactic further compounds the problem. These acute encounters with law enforcement and the ensuing interaction with the criminal justice system are often very traumatic experiences for exploited workers; the workers are perceived and treated as criminals. These types of negative experi-ences create another barrier for workers to trust any law enforcement who may try to assist them in the future (Chin et al 2019). The majority of workers also have an unstable immigration status, and as a consequence of arrest, women have a criminal record (Chin et al 2019). This makes it even more difficult for them to find work outside of the illicit massage industry.

Another barrier in eradicating the IMI is the lack of resources allocated to enforce legitimate business regulations. Many states have laws regarding health standards for massage parlors, and IMBs often do not meet these legal health requirements.

But the sheer volume of massage parlors in states like California, Florida, and New York create the seemingly insurmountable problem of actually enforcing health regulations.[17] As a result, IMBs operate with little to no negative consequences from regulatory authorities.

For jurisdictions that are addressing the industry, local law enforcement often uses a reactive "whack-a-mole" approach (Chin et al 2019). A local police station may engage an IMB after a community member submits a complaint, but even if a business closes down, it often re-opens down the street because no one is proactively monitoring the situation. The industry's overwhelming presence, the failure of stakeholders to recognize IMBs as trafficking, and the normalization of these storefronts as harmless in the dominant media narrative, has created an environment for these illicit businesses to operate and the industry to expand with little resistance and relative impunity.

5.2.3   Evidence of Progress

While the anti-trafficking field has historically faced many barriers in combatting trafficking, this is especially the case for the illicit massage industry. Nonetheless, there have been several examples of overcoming these challenges in recent years.

Culturally Connected and Relevant Service Provision

Service providers like Restore NYC, Garden of Hope, and Refugee Services of Texas have supported workers trafficked in the illicit massage industry in their transition out of the industry.[18] These organizations provided services like comprehensive case management and supported survivors of trafficking in accessing federal immigration relief. These services are delivered by staff members who share a common gender, ethnicity, culture, and/or native language with the population of industry workers. As discussed, the insider-outsider dynamic is a sensitive reality for the majority of Chinese women who work in IMBs. For example, a Chinese female immigration attorney who speaks Mandarin, who is trained in trauma-informed care and well versed on industry dynamics, can often form a strong connection with IMI workers who are also ethnically Chinese and Mandarin-speaking. Restore NYC regularly incorporates feedback from survivors of IMB trafficking to improve programming, as well as supports survivors who engage in outreach to their communities (Chap. 17) (both IMI workers and the Chinese immigrant community in general). These service providers have also developed survivor networks that

---

[17] According to Heyrick Research's analysis of Rubmaps.ch data, as of September 2020, California had the largest number of suspected IMBs (2499). Florida had the second highest (885), while New York was fourth highest (819).

[18] Visit https://restorenyc.org/, https://gohny.org/ and https://www.rstx.org/ for more information.

women can connect with as well. All these factors contribute to leveling the unequal power dynamic and closing the cultural gap that often exists between service providers and exploited IMB workers.

A critical service provision is the development of viable economic opportunities for workers who exit the IMI.[19] This is especially essential in light of how many trafficked in the IMI were in need of work and recruited with false promises about the nature of the job (Polaris 2018). A common factor that keeps women in illicit massage businesses is large amounts of debt and the need to financially support family members back home (Polaris 2018). Economic empowerment services from organizations like Garden of Hope, Sanctuary for Families, and Restore NYC, as well as worker cooperatives like Damayan, provide training, alternative work options, and community support for trafficking survivors to replace the exploitative environment of illicit massage. By connecting survivors to safe work, community-based organizations (CBOs) help reframe the workplace from a place of trauma to a source of empowerment.

Enforcing Existing Legislation

According to Heyrick Research, stakeholders have also used innovative or non-traditional approaches to combatting the prevalence of IMBs. These approaches often involve leveraging other entities, legal frameworks, or people that intersect with the problem but are rarely considered when considering possible solutions. For example, one approach is educating and engaging landlords (Heyrick Research 2020b). The process includes contacting landlords of IMB locations, informing them of the suspected illicit activity occurring on their properties, and educating them of the potential legal and financial consequences of continuing to host an IMB on their property. This approach motivates landlords to terminate or not renew leases for IMB tenants and successfully denies the storefront space that the illicit massage industry depends on for its revenue. In 2008, stakeholders in Washington, D.C., targeted landlords in a comprehensive strategy to shut down IMBs in the city (Heyrick Research 2020c). This technique, along with other tactics, was critical to the enduring success in both shutting down IMBs and keeping the D.C.'s IMB population at or near zero for 12 years. In February 2018, the San Jose Police Department began incorporating a landlord education program into their strategy to eliminate IMBs from their city (Heyrick Research 2020b). This resulted in the closure of 67% of the suspected IMBs in their jurisdiction (Heyrick Research 2020a). Other approaches include utilizing and enforcing existing regulatory requirements, including consumer protection laws and anti-deceptive trade practice laws. All of these methods

---

[19] See for example Garden of Hope (2004) "Project WE," Restore NYC "Economic Empowerment," and Sanctuary for Families (1984) "Economic Empowerment Program" (EEP); For workers cooperative information, visit https://www.damayanmigrants.org/ (Damayan Migrant Workers Association 2002).

target the industry where it is most vulnerable—the reliance on storefront locations and the need to appear and operate like a legitimate business.

Law Enforcement Shift in Investigative Practice

Law enforcement agencies have been successful in prosecuting IMB traffickers by shifting to an "all crimes" investigative approach, leveraging strong money laundering statutes, and focusing on labor trafficking in the industry. As discussed above, traditional prostitution "stings" by vice units more often than not result in poor outcomes for both exploited workers and law enforcement goals. By incorporating a broader investigative scope, law enforcement improves the identification of networked activity and other organized crime within the industry. This also moves the pressure off of victims by not being overly reliant on their cooperation and testimony to drive trafficking investigations. An "all crimes" approach against traffickers in the illicit massage industry has been successfully utilized by agencies at the federal, state, and local level, including the USAttorney's Office in the District of Minnesota, the Delaware State Police, and the Seattle Police Department.[20]

Cross-Sector Leadership and Capacity Building

The growing evidence of success across sectors against the illicit massage industry gave rise to the organizing of a national gathering in the fall of 2019. Six anti-trafficking organizations co-hosted the National Convening to End Trafficking in the Illicit Massage Industry in the Washington, D.C. area.[21] This 2-day conference hosted 240 attendees from 30 states. Attendees learned from their peers in different regions of the country, discussed effective strategies, highlighted successes, and addressed gaps in the field. It was an opportunity to foster a shared learning space, build capacity, and develop a stronger network of partnerships focused on countering this specific form of trafficking. It was evident at the convening that the old narrative of illicit massage businesses being harmless nuisances is finally being dismantled.

5.3   Conclusion

The present-day US illicit massage industry is a descendant of the historical "comfort" system. The setting has changed from the backdrop of explicit imperialism on foreign land to the profit motivations in storefronts that blanket the national

---

[20] See United States v. Michael Morris, et al., United States v. Sumalee Intarathong, et al., State of Delaware v. Da Zhong Wang, and Seattle Police Department's "Operation Emerald Triangle."

[21] Host organizations included Polaris Heyrick Research (formerly Praesidium Partners), Restore NYC, Children At Risk, Global Emancipation Network, and The Epik Project.

landscape, from the average suburban strip malls to big city commercial districts. Both now and then, the total number of those trafficked by these parallel systems is estimated to be in the tens of thousands. As with the footprint of imperialism, the primary people exploited in the industry today painfully mirror those from the past. At the time of this writing, the majority of women exploited in IMBs are East Asian, primarily Chinese; many others are Korean and Thai, and many reside in the United States with unstable immigration status. Like the military brothels of old, women regularly have to eat, sleep, and live in IMBs—the same physical space of their traumatic sexual encounters. Sex buyers who most frequent IMBs are wealthier, White males, with the added security of US citizenship. Both now and then, the gender, racial, national, and socioeconomic power imbalance between sex buyer and provider of commercial sex continues to be extreme. The intersectionality of oppressions, specifically racism, sexism, and poverty, continue to facilitate this form of trafficking.

From World War II to today, IMI traffickers have utilized attractive offers of employment and financial earning potential as a consistent recruitment tactic. While the trafficking of young women and girls in wartime brothels in East Asia routinely involved force, the means of trafficking in the modern illicit massage industry are much more coercive and culturally nuanced. Regardless, the outcome for traffickers is the same—a consistent supply of primarily Asian women to meet the demand of predominantly White male sex buyers from or in the United States. Historically, it was the formal agreements between allied nations, and racist and sexist stereotypes that laid the foundation for the rampant growth of prostitution surrounding US military bases. Today, there is no such agreement between IMBs and the government. Still, the dehumanizing stereotype of the hypersexualized Asian female remains. The failure to recognize trafficking in these illicit storefronts and ineffective law enforcement response has collectively produced the same result: a thriving criminal industry experiencing little to no formal resistance. In the end, the present-day industry echoes its historical predecessor by concealing the truth with euphemism. From "comfort stations" to "rest and relaxation centers," and from "comfort women" to "entertainers," now the harmful reality is "just a massage."

5.4   Recommendations

1. *The education of girls must be as valued as that of boys.* The vulnerability of girls and women forced and coerced into the IMI (and other exploitative situations) is due, in part, to their systematic under-valuation and under-education. For many, education contributes to a strong sense of self and worth (Chap. 16), as well as broadening job possibilities.
2. *Job availability should be based upon capacity to do the work, rather than gender.* In this way, more job opportunities can be open to qualified women, and IMI-work is not the only option to support family.

3. *US military laws against exploitation should be enforced and violators must be held accountable for purchasing sex while stationed in countries outside the United States.*

4. *Affirm and cultivate more robust, accurate, and diverse representations of Asian women in mainstream media*, while calling out harmful portrayals that perpetuate the racist, sexist, hypersexualized Asian female caricature.

5. *Utilize the expertise and specialization of culturally connected and relevant service providers like Restore NYC and Garden of Hope* for referrals, training, and best practices when working with women involved in the industry.

6. *Ensure legal and immigration services are accessible and offered to exploited workers*; among the expected services offered to survivors of trafficking (e.g., housing, medical care, trauma therapy, case management) foreign-national adult women who have been trafficked in the illicit massage industry are consistently interested in legal assistance and accessing immigration relief.

7. *Increase training of law enforcement, local regulatory authorities (e.g., Department of Health, Department of Licensing and Regulatory Affairs), immigration attorneys, and anti-trafficking service providers on the unique industry and cultural dynamics between traffickers and exploited workers*, specifically how trafficking presents in illicit massage businesses.

8. *Incorporate non-traditional approaches into a counter-IMB strategy*, including engaging landlords, utilizing existing regulatory requirements, and combatting these businesses with consumer protection or deceptive trade practices laws.

9. *Broaden the scope of law enforcement investigations by employing an "all crimes" approach* to cases involving illicit massage businesses and replicate successful models.

10. *Immediately stop arresting exploited workers for prostitution crimes, or other activities committed under duress.*

11. *Invest in and develop programs or organizations that provide exploited workers economic alternatives* to the illicit massage industry.

References

Bouche, V., & Crotty, S. M. (2017). Estimating demand for illicit massage businesses in Houston, Texas. *Journal of Human Trafficking, 4*(4), 279–297. https://doi.org/10.1080/23322705.201 7.1374080. Accessed 19 January 2020.

Chin, J. J., Takahashi, L. M., Baik, Y., Ho, C., To, S., Radaza, A., Wu, E. S. C., Lee, S., Dulfo, M., & Jung, D. (2019, November). *Illicit massage parlors in Los Angeles County and New York City: Stories from women workers.* http://johnchin.net/Article_Files/MP_Study_10.11.19_ FINAL.pdf. Accessed 31 October 2019.

Damayan Migrant Workers Association, est. (2002). https://www.damayanmigrants.org/.

Demand Abolition. (2018). *Who buys sex: Understanding and disrupting the Illicit demand market.* Research report. Washington, DC: Demand Abolition. https://www.demandabolition.org/wp-content/uploads/2019/07/Demand-Buyer-Report-July-2019.pdf. Accessed 18 November 2019.

Demick, B. (2002, September 26). Off-base behavior in Korea. *Los Angeles Times*. https://www.latimes.com/archives/la-xpm-2002-sep-26-fg-barwomen26-story.html. Accessed 12 February 2020.

Doucette, J. H. (2002, June 24). Fuji Spa a satellite of illicit sex circuit. *Times Herald-Record*. https://www.recordonline.com/article/20020624/news/306249999. Accessed 12 February 2020.

ECPAT International. (2020, February 13). *Trafficking in Thailand: The demand fuels child trafficking for sexual purposes*. ECPAT International. https://ecpat.exposure.co/thailand?utm_source=Website&utm_medium=Blog&utm_campaign=Trafficking%20in%20Thailand.

Fukushima, A. I., & Kirk, G. (2013). Military sexual violence: From frontline to fenceline. *Foreign Policy in Focus*. https://fpif.org/military_sexual_violence_from_frontline_to_fenceline/. Accessed 12 February 2020.

Garden of Hope, est. (2004). 501(c)3 nonprofit organization. https://gohny.org/.

Heyrick Research. (2020a). *Snapshot by the numbers – landlord engagement and storefronts*.

Heyrick Research. (2020b). *Snapshot – empowering landlords in the fight against the IMI*.

Heyrick Research. (2020c). *Snapshot – enduring IMB closures in the District of Columbia*.

Huang, B., & Woo, P. (2017). Restore NYC subject matter expert statements submitted for Polaris' report on illicit massage businesses, 9 November 2017 Partially quoted in Polaris (2018). *Human Trafficking in Illicit Massage Businesses, 21*, 27.

Hughes, D. M., Chon, K. Y., & Ellerman, D. P. (2007). Modern-day comfort women: The U.S. military, transnational crime, and the trafficking of women. *Violence Against Women, 13*(9), 901–922. https://doi.org/10.1177/1077801207305218.

Kubrick, S. (Director). (1987). *Full metal jacket*. Warner Bros.

Kulish, N., Robles, F., & Mazzei, P. (2019, March 2). Behind illicit massage parlors lie a vast crime network and modern indentured servitude. *The New York Times*. https://www.nytimes.com/2019/03/02/us/massage-parlors-human-trafficking.html. Accessed 19 January 2020.

Lee, J. (2018). East Asian "China Doll" or "Dragon Lady"? *Bridges: An Undergraduate Journal of ContemporaryConnections,3*(1),2.https://scholars.wlu.ca/bridges_contemporary_connections/vol3/iss1/2.

Levy, B. S., & Sidel, V. W. (2007). *War and public health*. New York: Oxford University Press.

Martin, L. (2017). *Sex buyers: The "demand side" of sex trafficking*, 12 U. St. Thomas J.L. & Pub. Pol'y 6. https://ir.stthomas.edu/cgi/viewcontent.cgi?article=1124&context=ustjlpp.

Min, P. G. (2003). Korean "comfort women": The intersection of colonial power, gender, and class. *Gender & Society, 17*(6), 938–957. https://doi.org/10.1177/0891243203257584.

Moon, K. H. S. (1997). *Sex among allies: Military prostitution in U.S.-Korea relations*. New York: Columbia University Press.

Nash, D. (2020, August 3). Discussion on sex buyers at illicit massage businesses. *Office of the Missouri Attorney General IMB working group meeting*, Johnson County Court House, Warrensburg, MO.

Nemoto, K. (2009). *Racing romance: Love, power, and desire among Asian American/White couples*. New Brunswick: Rutgers University Press.

Odenath, N. (2020, February 14). Interview. Conducted by Christopher Muller-Tabanera.

Polaris. (2018). *Human trafficking in illicit massage businesses*. https://polarisproject.org/wp-content/uploads/2019/09/Human-Trafficking-in-Illicit-Massage-Businesses.pdf. Accessed 18 November 2019.

Ratner, B. (Director). (2001). *Rush Hour 2*. New Line Cinema.

Redfern, C. (2019, November 18). In Philippine red-light district, an uphill struggle to battle trafficking and abuses. *The Washington Post*. https://www.washingtonpost.com/world/asia-pacific/in-philippine-red-light-district-an-uphill-struggle-to-battle-trafficking-and-abuses/2019/11/17/43a6470a-bad3-11e9-b3b4-2bb69e8c4e39_story.html.

Refugee Services of Texas, est. (1978). 501(c)3 nonprofit organization. https://www.rstx.org/.

Restore NYC. (2017). *IMB findings report*.

Sanctuary for Families, est. (1984). *Economic Empowerment Program (EEP)*. 501(c)3 nonprofit organization. https://sanctuaryforfamilies.org/our-approach/client-services/economic-empowerment-services/.

Schönberg, C.-M., & Boublil, A. (1989). *Miss Saigon*. Originally produced and performed at west end.

Soh, C. S. (2008). *The comfort women: Sexual violence and postcolonial memory in Korea and Japan*. Chicago: The University of Chicago Press.

Solutions to End Exploitation, est. (2009). 501(c)3 nonprofit organization. https://seefreedom.org/.

Tabassum, Z., & Cornwell, S. (2012, April 29). *U.S. military faces scrutiny over its prostitution policies*. Thomson Reuters. https://www.reuters.com/article/us-usa-agents-military/u-s-military-faces-scrutiny-over-its-prostitution-policies-idUSBRE83S09620120429.

Tanaka, Y. (2002). *Japan's comfort women: Sexual slavery and prostitution during World War II and the US occupation*. London: Routledge.

The Red Light Areas of Manila, Philippines. *The red light guide*. https://theredlightguide.com/the-red-light-areas-of-manila-philippines/.

Tongsuthi, J. (1994). Comfort women of World War II. *UCLA Women's Law Journal, 4*(2), 413–419. Retrieved from https://escholarship.org/uc/item/80f938hm.

Truong, T.-D. (1990). *Sex, money, and morality: Prostitution and tourism in Southeast Asia*. London: Zed Books.

US Department of Defense. (2019, January 9). *How we can recognize and combat it*. https://www.defense.gov/Explore/News/Article/Article/1727937/human-trafficking-how-we-can-recognize-and-combat-it/.

Vine, D. (2015). *Base nation: How U.S. military bases abroad harm America and the world*. New York: Metropolitan Books.

Woan, S. (2008). White sexual imperialism: A theory of Asian Feminist Jurisprudence, 14 Wash. & Lee J. Civ. Rts. & Soc. Just. 275. Available at: https://scholarlycommons.law.wlu.edu/crsj/vol14/iss2/5.

Yoshiaki, Y. (1998). *Comfort women: Sexual slavery in the Japanese military during World War II*. New York: Columbia University Press.

Chapter 6
Forced Labor in the US Construction Industry

Aaron Halegua and Katherine Chin

6.1 Introduction

Dr. Marty Rohringer was ending a graveyard shift at the lone hospital on Saipan, the exceptionally remote US island, when four Chinese men arrived with a body. The figure they had with them—a middle-aged man, also Chinese, naked but for his underwear—was unresponsive, and had clearly suffered severe trauma. As an orderly lifted him onto a gurney, the four men indicated in broken English that he had fallen from a hotel-room balcony. Rohringer began to evaluate the man under the ER's harsh fluorescent lights. His skin was pallid and turning blue, and it was obvious that he could not be revived. One of the men who'd arrived with the body started to mime chest compressions: Was there really nothing to be done? Rohringer pronounced the man dead just before 8 a.m. on March 22, 2017. Already, the medical staff suspected that the story of his fall was a lie.[1] (Campbell 2018)

The man who died that night was Hu Yuanyou, a construction worker who fell from the scaffolding of the Imperial Pacific casino project in Saipan. Hu was employed by one of the casino's contractors, despite lacking a legal work permit. After his fall, Hu's managers did not call an ambulance, choosing instead to rip off his uniform and drive him to the hospital, where they misled doctors about the cause of his injuries. During the prior year, hospital doctors in Saipan had noticed a worrying number of construction workers with severe injuries. They were also troubled that most workers who arrived at the hospital said very little to the doctors themselves. Instead, they were often accompanied by company representatives who would describe the accident, answer any questions, and sometimes order the patient

---

[1] Courtesy of *Bloomberg Businessweek*. Copyright Bloomberg L.P.

A. Halegua (✉)
Aaron Halegua, PLLC and New York University School of Law, New York City, NY, USA
e-mail: amh862@nyu.edu

K. Chin
Brown University Center for the Study of Slavery and Justice, Providence, RI, USA

© Springer Nature Switzerland AG 2021
M. Chisolm-Straker, K. Chon (eds.), *The Historical Roots of Human Trafficking*,
https://doi.org/10.1007/978-3-030-70675-3_6

be discharged and sent back to China—even when the doctors recommended otherwise.

Disturbed by this pattern, the doctors compiled a spreadsheet that listed 80 cases of serious injuries from the construction site in 12 months and sent it to the federal agency that oversees workplace safety (De La Torre 2016). This prompted a Hawaii-based investigator to fly over 8 hours to Saipan, inspect the worksite, and issue a few fines, but then construction continued as usual. Things only really changed after Hu fell and died, at which point the Federal Bureau of Investigation (FBI) raided the offices of the casino's contractors, found hundreds of confiscated passports, and discovered that hundreds of the construction workers had entered Saipan as "tourists" and lacked work authorization—uncovering what some experts have called "a pretty classic trafficking and forced labor scenario" (Yan 2018).

The forced labor scheme uncovered at the Imperial Pacific site in Saipan is not unique. The construction industry is notorious for poor working conditions and labor exploitation, including cases of forced labor and human trafficking. The International Labour Organization (ILO) reported that 24.9 million people were subjected to forced labor in 2016, and that the construction industry has the second-highest number of workers in forced labor situations worldwide, exceeded only by domestic work (International Labour Organization and Walk Free Foundation 2017). International media and advocacy groups have exposed some of these abuses. For instance, in 2014, the *Guardian* and Amnesty International reported that stadiums for the 2022 FIFA World Cup in Qatar were built by Nepalese men who worked for low wages under deadly conditions and were not allowed to return home without their employers' permission[2] (Doward 2014; Amnesty International 2014). Over 400 Nepalese migrant workers were reported to have died on these construction sites (Doward 2014). Around the same time, investigations by *The New York Times* and Human Rights Watch revealed that thousands of workers constructing New York University's campus in Abu Dhabi had incurred debt to pay huge recruitment fees based on what turned-out to be false promises of high salaries and good conditions and were then threatened with deportation if they complained (Kaminer and O'Driscoll 2014; Human Rights Watch 2015).

But this phenomenon is neither new nor limited to these "remote" places. Forced labor schemes pre-date the founding of the United States and then played a critical role in erecting prestigious universities,[3] constructing the nation's railroads, and building the country's vital infrastructure over the subsequent two centuries. More recently, in 2015, a settlement was reached to compensate 500 Indian workers

---

[2] Only in January 2020, after years of international pressure, did the Qatari government abolish the tenant of the *kafala* ("sponsorship") system requiring migrant workers to obtain their employers' permission in order to leave the country.

[3] Several universities have launched independent inquiries into their legacies of slavery and the role that slave labor played in their founding. Many found that their endowments were owed to patrons who made their wealth through the slave trade, but a few also revealed direct connections to slave labor in the physical construction of the schools, including the University of Virginia and Brown University.

subjected to forced labor by Signal International, a company that was repairing rigs and ships along the Gulf Coast after Hurricane Katrina (Chen 2015). In 2019, a jury convicted the head of US operations for the China-based Rilin construction firm for operating a forced labor scheme in New York City (US Attorney's Office, E.D.N.Y, Department of Justice 2019).

This chapter seeks to explain the prevalence of forced labor in the construction industry and illustrate the phenomenon through a few case studies, including the casino-builders in Saipan. Readers will be introduced to some features of the construction industry that make workers vulnerable to labor exploitation more generally and factors that make workers susceptible to various tools of force and coercion. Methods of control that employers often use include physically restraining workers, exploiting worker indebtedness, withholding wages, and fostering the workers' dependence on the employer. Such mechanisms were crucial in the use of forced labor to construct railroads in the 1800s and the more recent Saipan case mentioned above. The chapter then traces how strategies of coercion in the construction industry have remained surprisingly consistent over time and explores the extent of the problem in the United States. Finally, the chapter authors offer several recommendations (Sect. 6.4) for preventing and stopping forced labor in the construction sector.

6.2   Discussion

The ILO Convention on forced labor, promulgated in 1930 and ratified by almost every nation, defines forced labor as "all work or service which is exacted from any person under the menace of any penalty and for which the said person has not offered himself voluntarily." (International Labour Organization 1930). The critical feature that turns an abusive work situation into "forced labor" is that the work is not performed voluntarily, but compelled through some form of force, fraud, or coercion. Methods are not limited to physical restraints that prevent the worker from leaving, but also include threatening legal, economic, or psychological harm to the worker. This is reflected in the definition of forced labor in the federal Trafficking Victims Prevention Act (TVPA), passed in 2000: "*any scheme* … intended to cause the person to believe that, if that person did not perform such labor or services, that person or another person would suffer serious harm or physical restraint" (18 U.S.C.A. §1589).

In modern forced labor cases, some of the more common coercive tools include fraudulently representing the terms of the job, confiscating workers' identity documents, withholding wages, limiting mobility, threatening deportation, and exploiting workers' indebtedness—which is often incurred to pay exorbitant fees related to obtaining the job. The coercive effect of any particular measure differs based on the context. Therefore, to appreciate how these coercive tools operate in practice, it is important to first understand the underlying conditions and vulnerabilities of workers in that particular sector.

6.2.1 Exploitation and Forced Labor in the Construction Industry

Construction workers have many of the same vulnerabilities to employer exploitation as low-wage workers in other sectors. However, there are also certain features of the construction industry that exacerbate these vulnerabilities. This chapter discusses three such characteristics: (1) the project-based and location-specific nature of the work; (2) the prevalence of complex subcontracting arrangements; and (3) the practice of "payment upon completion."

Construction involves short-term projects that must be performed in a particular location. The short-term nature of the project makes it difficult for workers to develop any form of collective identity or organization that may build worker power, such as a union. Projects may also occur in less-populated areas, where established unions are not present and where government inspectors visit less frequently. As the local workforce is often insufficient to complete big projects, workers are often brought to the project site from other regions. Over half of unskilled construction workers in the United States are immigrants (Siniavskaia 2018). Migration is often expensive, and these costs frequently get passed onto workers through recruitment fees. Upon arrival, workers' dependence on their employer is often cemented by the requirement of living in company housing. Further, migrant workers generally lack familiarity with their surroundings, let alone the legal system or any social networks, and may not speak the local language. These conditions entrench a relationship of dependence in which the employer has great power over its workers.[4]

Complex subcontracting arrangements are prevalent on most construction projects, since they often involve multiple phases requiring different skills and work schedules (Stanford Law Review 1958). Accordingly, a general contractor may need to engage numerous subcontractors for discrete parts of the project, and contractors prefer to keep a flexible labor supply. Particularly in locations where finding workers is difficult, contractors may hire a subcontractor to recruit, hire, and pay the workers, even though the contractor directs their daily work on the site. These tiered, fluctuating labor systems obfuscate important issues such as who ultimately "employs" the worker or who is responsible for workers' safety. Government agencies seeking to enforce such standards must first overcome this obstacle of identifying who is in control.

The construction industry often operates on a "payment upon completion" financing structure; moreover, many contracts penalize contractors who do not

---

[4] This is not to suggest that only migrant workers are subject to abuse. Non-immigrant construction workers in the United States, particularly those who are not union members, also face various forms of exploitation, such as wage theft by their employers or being misclassified as independent contractors. However, based on the research and observations of the authors, many of the worst abuses do seem to involve immigrant workers, which is not surprising in light of their heightened vulnerability. Indeed, this seems to hold true across countries: an ILO report on the global construction industry finds that immigrant workers are more likely to suffer injuries, experience wage theft, be charged fees, and be subjected to forced labor (Buckley et al. 2016).

complete the work on time. Therefore, contractors want to finish projects as quickly as possible and minimize expenses incurred along the way. These incentives discourage investment in workplace safety, training, and equipment, as well as adherence to overtime regulations. The risks inherent to this financing structure also incentivize employers to withhold all or some of workers' wages until the work is complete and they have received payment themselves. Given the subcontracting chains that exist on many projects, it can often take months for payments to filter down from main contractors to the workers at the bottom of the supply chain (Business and Human Rights Resource Centre 2018). Where a contractor only receives partial payment because of unsatisfactory work, it may also try to pass that loss on to the workers.

In these distinct conditions of vulnerability, labor exploitation may develop into forced labor whereby certain "tools of coercion" are employed. Historically and currently, the most commonly-used tools can be generally classified into four categories: (1) physical coercion; (2) debt entrapment; (3) withholding wages; and (4) other measures to increase worker dependence on their employers, such as confiscating identity documents, employer-provided housing, restricting mobility, and threatened abuse of legal processes. The cases below illustrate how these tools operate in practice.

6.2.2 Historical Examples of Forced Labor in Construction

Forced labor played a significant role in the early part of the United States' physical and economic development. Prior to the American Revolution, it is estimated that between one half and two-thirds of all White immigrants to the US colonies were indentured servants, obligated to work off a debt to the employer who paid for their passage across the Atlantic—and risking physical punishment or death if they did not (Galenson 1984). As improving conditions in the English labor market made the cost of indentured White servants more expensive, the importation of African slaves began to grow. The legal institution of chattel slavery, which equated African American bodies with property and labor, existed in the United States from its colonial beginnings until the Thirteenth Amendment was passed in 1865[5] (Snyder 2013). Historians have found that Black slaves even laid the foundations of the White House and the Capitol building (Hannah-Jones 2019).

After slavery was formally abolished, the practice of forced labor continued and was intertwined with major construction and infrastructure projects, such as the

---

[5] While chattel slavery shares certain similarities with other forms of forced labor, there are also important elements that distinguish that institution. *See* Beutin, *Black Suffering for/from Anti-Trafficking Advocacy* (Beutin 2017). While the example of enslaving African Americans is most familiar, historians have also documented that Native Americans were enslaved by Spanish colonists as well as by the English and US colonists and settlers. *See* Reséndez, *The Other Slavery: The Uncovered Story of Indian Enslavement in America* (Reséndez 2016).

Transcontinental Railway and railroad infrastructure in the US South. In the former case, the railroad companies seeking to connect the coasts needed thousands of laborers for their project, but labor shortages led to only 800 applications from free laborers within the United States. The companies thus turned to Chinese merchant associations, who recruited "coolie" indentured laborers from China (Chap. 10).[6] The terms of their labor were negotiated by the merchant associations, who effectively placed the laborers in an indefinite system of debt bondage by charging high interest on their passage loans and selling their labor for incredibly low wages (Chang 2015). The Chinese workers' wages were paid directly to the associations, consolidating their continued control over the workers. These laborers—already in a foreign country with few social connections—were confined to living and working in remote sites, apart from non-Chinese workers, thus furthering their isolation. The state facilitated this system of bonded migrant labor; local police were enlisted to catch and punish workers who tried to run away.

The less-populated Southern states adopted similar strategies to fill the large labor needs for constructing railways there. In a period of just 5 months in 1907, one Florida town was reported to have placed hundreds of men in conditions of peonage (Carper 1976). The most notorious case of labor abuse was that of the Florida East Coast Railway (FEC). FEC agents recruited recent immigrants to New York and foreign laborers who came through the *padrone* system.[7] The company employed a debt entrapment scheme: it paid for the workers' passage to Florida, but misled them as to the cost involved and then required them to keep working until that debt was repaid. Upon arrival, laborers were placed under armed guard and faced physical punishment, including whipping, if they were unable to accomplish their tasks (Knetsch 1998). The company also withheld wages, promising workers a daily wage of $4 but paying a mere $1.25 a day (Carper 1976). Workers were kept in dismal living conditions and forced to purchase items such as blankets, shoes, and overalls for inflated prices that amounted to more than a day's wages, further ensuring that they would never repay their debt. If they ran away, workers were arrested, at which point they would face the impossible choice of returning to the FEC workforce or serving time in prison—which also leased-out inmates as laborers (Chap. 9) (Carper 1976).

---

[6] The term "coolie" is widely thought to have originated from the Tamil word for wages, or the Chinese word for "bitter labor." By the mid-nineteenth century in the United States, "coolie" was used to refer to indentured laborers imported from China and India, and became synonymous with Asian servitude (Chang 2015).

[7] The word "padrone" means "boss" or "manager" in Italian. The *padrone* system was a set of migration networks organized by labor contractors in the United States during the late 1800s and early 1900s. The contractors often recruited immigrants of the same national origin, finding them jobs, advancing their cost of migration for a cut of their wages, and providing other services for fees deducted from the immigrants' wages. These migration networks were typically concentrated in Italy, Greece, Turkey, Hungary, and Bulgaria (Sadowski-Smith 2008).

These early cases highlight how the features of the construction industry create fertile soil for exploitation and coercion. In each case, desperate for large numbers of cheap workers, companies engaged third-parties to recruit these workers from overseas or out-of-state. The cost of their passage became a debt that compelled workers to continue working in order to repay or face dire consequences. Workers were physically isolated and prohibited from leaving, often with the coercive power of the state helping to enforce this confinement.

6.2.3   Modern Manifestations of Forced Labor: The Imperial Pacific Casino in Saipan

Elements of the historical forced labor schemes involving chattel slavery or railroad workers can still be found in pockets of the US construction industry today. The persistent demand for site-specific, temporary, low-wage labor results in the importation of workers from overseas or other parts of the country. These migrant workers often accumulate large debts based on false promises and find themselves held captive to an employer that underpays and abuses them in a foreign land. For this largely migrant workforce, immigration rules have effectively replaced the earlier role of the police as coercive state power wielded by employers to prevent workers from escaping these conditions. Work visas tie these migrants' right to residency to one specific employer, meaning workers must endure their labor conditions or face deportation. Undocumented workers who lack visas may be deported at any time and are thus reluctant to disobey an employer who might notify immigration authorities.

The case of the Imperial Pacific casino project on the island of Saipan illustrates such a forced labor scheme. In 2014, Imperial Pacific obtained the exclusive license to operate a casino in Saipan. Soon thereafter, it hired multiple Chinese companies to do the construction. The Metallurgical Corporation of China (MCC), a state-owned Chinese firm, was hired as the general contractor, responsible for the building's foundation, steel frame, and electrical system. Numerous other companies, including Beilida, Gold Mantis, Grandland, Haitian, Jiangsu Provincial, Sino Great Wall, and CMC Macao, were contracted to handle other parts of the project. Each contractor hired its own workers, almost all of whom were brought into Saipan from China. Many entered Saipan on CNMI-Only Transitional Worker ("CW-1") permits—a guest worker visa specific to the Commonwealth of the Northern Mariana Islands (CNMI) that allows the employee to work for a particular employer for up to 1 year. When the visa quota was reached, however, the contractors hired subcontractors or recruiters that brought in several hundreds of workers to Saipan as "tourists."[8] These workers were generally promised good jobs in the United States

---

[8] A special parole program for the CNMI allowed Chinese nationals to enter Saipan without a visa for up to 45 days for the purpose of tourism. Due to abuses of this program, this period has since been shortened to 14 days (Encinares 2019).

on a multi-year project with high wages, overtime pay, and possibly a green card after a few years. Job ads were posted online and circulated through social media, and recruiters visited villages and homes. To pay the steep recruitment fees, most workers borrowed money, often from loan sharks at high interest rates, with their house or farm posted as collateral. It was only after arriving in Saipan and being coached on what to tell the customs agent, or even after starting work, that many realized they had been tricked and lacked the proper work authorization.

The conditions in Saipan were oppressive. The contractors required employees to work 13-hours per day, paid them less than minimum wage (or sometimes nothing at all), refused requests for rest days, and levied excessive fines for minor transgressions. Saipan's infrastructure was not prepared for an influx of thousands of workers, and the men were crammed into unsanitary dorms that sometimes lacked running water and fed meals of insect-infested food. Safety precautions were abysmal, as demonstrated by the case of Mr. Hu, and injuries frequent. Furthermore, the contractors refused to allow the undocumented workers medical treatment even after workers suffered burned legs, scalded hands, or crushed fingers; contractors told such workers that going to the hospital might get them deported.

The contractors coerced workers through various means. During daily meetings, managers would threaten workers that if they did not work hard, or if they disobeyed orders, they would be fired and deported back to China. Sometimes managers would ridicule workers about the large debts they incurred to get their jobs. The contractors also made the workers believe that complaining was futile. They said that no authorities would listen to the workers because they were working illegally. The contractors hid the workers from the authorities by telling them to stay in the dormitories when the worksite was being inspected. Most contractors also confiscated the workers' passports and threatened to fire any worker that refused. As one trafficking expert described the situation, "You have people with these debts. They're in the middle of the ocean. The isolation of the location is ripe for exploitation"[9] (Yan 2018).

The wages promised by the contractors often fell below the federal minimum wage and overtime pay requirements. Nonetheless, many contractors failed to pay even that amount: some workers labored for 3 or 4 months without any pay at all. The contractors often deflected complaints by stating that they too had not yet been paid by the developer, but everybody would be paid in full. The common practice of the companies was to be in arrears, or owing workers 2 to 4 weeks of wages at any given point. This meant that if a worker quit, they would effectively be forfeiting that money. When wages were dispersed, they were often sent to the workers' accounts in China, meaning the workers were generally cashless and thus dependent on their employers while in Saipan.

Government authorities did eventually crack down on the scheme. The FBI raided the offices of some of Imperial Pacific's contractors—although only after Hu's death—and found the confiscated passports and lists of "*heigong*" (a Chinese

---

[9] Copyrighted 2018. Associated Press. 2182900:1220PF. Used with permission.

term for individuals working illegally). Several project managers for the contractors were arrested and eventually pleaded guilty to illegally employing unauthorized aliens and served prison sentences. The federal Occupational Safety and Health Administration (OSHA) charged the Chinese firms with dozens of "serious viola-tions" of the workplace safety code and issued over $200,000 in fines. Imperial Pacific received no fines for the safety violations nor any criminal punishment.

The workers also received compensation through settlements reached between the US Department of Labor (USDOL) and four of the Chinese construction firms—totaling $13.9 million for over 2,400 employees. Quite significantly, that sum included not only compensation for owed wages, but also reimbursement for the recruitment fees paid by workers in China, which were often $6,000 or more. It is quite rare for workers to recover these fees because of the complex chain of brokers between the worker and the ultimate employer, and since it is often difficult to locate the recruiter after the worker returns home years later.

It is worth noting that neither the casino nor the contractors were criminally charged for trafficking or forced labor under the TVPA. The precise reason for this is unknown; however, one factor may be the difficulty in proving the elements of such crimes, such as coercion, whereas proving the employment of a worker lacking proper authorization is quite straightforward. A private lawsuit on behalf of some of the Chinese workers injured on the site—many of them received no medical atten-tion, let alone compensation—was amended in 2019 to add a forced labor claim under the TVPA. In addition to suing the contractors for engaging in the forced labor scheme, the litigation alleges that Imperial Pacific either participated in the scheme or, at a minimum, "knowingly benefitted" from it and therefore should also be liable. The case was still pending in the US federal court in Saipan at the time of writing.[10]

6.3   Conclusion

Worker exploitation and forced labor have been interwoven into the United States' construction industry since its inception and continues today. While these problems are not unique to the construction sector, certain characteristics of the industry, as demonstrated by the case studies, make it particularly ripe for such abuses; most notably: (1) the project-based and location-specific nature of the work, demanding large quantities of short-term, cheap labor be brought from other locations; (2) the reliance on subcontracting and the diffusion of accountability across subcontracting chains; and (3) the financing structure of the construction industry and the prevalent practice of paying subcontractors only upon completion of the work.

These conditions create a fertile environment for forced labor, and the mecha-nisms used by employers to effectuate such schemes have been remarkably consis-tent. First, physical restrictions on leaving the job were enforced by the police in the

---

[10] Chapter author Aaron Halegua is an attorney representing the workers in that litigation.

early railroad cases, but are more subtly effectuated today through the confiscation of passports, the threat of deportation, or the guarded supervision of worker residences. Second, construction firms continue exploiting worker indebtedness to maintain a compliant labor force: Chinese indentured workers' payments to merchant associations as passage loans look very similar to the high recruitment fees that workers paid for passage to Saipan to work on the casino project. Third, low pay and wage arrears remain a popular tool for making sure that workers stay indebted to their employers and thus stuck in their oppressive employment. The FEC only paid workers a quarter of their promised salary; in Saipan, contractors withheld several weeks of salary, paid below minimum wage, and sometimes paid no wages at all.

It is important to note how the state's coercive mechanisms are exploited to further coerce vulnerable workers. In earlier cases, the role was blatant and clear: police arrested workers who ran away. In modern times, immigration laws and the structure of guest worker programs have a comparable impact. Generally, a guest worker, whether under the H-2B or CW-1 program, may only work for the employer that sponsored them. Thus, whether undocumented or on a legal work visa, an indebted worker abused by their employer may only leave their employment at the risk of being deported.[11] This leaves workers essentially trapped and afraid to complain—a fact that employers readily exploit.

But how prevalent is this problem in the United States? While precise numbers are obviously difficult to obtain, Polaris has found that construction is one of the top 15 industries that contribute to human trafficking in the United States, identifying 144 human trafficking cases and 405 labor exploitation cases from 2007 to 2016 in that sector (Polaris 2017). Most of the workers involved were on H-2B visas or undocumented. However, this is likely only the tip of the iceberg. Polaris only classified 55% of the cases about which it was contacted because it lacked sufficient information regarding the others (Polaris 2017). Presumably, many exploited workers never reach out for help at all due to limited knowledge about their legal rights, skepticism that complaining will result in any positive outcome, and fear of retaliation or deportation (Halegua 2016).

Part of the problem is insufficient enforcement of the laws prohibiting labor exploitation or forced labor. The above-referenced settlement with Signal or the back-paid wages in the Saipan case may give the impression that traffickers are often held accountable and the workers receive some modicum of justice. However, of the cases brought to the government or private lawyers, only the most "winnable" may get prosecuted. It is not necessarily the most egregious cases or reprehensible violations that result in legal action, but those where the perpetrator can be located, the aggrieved are not too intimidated to testify, and the evidence is strong. Furthermore, the more "successful" trafficking schemes may never be detected by law enforcement. Most forced labor victims in the United States never receive any

---

[11] The CW-1 program does make some provision for a worker to switch employers, but only if the new employer files a petition to hire that individual as a guest worker within 30 days of their prior employment ending. *See* 8 CFR § 214.2(w)(7).

remedy, and construction is likely no exception. While Polaris alone identified 10,949 human trafficking cases in 2018, the Department of Justice only initiated 230 human trafficking prosecutions that year (Polaris 2018; The United States Department of Justice 2019). As for private lawsuits, only 299 cases were brought from 2003 to 2018 (The Human Trafficking Legal Center 2018). This is insufficient either to deter traffickers or to encourage abused workers to come forward.

So what else can be done to fight forced labor? This chapter primarily discussed instances of forced labor where the legal violations and the exercise of coercion were fairly clear. However, the workers in these case studies represent a narrow sliver of a much larger group of individuals working precarious jobs for low pay across industries, and who face differing degrees and forms of exploitation. Reducing these opportunities for worker abuse requires thinking not only about more robust government enforcement, but also considering more broadly how immigration law, employment regulations, and collective bargaining rights interact to shape labor markets and the power dynamics between employers and employees. In this regard, for instance, strategies to organize workers and increase unionization are crucially important to reducing their vulnerability. In the case of migrant workers, removing employers' ability to exercise total control over whether a worker can remain in the country (Chap. 3) would also decrease those firms' ability to coerce employees. These broader strategies to reduce the exploitation of all workers form an important piece of any effort to fight forced labor.

6.4 Recommendations

The recommendations offered here are more specifically focused on combatting forced labor in the construction industry, although they may still be applicable to other sectors.

1. *Hold property owners and developers at the "top of the chain" accountable for forced labor on their construction site by enforcing the "knowingly benefits" provision of the TVPA.*

It has long been recognized that combatting the effects of subcontracting requires holding the "top of the chain" accountable for abuses. These larger firms are often the only ones with the means to provide workers a remedy and the economic leverage to shape industry practices. In the construction context, this means holding the developer and general contractor responsible for the practices of any subcontractors or recruiters. In the United States, there are already mechanisms in the construction industry designed for this purpose, such as mechanics liens available under state law. These liens allow unpaid workers to claim an interest in any property that they helped to construct (NOLO 1958). Another accountability mechanism is OSHA's recognition of liability for parties exerting control over a property (as opposed to just control over the workers). So how can developers or construction firms be held accountable for forced labor?

There already exist legal instruments, though imperfect, for establishing the accountability of firms higher up the chain. For instance, under the TVPA, any enterprise that "knowingly benefits" from a forced labor venture may be liable for damages to the trafficked workers or face criminal prosecution. However, most litigation focuses on the actors that directly carry out the forced labor scheme. More cases, as in the case in Saipan discussed above, should be brought against those who knowingly benefit from the scheme.

2. *Ban entities that engage in or knowingly benefit from forced labor from bidding on future government projects.*

Regulations concerning federal contractors or grant recipients increasingly require that these entities implement compliance plans and procedures to monitor, detect, and terminate any employee, subcontractor, or subgrantee that engages in forced labor or human trafficking (E.O. 13627 § 2(a); H.R. 4310 § 1703). Further, if investigations reveal substantiated engagement in trafficking-related activities, that information will be recorded in the Federal Awardee Performance and Integrity Information System, which contracting officers must review prior to issuing any awards over $150,000 (H.R. 4310 § 1704; 2 C.F.R. § 200.205). Local governments and private developers should follow this approach of punishing firms found to benefit from forced labor and ban them from bidding on future projects.

3. *Deny guest worker visas to companies that engage in or knowingly benefit from forced labor.*

Developers or general contractors who engage companies found to use forced labor should also be prohibited from recruiting guest workers in the future. For instance, after the Saipan incident, the CW-1 program was modified to prohibit any business that "knowingly benefited" from trafficking from participating in that program (115 H.R. 5956). However, the government must *actually* exercise this authority and act against such companies in order for it to have the desired deterrent effect.

4. *Eliminate recruitment fees by making developers and employers liable for reimbursing any fees paid by workers on their site.*

The goal should be to eliminate the payment of recruitment fees by workers prior to migration, as they put already-vulnerable workers into deeper debt and thus make them more susceptible to coercion. Indeed, many advocates have called for "zero-fee" or "employer pays" systems, and this is the formal rule in some US guest worker programs.[12] However, enforcement is difficult. At a minimum, all actors along the migration chain, including the ultimate employer, should be liable if a worker is found to have paid an illegal fee. For instance, in the Saipan case, although many of the recruitment fees were paid in China, the USDOL settlement required

---

[12]The regulations for the H-2A and H-2B programs both prohibit collecting recruitment or job placement fees from workers, and require employers to prohibit any foreign labor contractors or agents recruiting on their behalf from collecting any fees. *See* 20 C.F.R. § 655.135(j), (k) (relevant H-2A provisions); 20 C.F.R. § 655.20(o), (p) (relevant H-2B provisions).

the contractors in Saipan to repay this money. This should incentivize employers to take steps necessary to stop the practice of charging fees, including bearing more expenses themselves, vetting the recruiters that they engage, and training workers while they are still in their home country (United Nations Global Compact).

5. *Require developers to establish independent, private monitoring and complaint mechanisms to fill the gaps left by inadequate government enforcement.*

Even if developers or general contractors could be held liable for forced labor in their supply chains, government enforcement alone will always be insufficient to detect the vast majority of cases. This point is starkly made by examining OSHA's enforcement of workplace safety in the United States: at current rates, it would take over 165 years for OSHA to inspect each of the country's eight million workplaces just once (Berkowitz). This is even more problematic in construction where the "worksite" may only exist for a number of months.

Developers must therefore establish their own mechanisms to prevent and detect forced labor practices. These schemes should address recruitment, worker training, worker safety, and wages and hours, and should be monitored by an independent third-party. If no union is in place, a complaint mechanism should also be established and workers offered a means of organizing. A crucial element is the "independent" aspect—meaning that even if the developer or employer is funding the mechanism, there must be ways to ensure the monitor is not influenced by that party's demands. Some progressive construction firms established the "Building Responsibly" coalition, adopting principles along these lines (Building Responsibly 2018). Monitoring schemes have also been tried at the Imperial Pacific site in Saipan, as part of a USDOL settlement (United States Department of Labor 2019). These types of coalitions are a necessary complement to more traditional, top-down government enforcement.

References

Amnesty International. (2014). *No extra time: How Qatar is still failing on workers' rights ahead of the World Cup.*

Berkowitz, D. *Enforcement declines to levels below Obama and Bush administrations.* National Employment Law Project. https://www.nelp.org/publication/workplace-safety-health-enforcement-falls-lowest-levels-decades/.

Beutin, L. P. (2017). Black suffering for/from anti-trafficking. *Anti-Trafficking Review 9.*

Buckley, M., et al. (2016). *Migrant work and employment in the construction sector.* International Labour Office. https://www.ilo.org/wcmsp5/groups/public/%2D%2D-ed_protect/%2D%2D-protrav/%2D%2D-migrant/documents/publication/wcms_538487.pdf.

Building Responsibly. (2018). Worker welfare principles. https://www.building-responsibly.org/worker-welfare-principles.

Business and Human Rights Resource Centre. (2018). *A human rights primer for business: Understanding risks to construction workers in the Middle East.*

Campbell, M. (2018). A Chinese casino has conquered a piece of America. *Bloomberg Businessweek.* https://www.bloomberg.com/news/features/2018-02-15/a-chinese-company-has-conquered-a-piece-of-america.

Carper, N. G. (1976). Slavery Revisited: Peonage in the South. *Phylon*.

Chang, K. (2015). Coolie. In C. J. Schlund-Vials, L. T. Vo, & K. S. Wong (Eds.), *Keywords for Asian American studies*. New York: NYU Press.

Chen, M. (2015). These guestworkers just won $20 million back from the company that trafficked them. *The Nation*. https://www.thenation.com/article/archive/these-guestworkers-just-won-20-million-back-from-the-company-that-trafficked-them/.

De La Torre, F. (2016). Federal warrant sought to inspect casino site. *Saipan Tribune*. https://www.saipantribune.com/index.php/federal-warrant-sought-inspect-casino-site/.

Doward, J. (2014). Qatar World Cup: 400 Nepalese die on nation's building sites since bid won. *The Guardian*. https://www.theguardian.com/football/2014/feb/16/qatar-world-cup-400-deaths-nepalese.

Encinares E. (2019). 14 days for Chinese tourists. *Saipan Tribune*. https://www.saipantribune.com/index.php/14-days-for-chinese-tourists/.

Galenson, D. (1984). The rise and fall of indentured servitude in the Americas: An economic analysis. *The Journal of Economic History, 44*, 1–26.

Halegua, A. (2016). Legal representation for New York's Chinese immigrant workers. In S. Estreicher & J. Radice (Eds.), *Beyond elite law: Access to civil justice in America*. Cambridge/New York: Cambridge University Press. https://papers.ssrn.com/sol3/papers.cfm?abstract_id=2551393&download=yes.

Hannah-Jones, N. (2019). Our Democracy's founding ideals were false when they were written. Black Americans have fought to make them true. *The New York Times*. https://www.nytimes.com/interactive/2019/08/14/magazine/black-history-american-democracy.html.

Human Rights Watch. (2015). *Migrant workers' rights on Saadiyat Island in the United Arab Emirates: 2015 progress report*. https://www.hrw.org/report/2015/02/10/migrant-workers-rights-saadiyat-island-united-arab-emirates/2015-progress-report.

International Labour Organization. (1930). *Forced Labour Convention* (No. 29), Article 2. https://www.ilo.org/dyn/normlex/en/f?p=NORMLEXPUB:12100:0::NO::P12100_ILO_CODE:C029.

International Labour Organization and Walk Free Foundation. (2017). *Global estimates of modern slavery: Forced labour and forced marriage*. https://www.ilo.org/wcmsp5/groups/public/@dgreports/@dcomm/documents/publication/wcms_575479.pdf.

Kaminer, A., & O'Driscoll, S. (2014). Workers at N.Y.U.'s Abu Dhabi Site Faced Harsh Conditions. *The New York Times*. https://www.nytimes.com/2014/05/19/nyregion/workers-at-nyus-abu-dhabi-site-face-harsh-conditions.html?auth=login-google.

Knetsch, J. (1998). *The Peonage Controversy and the Florida East Coast Railway*. Tequesta.

NOLO. (1958). *State-by-State Mechanics' Lien Laws*. https://www.nolo.com/legal-encyclopedia/state-by-state-mechanics-lien-laws; Mechanics' liens and surety bonds in the building trades. *The Yale Law Journal, 68*, 138–171.

Polaris. (2017). *The typology of modern slavery: Defining sex and labor trafficking in the United States*. https://polarisproject.org/wp-content/uploads/2019/09/Polaris-Typology-of-Modern-Slavery-1.pdf.

Polaris. (2018). *2018 U.S. National Human Trafficking Hotline Statistics*. https://polarisproject.org/2018-us-national-human-trafficking-hotline-statistics/.

Reséndez, A. (2016). The other slavery: The uncovered story of Indian enslavement in America. Mariner Books.

Sadowski-Smith, C. (2008). Unskilled labor migration and the illegality spiral: Chinese, European, and Mexican indocumentados in the United States, 1882-2007. *American Quarterly, 60*, 779–804.

Siniavskaia, N. (2018). Immigrant workers in the construction labor force. *NAHB Economics*.

Snyder, C. (2013). The long history of American slavery. *OAH Magazine History, 27*, 23–27.

Stanford Law Review. (1958). Special labor problems in the construction industry. *Stanford Law Review, 10*, 525–552.

The Human Trafficking Legal Center. (2018). *Federal human trafficking civil litigation: 15 years of the private right of action*. https://www.htlegalcenter.org/wp-content/uploads/Federal-Human-Trafficking-Civil-Litigation-1.pdf.

The United States Department of Justice. (2019). *Department of Justice Recognizes Human Trafficking Prevention Month and Announces Update on Efforts to Combat this Violent Crime*. https://www.justice.gov/opa/pr/department-justice-recognizes-human-trafficking-prevention-month-and-announces-update-efforts.

U.S. Attorney's Office, E.D.N.Y, Department of Justice. (2019). *Former Chinese Diplomat and Head of U.S. Operations for Chinese Construction Business Sentenced to 190 months' imprisonment for engaging in forced labor and related charges*. https://www.justice.gov/usao-edny/pr/former-chinese-diplomat-and-head-us-operations-chinese-construction-business-sentenced.

United Nations Global Compact. *Eliminating recruitment fees charged to migrant workers*. https://www.unglobalcompact.org/docs/issues_doc/labour/tools_guidance_materials/labour-recruitment-fees.pdf.

United States Department of Labor. (2019). *U.S. Department of Labor Secures $3.3 million judgment against Saipan casino developer for systemic wage violations by contractors*. https://www.dol.gov/newsroom/releases/whd/whd20190425-1.

Yan, S. (2018). *Chinese workers tricked into illegal work on Saipan*. Associated Press. https://apnews.com/4ceaac6873414bdf80d40e40b68ba6f7.

Chapter 7
Addressing Modern Slavery in Global Supply Chains: The Role of Business

Jean Baderschneider and Alison Kiehl Friedman

7.1 Introduction

The United States' relationship with slavery is older than the country's founding and inextricably tied to business (Chap. 2). This was the case in the 1600s when African slaves were brought to US shores. African slaves along with Indigenous slaves built much of the US infrastructure, including roads, buildings, churches, and even the original wall for which Wall Street is named in New York City (Pasley 2019). US school children's history books teach that slavery likely would not have taken such a hold in the United States had it not been for the cotton gin, but there is scarcely a business school class today that addresses the ongoing confluence of supply chains and modern slavery,[1] let alone the modern tools that can be used to combat it. Following the invention of the cotton gin in the 1790s, slave labor was used to hugely expand production of cotton, and the US became the global source for raw cotton, producing half the world's raw cotton crop by 1831 (Desmond 2019). The South produced the cotton, the North operated textile mills, and the trading merchants in US and European hubs created the framework for the global cotton

---

[1] "Modern slavery" is considered an umbrella term that encompasses human trafficking (labor and sex trafficking), forced labor, debt bondage, and commercial sexual exploitation. This is *not* a legal term, but a colloquial umbrella term that focuses attention on commonalities across these legal concepts. It involves exploitation by deprivation of a person's liberty through force, threats, violence, coercion, fraud, deception, and/or abuse of power. In this chapter, the term "modern slavery" will be used to connote deprivation of freedom, regardless of the precisely applicable legal terminology.

J. Baderschneider (✉)
The Global Fund to End Modern Slavery, Roslyn, VA, USA

A. K. Friedman
International Corporate Accountability Roundtable, Washington, DC, USA

© Springer Nature Switzerland AG 2021
M. Chisolm-Straker, K. Chon (eds.), *The Historical Roots of Human Trafficking*,
https://doi.org/10.1007/978-3-030-70675-3_7

commodity market (Baradaran 2019). This was the beginning of global supply chains built on the demand for and supply of slave labor.

Today, slaves are not picking cotton on US farms in the South, but there is large-scale systemic forced labor picking cotton around the world that will make its way into department stores across the US (Cotton Crimes 2016). Today, the "point of no return" in Senegal stands as a museum to a barbarism hundreds of years old, and yet nearby, there are children forced to pick the cocoa beans for chocolate bars (Chocolate Industry Tackles Child Slavery 2015) or mine the coltan necessary for cell phone batteries (Gibson 2014; Skinner 2012). The debt bondage associated with the construction of US railroads is gone, but throughout the East Asian Pacific region, men are trapped on boats forced to fish to meet US demand (Skinner 2012). US business still runs on the basic principles that cheap labor increases profits, and US business can still be inextricably linked to slavery in its modern form.

Slavery—antebellum and modern—was and is still driven by *demand for cheap labor* in supply chains, where a constant search for progressively lower costs and new sources of revenue has all too often led to forced labor, debt bondage, unethical labor brokering, and other forms of labor exploitation. Demand for slave labor to meet exploding cotton production in the early 1800s in the US South is mirrored today in the use of forced labor in apparel production across South East Asia and parts of Africa. Whereas supply chains were once limited by geography, technology, and communication, progress in globalization has led to deep and opaque supply chains and further complicated transparency and accountability. It is not uncommon to find labor exploitation buried more than six tiers deep into a supply chain, with US apparel brands built on raw material and production across numerous countries.

With increasing depth and opacity of current supply chains, a culture of permissible ignorance has developed around what corporations are expected to know about their supply chains. When there are health and safety concerns that threaten a brand, companies act to protect brand value. When there are effective enforcement mechanisms that threaten profitability (such as often exist related to health and safety), companies act to maximize profits by complying with regulations. All too often, however, labor abuses, including modern slavery, are buried deep within the supply chain and willfully ignored.

A globalized marketplace not only means that US consumers can order a product from China, Honduras, or South Africa from their home computer but it also means that businesses can build out deeper and more complex supply chains than ever before. In this way, businesses optimize where labor and raw materials best meet their cost and quality standards. Indeed, demand for fast and cheap fashion has led to innovation not dissimilar from the early quotas and mechanization in the cotton fields.

Through arbitrage, companies have been able to bring cheap materials and goods to cheap labor for production long before those products or workers touch operations owned or controlled by the brand-named companies that will ultimately sell the final product. This web of suppliers and subcontractors *is* more complex than supply chains of years past. However, business operations ultimately remain accountable to their consumers and shareholders and must comply with governmental regulations, to the degree they are enforced. This accountability requires following money and value flow along the entire value chain to ensure supply chains are responsible for eliminating the risk of modern slavery. While it is challenging to interrogate deep and opaque supply chains, *it is doable.*

This chapter will explore the ways modern supply chain management systems can be adapted to address modern slavery within a company's supply chain. It will provide concrete ideas for action that build on public and private support for meaningful leadership on this issue. Indeed, the last 20 years (2000–2020) of anti-trafficking activism has witnessed a huge rise in awareness, with bipartisan political leaders, religious leaders, business executives, workers, and survivors working to raise awareness and confront this crime's broader impact. However, there is not yet systemic and sustainable elimination of modern slavery. This chapter outlines actionable steps for businesses to achieve that end.

7.2   Discussion

To put these steps in context, it is important to understand the scale and scope of modern slavery. According to the International Labor Organization (ILO) and Walk Free, today 25 million people are subject to modern slavery (see Fig. 7.1). As it is a hidden crime, it is likely an underestimation.

Sectoral distribution of victims of forced labor exploitation in private sector 2016 (Alliance 8.7)
In percentages of cases where industry was reported (representing 65% of total cases of forced labor exploitation)

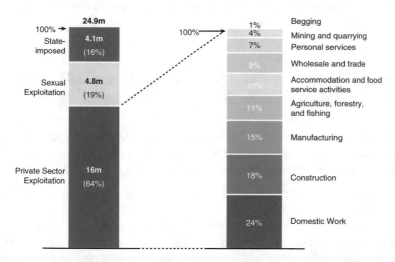

Fig. 7.1 Sectoral distribution of forced labor. (Source: Figure created by Global Fund to End Modern Slavery (GFEMS) with data from The International Labor Organization (ILO) and Walk Free Foundation in partnership with The International Organization for Migration (IOM)–*Global Estimation of Modern Slavery: Forced Labour and Forced Marriage,* ILO Office, Geneva, (2017, pp. 29 and 32). This is an adaptation of an original work by the ILO, Walk Free Foundation, and the IOM. Responsibility for the views and opinions expressed in this adaptation rests solely with the authors of the adaptation and is not endorsed by the ILO, Walk Free Foundation or IOM)

Modern slavery is a crime of economic opportunity with a massive footprint. It is present in every country, driven by supply of vulnerable populations and demand for cheap goods and services; exploitation is enabled by ineffective law enforcement, trafficker impunity, corruption, and systemic oppressions (Chap. 11). It exists in many industries (see Fig. 7.1) and is found in local product markets (e.g., brick kilns) and complex global supply chains. There are 148 global goods in 76 countries made by forced or child labor (US Department of Labor 2018).

The total spending by governments and nongovernmental organizations (NGOs) to fight human trafficking is about $400 million/year compared to more than $150 billion of illicit profits from the modern slave trade (ILO 2014). This imbalance makes sustainably ending trafficking extraordinarily challenging. With the buying power of businesses and socially responsible investors in the trillions, businesses and investors could dramatically shift the economic balance of power in this fight by *reducing the demand* for modern slavery through responsible business practices. Engaging the $70 trillion of private sector spending could create an inflection point long needed to end modern slavery by making it economically unprofitable.

While efforts by companies to address modern slavery are now discussed more frequently at company headquarters—in part due to requirements as laid out in the California Transparency in Supply Chains Law and U.K. Modern Slavery Act— these efforts have all too often failed to be incorporated into the business practices driving the demand for modern slavery. The presence of forced labor in supply chains is treated by businesses as regrettable but almost impossible to detect and assess. In reality, there are a number of concrete steps and standard processes currently used by some companies to make strategic business decisions that can be used to decrease modern slavery.

7.2.1   Businesses Face Significant Challenges in Addressing the Risk of Modern Slavery in Their Supply Chains

It is important to acknowledge that modern slavery has persisted in global supply chains even in the face of opposition because there are real and systemic challenges that thwart progress. Below are examples of these challenges:

1. *Complex and opaque supply chains make supplier engagement difficult in deep tiers.*
   Expanded globalization has enabled companies to source raw materials, which are often connected to forced labor (e.g., cocoa, cotton, and pig iron) from around the world. Many of the materials are from commodity markets, where raw materials are sold in bulk, at a floating price without visibility, into a source country, and then used for production. Often manufacturing and customer service operations are in different locations. The more distant from the end product, the more complicated tracing and engagement becomes.

2. *Corruption and criminal activity is associated with forced labor,* generating billions of dollars in illegal profits. Forced labor is a criminal enterprise. Often, the reputational risks with forced labor pass up the supply chain, without the financial savings. That is to say, companies may be paying fair market rates, but workers never see that reflected in their wages. The rates are diverted by labor recruiters (or other agents exploiting workers) to maximize their own personal profits, so companies see none of the savings. However, if modern slavery is found within a corporation's supply chain, the brand may well be negatively associated with abuse.

3. *Offshoring to progressively lower cost locations is difficult to reverse.*
   Decisions to site operations in remote locations to gain efficiencies are both capital- and time-intensive and are based on a commitment to continue to operate there for the foreseeable future to recoup the initial investment. This makes reversal costly.

4. *There are few proven practices.*
   Unions, rigorous independent monitoring, worker voice tools, and remedy provisions help to preclude and identify systemic worker abuse. Still, comparative data around particular promising practices beyond these do not exist at scale.

5. *Solutions are often philanthropy-based, not market-based.*
   Current philanthropic spending is dwarfed by corporate purchasing power. In addition to mobilizing trillions of dollars of buying power to clean up supply chains, proactive business engagement is needed to create market-based solutions to sustainably end modern slavery.

6. *There are also potential shareholder issues related to cost/benefit of acting against forced labor practices.*
   Much of a company's value is currently derived from short-term profit numbers that can incentivize unethical business practices. Businesses need to be able to demonstrate the medium and long-term impact on profits of clean supply chains and be rewarded for choosing a longer, more responsible time horizon.

7.2.2   What Can Business Do?

Eliminating Business Demand for Modern Slavery: 4 Key Areas of Engagement

As corporations work to maximize returns for shareholders, there are a number of business processes that can also be used to: (1) assess and understand the risk of modern slavery in supply chains; (2) develop mitigations when the risk of modern slavery is high (by leveraging Strategic Procurement); (3) demonstrate maximum returns to shareholders while protecting workers (using Total Systems Cost Analysis); and (4) build organizational cultures that responsibly address modern slavery when it occurs (by leveraging CEO Leadership and stewardship by operations and procurement executives).

Area 1(a)—Assessing the Risk of Modern Slavery in Supply Chains: Risk Management Every business has a process for assessing risk and ascribing a value to it in their decision-making processes. Businesses face many kinds of risk in pursuit of their goals to keep revenues up (money coming in) and operating costs down. These risks can cause serious loss of profits or even shut down the operations. Many companies have extensive risk management departments that limit a company's exposure to risk, evaluate the potential impact of risks, and create mechanisms to mitigate risk. Risk assessment processes identify threats and aim to determine when risks are highest, and rank risks in order of importance. This provides a pathway to risk mitigation by focusing on the risks with the greatest impact.

The main types of risk include:

A. Compliance Risk: companies evaluate compliance with laws and regulations based on where they produce, where they sell (their markets), and what they produce (e.g., organic foods require significant regulation). Compliance can change as companies move to new markets or locations. Compliance becomes more difficult in deep supply chains where there is a large geographic reach and there are multiple production steps.

B. Financial Risk: Virtually, all risk has a financial impact. Usually, that impact is an increase in costs and a reduction of revenue. For example, one buyer representing the majority of orders can lead to a financial crisis if that buyer turns to a different supplier. International operations can increase a company's risk as it is more difficult to follow money flow and track how and what is delivered. Fiscal returns can also fluctuate due to exchange rates, depending on the currency in which transactions are paid. This can trigger local producers to look for creative ways to reduce costs. In labor intensive industries, this can lead to lower worker wages, increased worker hours, and greater risk of exploitation.

C. Operational Risk: Failure in day-to-day operating procedures can have an immediate impact on revenues and costs and can also have a long-term impact on company viability. There are both internal and external causes of operational risk. Internal causes include worker performance (e.g., productivity, error rates, product rejection, or recycle due to quality issues), failure of equipment, poor infrastructure, etc. External causes range from natural disasters, economic trends, change in government regulations, or new competitors in the market. All of these issues can affect a company's ability to fulfill orders and deliver on contracts, which can mean loss of revenue and damage to reputation and risks to assets. They can also incentivize use of unauthorized subcontracting and informal networks of workers.

D. Reputational Risk: Reputation and brand value are everything to a business. When companies engage in behavior not accepted by consumers, buyers, or investors (such as modern slavery), there can be an immediate loss of revenue. Such behavior can start a vicious cycle at lower levels within a supply chain (below Tiers 1 and 2) of using unauthorized subcontracting and informal or "hidden production" alongside formal/public production. Informal production carries a greater risk of forced labor.

E. Strategic Risk: Businesses operate most effectively when decision-making is directed by a comprehensive business plan. As risks change, short-, medium-, and long-term strategic plans need to be adapted. Changes in technological innovation, mechanization, competitors, demand, and/or materials' cost can all affect a business's strategic plan. The key to assessing overall risk to a company's business plan is having the data and analytical knowledge of how to assess impact and frame mitigations.

While this summary is a simplification of the operation of risk management, what is relevant to the discussion here is that risk management is a well-defined function within most companies and assessing the risk of modern slavery could be included in this operation. Additionally, companies use their assessment and prioritization of each risk type to develop mitigations. For example, shrimp exporters in Thailand are able to trace every final product sold in the United States back to the individual pond. The exporters have decided the risk of a health problem arising and threatening their entire business is worth investing in greater granularity in their tracing (Association 2009). Fishing fleets have responded to US regulations requiring turtle excluder devices on their nets as a precondition of import, with nearly universal adoption of the practice (National Oceanic and Atmospheric Association 2020). McDonald's has invested significantly in ensuring the sustainability of its supply chain for Filet-O-Fish™ filet (Skinner 2012). Virtually, every company has a protocol for compliance with the Foreign Corrupt Practices Act, which holds companies—up to the C-suite or senior executives—accountable for bribes paid within their supply chain whether they know about them or not (Sect. 7.4).

Development of Risk Tools Each of the industries mentioned above have significant incidences of forced labor within their supply chain, but, to date, the presence of modern slavery has not brought with it the same risk calculations or clarity around required action that other risks have. Instead, due to long and opaque supply chains, companies often ignore what happens in a supply chain beneath the top tiers of production. These "hidden" tiers (often "informal" factories or "at home" work) become areas at high risk for violations in many of the risk areas, most notably operations and regulatory compliance (e.g., safety, environment, and human rights). Many companies argue that they cannot assess what goes on in these lower tiers. Given the length of many supply chains and the large number of potential suppliers in a supply chain, and despite the fact that 77% of CEOs reporting under the UK Modern Slavery Act think there is a likelihood of modern slavery occurring in their supply chain (Hult 2016), companies have not developed robust tools to evaluate risk of modern slavery in their supply chains. And yet, companies develop sophisticated track-and-trace protocols for activities they view as core to their operations, as with the shrimp exporters cited above.

There have been important first steps in developing tools to identify risks in supply chains, including FRDM by Made in A Free World (FRDM 2020), "Know the Chain" by Humanity United (Humanity United 2020), and the "Responsible

Sourcing Tool" (Verite 2020) and CUMULUS Forced Labor Screen (Verite 2018) by Verite. All these tools have provided key steps forward in understanding how to assess risk in supply chains. The challenge is to develop risk assessments that are actionable; this requires tracking each individual company's spend by commodity (raw materials through all production steps), by location, and by supplier and then matching that spend against measures/indicators of modern slavery for the same commodity, location, and supplier. Company spend data often hold the key to an operation's competitive advantage. As such, it is extremely difficult to get these data publicly and it is challenging to promote sharing within industries where such transparency could be most impactful. Indeed, it is even difficult for organizations with the expertise on these issues to secure the trust necessary to engage with corporate leadership around supply chain risks. Without this specificity, the risk of modern slavery is challenging to assess, let alone redress.

Building on these prior efforts, the Global Fund to End Slavery (GFEMS) is working to develop an artificial intelligence predictive screening tool to look for and quantify the risk of forced labor in corporate supply chains. This forced labor screening tool is designed to provide forced labor risk scores at various levels in a company, providing theoretical risk transparency throughout a supply chain. Every supplier would be scored. This is effectively a risk classification (high/low) based on elements that have a collective strong association with the presence of forced labor in a supply chain. These classifications can then be the basis for developing the appropriate mitigations.

At the time of this writing, GFEMS is developing a working prototype of this screening tool. GFEMS is pursuing prototype development with a private sector partner that has a machine-learning platform that can be used to analyze massive global databases (e.g., trade data, law enforcement data, human trafficking reports, media reports, financial information, and geography). This forced labor risk screening tool is designed to identify potential "hotspots"—like pig iron acquisition—so that a company can effectively correlate forced labor elimination efforts with the greatest areas of risk. The development of a robust tool to screen for risk of modern slavery in a supply chain is a key step forward in getting companies to integrate consideration of modern slavery into their risk management processes. Such a tool can be used as a first-pass screening by operations and procurement professionals, investors, regulatory enforcers, and stakeholders such as NGO "watchdog" groups.

It is important to note here that businesses need to recognize that the single best data source regarding—and frontline protection against—incidences of modern slavery in their supply chain lies with workers. Workers who feel empowered and safe to report abuse and suggest remedies on behalf of themselves and their coworkers (Chap. 3) can help act as researchers, insurers, and innovators. Companies that target and punish workers for organizing and speaking up when something goes wrong run a greater risk of modern slavery continuing unabated within their supply chains. As a result, grievance and whistleblower mechanisms should be incorporated into risk assessment processes. In the past few years, a number of tools have been developed to support the overall effectiveness of worker voice input (UNU 2019; Business and Human Rights Resource Centre 2020).

Area 1(b)—Assessing the Risk of Modern Slavery in Supply Chains: Data Analytics Risk screening tools will be important to help companies with long and opaque supply chains to focus their anti-modern slavery efforts on the most relevant parts of their supply chain. As the development of these screening tools takes time, companies need to utilize their own in-house data teams to develop key indicators of forced labor. Every company has its own operational data and associated analytics that *could* help interrogate their supply chain for these indicators as evidence of modern slavery. These analytical capabilities simply are not being used to screen for the risk of forced labor across a supply chain. Below is an example of a potential approach to screening for the probability of forced labor in a manufacturing environment.

Identifying Forced Labor by Comparing Exports with Labor Capacity in Apparel Factories Apparel factories in developing countries often produce products for well-known brands through short-term contracts that create a highly fragmented sector prone to hiring informal/temporary workers. These informal and temporary workers are often "hidden" in informal factories or home-based work, thereby placing them at greater risk for exploitation. Forced labor is very difficult to assess in this environment but is often driven by:

- *Demand* that is higher than *capacity* to produce; this can lead to both outsourcing and forced overtime work.
- Pressure to keep costs low (*price pressure*) can lead to unauthorized outsourcing; *margin pressure* (i.e., the pressure to keep the sales price well above the cost of production) in emerging markets can drive unethical practices in supply chains.
- *Outsourcing* by a few key exporters; firms receiving the majority share of export orders often seek progressively lower costs by moving operation to a location where they can be sourced more cheaply (*cost arbitrage*) (GFEMS 2019).

Given these conditions, GFEMS and Weave Services have designed a quantitative model, which uses actual production and export data, to estimate the prevalence of forced labor. That information is compared with "predicted" or expected production. *The core idea is to reconcile* export volumes, *which are converted into equivalent hours and available reported labor hours.* Any variation beyond a reasonable range could indicate the presence of forced overtime and unaccounted outsourcing. The following chart depicts the quantitative model (Fig. 7.2).

Companies in the apparel sector could execute a similar analysis across their production lines, analyzing predicted production levels versus actual production levels. Where actual factory export numbers are significantly higher than predictions, it may be an indication of "informal" factory and/or home-based production, both of which are associated with a higher probability of forced labor. While this is only one example, by utilizing their existing analytical capabilities, a company could identify factors that may be associated with forced labor in their supply chains. Examining company spend across units of production and comparing costs, tracking suppliers for any publicity concerning labor abuses, and analyzing pricing versus market indicators are just a few of the mechanisms companies could employ to identify exploitation.

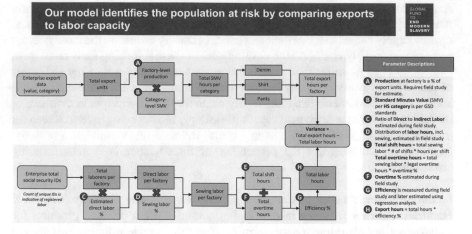

Fig. 7.2 Estimating prevalence of forced labor using factory operational data. Legend: HS: Harmonized Systems (refers to the international nomenclature for classification of products. HS allows countries to classify trade goods on a common basis). (Source: GFEMS (2019). Used with permission)

Area 2—Develop Mitigations when Risks of Forced Labor Are High: Strategic Procurement It is challenging to interrogate deep and opaque supply chains, *but it is doable.* Supply chain optimization and strategic procurement are well-defined functions in companies. Optimization of a company's entire purchase-to-pay process is not novel and can deliver key value. Investors want well run, effective supply chains and logistics. Companies can manage efforts to clean up their supply chains like any other risk in their business.

Once a risk is identified, the focus turns to risk mitigation and value generation, and here is where strategic procurement comes into play. Strategic procurement is designed to involve the entire company and includes the following:

- Understanding internal business needs: such needs assessment includes analyzing all organizational spending.
- Assessing market conditions and suppliers in the market: this includes understanding the need for sourcing of raw material, components, services, etc.
- Understanding specific suppliers: supplier selection is key to meeting needs and avoiding losses.
- Developing a sourcing strategy: this includes calculating total system costs of all major purchases to understand the costs incurred beyond the initial purchase price.
- Implementing the sourcing strategy: Will the company accept bids, use a single source, or develop a strategic partnership with a supplier? This includes evaluating winning bids (if applicable) and negotiating contracts.
- Choosing and then monitoring suppliers for effectiveness. While often considered a "lagging indicator," an audit may be helpful in providing a comprehensive picture of a supplier's operation.

- Developing recommendations for ongoing improvements and responses to market changes.

There are a number of procurement protocols along this process chain that can be used to mitigate the risk of modern slavery in the supply chain. They include:

- *Bid conditioning*: In setting up a bid for a particular product or service, companies often establish key requirements for those bidding. Technical expertise, production capacity, safety history, and evidence of environmental compliance are just a few examples of criteria required to ensure the supplier can meet performance expectations. This is where clear expectations on worker rights can be laid out, with companies requiring suppliers to outline what they have done to eliminate modern slavery from their supply chains.
- *Supplier authentication:* Companies should have well-defined supplier authentication processes that include evaluation of suppliers from independent sources and data. Where possible, site visits are an important part of the authentication process; a carefully executed site visit can be critical to evaluating for labor abuses. The authentication process can allow for evaluation of other indicators of modern slavery, such as workers' control of their identity documents, and recruitment fees charged to workers.
- *Contracting:* Companies usually take great care to ensure their "Terms & Conditions" in their contracts with suppliers outline expectations and protect the company from supplier nonperformance or supplier engagement in illegal practices. Every contract should include clear language outlining expectations regarding all employment practices. Each contract can also have a clear "roll down" provision that requires these same terms in any subsequent subcontracting.
- *Supplier monitoring:* The key to effective implementation of company policies that prohibit labor abuses is robust, ongoing supplier monitoring. Supplier monitoring protocols can look for evidence of worker exploitation or forced labor. This requires *random* inspections of supplier production sites, private interviews with workers, and effective operation of complaint mechanisms, such as hotlines and worker voice tools. Planned visits, while helpful, allow suppliers to hide many violations. Monitoring efforts must also ensure that no employer retaliation occurs against workers who speak up. There are emerging technology solutions that can increase the cost efficiency and effectiveness of supplier monitoring (GFEMS and IOM 2020). These solutions/tools will be particularly helpful where production is in remote locations and access constraints impede the ability to conduct on-site due diligence.
- *Supplier Relationship Management Programs (SRMs):* The development of a strategic relationship with a key supplier provides greater insight into their operation. SRMs involve sharing internal data, such as margins, in an effort to develop win-win approaches like performance-based contracting. This type of inside evaluation can ensure there are no hidden aspects of the production process that could be high risk for labor exploitation and forced labor.

While not a comprehensive list of procurement processes, the above processes represent substantive methods for mitigating and reducing the risk of (or opportunity for) modern slavery in a supply chain. In addition to these technical procurement processes, sourcing specialists' training is key to a company's awareness. This training must include total system cost (TSC) training to ensure companies understand the potential value of eliminating forced labor from their supply chain. Finally, it is extremely important that Procurement and Line Operations, not Corporate Social Responsibility (CSR) or sustainability personnel, are responsible for action related to fighting modern slavery. This ensures it is stewarded regularly at points in the organization that have the capacity to execute forced labor prevention and intervention actions.

Area 3—Demonstrating Maximum Returns to Shareholders While Protecting Workers: Total System Cost Analysis There are clearly potential shareholder issues related to the cost/benefit of addressing the risk of modern slavery in a company's supply chain. Businesses need to be able to demonstrate the medium- and long-term impact on profits of clean supply chains. There are a number of efforts underway to demonstrate improved returns from eliminating modern slavery from supply chains, and there is early evidence that improving key aspects of worker welfare is associated with higher productivity and higher retention rates, leading to improvement in profitability. More profitable factories, with more productive workers, also pay workers more (ILO 2015). Implementation of "progressive policies" (e.g., better wages, improved working conditions, safer environments, greater skill development, and worker transportation) has some correlation with improved profitability (measured by EBITDA: Earnings Before Interest, Taxes, Depreciation and Amortization) (Wazir 2019). These results lead to the perspective that a supply chain with rigorous protocols to prevent and address modern slavery could result in increased profitability.

Results such as increased productivity and the potential for a more committed and better trained workforce, need to be codified and empirically measured. This is where many companies with strategic procurement operations can utilize *Total Systems Cost* (TSC), also referred to as Total Cost of Ownership, to demonstrate that the lowest price for a good or service is not always the key to lowest cost overall. TSC is a fundamental supply chain management process that outlines a complete vision of all costs associated with a particular good or service. That is to say, TSC is the total of all costs in a production chain; it provides the basis for assessing the impact of decisions on all supply chain components related to cost and value. It often shows that acquisition costs are only a small portion of total costs.

The model in Fig. 7.3 is built on a hypothetical example of producing denim jeans. In the illustrative model, producing 100 pairs of jeans could cost 10.50 USD in a location known for low cost operations and higher risks of slave labor (note the relative proportion of labor costs to other costs). The drive for low-cost production has motivated global apparel brands to source from low- and low-middle income countries, where low cost production has been associated with labor exploitation.

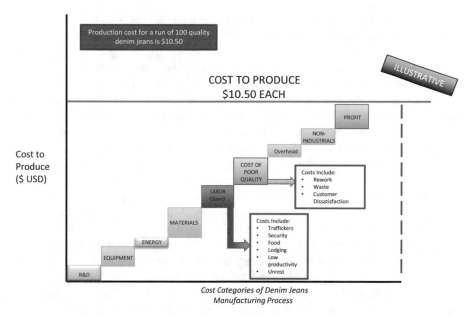

Fig. 7.3 Illustrative Total System Cost of denim jeans (assume slave labor)

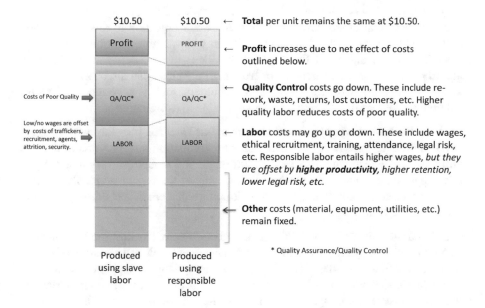

Fig. 7.4 Slave Labor vs Responsible Labor: Production cost for a run of 100 quality denim jeans (simplified, illustrative)

Most apparel producers are unaware of the actual cost of eliminating exploitative practices. The common assumption is that responsible labor practices drive up costs. The illustrative figure (Fig. 7.4) proposes that productivity improvement, quality enhancements that reduce product rejection or recycle, and so on can be associated with increased profits. This figure is a simple conceptual framework for examining garment manufacturing with, and without, modern slavery. The figure demonstrates how calculating a TSC model might provide a company insight into how responsible labor practices versus forced labor can *improve* profits. A well-run manufacturing process *with responsible labor* (meets global standards for wage and working conditions) could outperform a manufacturing process *with forced labor*. That performance advantage could deliver increased profits to the responsible business owner. This TSC model can be adapted to other manufacturing processes.

TSC analysis can be used to demonstrate how responsible labor practices could lead to increases in worker productivity, improved operational safety, better employee health, improved quality of goods produced with less rework/recycle and waste, better retention of workers, and, ultimately, increased profits. Obviously, actual data are needed to populate this model. This is where the procurement team can play a big role. They can add this framework to analysis, testing the assumption that replacing modern slavery with responsibly sourced labor will yield significant benefits. The purpose of this TSC example is to conceptualize a clear business case for eliminating modern slavery from the supply chain. This kind of analysis can demonstrate to shareholders that eliminating modern slavery can increase returns and, therefore, is in their financial best interest. It must also communicate to workers and other stakeholders that the work environment meets global standards for wages and working conditions. The TSC framework does not analyze costs associated with potential brand devaluation and consumer objection to products tainted with forced labor, but these elements can certainly be valuable additions to the analysis. The real advantage of the TSC framework is to help demonstrate that and quantify how eliminating forced labor from a supply chain can directly benefit corporate shareholders, workers, and other stakeholders, such as governments, NGOs, and civil society while protecting those vulnerable to exploitation.

Area 4—Building Organizational Cultures that Deal Responsibly with Forced Labor When It Occurs Organizational anti-exploitation culture starts at the top with the Chief Executive Officer's commitment to end modern slavery in a company's supply chain, but it must extend to all levels in the organization. Converting senior executive commitment to a corporate culture that eradicates this exploitation starts with the following:

- Bold public stances by the CEO and Board of Directors against modern slavery
- A commitment by the CEO and Senior Management to directly address and remedy incidences of modern slavery that arise throughout the supply chain, including holding anyone involved accountable. Ensuring that all modern slavery incidents receive appropriate and effective remediation reinforces a company's public commitment to end modern slavery. Such efforts may include establishing standards in line with the Consumer Goods Forum and providing detailed proce-

dures for frontline management to respond to incidences of modern slavery (Australia Business Pledge 2018)

- Implementation of an Ethical Code of Conduct that lays out clear expectations regarding responses to modern slavery
- Mandatory employer awareness training programs designed to train the entire organization on what modern slavery looks like and to galvanize the organization around anti-exploitation action, creating a cadre of frontline observers
- Requirement that all senior managers report, as part of their normal operations reporting and stewardship, their efforts to secure supply chains free from exploitation
- Senior management support for procurement and operations personnel in developing and implementing anti-exploitation protocols/processes
- Sourcing specialist training on strategic procurement tools designed to reduce the probability of modern slavery in supply chains and building TSC expertise to better understand the potential business advantage of eliminating this crime from supply chains

Finally, a key foundational element of a transparent culture, especially where a company and the consumer have limited visibility into where products originate, is the sanctioned use of worker voice tools and processes. As mentioned earlier, such tools can play a critical role in validating risk assessment processes. Where organizational culture does not provide workers and other supply chain stakeholders the opportunity to speak out, either because they lack the tools, such as a grievance procedure, or because of a lack of trust or fear of retribution, there is missed opportunity to mitigate modern slavery through collective information sharing and assessment. It is therefore important that worker voice tools be incorporated throughout business processes. This ensures that transparency is very much part of a business's culture. And, technology is rapidly developing to increase the efficiency of these worker voice tools (Farbenblum et al. 2018); social audit platforms such as Apprise can enhance worker voice (UNU 2019).

Businesses Role in Eliminating the Supply of Forced Labor

Companies can also work to reduce the "supply" of forced labor by investing in and growing businesses in local communities that can become local suppliers. By providing relevant training and skill development to local populations, companies can create sustainable jobs. This workforce investment has long-term value. For example, GFEMS is working with Business in the Community (BITC) to train vulnerable populations for jobs in the hotel industry in Việt Nam and India; trainees can then explore employment opportunities in the wider hospitality, tourism, and retail industries. There are many opportunities for companies to partner with communities to offer training and viable jobs as one part of the collective business strategy to end modern slavery.

There are numerous other opportunities to consider, including the use of *trade incentives*, which encourage governments to act and to support investment in companies that take anti-exploitation action. Additionally, responsible investors are finally considering supply chain issues to understand the impacts on a company's bottom line; interest in sustainable, responsible investing has been on the rise (Chasan 2019; Institute for Sustainable Investing 2020). The financial sector must also be engaged in order to take the fight directly to the traffickers and impact the supply of forced labor. Tracking and tracing money flows, enhancing financial investigations, and confiscating assets, for example, will change the risk calculus. It is instructive to note here that it was "the largest syndicated loan in history that underwrote the liberation of slaves in the British Empire" (Draper 2018).

7.3   Conclusion

What does all this mean practically for business? At the operational level, the risks for businesses of not addressing modern slavery are real:

- Use of forced labor could potentially *reduce* returns in the medium- and long-term.
- Modern slavery negatively impacts company efficiency, cost, effectiveness, and operations (e.g., worker productivity, product quality, worker safety, and security).
- Modern slavery in supply chains can negatively affect brand perception internationally.
- Governments and investors are increasingly expecting proactive efforts by companies to eliminate modern slavery from their supply chains.
- If companies do not act on their own, there is a risk of increasing government regulation/legislation, associated reporting requirements, and potential penalties, and reparations requirements.
- There are also indications of a potential correlation between modern slavery and environmental destruction (See, for example, Bales 2016).

The risks to companies associated with modern slavery cannot be ignored and need to be factored into business decisions.

Business Leadership Is Key

Finally, it is important to emphasize that business leadership is central to creating market-based solutions and sustainably ending modern slavery. The buying power of businesses and socially responsible investors is in the trillions of US dollars. Mobilizing those resources would be a game changer. Execution of the next steps outlined below requires unwavering CEO leadership and stewardship by senior operational executives; these actions should not be offloaded to a Corporate Social Responsibility (CSR) group. It requires leadership that shifts the norm to an explicit determination to find exploitation at any point in a supply chain and eliminating it wherever it is found. Furthermore, for solutions to be truly sustainable, businesses must develop their operations to be meaningfully accountable to all stakeholders – their workers, CSO and NGO representatives, and governments, which must similarly be accountable to the public trust they are responsible for stewarding. This could be done effectively through public-private partnerships that design and implement solutions that work in the market and also meet ILO core labor protocols at a minimum.

Modern businesses have developed robust processes and decision-making tools that are designed to maximize shareholder value. Over the years, private sector profits and modern slavery have intersected and intermingled in corporate supply chains. If successful businesses use existing data, analytics, and processes that maximize profits, they can significantly accelerate efforts to end modern slavery. The same levers that corporations use to optimize value from those supply chains can be adapted to identify and *make* modern slavery *economically unprofitable*.

7.4 Recommendations

Companies committed to eliminating modern slavery can engage in the following practices:

1. *Contribute to the development of Modern Slavery Risk Assessment tools by working with developers to provide spend data* according to commodity and location, social audit results, production and export data, trade data, and any claims regarding force labor. Efforts to develop risk tools need these data to increase robustness of forced labor assessments.
2. *Establish and utilize worker voice tools*, such as grievance and whistle blower mechanisms, which respect the role and voice of the worker and ensure that worker input is included in the formation of all anti-exploitation policies. These mechanisms can support "real-time" understanding of issues occurring at the operational level and may enhance company credibility and stakeholder trust.
3. *Develop protocols for utilizing internal data and data analytics capabilities to hone in on areas at high risk for modern slavery*. Designate key operational and procurement executives to develop and execute anti-exploitation protocols.
4. *Establish clear and focused mitigation steps directly correlated with identified risks and ascribe clear accountabilities*. Adoption of strategic procurement principles and processes (e.g., bid conditioning that includes anti-modern slavery commitments, random supplier inspections, etc.) can be done to both mitigate risk and reduce the probability of future forced labor entering a supply chain.
5. *Engage internal planning professionals (along with anti-modern slavery researchers) to generate a business case for eliminating modern slavery from supply chains*. The anti-exploitation argument would use TSC to demonstrate that a supply chain free of modern slavery is more profitable. This would involve using existing data on productivity, work force turnover, rejection/recycle due to

quality issues, and training to calculate a TSC that evaluates all costs associated with production and operation, to create modern slavery-free labor scenarios.

6. *Build internal governance and operational processes that reinforce an anti-modern slavery culture in a company.*
7. *Tout anti-modern slavery efforts and their return potential to enhance shareholder performance to investors.*

References

Association, H. o. T. F. F. (2009, October). *State Department Delegation to Samut Sakhon* [Interview].
Australian Business Pledge Against Forced Labour. (2018, June). The business response to remedying human rights infringements: The current and future state of corporate remedy. *Human Rights Remedy*.
Bales, K. (2016). *Blood and earth: Modern slavery, ecocide and the secret to saving the World.* Penguin: Random House.
Baradaran, M. (2019, August 18). Fabric of modernity: How southern cotton became the cornerstone of a new global commodities trade. *The 1619 Project New York Times*, p. 36.
Business & Human Rights Resource Centre. (2020, September 7). *New app helps detect labour exploitation in supply chains, according to report.*
Chasan, E. (2019, April 1). *Global sustainable investments rise 34 percent to $34.7 trillion*, Bloomberg report.
Chocolate Industry Tackles Child Slavery. (2015). [Film] Directed by Robin Curnow. West Africa: CNN.
Cotton Crimes: Forced Labor in Uzbekistan's Cotton Industry. (2016). [Film] Directed by Anti-Slavery International. UK: Anti-Slavery International.
Desmond, M. (2019, August 18). In order to understand the brutality of American capitalism, you have to start at the plantation. *New York Times*, p. 34.
Draper, N. (2018, September). *Some potential lessons from the British financial sector's role in perpetuating and ending chattel slavery.* UN University Centre for Policy Research.
Farbenblum, B., Berg, L., & Kintominas, A. (2018). *Transformative technology for migrant workers: Opportunities, challenges, and risks.* New York: Open Society Foundation.
FRDM. (2020). *FRDM.* [Online]. Available at: frdm.co. Accessed 31 Aug 2020.
Gibson, C. R. (2014, November, 10). How the iPhone helps perpetuate modern slavery. *Huffington Post*.
Hult Research in Partnership with Ethical Trading Initiative. (2016). *Corporate leadership on modern slavery: Summary report.* Hult International Business School.
Humanity United. (2020). *Know the chain.* [Online]. Available at: knowthechain.org. Accessed 31 Aug 2020.
ILO. (2014, May 20). *Profits and poverty: The economics of forced labour.* ILO.
ILO. (2015, March). *Working conditions, productivity and profitability: Evidence from better work Vietnam.* Research Brief, ILO.
Institute for Sustainable Investing. (2020, May 28). *Seven insights from asset owners on the rise of sustainable investing.* Morgan Stanley.
International Labour Organization (ILO) and Walk Free Foundation. (2017). *Global estimates of modern slavery: Forced labour and forced marriage* (pp. 29 and 32). Geneva: ILO Office.
National Oceanic and Atmospheric Association. (2020). *Turtle excluder device regulations.* [Online]. Available at: https://www.fisheries.noaa.gov/southeast/bycatch/turtle-excluder-device-regulations. Accessed 31 Aug 2020.
Pasley, J. (2019, September 6). 15 American landmarks that were built by slaves. *Business Insider*.

Skinner, E. B. (2012, February 2). The fishing industry's cruelest catch. *Bloomberg Business Week*.

The Global Fund to End Modern Slavery (GFEMS). (2019). *Unpublished report "Measuring prevalence of modern slavery" with Weave Services Ltd* (p. 16).

The Global Fund to End Modern Slavery (GFEMS) and the International Organization for Migration (IOM). (2020). *Predicting and verifying modern slavery risk: practical applications of artificial intelligence and data analytics (Webinar 3)*. https://www.gfems.org/event-webinar-series-responsible-recovery

UNU Institute in Macau and Mekong Club. (2019, October). *Apprise audit impact assessment report: Detecting labour exploitation in supply chains*. See also www.apprise.solutions.com

US Department of Labor. (2018, Septemeber). *2018 list of goods produced by child labor, required by the trafficking Victims Preotection Reauthorization Act of 2005*.

Verite. (2018, August 7). *Introducing CUMULUS Forced Labor Screen*. Verite.

Verite. (2020). *Responsible sourcing tool*. [Online]. Available at: responsiblesourcingtool.org. Accessed 31 Aug 2020.

Wazir Advisors. (2019, February 8). *Quantifying the business value of improved labor conditions in spinning mills in Tamil Nadu*. Submitted to the Global Fund to End Modern Slavery.

Part II
Governmental and Non-governmental Public Systems

Chapter 8
Governmental and Non-governmental Public Systems: Part II Introduction

Makini Chisolm-Straker and Katherine Chon

In 2020, the United States marked the 20th anniversary of the Trafficking Victims Protection Act, which established the legal framework for preventing human trafficking, protecting victims, and prosecuting perpetrators (Chap. 9). The whole-of-government approach at the federal level has received bipartisan support over multiple administrations with regular reauthorizations to expand these legal protections and authorization of funding resources. Every US state and territory also has local laws to integrate anti-trafficking efforts across child welfare, social service, health, education, labor, security, criminal and judicial, and other government systems. Increasingly Tribal governments, such as The Navajo Nation, are strengthening their own anti-trafficking laws and exercising their tribal sovereignty. In the US, a strong civil society, funded by private donors, corporate support, and government funding streams, implements the services essential to persons directly impacted by human trafficking, but tends to neglect longer-term systemic solutions.

On its surface, political will against and attention to human trafficking remain strong. The US has robust nongovernment anti-trafficking networks and growing leadership by survivors of human trafficking. Every year, the Federal Government provides public reports on progress of anti-trafficking efforts. State and local governments are increasingly releasing more information and data on human trafficking. However, there is insufficient understanding and accounting of how public systems, themselves, have knowingly or unknowingly contributed to human trafficking victimization and perpetration. This section provides a deeper understanding of the historical developments of governmental and nongovernmental systems and how their legacies have impacted levels of trust with populations, particularly those at disproportionate risk for human trafficking.

M. Chisolm-Straker (✉)
Institute for Health Equity Research, Department of Emergency Medicine,
Icahn School of Medicine at Mount Sinai, New York, NY, USA
e-mail: Makini.Chisolm-Straker@mountsinai.org

K. Chon
Center for the Study of Slavery and Justice, Brown University, Providence, RI, USA

© Springer Nature Switzerland AG 2021   123
M. Chisolm-Straker, K. Chon (eds.), *The Historical Roots of Human Trafficking*,
https://doi.org/10.1007/978-3-030-70675-3_8

"Government" is a way of controlling or managing a country, a group, or a people and its resources. Different doctrines of "social contract" determine the degrees to which people view their government as an authority figure and look to it for protection, support, and guidance in exchange for varying degrees of sacrificed individual freedoms. While there have been eras of greater trust with these public systems, historical analysis presented in this section illustrates how the US government has failed to implement the social contract equitably. Public systems face ongoing challenges in delivering purely benevolent services toward all people, privileging some groups over others—historically and now. In practice, the government does not lead every system that impacts US lives and civil society has been a critical force for regressive or progressive change. And while there is no US system (governmental or otherwise) that does not have an anti-trafficking role to play, diffusion of responsibility often obfuscates transparency and diminishes public accountability. Although multiple systems need to change, some require deeper systemic uprooting based on long histories of actively promoting or facilitating exploitation.

At the inception of the United States, slavery was legal and regulated. Even when the importation of slaves was outlawed, the slave trade remained a legitimate business and the use of slaves remained legal. Of note, legal slavery was based on race (nonWhites were "eligible" for enslavement); the government privileged the economic welfare and prosperity of landowning Whites over that of Indigenous and Black people (Chaps. 14 and 15). When slavery was made illegal throughout the United States, the economic well-being of Whites was still prioritized with the labor loophole of the 13th Amendment, which allows forced labor to be used as a form of government-sanctioned punishment. US leadership has supported the forced and coerced labor of the poor and people of color for centuries, and the criminal and judicial systems continue to effectuate mass incarceration and forced labor. In Chap. 11, Williamson and Flood explain how contemporary overfunding of law enforcement in the educational system contributes to the institutionalized policing of queer people and people of color in their childhood.

The United States' initial child welfare system was imported from that of the English empire. Orphaned and poor children were "placed" into indentured servitude until adulthood. This was considered better than the almshouses where children would learn no skills and were likely to be exposed to even more abuse (NFPA 2020). Historically, English children were commodities that could be used as collateral or purchased for apprenticeships. They, and poor White adults, served as the indentured servants and, with Indigenous and Black people, were used for the colonization of what would become the United States (Isenberg 2016). In the early 1700s, Benjamin Franklin suggested that children should replace indentured servants and slaves as the workers. This was ironic, given that Franklin was an indentured servant to his brother until the age of twenty-one and described "harsh and tyrannical treatment" (Franklin and Weld 1859); and indentured servitude was how many Whites came to the colonies. This overall idea ruled the century, and even Thomas Jefferson's elitist efforts to reform Virginia education by "raking the rubbish" for those with the most potential were dashed by the more popular belief that poor children were better suited for labor than education (Isenberg 2016).

In a twist on modern understandings of the purpose of education, starting in the 1800s, Native children were forcibly separated from their families, imprisoned in boarding schools, and punished for use of their language or traditions. Repeated over generations, the thin guise of edification was used to separate Native people from their Tribal histories, cultures, and knowledge. The establishment of government-sponsored child protective services was not until 1962, in response to concerns about child abuse (Myers 2008). It took centuries for the US to conceive of children as worthy of protection from abuse; still, the agency and insight of children are minimized and children continue to be used for political purposes, as Duane discusses in Chapter 12. As the federal government, including the Department of Education (only founded in 1979), has persistently underserved the nation's children—particularly the poor and those of color—systems of care other than those run by the US government have intervened. In Chapter 16, Hicks Greendeer and Weston hold up, for example, the Wampanoag Nation's work at self-determination via decolonization of education and a reclamation of educational sovereignty.

Health care, commonly considered a benevolent field, is another US system of care guilty of abuse and exploitation perpetuation. Chapters 14 and 15, by Chisolm–Straker and Warren, respectively, discuss the historical interactions of people of color with US "health care;" the interests of White slave owners and Whites in general were the driving force behind medical apartheid. The healthcare setting has also been used as a space of explicit harm for other people of color, including forced and coerced experimentation and sterilizations. The resultant consequences of lopsided morbidity and mortality of people of color continue in the twenty-first century. Rooted in racist and xenophobic ideologies, these disparities include Asian Americans. In Chapter 10, Cheng and Chang discuss how Chinese migrant workers (and then other Asian groups) were used for their labor but not welcomed as people with rights (allusions to contemporary anti-Latinx xenophobia and ethnocentrism are apparent). Asian Americans were initially largely unwelcome and later were and are used against other groups of color with the false narrative of the "model minority." This narrative has also contributed to the marginalization of less affluent Asian Americans, who are left out of conversations about race-based health and wealth disparities. Racial segregation in the US is illegal in name only.

The chapters in this section highlight examples of governmental and nongovernmental systems of care that have *contributed* to the abuse of many groups including people of color, the indigent, LGBTQIA2S+[1] people, immigrants, and more. Chronically oppressed groups have been and are targeted for exploitation; they remain incompletely protected and even harmed by practical policies and laws in various sectors and systems, including housing, education, law enforcement, health care, and immigration. These are also systems that have the capacity to serve and support all individuals living in the United States. The chapter authors, through in-depth historical examination, demonstrate what marginalized and oppressed communities here have experienced and known for decades and centuries. There are

---

[1] Lesbian, gay, bisexual, transgender, queer and/or questioning, intersex, asexual, Two-Spirit, and other non-heterosexual, non-cis identities and experiences.

multiple systems of care that must work toward equity and justice so that everyone has the opportunity to reach their highest levels of health; this is core to the practice of public health. The authors also challenge these systems of care to do better and they provide recommendations for action.

The recognition of human trafficking as a public health issue has opened the way for meaningful trafficking prevention work. Public health values secondary and tertiary prevention (intervention) work and *prioritizes* primary, or root-cause, prevention action that is grounded in context and evidence. The evidence has been mounting for centuries: the persistence of human trafficking is an expected product of White supremacy, classism, heteronormativity, xenophobia, and systems of patriarchy and unchecked capitalism (Chaps. 4 and 5). A public health response requires all three types of prevention efforts but especially primary prevention at policy and legislative levels, among diverse governmental and nongovernmental sectors. It took concerted, multidisciplinary efforts to reach the collective progress we have made so far; it will take the same to fully acknowledge the root causes and effectively eliminate the risk of human trafficking in future generations.

References

Franklin, B., & Weld, H. H. (1859). *Benjamin Franklin: His autobiography; with a narrative of his public life and services*. New York: Harper.

Isenberg, N. (2016). *White trash. The 400-year untold history of class in America*. New York: Penguin Books.

Myers, J. E. B. (2008). A history of child protection in America. *Family Law Quarterly, 42*(3), 449–463.

National Foster Parent Association. (2020). *History of Foster Care in the United States*. Retrieved 19 October 2020 from https://www.nfpaonline.org/page-1105741

Chapter 9
The Development of US Anti-slavery Law: A Historical Review

Luis C.deBaca and Griffin Thomas Black

9.1 Introduction

In May 1865, the guns of the US Civil War had barely gone silent when Frederick Douglass issued a stark warning to his victorious abolitionist partners. Rather than resting on what for any other person would have been a life's work—ending the legal, social, and economic system of chattel slavery into which he had been born—Douglass used his speaking turn at the meeting of the American Anti-Slavery Society to address an urgent task. The moment called not for a celebration and disbanding of the abolitionist movement, but continued vigilance against the evils of slavery:

> It has been called by a great many names, and it will call itself by yet another name; and you and I and all of us had better wait and see what new form this old monster will assume, in what new skin this old snake will come forth next. (Douglass 1865).

With this warning, and subsequent speeches cautioning against the exploitation of immigrant communities (Douglass 1867), Douglass challenged the nation to remain vigilant about slavery's ability to survive despite the defeat of the Confederacy. Similarly, the modern anti-slavery movement must defend against the temptation of state triumphalism and guard against backlash or dissipation of the political and policy advances of the last two decades. Indeed, one of the biggest risks facing the anti-trafficking movement is a false assumption that "modern slavery" is a new phenomenon and that the methods to combat it are equally new. Such an ahistorical approach can lead to misunderstandings about the social and legal mechanisms surrounding abolitionism that have taken the full length of US history to form. Thus,

L. C.deBaca
The Gilder Lehrman Center for the Study of Slavery, Resistance, and Abolition,
Yale University, New Haven, CT, USA

G. T. Black (✉)
University of Cambridge, Cambridge, UK
e-mail: gtb28@cam.ac.uk

© Springer Nature Switzerland AG 2021
M. Chisolm-Straker, K. Chon (eds.), *The Historical Roots of Human Trafficking*,
https://doi.org/10.1007/978-3-030-70675-3_9

when considering modern abolitionism, Douglass's theory of the endurance of slavery should be heeded. The fight against coerced labor and services has had a parallel continuity, one that must be considered to properly assess present-day policies, activism, and efforts.

A note on terminology: This chapter uses the terms "involuntary servitude" and "slavery" over "trafficking" to trace the development of US law. This is not for the sake of rhetoric. At multiple times since the ratification of the Thirteenth Amendment withdrew slavery's legal imprimatur, Congress and the courts have reaffirmed that slavery did not end with abolition, but remains an ongoing crime to be confronted wherever it may reappear. In its legislative findings, the applicable current US statute—the Trafficking Victims Protection Act of 2000 (TVPA)—makes it clear that it is addressing a modern manifestation of slavery, building on the legacy of 1865 and responding to Supreme Court interpretations of the historical involuntary servitude and slavery statutes that needed updating for the modern context.

A rough beginning of the modern anti-slavery movement—at least in the USA—could be placed in 1995. This one year contained three interlocking events: Florida crew leader Miguel Flores was convicted in a case that provided a model for a victim-centered, multidisciplinary approach; then-First Lady Hilary Clinton raised the issue of trafficking at the United Nations Conference on Women in Beijing; and a brutal sweatshop was discovered in El Monte, California, shocking US citizens. That perfect storm started a policy process that would lead to the formation of the US Worker Exploitation Task Force, to the formulation of the "3P Paradigm" of Prevention, Protection, and Prosecution, and to the passing of the TVPA as well as the promulgation of the United Nations Protocol to Prevent, Suppress, and Punish Trafficking in Persons (the "Palermo Protocol").

For many in the modern movement, even those antecedents are relatively unknown. Access restrictions on government records and a concentration by academics and other commentators on the ideological aspects of the Bush Administration's early implementation of the TVPA have left unwritten some of the modern history of the development of current law and practice. A quarter-century of activity comprises what many think of as the modern anti-slavery or modern anti-trafficking movement. But to limit the issue to that timeframe risks a misunderstanding of the legal and social development of the current laws and policies, which necessarily need to be understood as part of an anti-slavery project reaching back to the abolition of chattel slavery.

To make things even more confusing, the modern approach is a synthesis of two competing legal traditions: on the one hand, the rights-based approach of the US Thirteenth Amendment (or its international descendent, Article 4 of the Universal Declaration of Rights) for which slavery is the starting point; and the commerce-based approach of efforts to combat transportation of people for prostitution, for which slavery has often been used as a rhetorical tool. Therefore, this chapter seeks to shed light on modern laws and their application, as well as schisms and controversies within the modern movement, in light of the blending of these two disparate areas of law.

Slavery in its various manifestations has been contested in US law and policy-making since before the formation of the nation. While chattel slavery was still legal, much of the political and juridical battles were about defining its contours: confining it to particular parts of the country, assessing claims of kidnapped African

Americans that they had been free and thus were rights-holders, and allowing slave-holders access to state power to enforce their claimed property rights. Chattel slavery, stripping victims of their legal rights as well as agency in the personal sphere, was a race-based system of "social death" (Patterson 1982) that excluded Black people from membership in the United States' polity. In the late antebellum period, US legal systems confronted alternative forms of exploitation as westward expansion, colonization, and immigration came into contact with Spanish, Native American, and even Asian traditions of servitude.

After Emancipation, legislative and judicial focus switched from examining the status of the exploited worker to the activities of the employer— the analysis was no longer whether a person was a slave and therefore lacked all rights, but rather was what an employer did to obtain or maintain the labor or services of another coercive enough to be considered slavery or involuntary servitude and thus covered by the Constitutional guarantee of freedom. Southern states, seeking to reimpose a racialized social and economic system as close to antebellum slavery as possible, sought to evade federal protections through the use of legal loopholes. They twisted the Thirteenth Amendment's exclusion for prison sentences of hard labor to justify vagrancy enforcement and convict leasing schemes that fueled the economic development of the Jim Crow South by placing employment-age African Americans at the mercy of local sheriffs and landowners.

Although the late-1800s retrenchment of African American political, economic, and legal rights across the South was widespread and brutal, attempts to effectively reenslave the working-age population did not go wholly unanswered. Progressive Era federal agents and attorneys sought to address these abuses through a series of prosecutions, and civil rights activists brought *habeas corpus* cases to attack the convict leasing peonage system. At the same time, the country was confronting the wages of empire and immigration alike, as the abuse of conquered and colonized Native American and Mexican populations, and of Asian and European immigrants, could not be ignored. Legislative responses were both inclusive (such as the Padrone Statute, which sought to protect Italian children held as street musicians) and exclusionary (such as the Page Act, the Chinese Exclusion Act, and their state counterparts, which used perceptions of debt bondage and forced prostitution in Chinese communities to justify mass deportations and a closing of borders for more than a generation) (Chap. 10).

Simultaneously, notions of sex and morality—especially that of women of European descent seeking to migrate in an increasingly globalized world—fueled a competing legal framework, based on the Commerce Clause that made it illegal to transport someone across a border for prostitution. Despite legally requiring neither slavery nor whiteness, this concept was termed by the Victorians as "White Slave Trafficking." The cultural and bureaucratic pull of the White Slave Trafficking Act ("WSTA" or the "Mann Act") was so strong that for almost a century, women who were held in forced prostitution were assumed to be a form of transported contraband. They were at best co-conspirators with their "pimps"[1] and in practice were not afforded

---

[1] The term "pimp" has been in use since in English since at least the 1600s, roughly co-terminus with Anglo settlement on the North American continent. The less vulgar "pandererer" was often used in more formal legal settings. "Pimp" is often used to suggest a seedier, more illicit relationship with the clients and prostitutes.

the protection of the Thirteenth Amendment. Racial inequities in its application—whether in barring the immigration of women of color or using the law to punish Black men for miscegenation—left a dubious legacy for the Mann Act that positioned it not within the civil rights context, but as a heavy-handed tool of vice enforcement.

During the twentieth century, with the gains of the Civil Rights movement, anti-slavery enforcement took on the feel of a rearguard action, mopping up the bad apples who might use coercion to hold a captive workforce but not questioning the systemic underpinnings of exploitation in low-skilled work or the US sex industry (Chap. 2). From 1865 on, pushback from the business community and those who benefit from worker exploitation has been as much a part of this issue as have been the periodic gains and breakthroughs. The push and pull over definitions and application of the law have continued unabated, whether through the adoption of convict leasing schemes in response to Emancipation, or the North Carolina growers' push for guest worker programs in the 1980s in response to a string of successful farmworker prosecutions.

In the 1970s and 80s, an uptick in federal Civil Rights enforcement incorporated understanding of psychological coercion and the power dynamics around servitude, much as law enforcement was coming to new ways of addressing domestic violence and sexual abuse. But in *United States v. Kozminski*, the Supreme Court instead looked to more concrete coercion, limiting the application of involuntary servitude and slavery laws to those cases involving force, threats of force, or threats of legal coercion tantamount to imprisonment. A few years later, the unlocking of the Soviet Bloc replicated the 1890s' dodgy labor recruitment and abusive working conditions for immigrants in Western Europe and the Americas, a phenomenon once again first recognized by the sex industry.

The domestic legislation that responded to the *Kozminski* case and increased attention to the international sex trade, the Trafficking Victims Protection Act (TVPA), incorporated both the lessons of the prior two centuries and some of their shortcomings. Legacies of freedom, workers' rights, and inclusivity exist in tandem with failed promises, evasion, exploitation of loopholes, and misuse of rhetoric. Current shortcomings in the anti-slavery response, such as the overemphasis on the vice approach and an uneasy fit with the Trump Administration's hardline immigration policies, are more understandable when seen as part of the long-term development of this legal regime (Chap. 12). Understanding how the USA arrived at the TVPA is critical in implementing it for the benefit of the victims of modern slavery.

9.2   Discussion

9.2.1   Legislative Action in a Time of Legal Slavery

It has taken the USA 250 years of legal reform, retrenchment, and innovation to reach its current victim-centered approach to anti-slavery legislation, as set forth in the TVPA and the Palermo Protocol. The legal paradigm the country now inhabits can only be fully understood by taking the entire quarter-millennium arc into account. A discussion of US modern slavery efforts must begin with the sobering reality that the US Constitution was consciously crafted to protect, enable, and indeed encourage legal chattel slavery in order to knit together a country out of both slave and free states. It is likely that the USA's modern anti-trafficking regime would have developed radically differently had slavery not been so deeply entangled with the national point of departure.

Writing in the late 1970s, legal scholar Richard Delgado identified four policy goals that run through US anti-slavery laws and enforcement:

> [P]revention of the degradation of the human personality likely to result if persons are treated like items of property; prevention of the slaves' misery and suffering; prevention of the corruption of the master as the result of his unnatural control over other human beings; and prevention of social stagnation resulting from the institution of slavery itself. (Delgado 1979).

The chapter authors argue that, in addition to these goals, there are three additional through-lines that have influenced federal efforts to confront slavery and trafficking: (1) the tension between a focus on the oppressed identity of the victimized (e.g., Black, immigrant, woman) and a focus on the victim as a rights-holder; (2) the tension between a freedom-based, civil rights approach rooted (since 1865) in the Thirteenth Amendment, and a commerce-based transportation/movement approach; and (3) the extent to which laws should be based on objectively observable coercive techniques (e.g., threats, force) as opposed to subjective experience of the victim (e.g., perceptions of serious harm, particular vulnerabilities, psychological coercion). All of these issues continue to impact the application of US anti-slavery laws to the present day.

9.2.2 An Extensive Legislative History, Even While Slavery was Legal

In his path-breaking dissertation and first monograph, *The Suppression of the African Slave-Trade*, W.E.B. DuBois charted over 300 legislative or executive actions from 1641 through 1871, spanning from British Rule to the aftermath of the US Civil War. Throughout that time, the slave trade was contested, condemned (even by many slaveholders), and legislated. Extensive laws and regulations were promulgated. But slavery continued unabated, and the few restrictions on the trade were routinely flouted. Despite positive legislation enacted in the Federal period (1790–1830) to stop the international trade of slaves (1808), the proslavery provisions of the Constitution would sustain the enslavement of millions until war exorcised these compromises from the text.

From the nation's founding to the ratification of the Thirteenth Amendment in 1865, slavery was legally sanctioned in the USA. Despite the supposed commitment to the "principle that all men are created equal," the country's early survival, expansion, and economic growth were predicated on the brutal dehumanization and forced labor of individuals of African descent, along with the dispossession of Native communities (see Morgan 1975). This ideological paradox had to be legally supported. While slavery did not develop uniformly throughout the States (many States in the North began to phase out the institution in the years following Independence), when the Framers met in Philadelphia in 1787 to draft a constitutional charter, the result was a new federal structure that actively bolstered non-White chattel slavery.

9.2.3 The US Constitution, the Slave Trade Act, and the Northwest Ordinance

While the Constitution avoided mentioning slavery or slaves outright (euphemisms such as "such persons" abound), the Framers incorporated a series of concessions to the slave interest in the Southern states that would protect and perpetuate the sectional "peculiar institution" with federal force. For instance, the slaveholding states were granted unique political power through their ability under the Constitution to count sixty percent of their enslaved populations in determining Congressional and Electoral College representation despite slaves' lack of civil rights. This had the effect of nearly doubling the political power of each landowning Southern White male's vote. Fugitive slaves were to be returned, and the Federal Government's police powers extended to putting down slave insurrections. Additionally, as part of a legislative compromise, the Framers banned the introduction of legislation regarding the abolition of the slave trade for twenty years; some imagined that would be enough time for the practice to naturally end and others intended to use those twenty years to marshal their political forces to prevent its abolition (Farrand 1913; Rakove 2009).

Notwithstanding this twenty-year compromise, federal statutes were passed in the early republic to narrow and regulate US citizens' direct involvement in the slave trade. For instance, the 1794 Slave Trade Act prohibited slave ships from being built in the USA and US ships from carrying out the traffic; this law was amended and supplemented several times in the ensuing decade in an attempt to slow the trade. Much as would happen over 200 years later, the political rhetoric of ending the traffic in slaves was more politically palatable than ending the exploitation itself. The one exception to this basic rule was to be found as part of the country's westward expansion, a trend initiated by the Northwest Ordinance of 1787, which prohibited slavery in the newly acquired region that was to become Ohio, Michigan, Indiana, Illinois, Wisconsin, and portions of Minnesota. The Northwest Ordinance, written in no small measure by Thomas Jefferson, mandated that there "be neither slavery nor involuntary servitude in the said territory, otherwise than in the punishment of crimes whereof the party shall have been duly convicted." The exception for servitude as a consequence of a criminal conviction reflected penal practice of the time, when options of capital punishment or hard labor, such as penitentiaries and formal corrections infrastructures, had not yet been devised. Much of the political and legal conflicts of the succeeding generations were to flow from the legacy of the Ordinance's geographical division of slave and free states, especially as new territories were "opened up" by conquest and colonization. In 1865, the words of the Northwest Ordinance were so familiar and well-established that they were a politically palatable construction with which the Thirteenth Amendment could prohibit slavery in *all* locales subject to the USA's jurisdiction. But, by adopting the Ordinance almost verbatim and including its outmoded punishment clause, the framers of abolition provided a means of evasion that states were quick to exploit.

9.2.4 The Slave Trade Acts of 1808 and 1818

It is a measure of the US political consensus against the slave trade that President Thomas Jefferson—a wealthy slaveholder himself—made it a priority to act against the trade on the earliest occasion constitutionally possible: January 1, 1808. Jefferson took care to highlight this goal in his annual message to Congress:

> I congratulate you, fellow-citizens, on the approach of the period at which you may interpose your authority constitutionally, to withdraw the citizens of the United States from all further participation in those violations of human rights which have been so long continued on the unoffending inhabitants of Africa, and which the morality, the reputation, and the best interests of our country, have long been eager to proscribe. Although no law you may pass can take prohibitory effect till the first day of the year one thousand eight hundred and eight, yet the intervening period is not too long to prevent, by timely notice, expeditions which cannot be completed before that day (Jefferson 1806).

Notably, as with his own personal affairs, Jefferson's urging of Congress to regulate the trade did not extend so far as challenging the ongoing practice of slavery itself. Despite a series of laws that on paper were vigorous anti-slavery provisions, funding and prioritization lagged and in subsequent years the slave trade statutes of the early 1800s were undercut by evasion and outright flaunting of the law, made all the easier by the legality of a thriving domestic slave trade that quickly made up for any restrictions on bringing in foreign victims.

Though forced into a clandestine gray market, the transatlantic trade continued to some extent even after it was made illegal in 1808. Amendments in 1818 stiffening penalties and directing more robust enforcement had a temporary effect. US ships joined the Royal Navy on slave patrols in the Atlantic, but never at the level of commitment displayed by the British. Under cover of the southern coastal trade, through which slaves in the USA were transferred by sea, newly kidnapped Africans were landed; through the use of flags of convenience, US slavers hid behind a robust continuing slave trade in Cuba and Brazil. The trade, though banned by law had continued "in a Spanish dress," disguising its US character. (DuBois 1896).

9.2.5   Antebellum Legislation not Limiting Slavery, but Advancing the "Slave Power"

Much of the diminution of the transatlantic slave trade in the early 1800s came not from new laws and enforcement efforts, but stemmed from the development of a robust internal slave trade within the USA. For many of the planter class, newly imported Africans were less profitable than the "natural increase" of their enslaved property. For a generation, colonization of the western South and its transformation of former Indian lands into the "Cotton Kingdom" brought immense wealth to the slaveholding population, not only in commodities' prices but in their human capital.

By the early 1850s, that calculus began to change. Labor shortages and price pressures made keeping the slaves one had—and cutting off their avenues of escape—critical. In this atmosphere, Southerners became increasingly vocal in the national political sphere. They contested earlier compromises that had limited slavery to certain regions and forced through the Fugitive Slave Act which required Northern states to return escapees to their masters (Oakes 2014). The Supreme Court's decision in *Dred Scott v. Sandford* cast the Northwest Ordinance into question and articulated a vision of the country in which Blacks had no civil rights at all. In light of these legislative and judicial victories, some of slavery's proponents sought to reopen what everyone thought was long-resolved: the transatlantic slave trade.

Despite proslavery governmental developments, the reopening of the transatlantic trade was clearly a nonstarter within the broader US political sphere. The Southern Commercial Convention of 1859, confronting labor shortages and a groundswell of sentiment in favor of reopening the transatlantic trade, proposed bringing African workers into the USA as temporary "apprentices" (DuBois 1896). This episode, overcome by the events of the Civil War, was eerily prescient of Southern growers' eventual success in bringing in foreign guest workers over a century later (Chap. 10). Twentieth-century guest workers entered the USA via the expansion of the H-2B visa category, which occurred in the wake of a series of successful federal involuntary servitude prosecutions that again risked cutting off Southern growers' access to exploitable Black labor in the early 1980s.

9.2.6   Anti-slavery Social and Political Movements—The Abolitionists

Various strains of abolitionist ideology and activism had been present in the New World since the colonial period, the first rumblings of which emanated from Quaker communities in Pennsylvania. Importantly, even this earliest stage of anti-slavery work was transatlantic in nature, predicated on international coalitions and political pressure (Fladeland 1972). As New World Quakers sought to influence the policy decisions of their congregational brethren in the British mainland, they were inaugurating a tradition of transnational abolitionism that exists to this day (McDaniel 2013; Blackett 1983; Fladeland 1972; Rice and Crawford 1999; Mason 2002) and was reflected in the policy dialog between the 2012 California Supply Chain Transparency Act and the UK Modern Slavery Act of 2015 (Chap. 7).

After the American Revolution, the main political drama of the Atlantic anti-slavery movement took place in the British Empire. The British effort culminated in West Indies Emancipation in 1833 and the final fall of a transitional apprenticeship system in 1838. US activists played a role in these changes, but at the dawn of the 1830s, the USA was fast becoming the stronghold of proslavery policy and economic thought (on British anti-slavery, see Huzzy 2012; Brown 2006; Anstey 1975; Temperley 1972).

A new coalition of activists committed to the immediate and uncompensated abolition of slavery arose, led by Massachusetts printer William Lloyd Garrison. The emergence of immediatism and its Garrisonian proselytizers marked an intensification of the slavery debate in the USA as southern intransigence became intensified and sectional lines deepened (Davis 1962; Kraditor 1969; Mayer 1998; Blight 2008). It is important to remember, especially when assessing modern anti-slavery work, that abolitionism has always been an internally fractious and divisive business. Garrison led the American Anti-Slavery Society, but by 1840 internal disagreements over political participation and the role of women reformers resulted in a group of activists splitting off to form the American and Foreign Anti-Slavery Association (for more on the many internal ruptures of the US abolition movement, see Harrold 2019; Perry 1973; Sewell 1976).

It is important to acknowledge, from a medical and public health standpoint, that this was an era of racial "science." Theories proliferated that sought to stratify human populations and scientifically cement ideas of racial difference. Pseudo-scientific theories were deployed to justify the enslavement and colonization of peoples deemed racially inferior (Chap. 15). In this regard, science was used as a powerful tool of empire and enslavement (Livingston 2008; Fabian 2010; Mitchell and Michael 2019; Gates and Gates 2019). For example, it was commonly claimed that US slaves of African descent were biologically predisposed to the labor and climate of plantation life. Moreover, it was argued that they were mentally and physically fitted for conditions of servitude. These scientific ideas of racial difference were often paired with religious—supposedly biblical—justifications for slavery, resulting in a nefarious amalgam of oppressive ideologies. The racist assumptions of early psychology and ethnography were so dominant that even anti-slavery scientists were drawn into using racial science. For example, George Combe, a leading phrenologist of the day (and an anti-slavery sympathizer) took the opportunity of Frederick Douglass's exile in the U.K. to analyze his skull, utilizing a host of racialized theories and assumptions (Blight and Black 2020; Black 2020). Combe expressed surprise that such an impressive man (Douglass) could have "been born and reared in slavery" (Combe 1846). One might hope racial prejudice would not similarly be reflected in modern scientific assessments, but that hope might be easily dashed. Healthcare resources are still allocated based on race, and such practices are promoted by reputable professional organizations, no less (Peterson 2010; Levey 2009; Grobman 2007) (Chap. 14).

9.2.7   Fugitive Slaves: Activists, Symbols, and Flashpoints

US abolitionism cannot be understood without centering the actions of fugitive slaves (Blackett 2018; Brooke 2019). Politically, runaways were constant reminders to both Northerners and Southerners of the injustice of slavery, its utter reliance on force and coercion, and the unsteady nature of its continued existence. Culturally, abolitionist fugitives, through their narratives and activism, showed the lie of White supremacist tropes of Black unimprovability or the "need" for slavery as a civilizing and paternalistic blessing. Economically, fugitive slaves were a risk to not only the slave owners' bottom line, but were a living affront to the idea that people could be property.

Article IV of the Constitution committed the Federal Government to return captured fugitives, but Southerners were perennially dissatisfied with the lackluster enforcement of the clause. Contentions over the issue led to the passage of the Fugitive Slave Act as part of the Compromise of 1850. The Act dictated a far more stringent legal regime for the return of fugitives that many Northerners saw as a massive infringement on the right of their States to legislate on such matters. The law went so far as to allow slave catchers and law enforcement to forcibly deputize and compel citizens to aid in the arrest of supposed fugitives.

To the average Northern citizen who had viewed abolitionism as an activism to be mildly tolerated, it suddenly seemed as if the Southern slave power was infiltrating the North. The South's great legislative victory was too big of a win, bringing slavery directly into Northern households. As a result, previously uninvolved communities began to engage with Free Labor ideologies (Chap. 14). Southern politicians suddenly felt the ground slipping from under them and were determined to preserve slavery by whatever means necessary. Having lost their political advantage within the Union, they sought to disband the country. As W.E.B. DuBois remarked, "[i]f nationalism had been a stronger defense of the slave system than particularism, the South would have been as nationalistic in 1861 as it had been in 1812" (DuBois 1928).

9.2.8   Emancipation and Abolition

The Civil War brought about the central legal paradigm shift in the US anti-slavery movement. In the short period between the bombardment of Fort Sumter in April 1861 to the ratification of the Thirteenth Amendment in December 1865, the USA transformed from a nation with economic, social, and political structures built around chattel slavery to one with a legal apparatus for combating involuntary servitude. This moment of Emancipation and ultimate abolition is crucial for consideration not only because it was the culmination of generations of anti-slavery activism (Berlin 2015) but also because it is the cornerstone of US anti-slavery policy both domestically and internationally to this day.

9.2.9 Emancipation: Freedom by Executive Order

Abraham Lincoln's successful run for president in 1860 lead to a cascading sequence of secession and disunion. Rather than submit to what they saw as an abolitionist victory that would lead to emancipation, eleven southern states broke away from the USA and formed a new confederacy to preserve slavery. While he was the first president elected on an anti-slavery platform, Lincoln stressed the maintenance of the Union above all else as he took office. His anti-slavery policies were largely expressed through his decision to allow the execution of a US sea-captain who was one of the few US citizens to be charged under the Slave Trade Acts (Soodalter, 2006). Two years into war, however, Lincoln saw in emancipation the convergence of his moral convictions and military obligations.

Invoking his wartime powers as commander-in-chief, Lincoln's Emancipation Proclamation went into effect on January 1, 1863. The document declared that all slaves held in rebelling areas of the country "are, and henceforward shall be free; and that [the Executive Branch,] including the military and naval authorities thereof, will recognize and maintain the freedom of said persons." Lincoln justified the Proclamation out of "military necessity" (Foner 2019).

The Proclamation was not just a freedom order, but for Radical Republicans also one based on the equality principle—it invited newly freed African American men to join the US Army and Navy, a badge of citizenship in a country that had denied their membership in the US polity since the Founding. Survivors of slavery were suddenly not simply free, but could become soldiers in an army of liberation. In practice, equality was not so simply achieved and African American soldiers served in segregated units. Still, the armed Black rebellion that had dominated Southern fears since Haitian independence came to fruition in Union blue uniforms.

While a watershed moment, the Emancipation Proclamation did not solidify abolition—far from it. The military still had to defeat the Southern rebellion and make the guarantees of the Proclamation real. Further, under the Proclamation, slavery technically still existed in the border states that had remained in the Union and in other regions of the South that were already under federal military control. An Executive Order such as the Proclamation—and especially one based on emergency wartime powers—did not have the legal force necessary to abolish slavery entirely. Abolition had to be cemented in the US Constitution, where it would override all other laws and be protected from subsequent repeal or change. While celebrating the Proclamation, abolitionists immediately agitated for Congress to bolster it with legislation and ultimately a constitutional amendment.

9.2.10 Abolition: Legal Freedom by Constitutional Amendment

The text of the Thirteenth Amendment was submitted by the Senate Judiciary Committee led by Senator Lyman Trumbull of Illinois. Written to echo the Northwest Ordinance of 1787, the first clause reads: "Neither slavery nor involuntary servitude, except as a punishment for crime whereof the party shall have been duly convicted, shall exist within the United States, or any place subject to their jurisdiction." The second clause equips the Federal Government with the necessary authority to ensure the freedom of US citizens: "Congress shall have power to enforce this article by appropriate legislation" (US Const. Amend. XIII).

Writing later, then-congressman James G. Blaine described how, through the Amendment, "the relation between the national and state governments, respecting the question of human liberty, was radically changed. … Freedom of the person became henceforth a matter of national concern" (Foner 2019). The Amendment was eventually passed by the House of Representatives on January 31, 1865, countersigned by President Lincoln the next day to demonstrate its importance, and sent to the states for ratification. The Amendment was fully ratified on December 18, 1865. Multi-generational chattel slavery of African Americans, negating their civil rights, denying their citizenship, and reducing them to property, was no longer legal. The status of "slave" was legally no more.

9.2.11   The Thirteenth Amendment as a Forward-looking Rights Guarantee

The Thirteenth Amendment did not simply end legal chattel slavery in 1865. Keeping with Douglass's warning a few months later, the Amendment recognized that, if denied the comfort of state support, slaveholders would hold others in service through other strategies of force, violence, and threats. By including the term "involuntary servitude" into its provisions, both the Thirteenth Amendment and its predecessor (the Northwest Ordinance) recognized that there were different forms of unfree labor in the USA, in addition to chattel slavery. This was to prove critical in the years following the Civil War, as government, business, and vulnerable communities sought to navigate a system in which forms of enslavement were no longer based on the status of the person, but on the actions of the employer in compelling their service (Scott 2017).

Furthermore, the Thirteenth Amendment made chattel slavery of African Americans illegal, but did so without naming them specifically as the only involved group, as had antebellum anti-slavery policies. Soon after enactment and ratification of the Amendment, at a time when the postwar economy was improving, new labor arrangements were needed. In a time of transition with dramatic territorial expansion and the arrival of new immigrant communities, alternate forms of exploitation—not always arranged on the Black/White binary but often still arranged by race or ethnicity—became apparent. The applicability of the Amendment's protections to all parts of the country and to populations other than formerly enslaved African Americans was recognized by the Supreme Court in *The Slaughterhouse Cases*. But, even as federal laws and additional constitutional amendments were promulgated to protect and advance hard-won freedom, former masters in the South were exploring legal loopholes in an attempt to replicate their prior economic and social power in a post-Emancipation world.

9.2.12   Expansion to Other Groups—The Peonage Act and the Padrone Statute

The Multicultural, Multiracial West: Mexicans, Native Americans, and the Peonage Act

Soon after the ratification of the Thirteenth Amendment, Congress enacted a statute which dominated US anti-slavery jurisprudence for much of the next 75 years: the Peonage Act. While it was a product of a postwar Free Labor consensus (Reséndez 2017), the statute actually had its roots in the antebellum colonization of Northern Mexico in the late 1840s. With western US expansion came tough political questions; one of the national political flashpoints around 1850s' slavery policy was the newly acquired Territory of New Mexico. As they had for decades, the slave states pursued the westward expansion of slavery lest they lose their sectional advantage and voting power in Congress. But even as Congress debated whether African American chattel slavery would be imposed on the seized lands, the occupying US Army was wrestling with another form of slavery, outside of the Anglo-American legal tradition and the Black/White paradigm.

In New Mexico, peonage took several forms, but as in most of Spanish America, it did not extinguish the enslaved persons' civil, social, and natal rights as did chattel slavery in the English-speaking Atlantic world. As the cash economy began to emerge with the opening of trade routes to the USA, peonage became linked to repayment of debts, rather than village-level economic and security responsibilities reminiscent of feudal-era Spain. Another group of enslaved people came from sporadic raiding; while New Mexican children kidnapped by Native raiders were often incorporated into tribal life, Native children kidnapped by New Mexicans were often sold into families as domestic servants. Newly imposed US laws and enforcement efforts were often ineffective in detangling this swirl of "complex relations of captivity, slavery, debt peonage, household dependence, and kinship ties born of centuries of borderlands raiding and trading" (Smith 2015). With colonization by the USA, racial classifications of Spanish and Mexican social systems were scrambled—New Mexicans who had considered themselves White and Christian in comparison to the independent Native communities around them were suddenly assigned racial minority status and their Catholicism dismissed as naïve superstition (Weber 1973).

Territorial officials wrestled with the practice of peonage, especially since chattel slavery was legal in so much of the USA, as was noted by the New Mexico Supreme Court in *Jaremillo v. Romero*, 1 N.M. 90 (1857). In refusing to allow the forcible return of an escaped woman to her master, the Territorial Court declined to grant New Mexican landowners the same property rights enjoyed by their Southern counterparts. After Emancipation, military officials used the Thirteenth Amendment to free *peones* from service, but ran up against widespread evasion by landowners who continue to hold their servants in bondage and had even used the confusion of the Civil War to raid Indian villages for additional child slaves (Rael-Gálvez 2002).

Accordingly, a frustrated Congress in 1867 passed the Peonage Act. While the debates were not extensive, the attention paid to the racial aspects of New Mexico demonstrates that the framers of the Peonage Act[2] were purposeful in expanding the freedom right to all racial groups.

Senators seemed to not quite know how to classify the residents of the Territory along US racial hierarchies. For Senator James Doolittle, who had been leading a Congressional inquiry into the conditions of Native Americans, including those in New Mexico, the racial distinction between Indians and New Mexicans was blurry: "a majority of the Mexicans are of Indian blood, with some Spanish blood intermixed" (US Congress 1867a).

For Senator Henry Wilson, on the other hand, Mexicans—not being Black— were White:

> It is certainly a most wretched system. It applies not to negroes, but to White men; and while I have great faith in the negro I believe a White man is as good as a negro and while I have been against negro slavery I am also against slavery of this kind for White men. I hope we all put the bill on its passage, and I have no doubt good results will grow out of it (US Congress 1867b).

Regardless of the racial classification of the peonage system, Congress could agree that it had not faded away by virtue of the *Jaremillo* case and federal investigations. Senator Charles Buckalew perhaps summed up the immediate postwar consensus about any form of slavery being anathema: "It is a system which degrades both the owner of the labor and the labor itself, and in my opinion the sooner we terminate the better" (US Congress 1867c).The new statute's expansion of the Thirteenth Amendment's coverage to the Latino and Native American communities was to prove important, not only as it stood for the universality of the right beyond the newly freed African American community, but because the Peonage Act itself was to eventually find its most important use not in New Mexico, but as a way for Progressive Era civil rights activists and reformers in the Federal Government to attack what has been termed "the re-enslavement of Black Americans" in the South (Blackmon 2008).

New Mexico was not the only colonized area in which the expanding USA encountered traditional slavery systems. In Alaska—obtained by purchase after the promulgation of the Thirteenth Amendment—a highly developed slavery system existed with social, economic, and religious aspects, including ritual mutilation and the killing of some slaves upon their masters' death. US courts in the sparsely populated territory wrestled with extending US laws to the Native Alaskan community, both in cases of slavery and in high-profile public cases of domestic violence. In *In re Sah Quah*, the US District Court freed an enslaved Native Alaskan and abolished slavery among the Tlingit as inconsistent with the Thirteenth Amendment and the 1866 Civil Rights Act. But as in New Mexico, the expansion of such protections to previously powerless parts of Alaskan society was not received enthusiastically. The *Sah Quah* decision was seen by some not as a welcome application of federally

---

[2]Act of March 2, 1867, US Statutes at Large, 29th Cong., Sess. II., Chp. 187, p. 546.

protected rights, but as having been a setup to strip the Tlingit of their tribal sovereignty.

Urban Immigrants: The Padrone Act

In 1874, Congress passed the "Padrone Statute,"[3] the official title of which was "An Act to protect persons of foreign birth against forcible constraint or involuntary servitude," intending to "prevent the practice of enslaving, buying, selling, or using Italian children, a practice which [was] so common in the large cities of our country" 2 Cong. Rec. 4443 (1874) (Rep. Cessna). The statute was soon tested in a criminal case, *United States v. Ancarola*, in which several traffickers were convicted for trafficking children into street entertainment by making false promises to their parents of a better life in the United States.

Notably, the Padrone Statute recognized that confronting unscrupulous recruitment and inveiglement of immigrants was an integral part of a post-Emancipation freedom agenda. In tandem with the Peonage Statute, this law would over the coming decades shift the ultimate question in slavery litigation to one of how victims were placed into or held in compelled service (as opposed to antebellum court cases which typically turned on whether a person was not a slave and should be released or returned to service). Such a legal approach brought what would otherwise be state-level assaults and threats into federal purview—a powerful tool in situations where Southern law enforcement collaborated with employers to maintain a system of debt bondage. For the federal statutes to fully reach that promise would take decades. However, the dominance of the Peonage Statute had the unintended consequence of excluding cases from federal action in which flat-out coercion was used to compel and maintain service, rather than service in repayment of a debt. It would not be until 1941 that the USA conclusively shifted away from the concept of debt as a determinative evidentiary threshold for even bringing a prosecution.

9.2.13   The South and the "Reenslavement" of Black Americans

As predicted by Douglass, White Southerners moved to quickly replace slavery with a simulacrum of the system under which they had profited. Part of a broad-scale stripping of African American communities of rights, the reestablishment of servitude in the late 1800s through sharecropping, debt bondage, and various forms of convict labor schemes set a pattern of brutality and exploitation, covered with a thin veneer of legality, that has marked Southern agriculture and other forms of labor to the modern day. Initial attempts to use debt bondage to reenslave newly

---

[3] Act of June 23, 1874, ch. 464. 18 Stat. 251.

emancipated communities ran up against a vigorous federal resistance from the Grant Administration. The Administration used the military and the Freedman's Bureau not only to prevent violence against African Americans but also to ensure that they obtained the benefit of the freedom and equality principles of the Thirteenth and Fourteenth Amendments and the political participation of the Fifteenth Amendment. But by the late 1870s, the Federal Government's political capital to sustain such efforts had already faded and with it the protections accessible to the African American community. Southern states quickly set up integrated corrections and economic systems, once again tapping the coercive power of the state to ensure availability, compliance, and cheap labor from the African American community.

Southern state legislatures took advantage of the Thirteenth Amendment's exclusion of labor as a consequence of a crime for which one had been duly convicted to allow for convict leasing. In this way, employers could rent convicts from the state, or even from local jails. The combination of zealous policing, profit motives for local sheriffs and justices of the peace, and the desire of unscrupulous employers for exploitable labor was too great a temptation. Despite a series of successful prosecutions and Supreme Court cases over an almost fifty-year period, the practice did not officially come to an end until 1944, and its echoes live on in current systems of incarceration, prison labor, and policing (Chap. 11).

9.2.14   The 1909 Recodification of US Criminal Statutes

In 1908, as part of a wholesale revision of federal criminal law, Congress recodified the various strands of anti-slavery legislation. This effort is most notable as the moment in which the anti-involuntary servitude and anti-slavery statutes were deracinated. These laws were combined into a unified statute that would apply to all individuals rather than having piecemeal laws for different racial or ethnic groups.

In considering the updates, some legislators, like Senator Frederick Hale of Maine, resisted inclusion of anti-slavery provisions in the new version of federal law. Hale claimed that slavery statutes "sound like echoes of the dead past" that were rendered useless by the mere fact of the Thirteenth Amendment's ratification years before. On the Senate floor, he sarcastically noted that had lawmakers "found upon the statute books, lurking there unobserved from the traditions of the past, provisions for the punishment of witchcraft, we would be confronted with a situation not more practical and not less commending itself to our attention and to our legislation than these" anti-slavery laws. (Congressional Record—Senate, January 27 1908a, p. 1114).

In contrast, the manager of the bill, Senator Heyburn of Idaho, while admitting that the institution of African American chattel slavery had been extinguished by ratification, argued that "other conditions have arisen" which demanded the extension of these laws to protect those of all races. Heyburn warned of the coerced labor of Japanese and Chinese immigrants (Chap. 10) and reminded his colleagues that "[m]any of these people who have been brought to this country even up to the present day for the purposes of slavery, or what amounts to slavery" were not of African descent, yet they required legal protection from involuntary servitude. Senator Heyburn worried that if the slavery laws were not brought forward in the new statutes, the language of the Thirteenth Amendment alone was not enough to prevent all forms of human trafficking. "The sections under consideration give life, virility, and meaning to that provision of this Constitution," he proclaimed.

Senators were not just concerned about slaveries that might persist on the soil of the mainland USA, but were particularly cognizant of the problems of the US Empire. Senator Heyburn, in justifying the need to keep the anti-slavery statutes on the books, argued that the recent acquisition of the Philippines from Spain made it "particularly necessary that such legislation should be kept upon the statute books, since we have obtained the responsibility as well as the control of some lands in which other customs than those with which we have of late been familiar obtain." In order to "protect those helpless people" the USA needed "this real weapon of law" (p. 1114–6, Congressional Record—Senate, January 27 1908b).

Another key moment in the Senate debate occurred when Senator Henry Cabot Lodge of Massachusetts described his previous work on the Padrone Statute:

> I happened to be one of those who made investigation into what was known as the padrone system. The padrones were men in New York who brought boys out from Italy and let them out for various purposes – shoeblacks, and one tiling and another of that sort – and the boys were held in a condition of practical slavery. We have tried to meet some of these difficulties by our immigration laws, but the fact that slavery has been abolished, the fact that it is a crime, does not seem to me to make it desirable, therefore, to do away with all the statutes which were designed to punish the crime and which make it a crime. The declaration of the thirteenth amendment to the Constitution is not of itself sufficient...

Putting his considerable political weight behind Heyburn, Lodge argued that a proper recodification and strengthening of anti-slavery laws were necessary because forms of slavery did in fact still exist in the USA and the Thirteenth Amendment needed subsequent legislation to make its promise of freedom a reality. It was Congress's duty to pass such legislation, as the Constitution itself was "not self-executing" (p. 1122, Congressional Record—Senate, January 27 1908c).

The recodification statutes faced other opposition. On the House side, Representative Brantley of Georgia invoked "state sovereignty" and sought to amend the peonage laws to "require the Government to prove, in addition to all that must now be proved, the further fact that the act committed was permitted or sanctioned by the State." Brantley's efforts aimed to dilute the Federal Government's ability to implement anti-slavery laws against private actors by forcing the government to prove that a "system" of peonage existed. Such loopholes had been proffered in courts by Southern employers, but had been rejected by the Supreme Court (pp. 2587–9, Congressional Record—House, Feb. 17 1909).

Congressman Brantley's amendment lost, but was one of many similar attempts to water down the anti-slavery statutes if they could not be omitted entirely. As in the Senate, representatives from states whose economies were still organized around exploited African American or immigrant labor were particularly vocal in trying to characterize anti-slavery laws as no longer needed in the modern era. These attempts failed, and the disparate criminal laws of the 1800s were combined into two main categories: peonage and kidnapping/inveiglement for slavery.

The 1909 Recodification was not an entire success because of a competing framework that undercut the very arguments the Progressive reformers were making in defense of the anti-slavery statutes. Outlining legal ideas still vital to US anti-slavery law, Senator Heyburn explained that "[w]hether this service be for manual labor or whether it be for immoral purposes [prostitution] is immaterial; if it is a service enforced upon those parties against their will or without their consent or pursuant to a contract to which they are not a party, all of these conditions would be slavery within" federal law. (p. 1116, Congressional Record—Senate, January 27 1908b). But Senator Heyburn's bold statement of the coverage of modern, deracinated, service-neutral anti-slavery statutes was to be contradicted within a year, through the passage of the White Slave Trafficking Act. This law separated antiprostitution from anti-slavery statutes and assumed the experience of White women in prostitution as one of exploitation *per se*. That bifurcation was to characterize the next ninety-years of anti-slavery law, with the WSTA and the civil rights statutes developing not only separate jurisprudences, but separate enforcement cultures and bureaucratic structures.

9.2.15 An Alternative Origin of Anti-trafficking: Women, Cities, and "White Slavery"

Periodic anti-slavery reforms in the USA have often been quickly subsumed into competing and more entrenched efforts with less progressive intent. They may take the form of exclusionary immigration policies (Chap. 10), the use of criminal enforcement to maintain "social order," or the regulation of public morals, gender, and racial roles.

"White Slavery": A Concept that Requires Neither Whiteness nor Slavery

What is "White slavery" and why was transportation for illegal sexual activity (the modern title in the US Criminal Code) described in those terms? In the Victorian Era, reformers in both England and the USA—either abolitionists themselves or children of leading abolitionists—often looked to the success of the anti-slavery project for inspiration and guidance. Reform work against social ills that could be characterized as an extension of prior anti-slavery activism received the benefit of moral or political high ground, historical legacy, and a ready-made cast of activists who could be rallied around the current political and social incarnations of the social justice fight (Lui 2009). In the late 1800s, social movements often had a distinct gender aspect, with the protection of women's "morality" being highly valued. Women's "morality" was particularly in the limelight during this time in which traditional Western family and social roles were changing and young women were obtaining work in urban areas away from their families or communities.

The British and French experience with migratory prostitution centered around White discomfort with European women being used for prostitution with Arab men.

Those nation's efforts to control White women's prostitution were reminiscent of the early years of anti-slavery activism in the United States and Britain. In the migratory prostitution arena, Britain and France focused on legal instruments attacking the trade (or "traffic") as opposed to actual enslavement. "White slavery," a term initially coined to describe the plight of child laborers, such as the London match girls who had gone on strike rather than suffering continued death and disfigurement (Chap. 3), quickly became a euphemism for the transnational prostitution of White women and girls. Attempts by non-White women and their defenders to seek protection – whether from abusive "pimps" or the state's deportation power, such as in the case of *In re Ah Sou* – were unsuccessful. Non-White women did not fit comfortably into racialized discourses around sex trafficking in a post-Reconstruction United States that was eager to overlook the continuing exploitation of Black citizens and paper over the realities of chattel slavery in the cause of reunion (Blight 2001). As Jessica Pliley points out, the new focus on "White Slavery" created a mythology that stripped chattel slavery of its "sexual and reproductive component" and reduced it to being understood only as a labor system rather than a "racial caste system." The 1890s' anti-trafficking discourse therefore posited that chattel slavery (once it was recast as only a problem of unpaid labor) was not as damaging as prostitution, in which the women were marked "with the loss of virtue" (Pliley 2014).

From a legal perspective, the rhetoric of slavery and exploitation that permeated the "White slave trafficking" diplomacy and activism of the time was just that— rhetoric. The laws passed under its banner did not require demonstration that someone be held in compelled service or indeed that she be White. Rather, the crime was to recruit or transport a woman[4] to cross a border for the purpose of immoral activity.

The term "traffic" immediately posed a problem. In Congressional debates, officials attempted to distinguish the traffic of "persons" from the traffic of "things," while others argued that, since it is an issue of morality, its regulation should be left up to the states. Supporters maintained that the states lacked the capacity to effectively regulate the "White slave" trade because of its cross-border and international dimensions. But passing a law that focused on the trade, rather than on the conditions of service, cast the women involved as a form of contraband, rather than individuals whose constitutional rights had been violated. Such a frame dehumanized the women, elided real-world relationships and experiences (Laite 2017), and when put into practice did not challenge law enforcement assumptions that they were co-conspirators with their "pimps." Such a divergence between legal reality and political rhetoric had consequences. Confronted with the reality that at least *some* percentage of women in transnational or interstate prostitution were not kidnapped or inveigled, law enforcement (and generations later, historians) began to discount the possibility that *any* were abused and in need of protection.

So too, the racial aspects of the law were troubling. First, the emotive power of the term "White" in the accepted label for cross-border vice offenses overrode in

---

[4] In the modern era, the White Slave Trafficking Act, as with all federal criminal laws, is gender-neutral (18 U.S.C., Section 2421) and sex trafficking is understood to affect all communities. For reformers and legislatures of the early 1900s, however, prostitution and trafficking were seen as a crime involving women and girls.

practice what might have been a helpful tool to protect women of color from abuse at the hands of traffickers. While some federal prosecutors of the time sought to use both the anti-peonage statutes and the new "White Slavery" statute to address the forced prostitution of African American women in turpentine camps through a civil rights lens (*New Orleans Times-Picayune* 1911), in the public's mind, the archetypal victim was White, US-born, innocent, and lured and trapped in prostitution in a city. Their traffickers were often assumed to be not the owner of the local juke joint or hotel, but foreign-born men (typically Chinese, Italian, or Jewish Eastern Europeans), or predatory African Americans. Not surprisingly, the White Slave Trafficking Act quickly became a tool to enforce anti-miscegenation attitudes, such as in the high-profile prosecution of boxer Jack Johnson. Such was the immediate dominance of the WSTA approach that with limited exceptions (such as in *Bernal v. United States*) the protections of the Thirteenth Amendment were not extended to women in brothels or other sites of the sex industry for almost a century.

The Precursor of the White Slave Trafficking Act: the Page Act

The focus of the WSTA on White womanhood and its attendant morality is actually in contrast to some of the initial political and policy uses of sex trafficking. Initially, the focus was on Asian immigrant populations, most specifically Chinese women in prostitution on the West Coast (Chap. 5). The WSTA must be viewed in light of a similar, more narrowly focused law from a generation earlier: the Page Act of 1875. After the Civil War, the US press was becoming nationalized and technology allowed for broad distribution of illustrated newspapers on a national scale. Horrifying images of people locked in cages in Chinatown brothels circulated widely and were eagerly seized upon by immigration restrictionists who were eager to cut off Chinese immigrants from competing with Whites as laborers and as nascent business leaders (Chap. 10).

The Page Act, crafted as a criminal statute to avoid abrogating a treaty between the USA and China that governed immigration policy, claimed to prohibit the recruitment or importation of Chinese men for forced labor and Chinese women for prostitution. It was actually used to cut off migration flow by denying Asian immigrants' entry, supposedly for their own protection from such abuses. Rather than seeking to vindicate Asian immigrants' right to be free from involuntary servitude, the Page Act (and its progeny the Chinese Exclusion Act) misused the rhetoric of free labor and sexual morality to deny rights to an entire race. While it is often seen as a precursor to the now regulated and securitized border, the Page Act can also be read as a White supremacist protectionist labor law. It was enthusiastically enacted despite attempts by the (at this point) weakening anti-slavery coalition to prevent such an injustice against a community that should have been allowed to contribute to a "Composite Nation" (Douglass 1867). The legacy of the racially exclusionary Page Act and the subsequent WSTA have fueled contemporary critiques of the modern anti-trafficking movement as merely a continued attempt to regulate women of color's sexuality and a rejection of the capacity of women to exercise agency (see, e.g., Pliley 2014; Peña Delgado 2012; Dozema 2010).

9.2.16   The Progressive Era: Robust Federal Activities Driving Jurisprudence

US law has developed not just via legislative action but through the enforcement patterns, practices, and litigation strategies of the various presidential administrations. Even at the height of explicitly institutionalized racism when Southern legislatures were codifying Jim Crow restrictions in new state constitutions, African American activists such as Booker T. Washington and White allies in philanthropy and government were pursuing strategic litigation to undercut the system of convict labor and debt bondage in the South. Some of the servitude was compelled and maintained through debts, beatings, and murders. Much of it, however, was conducted with a legal imprimatur: "a gigantic system of peonage with the aid of corrupt local law enforcement officials and justices of the peace" who leveraged such petty crimes as loitering and vagrancy to create debts that could be sold to employers whose workers would thus be bound to them by threat of arrest (Daniel 1970).

By the 1890s, while no longer able to hold legal title to Black workers, employers could once again access the state's police power to control and maintain their workforce, by leasing schemes that were allowable under the Thirteenth Amendment's prison labor exception. Under President Theodore Roosevelt, who was intent on providing a "Fair Deal" to Black citizens, a series of investigations and prosecutions, brought under the anti-peonage statute and led by a cadre of reformist Southern federal attorneys and judges, caught Southern political and business leaders off-guard. For the first time in a generation, there was vigorous enforcement against farmers and employers who enslaved Black workers.

Anti-slavery efforts were not limited to protecting African Americans, but extended to immigrant communities, with cases brought involving Italians who had been lured to the South for railroad building and other infrastructure projects (Daniel 1973). Anti-peonage enforcement continued into the Taft Administration, which tasked the US attorneys to submit periodic reports on cases under investigation. This was the beginning of a centralized civil rights program in the US Justice Department that would later be made official with dedicated staffing and bureaucratic structures within the agency.

The burst of anti-slavery enforcement activity in the Progressive Era was in keeping with the newfound spirit of government intervention and anti-poverty work that was to give that era its name. Reform efforts that have since been relegated to convenient silos (e.g., urban poverty reform, workers' rights, health and safety reforms in slaughterhouses, anti-sweatshop activism, immigrant rights) appear to have been much more interconnected in goals and personnel than convenient historical categorization, or ahistorical anti-trafficking efforts, would suggest.

9.2.17   The Jurisprudence of the Peonage Era

Much of the case law that was developed during the Progressive Era anti-peonage push was actively used up to the passage of the TVPA, and while the language is from a more formal time, the issues and rulings will be familiar to current anti-trafficking practitioners. Most notably, Judge Thomas G. Jones' detailed instructions to an Alabama federal grand jury in 1903's *Peonage Cases* define the offense squarely as a violation of rights, and in many ways, his instructions remain the definitive description of the offense:

> The condition of peonage, therefore, to which it is forbidden to hold or return any person, by the express words of the statute, means the situation or status in which a person is placed, including the physical and moral results of returning or holding such person to perform labor or service, by force either of law or custom, or by force of lawless acts of individuals unsupported by local law, "in liquidation of any debt, obligation, or otherwise." The phrase "condition of peonage" means the actual status, physical and moral, with the inevitable incidents to which the employee, servant, or debtor was reduced under that system, when held to involuntary performance or liquidation of his obligation—the effect thereby produced upon the person, liberties, and rights of a man held in such a situation (The Peonage Cases 1903).

The Thirteenth Amendment's prison labor exception was misused to perpetuate compelled labor, but it was not an absolute carve-out.[5] Challenges were brought not only by federal prosecutors but by attorneys secretly acting on behalf of Booker T. Washington, who supported the development and litigation of *Bailey v. Alabama*. This was a complex case that went to the Supreme Court on two separate occasions before finally invalidating the Alabama convict leasing scheme. Beginning in the late 1890s, the Supreme Court found itself repeatedly addressing forced labor practices through a series of cases that eventually wore down the practice by revealing the bad faith of the Southern legislatures. They had carefully constructed convict leasing schemes to evade the Thirteenth Amendment's guarantee of freedom. Their attempts to maintain this "slavery by another name" (Blackmon 2008) were couched in the pro-business sensibilities of the day, in which the dominant legal approach was to defer to the primacy of contract. This approach was prominently displayed by United States Supreme Court Justice Oliver Wendell Holmes' pattern of "tender regard for both sectionalism[6] and the right of employers" (Daniel 1970). Eventually, Southern legislators' continued evasion of the spirit of the Supreme Court cases exhausted even Holmes' patience. In 1914, he joined his colleagues in holding Alabama's convict leasing scheme unconstitutional in *United States v. Reynolds* and finally recognized that the state statutes were constructed not to preserve freedom of contract but to create a system of forced labor through sham debts.

---

[5] "Carve-out" is the legal term for something written in a law that creates an exception for a particular group or situation.

[6] Judges and policymakers of the time routinely tempered anti-slavery rulings or legislation by disavowing any hint of servitude being a Southern phenomenon. Localized peonage of Scandinavians in Northern logging camps and labor conditions of European immigrants in urban areas were used in political discourse to set up a false equivalence that supported the project of national reconciliation at the cost of African American civil rights and a whitewashing of the causes of the Civil War (Blight 2001).

9.2.18 An Industry-Specific Approach: the Seaman's Protection Act

The idea that certain sectors were outside of the reach of the Thirteenth Amendment was not limited to prison labor, and Southern business interests were not alone in seeking to exclude "their" economic sectors from its coverage. The shipping industry had long relied on its ability to use law enforcement to return runaway seamen to their ships even if they had been forcibly impressed. In 1897, in the case of *Robertson v. Baldwin*, the Supreme Court was faced with a federal statute that authorized warrants for the return of deserting sailors to their captains. For the majority, it seemed dispositive that, "[f]rom the earliest historical period, the contract of the sailor has been treated as an exceptional one, and involving, to a certain extent, the surrender of his personal liberty during the life of the contract," lest "the sailor...desert the ship at a critical moment or leave her at some place where seamen are impossible to be obtained." That the sailor might have, in the first instance, been kidnapped or drugged was of no import.

Justice Harlan's dissent in favor of the freedom principle of the Thirteenth rings today louder than the majority opinion:

> The Thirteenth Amendment, although tolerating involuntary servitude only when imposed as a punishment for crime of which the party shall have been duly convicted, has been construed by the decision just rendered as if it contained an additional clause expressly excepting from its operation seamen who engage to serve on private vessels. Under this view of the Constitution, we may now look for advertisements not for runaway servants as in the days of slavery, but for runaway seamen. In former days, overseers could stand with whip in hand over slaves, and force them to perform personal service for their masters. While, with the assent of all, that condition of things has ceased to exist, we can but be reminded of the past, when it is adjudged to be consistent with the law of the land for freemen, who happen to be seamen, to be held in custody that they may be forced to go aboard private vessels and render personal services against their will. (*Robertson v. Baldwin*, 165 U.S. at 288, Harlan, J. dissenting)

The Supreme Court's conservative reading of the Thirteenth Amendment in *Robertson* would lead to Congressional action, as abuses at sea mounted. The 1915 Merchant Seamen Welfare Act not only demonstrates the multifaceted manifestations of compelled service, but the USA's repeated tendency to address exploitation in a piecemeal or sectoral manner, rather than through a unified anti-slavery guarantee.

Shocked by revelations in the press and concerned about the *Robertson* decision having exempted sailors from the protection of the Thirteenth Amendment, Congress engaged in lengthy hearings about involuntary servitude on ships. But, as with the debates around the WSTA five years earlier, representatives initially disagreed about the proper course of action. While some believed that regulation was necessary across the board, others raised concerns about the effect of federal action on "independent" ship owners who may be pushed out of business if they had to abide by stringent regulation. The scope of debate was extensive, ranging beyond simply involuntary servitude, but also confronting workplace safety regulations. Reflecting a commerce-based sectoral approach rather than a freedom-based analysis, many attempts were made to tailor the legislation's reach for different types of ships, practices, and industries.

9.2.19   The War on Crime, the New Deal, and the Creation of the Civil Rights Section

The 1920s saw the growth of federal law enforcement, especially in the form of the Federal Bureau of Investigation. The first leader of what was initially called the Bureau of Investigation, Stanley Finch had been the lead investigator on a number of Peonage Cases, and was thereafter given the task of implementing the WSTA. Even as he set up the enforcement mechanisms for the new law, he questioned its necessity, telling Congressional committees that forced prostitution should have been addressed under the Thirteenth Amendment rather than the commerce clause. He called out the shortcoming of the federal servitude statutes that required showing that a "person had been, in the first instance, kidnapped or carried away or bought or sold" (Pliley 2014).

Under J. Edgar Hoover, the Bureau dramatically shifted its attention away from the politically and racially relevant peonage cases. The FBI leveraged the anti-vice enforcement regime of the WSTA, not as an opportunity to vindicate the rights of abused prostitutes or to fight for their redemption as Finch might have wanted, but rather to build agency authority vis-a-vis other federal agencies and local police forces as part of a national War on Crime. Political priorities shifted from combatting prostitution to punishing sexual practices (such as pedophilia, miscegenation, and adultery) crimes which previously would have been handled by local law enforcement, if at all. As US ideas of morality and women's sexuality changed, so too did the FBI's, until the women in WSTA cases became seen not as the victims of cruel traffickers and lecherous clients, but instead as cogs in the machine of organized crime or as tough co-conspirators with their "pimps." These women were now seen as a public health threat to respectable women whose husbands used prostitutes' services (Pliley 2014). For the 1930s FBI, riding high on its highly publicized war against organized crime, using the anti-slavery statutes to protect Black people who were held in servitude was a low priority because of Blacks' low social value; similarly, the efficacy of using the WSTA or any other law to protect prostituted women and girls from abuse was cynically relegated to a reformers' fantasy.

9.2.20   The New Deal: Worker Protections Through both Free Labor and Anti-slavery Lenses

The civil rights lens came back into play under Roosevelt's New Deal. The 1930s saw increased anti-slavery enforcement on the part of the Justice Department, in part due to public pressure from civil rights and workers' organizations concerned about the continued practice of peonage in the South. The time saw the establishment of civilian anti-peonage societies and the formation of DOJ's Civil Rights Section to guide investigations and prosecutions from headquarters rather than simply serving an advisory function as in the Progressive Era. Section prosecutors developed an expanded vision of the Thirteenth Amendment, going beyond debt bondage for agricultural labor to include domestic service, forced prostution, and even labor rights at work (Goluboff 2009).

The Fair Labor Standards Act

But, simultaneously, New Deal wage protections under the Fair Labor Standards Act (FLSA) specifically omitted from coverage two areas that had traditionally been concentrated in African American or immigrant populations: domestic work and agricultural labor. Child labor was also not initially regulated, on the now-outdated assumption that the bulk of US agriculture was on small, family-owned farms.

Just as convicts were specifically excluded from the Thirteenth Amendment, as seamen were excluded from its protection by the Supreme Court in Robertson, and as prostitutes were excluded from its protection by the application and assumptions surrounding the WSTA, the exclusion of farmworkers and domestic servants from the Fair Labor Standards Act left them vulnerable to exploitation. The FLSA limited the reach of labor inspectors and others who might ameliorate poor working conditions or uncover involuntary servitude. In response to Edward R. Murrow's 1961 documentary "*Harvest of Shame*" and the farmworker activism of the 1960s, the Agricultural Worker Protection Act (later renamed the Migrant and Seasonal Worker Protection Act, or MSPA) was passed, bringing some modicum of coverage to the agricultural sector though not the full protections of the FLSA.

Such exclusions from coverage of administrative labor protections have a domino effect. If FLSA or MSPA, or other labor laws, do not apply to a segment of the economy, then an industry's only regulation ends up being law enforcement's application of the involuntary servitude statutes. And even at the time of this writing, rather than the myriad daily humiliations suffered by domestic servants and farmworkers, anti-involuntary servitude statutes only cover the worst and most discoverable abuses. Anti-slavery and workers' rights groups have revealed structural issues within employment-based immigration, including temporary guest worker programs; workers who are brought into the country by diplomats; or students who work while in a cultural exchange program.

The Roosevelt and Truman Administrations: the Rise of Involuntary Servitude

In the late 1930s, the newly formed Civil Rights Section of the Justice Department's Criminal Division was the locus of federal peonage work. Anti-peonage societies— the precursor to the modern civil rights movement—pushed the government to revisit the persistent, exploitative practices in the South. The activities of the civil rights prosecutors were given a major boost in 1941, with the issuance of the "Biddle Memo." Coming the week after the attack on Pearl Harbor, this directive to the field is often seen by scholars as a US response to Nazi and Japanese propaganda, which highlighted the unjust conditions of African Americans in the US South. The Nazis and Japanese used these truths in an attempt to undercut African American participation in US mobilization and to push back against US diplomatic objections to their treatment of occupied China or the European Jewish community.

In the memo, Attorney General Francis Biddle communicated to federal prosecutors and agents that involuntary servitude cases were to be given high priority and that they should no longer confine their activities to cases involving a debt (peonage), but should take on all cases of compelled service. To drive this point home, the official title of the federal effort was changed from "Peonage" to "Involuntary Servitude and Slavery," a title that the enforcement program would carry for the next sixty years. To ensure uniformity in bringing and dismissing cases, and to signal prioritization, an internal reporting regime was announced. The scheme required immediate notification of new matters to the Civil Rights Section and mandated that indictments be approved by headquarters.

The Biddle memo spoke to many of the issues that needed to be addressed in implementing the Palermo Protocol decades later: the abuse of a position of vulnerability; the irrelevance of initial consent after coercion; and the difficulty of victim identification. The Biddle Memo mandated a holistic inquiry, in which overt force, threats, or intimidation need not be shown; the federal statutes applied whether the victim was made *either* to enter into or remain in service; and occasional kind treatment of the victim by the exploiter was not a defense.

The resulting Involuntary Servitude and Slavery enforcement push gathered many of the concepts that would later be enshrined in the TVPA and the Palermo Protocol as a global standard. It also demonstrated a transformed understanding of what involuntary servitude cases could look like. Previously, the "typical" peonage case, in both legal application and cultural assumptions, involved African American men in agricultural labor, often under a contract or bonding scheme. This vision of slavery was so broad that it allowed for the wholly different approach of the WSTA; previously, policymakers and activists did not conceive of slavery statutes as applying to women (even though African American women were obviously also enslaved in chattel slavery, and sexual abuse and even enslavement for commercial sexual activity were common).

Following the Biddle Memo, federal prosecutors began to bring cases involving female domestic servants and even used the ISS statutes rather than the WSTA in a sex trafficking case (*Pierce v. United States*). At the time, the commonly invoked slavery trope involved a Black male field hand as the victimized; this relied on an incomplete picture of the genders of Blacks enslaved. The new approach began to make good on Senator Heyward's admonishment in the 1908 recodification debates: The anti-slavery laws did not only protect against the abuse of a segment of the population (enslaved male field hands) but against the violation of *anyone*'s right to be free from involuntary servitude, regardless of their gender or industry of exploitation.

The 1940s also saw the final court cases against the convict leasing system, which had lived on in Florida and Georgia despite the successful cases against it in Alabama. In *Pollock v. Williams* (1944), which effectively ended the practice, Justice Robert Jackson characterized the 1867 Peonage Act as effectuating the Thirteenth Amendment by having "raised both a shield and a sword against forced labor." As a shield, the amendment protected against state supported exploitation, and as a sword, it was used by the state to punish and prevent private actors who would hold someone in servitude.

9.2.21   *Quantum of Coercion versus Type of Coercion*

With White businessmen moving away from use of debt peonage to involuntary servitude and the Department of Justice following the standards of the Biddle Memo, a new problem faced investigators, prosecutors, and victims' advocates in the National Association for the Advancement of Colored People and other organizations: how to demonstrate victim compulsion without the "objective" fact of an underlying debt. Much of the law since the 1940s has wrestled with this balancing test and it continues to play out in the TVPA era in both civil and criminal cases. Courts have long wrestled with this tension: If the crime is one of overbearing someone's will (a subjective condition) to compel service, are courts to merely accept a worker's claims as to their then-existing mental state, or should there be more objectively observable facts? Are there some managerial activities that are abusive or offensive, but should not be seen as unconstitutionally compulsive? Much as the debt had served as a proxy in the Peonage practice years, during the ISS years, the objective aspect of these cases came in the form of judicially recognized objective means of coercion. These included the use of force, threats of force, or threats of legal coercion tantamount to imprisonment. Such an approach, however, failed to fully capture the psychological dimensions of the crime.

Prosecutors of the postwar era turned to psychologists for help in explaining to finders of fact why a slavery victim might not "just leave." In *United States v. Ingalls*, notable as a high-profile 1940s use of the slavery statute rather than the peonage section, a psychiatrist testified on behalf of the prosecution. In that case, domestic servant Dora Jones had been held in servitude for much of her life, under threats of being turned over to the police for an illegal abortion obtained after the defendant's first husband had raped her as a teenager. Not only was Ms. Jones' reproductive history and mental state put before the jury as a way to explain her decades of work, but she was allowed to show the jurors her deformed hands from years of caustic cleaning chemicals on Mrs. Ingalls' behalf (Arnold 1947).

Dora Jones' bravery in testifying against her wealthy abuser made national news, especially in many African American communities which had thought that they had left such practices behind them in the Great Migration;[7] African Americans who observed trial proceedings commented on slavery happening in California, rather than the South (Arnold 1947). The *Ingalls* case was also noteworthy for being one of the first cases in which restitution was ordered. For many years, especially in cases involving undocumented immigrants or prostitution, restitution was not front of mind for courts. Accordingly, the TVPA required mandatory restitution—a requirement that, at the time of this writing, is only imperfectly being met (Levy and Vandenberg 2015).

---

[7] Beginning in 1916, a massive internal migration took place in the USA. Over an approximately fifty-year period, as many as 6 million African Americans moved away from the US South in the face of racial violence, peonage, police brutality, and segregation.

9.2.22   The 1948 Recodification: The Creation of Chapter 77

In 1948, the USA undertook a massive recodification of existing federal laws. The architects of the recodification claimed that they were not making new laws, but simply streamlining the preexisting statutes. While that was the case for the Peonage Statute, which was recodified as Section 1581 but essentially unchanged, the Involuntary Servitude Statute saw important changes. No longer based on the treatment of someone who had been imported from another country, the redrafted Section 1584 positioned the holding of a person in servitude as the central aspect of the crime:

> Whoever knowingly and willfully holds to involuntary servitude or sells into a condition of involuntary servitude, any other person for any term, or brings within the United States any person so held, [shall be guilty of an offense].
> 18 U.S.C., Section 1584.

The revised Involuntary Servitude statute, Section 1584, was heavily influenced by the *Ingalls* case, where under the prior law, the government had to show not just that the defendants had held Ms. Jones in servitude, but that the defendants had transported her "with the intent that [she] be held as a slave." After the 1948 revisions, one could establish involuntary servitude simply by demonstrating that someone was held in compelled service for a term, without having to establish movement. This focused the crime once and for all on the compulsory service, as opposed to proxies such as a debt (Section 1581, Peonage) or recruiting and inveigling (Section 1583, the modern version of the Padrone statute).

The 1948 Criminal Code revision had closed the recruitment/transportation loophole that Bureau of Investigation Director Stanley Finch raised to Congress in 1912. However, it did not move forced prostitution cases under the protection of the Thirteenth Amendment as he had appeared to suggest (Pliley 2014). While, for the next fifty years, Section 1584 was to become the workhorse of the anti-slavery, Civil Rights enforcement program, the WSTA—with its focus on morality—remained the primary lens through which forced prostitution was viewed in the federal system. For most of the twentieth century, forced prostitution was officially a problem of criminal vice, rather than human rights.

9.2.23   The Activist ISS Program of the 1970s and 1980s

In the 1970s and 1980s, civil rights enforcement took place at the same time as labor investigations and other structural responses. An activist Civil Rights Division[8] not only expanded application of the Thirteenth Amendment protections to new areas

---

[8] In 1957, reflecting the growing importance of the civil rights, the practice area in the Department of Justice was elevated to the status of a Division, retaining the criminal prosecutions mission (involuntary servitude/slavery, official misconduct, and racial violence) and adding civil enforcement around issues such as housing, education, employment, voting, and other civil rights.

but also developed case law recognizing the psychological aspects of compelled service. But, despite advances in other areas of the criminal law that recognized the power dynamics inherent in domestic violence and sexual abuse, in 1988 the Supreme Court looked back to 1865 to interpret the scope of the Amendment and its enacting legislation. And, just as had been the case in earlier years, workers' rights gains faced backlash. Restrictions were placed on legal aid, labor enforcement was weakened, and the adoption of guest worker programs undercut attempts to organize and empower farmworkers.

The Involuntary Servitude and Slavery Program: New Sectors, Psychological Coercion

The enforcement efforts of the 1970s and 1980s undertook a linked approach, with labor inspectors, FBI and Immigration and Naturalization Service (INS) Agents, and Civil Rights Division prosecutors working together to investigate and prosecute farm labor contractors whose abuse of their workers rose to the level of involuntary servitude. In the late 1970s, an active group of attorneys established linkages with migrant worker groups, immigrant advocates, and legal aid providers to investigate and prosecute slavery cases. For the first time, the Department of Justice appointed a lead prosecutor for the effort; the creation of the Involuntary Servitude and Slavery Coordinator position enabled the Civil Rights Division to begin to function not just in the courtroom but as a policy clearinghouse within the US government.

The cases of the ISS era sought to move beyond a restrictive reading of Section 1584 that had been set forth in the early 1960s in the appellate case *United States v. Shackney*. *Shackney* overturned a Connecticut prosecution in which a farmer recruited and enslaved a Mexican family on a chicken farm using veiled threats of deportation as opposed to overt force, threats of force, or threats of legal coercion tantamount to incarceration. The *Shackney* Court shied away from a subjective inquiry into the psychological effect of a pattern of coercion, opting instead for a more objectively observable bright-line test concerning the type of coercive force used by the employer. For the *Shackney* Court, threats of deportation (which it characterized as an administrative action rather than a legal punishment) were less threats to turn the workers over to law enforcement than they were a promise to release them from service and send them home.

Addiction,[9] Disability, and Psychological Coercion

As the Civil Rights Movement began to change the poverty and social exclusion that had allowed involuntary servitude to persist a century after Abolition, growers on the East Coast responded to the resulting labor pressures. They turned to immigrant populations as a source of cheap and exploitable labor.

---

[9]This was the term of the time and does not reflect modern understandings of substance use disorders.

Cases increasingly involved unscrupulous bosses manipulating the vulnerabilities of immigrants, the developmentally disabled, and the addicted, as opposed to reaping the benefits of Jim Crow and its aftermath. The *Shackney* majority's trusting characterization of employers with immigrant workers was to be tested over the coming decades as the percentage of immigrants in the country's dirty, dangerous, and demeaning jobs exploded and immigration enforcement became more punitive.

For those who sought to assist immigrant victims or US migrant workers lured from soup kitchens or the streets with cheap wine or drugs, understanding the effects of psychological and structural coercion became as important as uncovering physical abuse. It is telling that one of the early ISS Coordinators, Susan King, came to the Justice Department after representing indigent mentally ill persons in civil commitment proceedings. She and her colleagues pursued a litigation strategy to broaden the application of the servitude statutes to include psychological coercion, notwithstanding the *Shackney* decision. Such cases as *United States v. Booker*, *United States v. Bibbs*, *United States v. Harris*, *United States v. Warren*, and *United States v. Mussry* advanced judisprudential recognition of important elements of servitude. For example, these cases highlighted the effect of witnessing third-party injury or threats in creating a "climate of fear," the lack of an affirmative duty of an enslaved person to attempt escape when their will has been overborne, and the effect of psychological and structural manipulation.

The ISS era is also notable for again expanding the types of service work to which the Thirteenth Amendment was applied. Just as the civil rights attorneys of the Roosevelt and Truman era pushed to include domestic service (and even in limited circumstances, prostitution) into Thirteenth Amendment coverage, their successors increasingly worked in immigrant as well as Black communities. They even recognized the applicability of the ISS statutes in cases involving religious cults, especially in the wake of the mass suicide of cult members in Jonestown, Guyana. Blending psychological as well as physical manipulation, cases addressing servitude in sects such as the House of Judah (*United States v. King*) the Ecclesia Athletic Association (*United States v. Van Brunt* (unreported)), and the Church of God and True Holiness (*United States v. Cain*) were an important testing ground for the modern understanding of dependency and compulsion in servitude prosecutions.

The 1980s did not, however, see the use of anti-slavery statutes in the sex industry, even in cases of forced prostitution. Within the Justice Department, such cases were brought by US Attorney's Offices and monitored by the newly formed Child Exploitation and Obscenity Section of the Criminal Division, which grew out of the Attorney General's Commission on Pornography (the "Meese Commission"). The WSTA being assigned to an office whose primary focus and responsibility were child pornography and the sexual exploitation of children relegated adult prostitution cases (including forced prostitution) to the sidelines of federal enforcement. To the extent that the more established Organized Crime and Racketeering Section of the Criminal Division continued to pursue WSTA cases, it was in furtherance of dismantling organized crime networks rather than with the intention of vindicating the rights of abused persons in prostitution.

9.2.24 *A Setback:* United States v. Kozminski

By the late 1980s, the momentum of the Civil Rights Division ISS Initiative slowed. Legal aid funding was restricted, undercutting the Division's nongovernmental partners' ability to work on behalf of vulnerable groups. The Farm Bureau and other industry groups fought worker protections and succeeded in expanding agricultural guest worker programs and opening up a new supply of exploitable field labor. And in 1988, the Supreme Court in *United States v. Kozminski*, dealt what seemed at the time to be a death blow to the program, rejecting the psychological coercion standard that had developed in the prior decade. The Court examined the development of the federal slavery statutes through the years, through both legislative action and court cases. Like in the debates around the 1909 recodification, the Court wrestled with how best to capture the prohibited means by which employers hold their victims in servitude. In *Kozminski*, the victims were adult White men, made vulnerable by their developmental disability and homeless by the 1980s' deinstitutionalization of mental health care (Chap. 13). Rather than accepting that the Kozminskis had successfully held the men in servitude on their Michigan dairy farm through psychological coercion, the Supreme Court ruled that the slavery statutes only reached cases involving overt force, threats of force, or threats of legal coercion.

There was a small silver lining in the majority opinion: a means through which to examine the subjective reality of the victims. According to Justice O'Conner, the vulnerabilities of victims were not wholly off-limits and could be considered when determining if a particular threat was sufficient to overbear the particular person's will, especially given Congress's concern for the Italian children in the Padrone Act. Anything more, the Court suggested, would require further Congressional action.

9.2.25 *Rebuilding post-Kozminski: Worker Exploitation, Trafficking, and the TVPA*

The Congressional action that Justice O'Connor invited did not come right away. Jolted by the defeat in *Kozminski* and weighed down with a crushing caseload of racial violence and police brutality cases,[10] the ISS Program in the main receded into a collateral priority, though cases involving domestic servants and migrant farmworkers continued occasionally. But the march of history does not wait; in the 1990s, globalism and the fall of the Soviet Union resulted in an explosion of global migration similar to that of the late 1800s, replete with the abuses and trafficking patterns reminiscent of the earlier time period. Just as in the 1890s, women in Eastern Europe seeking alternatives to economic and political destabilization were targeted by unscrupulous recruiters and abusive employers. And just as in the late

---

[10] These included the high-profile investigation and prosecution of Los Angeles Police officers who had beaten motorist Rodney King; this case dominated the Civil Rights Division's activities of the time, and the then-ISS Coordinator was shifted to lead one of the teams on the King case.

1800s, workers from Asia and Mexico were exploited in sweatshops and agricultural fields from California to Florida and sometimes in the very fields in which peonage prosecutions had been brought in the 1940s or 1970s. High-profile cases in the USA (Chap. 3), and scandals of sexual slavery around the military action in the former Yugoslavia (Chap. 5), compelled a new attention to the US anti-slavery legal regime.

The reemergence of servitude in the public eye provided not only the impetus for a new interagency effort led by the ISS Program (the National Worker Exploitation Task Force), but an opportunity to undo the damage of the *Kozminski* case and anti-immigrant legislation that had made investigations, prosecutions, and victim care more difficult. While much of the sex trafficking discourse of recent years seems delinked from labor issues, that has not always been the case: the Clinton Administration's Task Force worked to empower labor inspectors, and the Task Force developed a legislative agenda that would raise penalties under the MSPA as well as updating the servitude statutes. But the Task Force's work was not focused wholly on labor trafficking. Much like the innovations of the early ISS years, in the 1990s the USA again applied the slavery statutes to forced prostitution as well as forced labor, recognizing in cases such as *United States v. Cadena*, *United States v. Kwon Soon Oh*, and *United States v. Pipkins* that people held in the sex industry were rights-holders under the protection of the Thirteenth Amendment just as were their counterparts in forced labor.

The Clinton Administration, led by First Lady Hillary Rodham Clinton and the President's Interagency Council on Women, articulated an organizing principle for anti-slavery activities in the modern era: the "3P Paradigm." Prevention and protection were to be seen as coequal to the state's interest in prosecution. The Administration pursued both an international instrument, which was to become the United Nations "Palermo Protocol," and domestic legislation.

The resulting domestic statute, the Trafficking Victims Protection Act of 2000, is a strong modern anti-slavery law. While initial drafts introduced in the House were in many ways restatements of the White Slave Trafficking Act, the version that was eventually enacted was an update of the post-Civil War slavery statutes. It was designed to bring the promise of 1865 to a modern era. Indeed, during the Senate consideration of the bill, cosponsor Sam Brownback from Kansas stated, "This legislation is the most significant human rights bill of the 106th Congress, if passed today, as hoped for. This is also the largest anti-slavery bill that the United States has adopted since 1865 and the demise of slavery at the end of the Civil War" (United States Congress 2000).

9.2.26   A Culmination, not a Beginning: The Trafficking Victims Protection Act of 2000

The passage of TVPA in 2000 in many ways resolved the various issues of the prior two centuries. While sex trafficking dominated the politics of the TVPA, the statute itself focused on involuntary servitude, rather than the type of labor or services that were performed. Because it cast victims as rights-holders, rather than as illicitly moved contraband or culpable coconspirators with the traffickers, victim protection and restoration were a necessary response in vindicating their rights. And so, by organizing itself around the "3Ps" of prevention, protection, and prosecution, the TVPA for the first time articulated an anti-slavery response that was not simply carceral. The TVPA's victim care provisions and creation of bureaucratic and grant structures were an exciting opportunity to shift the federal response away from one that was driven wholly by the needs of investigators and prosecutors. By providing "teeth" to the Migrant and Seasonal Workers Protection Act and encouraging inter-agency structures involving not just criminal enforcement offices but also the Department of Labor, the TVPA in a small way began to extend protections to the farmworkers and domestic servants who had been excluded from the Fair Labor Standards Act.

9.2.27 Reclaiming Psychological and Structural Coercion, and Unifying Concepts

On the statutory side, the TVPA created in the Slavery/Peonage Chapter of the Criminal Code (Chapter 77), Section 1589, which brought back the psychological basis for liability, reviving the standard rejected by *Kozminski*; Section 1591 (addressing sex trafficking), and Section 1592 (addressing servitude maintained through the confiscation of documents). While the traditional statutes remain in the federal Criminal Code, the TVPA statutes have in practice replaced the Peonage and Involuntary Servitude statutes as the lodestar of anti-slavery enforcement for the new millennium. The new criminal statutes' focus could apply to any person in any part of the economy. The TVPA finally bridged the objective/subjective problem identified in *Shackney* by articulating a hybrid inquiry suggested by the *Kozminski* decision: Was a threat of serious harm one that would "compel a reasonable person of the same background and in the same circumstances" as the victim? And, most importantly, it rejected the limitation of the Thirteenth Amendment to force, threats of force, and threats of legal coercion. Rather, it adopted the psychological coercion standard rejected by the *Kozminski* Court. Cases such as *United States v. Bradley* and *United States v. Calimlim* applied ISS Era precedent to flesh out the new standard of coercion under the TVPA, such as the lack of an affirmative duty to escape and the effect of witnessing or hearing of abuse or threats to coworkers in creating a "climate of fear."

The TVPA sex trafficking provision, Section 1591, addressed the original structural problem of the WSTA that assumed that persons transported for prostitution were themselves culpable or contraband; the provision harnessed the post-*Kozminski* psychological standards of Section 1589 for sex trafficking as well as labor trafficking situations. It also extended to cases in which the sex traffickers' activities *affected* interstate commerce, rather than requiring that the offenses occur *in* interstate commerce. The TVPA thus moved away from a conception of the social harm being the transportation across state lines and began to focus on what was done to the persons involved. "Regular" cases of transportation for illegal, commercial sexual activity without coercion can still be handled under the WSTA, but under TVPA Section 1591 victims can finally be recognized as such.

The anti-child sex trafficking tools of the TVPA are somewhat redundant to the WSTA's provisions, but the new law provided an opportunity to change law enforcement and social services paradigms by highlighting the need to see sexually exploited children as dependent, rather than delinquent. Because the child sex trafficking provisions of Section 1591 are strict liability provisions—there need be no showing of force, fraud, or coercion to establish a commercial sexual offense against a minor[11]—that Section was promulgated under the Commerce Clause, effectively marrying the WSTA and the anti-slavery statutory lines in one section.

While the TVPA does not refer directly to the Merchant Seaman's Welfare Act, the Civil Rights Division's ISS Program dealt with several such allegations and the modern anti-trafficking policy and regulatory framework has been used to address forced labor at sea. Moreover, while the Thirteenth Amendment's coverage is limited only to "places subject to [US] jurisdiction," the Trade Facilitation and Trade Enforcement Act of 2015 (TFTEA) provided mechanisms to prohibit the importing of slave-made goods (Chap. 7), thereby extending criminal anti-slavery enforcement to the global marketplace. One of the first actions under TFTEA was to ban seafood imports from ships notorious for forced labor.

This chapter does not trace the subsequent history of the TVPA, but two aspects of reauthorizations and implementation are noteworthy in examining the development of anti-trafficking law in the USA. First, civil cases, made possible by amendments to the TVPA in 2003, have amplified the voices of victims; a substantial percentage of forced labor cases are now brought directly rather than through the government. Unlike the civil cases of the Progressive Era, which often had to be brought as *habeas corpus* proceedings, modern civil anti-slavery cases can seek damages and remediation. Civil cases are being brought in domestic service, shipbuilding, forestry, hospitality, and prostitution arenas, as well as being harnessed to address the prison labor loophole in both immigration detention and private prisons. Nowadays, development of case law is as likely to stem from civil as criminal actions. Second, state anti-trafficking statutes, many based on the TVPA, are providing an avenue for a more localized law enforcement response. Still, at the time of this writing, state and local activities are overwhelmingly concentrated on vice and commerce aspects of cases involving US citizen child victims rather than on the freedom principle, demonstrating the continued staying power of the "White Slave Trafficking" lens of yesteryear.

In addition to the TVPA, Congress has turned to the Thirteenth Amendment to justify federal action against bias crimes, extending protections to lesbian, gay, bisexual, transgender, and queer (LGBTQ) communities and streamlining

---

[11] Like the FLSA in the 1930s, the TVPA was impacted by US cultural understandings of child labor stemming from traditional family businesses such as farms. As a result of compromises with Senator Orin Hatch, the strict liability only applies in child prostitution cases; force, fraud, and/or coercion still must be established in a child forced labor case.

traditional federal hate crimes enforcement in the Matthew Shepard and James Byrd Jr. Hate Crimes Prevention Act of 2009, codified at Title 18, US Code, Section 249. States are removing the prison labor exception from their corresponding constitutional provisions, and, in the summer of 2020, Oregon Senator Jeff Merkley announced his intention to introduce legislation to strip the prison labor exception from the Thirteenth Amendment, thus closing the federal loophole that allows the freedom principle to be perverted through strategic evasion (KOIN 2020).

While the TVPA—which interweaves the rights-based abolitionist tradition and the commercial-based, anti-prostitution framework of the WSTA tradition—marked a watershed change in anti-slavery legislation, it remains essential that practitioners understand these, at times competing, lineages. The WSTA paradigm is still culturally and politically strong; its influence has the potential to drown out the crucial historical and legal import of a rights-based approach founded on the Thirteenth Amendment and the UN Declaration on Human Rights. The TVPA rightly stands as a vindicator of victims' rights, but if the central tenants of human rights and victim agency are overshadowed the TVPA could simply become a tool for vice enforcement or border security (Chap. 12). The TVPA has been the subject of intense political and ideological debate from within the ranks of anti-trafficking reformers who are as passionate as their Abolitionist and Progressive forbearers. But recent trends of focusing on sex trafficking while downplaying labor rights or immigrant rights (a trend steeped in the rhetoric and philosophy of the WSTA) should not overpower the longer narrative of freedom that brought the nation to the TVPA.

9.3 Conclusion

9.3.1 A blend of old and new

In 2020, 233 years and many laws since the founding of the nation, the anti-slavery chapter of the Federal Criminal Code is an intriguing blend of ancient and modern. The Peonage Statute continues with pride of place, and the Padrone Statute lives on as part of the Involuntary Servitude Statute. Centuries-old slave trade acts that prohibit the fitting out of vessels for the slave trade and kidnapping people into slavery exist side by side with modern sections that address restitution, psychological coercion, and document servitude. But the presence of those archaic statutes serves a purpose. In the words of former House Judiciary Committee Chairman and Civil Rights icon Congressman John Conyers, Jr., "Emancipation wasn't a one-time event; it is a promise written in the blood of all who have ever been held in bondage" (Conyers Jr. 2008). That promise cannot be ignored in a US Criminal Code that blends old and new, forcing those who grapple with modern slavery to at least pass by the hard-fought statutes that sought to restrict antebellum slavery.

That slavery/freedom frame forces one to consider victim protection, labor rights and conditions, therapeutic responses, and the placement of the modern movement in its historical context. The competing commerce frame does not and, as was seen under the WSTA, too often can result in overly carceral responses based on immigration restriction and middle-class morality. The slavery/freedom frame forces one to focus on the survivors. The rights-centered framework of the anti-slavery laws necessarily leads to a victim-centered approach. While criminal enforcement and administrative enforcement are a necessary part of the resulting rights-based legal regime, they must be meaningfully and sustainably joined by prevention and protection. The slavery/freedom frame forces one to abandon notions of state triumphalism and assumptions of continuous forward progress. The USA's constitutional and legal path to its modern anti-slavery policy has been meandering, inconsistent, and marked by both advances and retrogression. That said, the nation has used its complex legal history as a guide to lead the world in the establishment of a comprehensive anti-trafficking framework (the 3P approach); the framework provides precedential support for concepts such as the irrelevance of initial consent and the nonpunishment of victims and has informed the development of victim care flowing from a rights-based approach.

The central import of US emancipation, abolition, and reconstruction in spawning the modern anti-slavery legal regime must not be overlooked. Contemporary ideological debates rage over prostitution policy in ways that mirror the commerce-based legacy of the WSTA. Contemporary institutional racism and xenophobia often take on a divisive tone reminiscent of Jim Crow or the Chinese exclusion law. The desire for profits fuels guest worker programs and attacks on workers' rights. It is critical to remember the freedom guarantee and the principles from which the TVPA arose. The modern anti-slavery movement is a continuation of the long, sometimes clumsy, and presently incomplete US project of liberation and freedom.

Emancipation was not a one-day event, and abolition was not perfect. As Frederick Douglass warned mere days after the Confederate surrender, Jubilee had to be maintained through hard-fought political, legislative, and judicial battles. There were decades in which loopholes, evasion, and racism seemed to carry the day. The fight for abolition continues.

One can only imagine Douglass's reaction if he could see that the USA continues to work against powerful interests' desire to come up with new slaveries under new names. He would see workers of color successfully organizing for their rights in the very fields in which generations had lived and died in chattel slavery. He would see activists confronting not only the Thirteenth Amendment's prison labor loophole, but challenging the glorification of those who treasonously fought to prevent Emancipation. He would see how his descendants have themselves been part of the modern anti-slavery advocacy coalition that has brought forward the end-user liability of the TVPA, the victim protections, and the creation of survivor advisory groups so that others can make their voices heard as he did.

And what if Douglass could see how the modern statutes, honed against 150 years of cruelty and evasion, have been brought to bear on behalf of abused workers from around the world? No matter their imperfections and loopholes, no matter the halting nature of their application, this Constitutional provision and its effectuating statutes were worth the fight. In all probability, Douglass's reaction would be one of continued determination and a recommitment to the ongoing anti-slavery fight. Because of all people, Frederick Douglass knew that when dealing with a snake— no matter what skin it wears—one needs to carry not just a shield, but a mighty, swift sword.

9.4 Recommendations

Public health professionals must play a prominent role in a rights-based, victim-centered approach to human trafficking. They are pivotal in the success not only of the TVPA's ethos of "Prevention, Protection, and Prosecution," but also of restoration and rehabilitation efforts. As such, public health professionals and others should:

1. *Understand the myriad forms that human trafficking and modern slavery can take*. Slavery and its victims do not all appear in a single industry.
2. *Give due credit to the (at times competing) contributions of the different cultural strands of present-day abolitionism* (i.e., feminist, labor-centered, and those in the Mann Act legal tradition) *while centering practice on the rights-based approach* of the anti-slavery lens.
3. *Legally recognize the myriad forms of nonobjectively observable coercion* (e.g., emotional and mental abuse) *that traffickers use* to hold victims in involuntary servitude; a dialectic of overt force alone is counterproductive and allows for forms of servitude to be overlooked.
4. *Address legal loopholes used by unscrupulous employers* to keep workers in slavery-like conditions, historically and in current practice.
5. *Accept the truth of the long and continued legacy of race-based chattel slavery and exclusionary immigration policies in USA* and world history, in both racial and labor settings.
6. *Recognize and confront instances of human trafficking as* not simply isolated instances of assault or sexual abuse, but *part of a systemic arrangement of power and access*.
7. *Acknowledge the ways in which the USA's anti-slavery legal trajectory has shaped the global fight against contemporary forms of slavery, while being wary of narratives of US exceptionalism.*
8. *Reassess the current potential and promise of the Thirteenth Amendment as a legal tool for continued reform.*
9. *Incorporate awareness and use of not only the existing criminal laws but also of labor regulations, wage protections, workers' ability to organize, and the closing of contracting and other loopholes* that unscrupulous employers use to shield themselves from liability.
10. *Interrogate carceral policy, especially labor schemes in prison and detention settings*, in light of the historical misapplication of the Thirteenth Amendment's prison labor exception to evade anti-slavery laws and policies.

References

Arnold, C. M. (1947, July 10). Dora Jones on stand in day long grilling. *Los Angeles Sentinel*.

Anstey, R. (1975). *The Atlantic slave trade and British abolition, 1760–1810*. London: Macmillan.

Berlin, I. (2015). *The long emancipation: The demise of slavery in the United States*. Nathan I. Huggins Lectures. Cambridge, MA: Harvard University Press.

Black, G. (2020, October 12). The Whitewashing of Black Genius: Frederick Douglass, Antonio Maceo and the Outrages of 'Racial Science'. *Scientific American*.

Blackett, R. J. M. (2018). *The captive's quest for freedom: Fugitive Slaves, the 1850 Fugitive Slave Law, and the Politics of Slavery*. Slaveries Since Emancipation. Cambridge: Cambridge University Press.

Blackett, R. J. M. (1983). *Building an antislavery wall: Black Americans in the Atlantic abolitionist movement, 1830–1860*. Baton Rouge: Louisiana State University Press.

Blackmon, D. A. (2008). *Slavery by another name: The re-enslavement of Black People in America from the Civil War to World War II*. New York: Anchor Books.

Blight, D. W. (2008). William Lloyd Garrison at two hundred: His radicalism and his legacy for our time. In J. B. Stewart (Ed.), *William Lloyd Garrison at two hundred: History, legacy, and memory* (pp. 1–12). New Haven: Yale University Press.

Blight, D. W. (2001). *Race and reunion: The Civil War in American Memory*. Cambridge, MA: Belknap Press of Harvard University Press.

Blight, D. W., & Black, G. (2020, June 25). Black People aren't naturally vulnerable to Covid-19. That's junk race science. *Washington Post*.

Brooke, J. L. (2019). *"There Is a North": Fugitive slaves, political crisis, and cultural transformation in the coming of the Civil War*. Amherst: University of Massachusetts Press.

Brown, C. L. (2006). *Moral capital: Foundations of British abolitionism*. Chapel Hill: University of North Carolina Press for the Omohundro Institute of Early American History and Culture.

Combe, G. Diary entry for June 8, 1846, MSS. 7425, "Continuous Diary of George Combe, 1841–1858," Papers of George Combe, National Library of Scotland, Edinburgh.

Conyers, Jr., J. (2008). Comment on Benjamin Skinner's *A Crime So Monstrous*, accessible at Skinner, Benjamin. "A Crime So Monstrous – Praise and Reviews," Accessed 21 oct 2020. https://acrimesomonstrous.com/.

Daniel, P. (1970). Up from slavery and down to Peonage: The Alonzo Bailey case. *The Journal of American History, 57*(3), 654–670.

Daniel, P. (1973). *The Shadow of Slavery: Peonage in the South, 1901–1969*. Urbana: University of Illinois Press.

Davis, D. B. (1962). The emergence of immediatism in British and American antislavery thought. *The Mississippi Valley Historical Review, 49*(2), 209–230.

Delgado, R. (1979–1980). Religious totalism as slavery. *New York Review of Law and Social Change, 9*(1), 58–68.

Douglass, F. (1865, May 26). *Floor statement*, Proceedings of the American Anti-Slavery Society, May 10, 1865, New York, New York, in The Liberator.

Douglass, F. (1867). "The Composite Nation" Lecture in the Parker Fraternity Course, Boston. Available online at https://www.loc.gov/item/mfd.22017/.

Dozema, J. (2010). *Sex slaves and discourse masters: The construction of trafficking*. London: Zed Books.

DuBois, W. E. B. (1896). *The Suppression of the African Slave-Trade to the United States of America, 1638–1870*. Cambridge: Harvard.

DuBois, W. E. B. (1928, March). *Robert E. Lee*, The Crisis, Vol. 35, n.3

Fabian, A. (2010). *The skull collectors: Race, science, and America's unburied dead*. Chicago: University of Chicago Press.

Farrand, M. (1913). *The framing of the constitution of the United States*. New Haven: Yale University Press.

Fladeland, B. (1972). *Men and brothers: Anglo-American Antislavery Cooperation*. Urbana: University of Illinois Press.

Foner, E. (2019). *The second founding: How the civil war and reconstruction remade the constitution*. New York: W. W. Norton & Company.

Gates, J., & Gates, H. L. (2019). *Stony the road: Reconstruction, White supremacy, and the rise of Jim Crow*. New York: Penguin Press.

Goluboff, R. L. (2009) *The Thirteenth amendment in historical perspective*, 11 U. Pa. J. Const. L. 1451.

Grobman W. A., Lai, Y., Landon, M. B., et al. (2007). Development of a nomogram for prediction of vaginal birth after cesarean delivery. *Obstetrics & Gynecology, 109*, 806–812.

Harrold, S. (2019). *American abolitionism: its direct political impact from Colonial Times into reconstruction. A nation divided: Studies in the Civil War Era*. Charlottesville: University of Virginia Press.

Huzzy, R. (2012). *Freedom burning: Anti-slavery and empire in Victorian Britain*. Ithaca: Cornell University Press.

KOIN 6 News Staff. (2020, July 1). Merkley Pitches Constitutional Amendment to Ban Forced Labor. *KOIN.com*. https://www.koin.com/news/oregon/merkley-pitches-constitutional-amendment-to-ban-forced-labor/.

Kraditor, A. S. (1969). *Means and ends in American abolitionism: Garrison and his critics on strategy and tactics, 1834–1850*. New York: Pantheon Books.

Laite, J. (2017). Traffickers and Pimps in the era of White Slavery. *Past & Present, 237*, 237–269.

Levy, A. F., & Vandenberg, M. E. (2015). Breaking the law: The failure to award mandatory criminal restitution to victims in sex trafficking cases. *Saint Louis University Law Journal, 60*(1), 43–72.

Levey, A. S, Stevens, L. A, & Schmid, C. H, et al. (2009). A new equation to estimate glomerular filtration rate. *Annals of Internal Medicine, 150*, 604–612.

Livingston, D. N. (2008). *Adam's ancestors: Race, religion, and the politics of human origins*. Baltimore: Johns Hopkins University Press.

Lui, M. T. Y. (2009, September). Saving young girls from Chinatown: White slavery and woman suffrage, 1910–1920. *Journal of the History of Sexuality, 18*(3), 393–417.

Mason, M. (2002). The battle of the slaveholding liberators: Great Britain, the United States, and slavery in the early Nineteenth Century. *The William and Mary Quarterly, 59*(3), 665–696.

Mayer, H. (1998). *All on fire: William Lloyd Garrison and the abolition of slavery*. New York: St. Martin's Press.

McDaniel, W. C. (2013). *The problem of democracy in the age of slavery: Garrisonian abolitionists and transatlantic reform*. Baton Rouge: Louisiana State University Press.

Mitchell, P. W., & Michael, J. S. (2019). Bias, brains, and skulls: tracing the legacy of scientific racism in the Nineteenth-Century works of Samuel George Morton and Friedrich Tiedemann. In J. A. Thomas & C. Jackson (Eds.), *Embodied difference: Divergent bodies in public discourse* (pp. 77–98). Lanham: Lexington Books.

Morgan, E. S. (1975). *American slavery, American freedom: The Ordeal of Colonial Virginia*. New York: Norton.

Oakes, J. (2014). *The Scorpion's sting: Antislavery and the coming of the civil war*. New York: Norton.

Patterson, O. (1982). *Slavery and social death: A comparative study*. Cambridge, MA: Harvard University Press.

Peña Delgado, G. (2012, Summer). Border control and sexual policing: White slavery and prostitution along the U.S.-Mexico Borderlands, 1903–1910. *Western Historical Quarterly, 43*(2), 157–178.

Perry, L. (1973). *Radical abolitionism: Anarchy and the government of god in antislavery thought*. Ithaca: Cornell University Press.

Peterson, P. N., Rumsfeld, J. S, Liang, L, et al. (2010). A validated risk score for in-hospital mortality in patients with heart failure from the American Heart Association Get with the Guidelines program. *Circulation: Cardiovascular Quality and Outcomes, 3*, 25–32.

Pliley, J. (2014). *Policing sexuality: The Mann Act and the making of the FBI*. Cambridge, MA: Harvard University Press.

Rael-Gálvez, E. (2002). *Identifying captivity and capturing identity: Narratives of American Indian Slavery, Colorado and New Mexico 1776–1934*. (PhD diss., University of Michigan), pp. 221–22.

Rakove, J. N. (2009). *The annotated U.S. Constitution and declaration of independence.* Cambridge, MA: Belknap Press of Harvard University Press.

Reséndez, A. (2017). North American Peonage. *The Journal of the Civil War Era, 7*(4), 597–619.

Rice, A., & Crawford, M. (Eds.). (1999). *Liberating Sojourn: Frederick Douglass and transatlantic reform.* Athens: University of Georgia Press.

Smith, S. L. (2015). Emancipating peons, excluding coolies: Reconstructing coercion in the American West. In G. Downs & K. Masur (Eds.), *The world the civil war made* (pp. 46–74). Chapel Hill: University of North Carolina Press.

Scott, R. J. (2017). Social facts, legal fictions, and the attribution of slave status: The puzzle of prescription. *Law & History Review, 35,* 9.

Sewell, R. H. (1976). *Ballots for freedom: Antislavery politics in the United States, 1837–1860.* New York: Oxford University Press.

Soodalter, R. (2006). *Hanging captain Gordon: The life and trial of an American slave trader.* New York: Atria.

Temperley, H. (1972). *British Antislavery, 1833–1870.* London: Longman.

Weber, D. (1973). *Foreigners in their native land: Historical roots of the Mexican Americans.* Albuquerque: University of New Mexico Press.

Case Law

Dred Scott v. Sandford, 60 U.S. 393 (1856)

Jaremillo v. Romero., 1 N.M. 90 (1857)

United States v. Ancarola, 1 F. 676, 683 (Cir. Ct. S.D.N.Y. 1880)

In re Sah Quah, 31 Fed. 327 (1886)

Robertson v. Baldwin., U.S. 275 (1897)

Peonage Cases, 123 F. 671 (M.D. Ala. 1903)

In re Ah Sou, 132 F. 878 (D.WA. 1904), rev'd, 138 F. 775 (9th Cir. 1905)

Bailey v. Alabama, 219 U.S. 219 (1911)

United States v. Reynolds., 235 U.S. 133 (1914)

Pollock v. Williams., 322 U.S. 4 (1944)

United States v. Ingalls, 73 F. Supp. 76, 77-78 (S.D. Cal. 1947)

United States v. Shackney, 333 F.2d 475, 486 (2d Cir. 1964)

United States v. Bibbs, 564 F.2d 1165, 1168 (5th Cir. 1977)

United States v. Booker, 655 F.2d 562, 566 (4th Cir. 1981)

United States v. Cain, 653 F.2d 883 (4th Cir. 1981)

United States v. Harris, 701 F.2d 1095, 1100 (4th Cir. 1983)

United States v. Warren, 772 F.2d 827, 833-34 (11th Cir. 1985)

United States v. Mussry, 726 F.2d 1448 (9th Cir. 1984)

United States v. Kozminski., 487 U.S. 931 (1988)

United States v. Garcia, No. 02–CR–110S–01, 2003 WL 22938040 (W.D.N.Y. Dec. 2, 2003)

United States v. Bradley and O'Dell, 309 F.3d 145 (1ˢᵗ Cir. 2004)

United States v. Calimlim, 538 F.2d 706 (7ᵗʰ Cir. 2008)

Statutes and Executive Orders

The Slave Trade Act, Pub. L. No. 3-11 (March 22, 1794)

Fugitive Slave Act of 1850, Pub. L. No. 31-60 (Sept. 18, 1850)

Trafficking Victims Protection Act of 2000 (TVPA), Pub. L. No. 106-386 (Oct. 28, 2000)

The Matthew Shepard and James Byrd, Jr., Hate Crimes Prevention Act of 2009, 18 U.S.C. § 249, *enacted as* Division E of the National Defense Authorization Act for Fiscal Year 2010, P.L. 111-84 (Oct. 28, 2009)

Trade Facilitation and Trade Enforcement Act of 2015, Pub. L. No. 114-125 (Feb. 24, 2016)

U.S. Const. amend. XIII.

Congressional Materials

President Thomas Jefferson, Sixth Annual Message to Congress, December 2, 1806, available online at https://avalon.law.yale.edu/19th_century/jeffmes6.asp
U.S. Congress, Record of Debate, Peonage Act, Cong'l Globe, February 19, 1867a, p. 1571 (statement of Senator Doolittle)
U.S. Congress, Record of Debate, Peonage Act, Cong'l Globe, February 19, 1867b, p. 1571 (statement of Senator Wilson).
U.S. Congress, Record of Debate, Peonage Act, Cong'l Globe, February 19, 1867c, p. 1571 (statement of Senator Buckalew)
U.S. Congress, Record of Debate, Padrone Statute, 2 Cong. Rec. 4443 (1874) (statement of Representative Cessna)
U.S. Congress, Record of Debate, Criminal Code Revisions—The Slave Trade and Peonage, Cong. Rec.—Senate, January 27, 1908a, p. 1114 (statement of Senator Hale)
U.S. Congress, Record of Debate, Criminal Code Revisions—The Slave Trade and Peonage, Cong. Rec.—Senate, January 27, 1908b, pp. 1114-6 (statements of Senator Heyburn)
U.S. Congress, Record of Debate, Criminal Code Revisions—The Slave Trade and Peonage, Cong. Rec.—Senate, January 27, 1908c, pp. 1122 (statements of Senator Lodge)
U.S. Congress, Record of Debate, Criminal Code Revisions—The Slave Trade and Peonage, Cong. Rec.—House, February 17, 1909, pp. 2587-9 (statements of Representative Brantley)
U.S. Congress, Record of Debate, Trafficking Victims Protection Act, 146 Cong. Rec. S10164-02 (2000) (statement of Senator Brownback)

Bibliography

Case Law

Slaughter-House Cases, 83 U.S. 36 (1872)
Bernal v. United States, 241 F. 339 (5th Cir. 1917)
Pierce v. United States, 146 F.2d 84 (5th Cir. 1944)

Statutes and Executive Orders

Northwest Ordinance, Art. VI, 33 Journals of Continental Congress 343 (1787)
Act to revise, codify, and enact into positive law, Title 18 of the United States Code, entitled "Crimes and Criminal Procedure", Pub. L. No. 80–772 (June 25, 1948)

Section 1581 (Peonage) Precursors

Act to Abolish and Forever Prohibit the System of Peonage in the Territory of New Mexico and other Parts of the United States. *United States Statutes at Large*, 39th Cong., Sess. II., Chp. 187, p. 546 (1867)
Act of March 4, 1909a, ch. 321, § 269, 35 Stat. 1142 (Peonage)
Act of March 4, 1909b, ch. 321, § 270, 35 Stat. 1142 (Obstruction of Peonage Enforcement)

Section 1584 (Involuntary Servitude) Precursors

Act of March 2, 1807, ch. 22, § 6, 2 Stat. 427 (1808) ("Slave Trade Act" banning purchase or sale, or holding to service, of "any negro, mulatto, or person of colour" imported into the United States)

Act of April 20, 1818, ch. 91, 3 Stat. 452 (1818) (increased penalties for activities criminalized in earlier Slave Trade Act)

Act of June 23, 1874, ch. 464, § 1, 18 Stat. 251 (1874) ("Padrone Statute" banning recruiting/enveiglement with intention to hold in involuntary servitude)

Act of March 4, 1909, ch. 10, 248, 35 Stat. 1139 (1909c) (abandoning racial or ethnic characterizations for "any person" subjected to involuntary servitude)

Act of March 4, 1909, ch. 10, § 271, 35 Stat. 1142 (1909d) (abandoning racial or ethnic characterizations for "any person" kidnapped or enveigled into slavery)

Chapter 10
Immigration, Precarity, and Human Trafficking: Histories and Legacies of Asian American Racial Exclusion in the United States

John Cheng and Kimberly Chang

10.1 Introduction

10.1.1 Trafficking and Precarity

There is no singular profile of a person at risk of being trafficked. Trafficked persons span all ages, races/ethnicities, genders, socioeconomic backgrounds and class, and national origin and citizenship status (Banks and Kyckelhahn 2011). However, examination of the dynamics of power, economics, exploitation, and marginalization reveals broad categories of social dynamics as well as personal characteristics that increase the vulnerabilities of populations and individuals to being trafficked (United Nations Office on Drugs and Crime 2008). Because human traffickers target people who are poor and disempowered, policies that create disparity and precarity, weaken social safety nets, or lead to social exclusion increase risk for exploitation, including human trafficking. Conditions that produce such dynamics include political instability, natural disasters, poverty, policies leading to lack of legitimate employment, the continued legacy of colonialism (Chap. 2), structural racism, cultural norms of gender inequality and misogyny (Chap. 5), and other systemic inequities. Ultimately, risk of human trafficking increases with unchecked power differentials and the demand for inexpensive labor or sex – and the continuing abusive exploitation of human bodies.

In this sense, social marginalization increases vulnerabilities to human trafficking (Bryant-Davis and Tummala-Narra 2018). Marginalization occurs when any

J. Cheng
Binghamton University, Binghamton, NY, USA

K. Chang (✉)
Asian Health Services, Oakland, CA, USA

© Springer Nature Switzerland AG 2021
M. Chisolm-Straker, K. Chon (eds.), *The Historical Roots of Human Trafficking*,
https://doi.org/10.1007/978-3-030-70675-3_10

group exists at the periphery of power in society, most notably minority[1] populations. Fundamentally, policies that do not seek to include minority populations
explicitly amplify and exacerbate marginalization; indeed, policies often *create*
marginalization. The modern US immigration system creates marginalization based
upon immigration status and differential classes of documentation. Immigrants with
work visas are able to secure legitimate forms of employment but are still at higher
risk of exploitation compared to US citizens; immigrants without documentation
are at a much higher risk of being trafficked due to their lack of work authorization
and subordinated lack of power in labor relations. Without membership in the group
with citizenship, or work visas, people without immigration documentation fundamentally lack or reasonably perceive a lack of access to institutional systems of care
and protection. Writing about early twenty-first-century conditions of war, Judith
Butler defined precarity as the conceptual frame within which the precariousness of
lives – those whose threatened existence may be recognized and grieved and those
who may not – is understood. Precarity, in her usage, is a specifically political
notion that illuminates relational inequalities in and for precariousness, regulating
between those who are secure and those who are not (Butler 2004; Butler 2009).
Precarity is similarly useful in evaluating systems of oppression, and of care and
protection, when considering how root causes that predispose populations to risks
of exploitation and abuse become institutionalized through definition and practice.

The modern legislative definition of human trafficking in the United States begins
with the Victims of Trafficking and Violence Protection Act (TVPA) (Chap. 9),
signed into law on October 28, 2000. This legislation defines "severe forms of trafficking in persons" as: (A) sex trafficking in which a commercial sex act is induced
by force, fraud, or coercion, or in which the person induced to perform such act has
not attained 18 years of age; or (B) the recruitment, harboring, transportation, provision, or obtaining of a person for labor or services, through the use of force, fraud,
or coercion for the purpose of subjection to involuntary servitude, peonage, debt
bondage, or slavery (TVPA 2000). It clarifies further that the term "sex trafficking"
is the recruitment, harboring, transportation, provision, obtaining, patronizing, or
soliciting of a person for the purpose of a commercial sex act and clearly specifies
that a person younger than 18 years old need not experience "force, fraud, or coercion" to be considered victimized by sex trafficking. The TVPA's definition establishes benefits and protections to those meeting its criteria and has become the most
commonly cited contemporary definition of "trafficking." Its focus on "severe"
forms of trafficking, however, has contributed to popular and public discourse that
conflates sex trafficking with prostitution and views of trafficking as either sex or
labor trafficking rather than the broader range of trafficking's exploitative and

---

[1] Tatum's seminal work on "otherness" defines seven core minority groups based on race or ethnicity, gender, religion, sexual orientation, socioeconomic status, age, and physical or mental ability.
Tatum notes that "each of these categories has a form of oppression associated with it: racism,
sexism, religious oppression, heterosexism, classism, ageism, and ableism, respectively. In each
case, there is a group considered dominant (systematically advantaged by the society because of
group membership) and a group considered subordinate or targeted (systematically disadvantaged)" (Tatum 2000).

abusive practices. Importantly, it has also limited entitlements, services, and relief, including immigration relief, to people victimized by trafficking (Lee and Lewis 2003). No grounds exist to prosecute forms of sex trafficking that are not severe in its terms (that is, adult victims who do not experience force, fraud, or coercion) and those who consequently suffer are not eligible for the services and safeguards offered for "severe" trafficking. These definitional categories determine who has access to systems of care and protection and who do not.

It is critical, therefore, to broaden the concept of trafficking and to consider its historical antecedents and contexts. Specifically, a direct line connects the modern definition of human trafficking as laid out in the TVPA to the 13th Amendment of the United States Constitution (Chap. 9). While Section One of the Amendment abolished slavery and involuntary servitude, Section Two gave Congress the power to enforce that abolition through legislation (US Const., Amend. XIII). The TVPA's enforcement provisions stem directly from that authority in the 13th Amendment. Moreover, as contemporary legal scholars note, the 13th Amendment, passed during Reconstruction, sought not only to abolish economic subordination and hierarchy and other forms of unfree labor generally, but also to eradicate its racial basis (Kim 2020). In this sense, understanding human trafficking requires a race-conscious perspective to recognize the role of restrictive and exclusionary immigration policies in increasing the risks of populations to exploitation and trafficking. While the 13th Amendment declared formal slavery and involuntary servitude unconstitutional, the desire for inexpensive labor in the United States persists throughout its history (Chaps. 2 and 7); labor that, in many cases, comes from people with origins in other sovereign entities, including Indigenous peoples, and takes advantage of their marginalization. Racial notions, in turn, inform views of non-White migrants as temporary, non-citizen laborers, separating "labor" from the human beings providing it. Such notions facilitate and justify restrictive and exclusionary immigration policies against non-White migrants, as well as their exclusion from legal rights and protections, and access to systems of care and protection. These restrictive and exclusionary policies and practices are at odds with the spirit of the 13th Amendment. While the formulation of policies to address human trafficking are historically and inextricably linked to ideas of race, so too are immigration policies. Immigration policies have always informed the precarity – particularly racial precarity – of human trafficking within the United States.

10.1.2   Asian Exclusion, Immigration, and Race-Based Vulnerability

This chapter traces the history of United States immigration policies regarding peoples from Asia and the Pacific to consider race-based policy connections and contributions to trafficking, broadly understood. The modern racial notion of "Asian American" derives from this history, from the dynamics of inter-posing and counter-posing shifting associations of "Asian" against and within "American."

Historians, social scientists, and other scholars of race agree that race is not a real or natural expression of biological difference (AAA 1998; AAPA 1996; SSRC n.d.). Instead, racial categories are social constructs whose contours expressed tensions and anxieties about the nature and place of specific groups within the United States and in the world; while race has never been real, racism, the disparate and inequitable consequences of its perceived difference, has always been. For Asians and Pacific Islanders – whose combination is itself a contested construction – these tensions centered around migration, gender, family formation, and class within the dynamics of national citizenship and transnational colonialism and empire.

In the late nineteenth century, following the abolition of slavery in the United States, racial animus facilitated the passage of restrictive policies against labor migration from Asia, which had developed as an alternative source of labor in the Americas as a result of British efforts to end the African slave trade earlier in the century. Racialization in immigration policy expanded to efforts to categorically exclude Asians from citizenship and within US society. Although Asians born in the United States successfully defended their citizenship, Asian immigrants who entered the country found themselves on the opposite, precarious side of an emergent color line, permanently ineligible for citizenship and denied its legal protections and economic opportunities. Racial precarity, moreover, informed and shaped gender precarity and limited family formation, falsely equating Asian women to prostituted women, barring White women from marrying Asian men, and stripping US citizenship from women[2] who married Asian immigrant men. Tolerated for their imported labor, well into the twentieth-century Asian Americans were relegated to a subordinate social status whose restrictive and marginalized conditions facilitated vulnerability and exploitation and, because of their connection to migration and immigration policies, to human trafficking (Cacho 2012; Card 2003; Paik 2016; Patterson 1982; Price 2015).

The consequences of these racial policies continued even after their formal repeal and as the Asian American population and racial demographics of the United States changed. Anti-Asian immigration restriction and exclusion left a legacy of legal precedent and administrative practice intended to monitor immigrants' entry and question their purpose: identification papers, entry and exit documents, detention, inspection, and examination. Indeed, the development of federal immigration infrastructure followed examples set first in Asian exclusion; the Bureau of Chinese Inspection, for instance, pre-dated the Bureau of Immigration as a federal agency.[3] Examining the historical racial context of exclusionary immigration policies and practices illuminates how racial precarity in contemporary immigration policy continues to facilitate human trafficking. Observing that immigrants of color comprise the majority of labor trafficking victims (Armstrong 2019), legal scholar Kathleen Kim argued that "immigration restrictions are inextricably connected to labor trafficking" and their connections to employment conditions make "noncitizen

---

[2] Not all women who were expatriated were White.

[3] The Bureau of Chinese Inspection was created in 1882 to enforce the Chinese Exclusion Act. The 1891 Immigration Act created the federal Office of Immigration, which subsequent legislation in 1895 promoted to the Bureau of Immigration.

workers of color . . . among the most vulnerable to workplace exploitation" (Kim 2020). Trafficking, in this sense, involves more than labor or sex exploitation; it includes the precarity within which many of its potential victims live and work, and their unequal access to and practical exclusions from systems of care and protection.

10.2   Discussion

10.2.1   Asians, Servitude, and Exclusion

Asians first arrived in the Americas as a result of the Manila galleon trade, between Spanish colonies in the Philippines and Mexico, in the mid-sixteenth to the early nineteenth centuries. Conscripted to serve on ships' crews, Filipino deserters in the mid-eighteenth century helped establish a maroon settlement in Saint-Malo, on the Gulf Coast of present-day Louisiana (Bonner 2014). In the early nineteenth century, large numbers of South Asian and Chinese indentured laborers were contracted, often through coercion or deception, and brought to the Caribbean, notably Cuba, Jamaica, Trinidad and Tobago, and British Guiana, for plantation work. They were a part of the global "coolie" trade that emerged after British abolition of slavery and blockade of the African slave trade (Lai 1993; Lowe 2015).

The United States' concern about Asians and Asian migration was similarly informed by and centered on their position as racialized labor. Small numbers arrived prior to the Civil War, with Chinese involved in the Hawaiian sandalwood trade and the California gold rush, where they faced discriminatory taxes. During the war, Confederate sugar plantation owners in Louisiana recruited Chinese workers to replace enslaved African Americans even while the United States banned participation in the coolie trade (Jung 2006). After the war, during Reconstruction, debates about the 14th Amendment and naturalization law related Chinese people to African Americans, arguing on the one hand, the relative merits of servitude versus slavery, and on the other, racial eligibility for citizenship: While their labor was morally preferable to chattel slavery, the Chinese were deemed inappropriate and ineligible for citizenship. As larger numbers of Chinese people migrated to work on sugar plantations in Hawai'i, on building rail lines – famously, but briefly on the transcontinental railroad – in mining, and in agriculture in the trans-Mississippi west, rising anti-Chinese sentiment led to passage of the 1882 Chinese Exclusion Act. Chinese people also experienced an increase in racial harassment, discrimination, residential segregation, and violent uprisings resulting in death and forced expulsion from their homes and communities (Chang and Fishkin 2019; Karuka 2019; Lee 2003; Lew-Williams 2018).

"Exclusion," which remained in force until the mid-twentieth century, maintained the tension between race, labor, and citizenship. Exclusion banned Chinese workers from immigrating, but allowed exceptions for merchants, students, religious leaders, and their families. At the same time, it also required all Chinese to carry identification and excluded all Chinese from naturalizing. The 1892 Geary Act, which extended the exclusion's original 10-year term, also authorized detention and up to a year of hard labor for Chinese without documentation; in its framing, to be Chinese was to be precarious (Geary Act 1892). While the Supreme Court later ruled the forced labor unconstitutional, it authorized the detention, establishing the precedent and basis for incarcerating migrants pending their deportation, declaring it was "not imprisonment in a legal sense" (*Fong Yue Ting v. United States* 1893; *Wong Wing v. United States* 1896). This practice continues in the twenty-first century with the detention of migrants and their families at the southern US border (Chap. 12), pending resolution of their immigration status (Jones 2016; Longo 2018; Hernández 2017). Proponents of exclusion argued it even extended to citizenship generally such that Chinese born in the United States were Chinese subjects and therefore exempt from the 14th Amendment's definition of citizenship. In a case involving a San Francisco cook, Wong Kim Ark was denied re-entry on these grounds. However, in 1898 the Supreme Court ruled his birth granted him citizenship, establishing birthright citizenship as an US legal principle beyond racial considerations (*United States v. Wong Kim Ark* 1898).

Migrants from other regions in Asia to the United States faced similar cycles of recruitment, resentment, and exclusion. In the late 19th and 20th centuries, tens of thousands of Japanese and smaller numbers of Koreans and South Asians filled Chinese exclusion's labor void in agriculture in Hawai'i and the West Coast, as well as in the lumber and fishing industries. Stoking racial animus against them, labor unions and state and local officials gained popular support to expand Chinese exclusion into a generalized "Asiatic" exclusion. Legislation in 1917 and 1924 as well as judicial rulings in the years in-between barred East, South, and Southeast Asians as well as Pacific Islanders – natives of an eponymous "Asiatic Barred Zone" as well as China, Japan, and Korea – not only from immigration, but also from naturalization (Immigration Act 1917; Immigration Act 1924).[4] That exclusion, under the rubric of "aliens ineligible for citizenship," (Immigration Act 1924; Ngai 2004) also formed the basis for discriminatory "alien land laws" that more than 15 states enacted barring these groups from owning land, forming corporations, and other economic pursuits (Aoki 1998; Chin 2001; Lazarus III 1988; Villazor 2009). Because the Philippines had become a US colony at the turn of the century in the aftermath of the bloody Philippine-American War, Filipinos remained eligible to enter the United States. They were recruited in large numbers to meet the continuing demand for labor (Chap. 14), particularly in Hawai'i and as migrant workers in California's emerging industrial agricultural system. While they were not "alien" immigrants because they did not migrate from another sovereign state, the United States designated them, along with other natives of US overseas colonies (e.g., Guamanians, Chamorro, and Samoans), "nationals" who were also ineligible for naturalized citizenship (Baldoz 2011).

---

[4] In its 1922 Ozawa and 1923 Thind cases, the US Supreme Court ruled that Japanese and Indians, as well as other natives of the barred zone, were racially ineligible to naturalize (*Ozawa v. United States* 1922; *United States v. Thind* 1923).

10.2.2   Imperialism, Gendered Labor Migration, and Racial Family Formation

Asian migration to the United States in the 19th and 20th centuries involved more than the prospect of US economic opportunity. European and US imperial interests in that period applied tactics ranging from diplomacy, economic coercion, physical violence, and military intervention to frank state warfare in order to gain territorial colonies, extra-territorial sovereignty, and economic advantage throughout Asia. The resulting social, economic, and political dislocations drove millions of Asians into overseas diaspora to fulfill the expanding labor needs of global capitalism (Chap. 5). Inter-regionally, Asians moved within Asia and the Pacific Islands, and also to Australia and New Zealand, North and South America, and Africa. Asian labor migration often followed the specific contours of colonial empires: Chinese and South Asians throughout the British Empire; Chinese, Japanese, Koreans, and Filipinos to Hawai'i and later to the continental United States. In response, emerging White settler colonies in the world, notably Canada, Australia, New Zealand, and South Africa, enacted similar racial exclusionary policies to the United States against Asian – and in some instances, Pacific Islander – labor migrants (Lake and Reynolds 2008).

Racial attitudes and assumptions, which were not always consistent, informed US and European imperial powers' perspective on Asia. On the one hand, the logic of racial hierarchy justified their colonial ventures globally as "civilizing" missions to improve the conditions of colonized regions and peoples. On the other hand, Japan's entry into empire, following Western models of industrialization and modernization, elicited concerns about its "Yellow Peril" after its defeat of China in the Sino-Japanese War in 1895. Those concerns gained further significance when Japan's defeat of Russia 10 years later inverted assumptions of European superiority. Nevertheless, despite Japanese efforts to distinguish themselves, Japan's specific peril as an imperial rival was assimilated into existing Western racial views of Asians and Asian migration (Tchen and Yates 2014). A 1906 San Francisco school board decision to include Japanese and Korean children with Chinese children in a segregated "Oriental"[5] school sparked tensions and fear of war between the United States and Japan; the situation required a negotiated settlement between the two countries. In an unofficial "Gentlemen's Agreement," Japan agreed to restrict labor migration to the continental United States in exchange for US allowance of Japanese American children's public school attendance, acceptance of already-resident Japanese immigrants, and family reunification.[6] However, that negotiated resolution

---

[5] The term, "Oriental," has long historical roots in European language and thought that, on the one hand, employed the "Orient" as a synonym for the general geographic notion of the "East" while, on the other hand, also connected it to cultural associations of exoticism, difference (specifically Islam's religious difference with Christianity), invasion, and degradation. With the emergence of European colonialism in the 18th and 19th centuries, these associations were redeployed to justify Western subjugation of the "Orient" (Said 1978).

[6] "The Japanese government agreed to stop granting passports to laborers who were trying to enter the United States unless such laborers were coming to occupy a formerly-acquired home, to join a

was short-lived; continued efforts against Japanese migration, particularly of "picture brides" – women whose arranged marriages to immigrant men allowed them entry to the United States – led to their exclusion as part of the general exclusion of "ineligible aliens" by 1924.

Concern about picture brides made explicit the gendered dimensions of Asian migration that were intrinsically connected to, and inseparable from its racial and economic dimensions. Historically, the large majority of Asian migrants (to the United States and globally) were men. The emergent conditions of global labor migration revised the social paradigm of chattel slavery. Labor recruitment separated men, both single and married, geographically and across national borders from their families. Its reductive focus on work argued, on the one hand, that they were temporarily resident "sojourners," despite the reality that many spent the majority of their lives in the United States and other countries where they worked. On the other hand, the reductive focus displaced family formation and relations overseas, requiring a return for the possibility of family creation and connection. Within the transnational circuits of their migration, the communities that Asian migrants formed out of adaptive social necessity were noted for their gender imbalance. Filipino migrant farm workers forged common bonds as "*manong*" (brothers) as they traveled from region to region to harvest seasonal crops. Overseas Chinese settlements were known as "bachelor" societies despite the fact that those who were able returned to China to marry and father children before departing again for work – a cycle that some families repeated for generations.[7] Despite his native birth in the United States, Wong Kim Ark traveled to China several times to marry, father children, and visit his overseas family; his denied re-entry on one trip precipitated his citizenship case to the Supreme Court. Born abroad, but citizens because of their father's status, his four sons came to the United States and faced similar – racially precarious – conditions and choices regarding work and family (Berger 2016).

By the same reductive logic, the few Asian women who migrated were assumed to provide sexual service, disregarding their fuller social capabilities and roles – and assigning their racialized labor and bodies additional gendered precarity. The 1875 Page Act, which preceded the Chinese Exclusion Act, banned the importation of women for prostitution and required checking whether immigrants from "China, Japan, or any Oriental country" were contracted for "lewd or immoral" services, effectively connecting the two concerns (Peffer 1992, 1999). Wives and daughters of merchants and other Chinese individuals exempt from exclusion remained suspect and were concerns for Christian missionary reformers who sought to rescue these women (Pascoe 1990). Conversely, relations between Asian men and White women were fraught. Concern about Chinese men's abduction and sexual predation of White women informed discussion of and legislation against the "White slave trade" (Lui 2005). Anti-miscegenation laws in many states banned Asians from

---

parent; spouse; or child, or to assume active control of a previously-acquired farming enterprise" (Browne 1921).

[7] Madeline Hsu estimates 2/5ths of Chinese workers in the United States had family in China (Hsu 2000).

marrying Whites. Even when legally married, beginning from 1907 to the early 1930s, women who married "ineligible aliens" – that is, Asian immigrant men – were automatically expatriated, or, stripped of their US citizenship (Bredbenner 1998; Gardner 2009; Volpp 2005). Their status, moreover, was not automatically reversed with reforms in the mid-1930s, because women, including native-born women, were required to apply to repatriate, some remained stateless into the late twentieth century.

Women's presence among male immigrants, moreover, represented not only sexual relations, but the potential of children and family formation within the United States – challenging the racial and gendered logic of transnational labor migration. The California State Board of Control's 1922 report, "California and the Oriental," included sections on population, birth rate, and picture brides, which included not only a tabulation of the number of such arrivals in 1918 but also who had given birth within a year. Japan agreed to end picture bride emigration in 1921, seeking to avoid full abrogation of the Gentlemen's Agreement. The gesture was futile, however, as the US Supreme Court's 1922 ruling that Japanese were not eligible to naturalize, combined with the 1924 Immigration Act's exclusion of "aliens ineligible for citizenship," effectively ended the agreement.

US race concerns and anxieties (of Whites) about Asians culminated in the internment of Japanese during World War II. The United States forcibly evacuated 120,000 Japanese Americans from their homes, then incarcerated them in government-run "relocation centers" – which were concentration camps – under the logic, following immigration exclusion, that they were unassimilable aliens. Two-thirds, however, were native-born citizens while the others, many their immigrant parents, were permanently barred from citizenship. They were all, nevertheless, "impossible subjects," whose race trumped the rights and due process citizenship was supposed to guarantee (Ngai 2004). Family formation was equally suspect. Internment affected all "persons of Japanese ancestry," which included mixed-race Japanese Americans, and forced non-Japanese spouses to decide whether to accompany their families, and in particular their children, into incarceration. Japanese internment, moreover, was not confined to citizens of the United States. Canada operated a similar set of camps for Japanese Canadians while several Latin American nations exported their Japanese citizens (the largest number from Peru) to be interned in camps in the United States; these camps differed from the camps housing Japanese Americans (Gardiner 1981; Mak 2009; Sunahara 1981).

10.2.3   Post-World War II Global Era: Defining "Asian American"

The United States' emergent global position at the end of World War Two and into the Cold War marked a turn in the racialization of Asians and Asian migration. On the one hand, the United States' prominent leadership role in the formation of a new international order, amid the decolonization of former European empires, required reconsideration of its racial history and reform, at least in principle, of racial policies (Cheng 2013; Dudziak 2002). Adoption of the Universal Declaration of Human Rights in 1948 provided a basis for the dismantling of racially discriminatory laws including those targeting ineligible aliens and was an impetus to pursue civil rights (Chap. 9). Following the repeal of Chinese exclusion and similar exclusions against Filipinos and Indians during and after the war, the 1952 Immigration and Nationality Act removed racial and marriage eligibility requirements for naturalization and abolished the "Asiatic Barred Zone," although its reconfiguration in an "Asia-Pacific Triangle"[8] maintained a restrictive minimum immigration quota. The 1965 Immigration Act abolished those and other race-based "national origins" quotas established in 1924 and led to a dramatic increase in Asian immigration that continues to this day (Hong 2019; Yang 2020).

At the same time, opposition to the expansion of communism led to US wars in Korea and southeast Asia and its increased influence and presence throughout Asia and globally (Man 2018). Temporary provisions for service members to bring military brides to the United States in the immediate aftermath of World War II became a small, but regular source of migration. It resulted in the establishment of a system of largely permanent overseas military bases and installations – which also gave rise to associated camp-town settlements and economies, including militarized prostitution (Yuh 2002) (Chap. 5). Dislocation from war, conflict, and their political, social, and economic fallout drove migration of those specifically and directly impacted: refugees and asylum seekers, adopted children, and reunion of mixed-race children of military personnel with their extended family as well as immigration of Asians to the United States generally. Many were from areas, including South and Southeast Asia, without large previous emigration.

As a result, the Asian American population in the United States has both increased and changed significantly. Asians are the fastest growing segment of the US population, growing more than four times faster than the overall population and comprise a quarter of all immigrants to the United States since 1965 (Hoeffel et al. 2012). Asian Americans today are also more ethnically diverse than historically. Where previously, the large majority were predominantly from East Asia (specifically China and Japan) and the Philippines, many now are from Southeast and South Asia; South Asians, in fact, are the fastest growing group by percentage. Indians, Vietnamese, and Koreans, whose historical numbers were small to non-existent, are (at the time of this writing) among the largest national groups with Chinese, Filipinos, and Japanese who, well into the twentieth century, were the largest Asian American national group. Beyond those six, which the US Census enumerates explicitly, the Census Bureau tabulated significant numbers of more than a dozen other Asian ethnic/national groups (Hoeffel et al. 2012; Pew Research Center 2012). Moreover, while historical migration originated from specific regions within Asian

---

[8] The "Asia-Pacific Triangle" included all of Asia and the Pacific between the 60th meridians (east) and 125th meridian (west) of longitude and north of the 25th parallel of southern latitude.

nations, contemporary migration often spans multiple regions from the same nation. Those differences beyond national origin are represented in a wide range of spoken and written languages as well as religion. Asian Americans also include non-national ethnic groups; Hmong are the largest, but also substantively present are Mien and several others.

With these inter-related shifts in policy and population, the perception of Asians within the United States also shifted in its tone (Hsu 2015; Wu 2015). In the 1960s, public commentary began noting Asian American "success," which was initially seen as modest. In the 1980s, when Asian household incomes began to exceed national averages, surpassing even those of White households, these observations turned into laudatory acclaim for extraordinary success. Within an emergent discourse of equal opportunity meritocracy, Asian Americans, whose immigration exclusion a few decades earlier were based on their un-assimilability, were now celebrated as a "model minority." Part of this new "success" came from repeal of racial restrictions as well as employment protections in civil rights legislation in the 1960s. Preferences in immigration-based employment, particularly in science, engineering, and medicine, however, also contributed to this new view of Asian Americans. The social capital they brought with them, with the economic resources they accrued once they arrived, provided these new immigrants and their families, including children, opportunities previously unavailable to Asians.

The increasing population of Asian Americans complicates and belies the idea of the "model minority" and reveals the tension within its racial paradigm: Where before, simply to be an Asian in the United States was to be precarious, now, because Asian Americans are successful, they cannot be precarious – even while many remain so. Close examination shows that the Asian American population in the United States is bi-modal, the result of new professional immigration and continued labor migration. While one portion is well-educated, affluent, and suburban, another, not insubstantial portion is less-educated, lower income, and urban. While the Asian American poverty rate (12.1% in 2015) is slightly lower than the national poverty rate, the percentage of Asian Americans living in poverty was among the fastest growing in the 2010s, and at the time of this writing, Asian income inequality is rising more rapidly than among any other group in the United States (Ishimatsu 2013; Kochhar and Cilluffo 2018). These migrations, moreover, are neither separate nor distinct, but are often connected; Asian immigrants use family reunification preferences in the 1965 immigration act in concert with professional preferences and vice versa to bring networks of extended family members together in the United States. Disaggregation of Asian ethnic populations reveals important income and education differences between them: Cambodians, Laotian, Hmong, Burmese, Nepalese, and Bhutanese are among those with the lowest income and education levels and Indian, Filipinos, Japanese, and Sri Lankans are at the high end (Budiman et al. 2019). Furthermore, economic bi-modality exists within all Asian American groups, particularly within groups with higher incomes, the success of some obscures recognition of others who work low-income jobs, live in poverty, and/or are undocumented.

Higher income and professional status, moreover, do not insulate Asian Americans from either racism or other forms of social vulnerability, including trafficking. When calibrated for the number of household earners, educational attainment, and other factors, income figures for Asian Americans fall below expected levels (Lee and Tran 2019; Lee and Zhou 2015; Tran et al. 2019). Similarly, workplace practices in the corporate world continue negative racial and gender associations about Asian Americans and institutionalize detrimental dynamics, constituting a "bamboo ceiling" that limits Asian Americans' upward mobility (Chin 2020). While immigration preferences facilitate professionals' entry into the United States, they can also expose them to labor exploitation and human trafficking. Recent cases of nurses from the Philippines demonstrate the ways that unscrupulous employers subordinated their immigration status, threatening deportation, to gain advantage in their labor relations. Employers leveraged Filipino nurses' precarity to deny their rights and traffick their labor and bodies (Bump 2019; Michelen 2019; Roy 2019).

The complications of contemporary perception extend to awareness of Asian American racialization historically, including among Asian Americans themselves. Because many Asian Americans are immigrants, those who arrive as adults have little knowledge or education about US history, particularly its racial history. Those who arrive as children are taught historical curricula determined at the state and local level, and those ethnic studies components explore contributions from the United States' multicultural, ethnic, and immigrant past with scant reference to specific racial context and critique (Chap. 16). Similarly, while an awareness of events in Asian American history are now part of public discourse, less engaged are the specific, broader contexts that informed and gave rise to them.

This disconnect extends even to the terms "Asian American" and "Asian Pacific Islander" which have different origins, histories, and valences that remain largely unexamined. Both are used commonly and interchangeably with the assumption that they refer generically to Asian immigrants to the United States. The one, "Asian American," however, stems from the founding of the Asian American Political Alliance, a grassroots community organization formed by student activists at the University of California, Berkeley, in 1968. Drawing inspiration from global movements for Afro-Asian solidarity, the group rejected the racist associations of existing terms such as "Oriental" and "Asiatic." Rather, they argued for Asian American participation in a multi-racial coalition seeking self-empowerment beyond civil rights, including education in comparative ethnic studies that situated its anti-racism within a critique of US militarism and imperialism (Maeda 2009; Maeda 2012). The other, "Asian Pacific Islander," is a derivation of a government category, "Asian or Pacific Islander," first articulated in the 1970s by the Office of Management and Budget that was itself derived from historical designations of the Asia-Pacific Triangle and the "Asiatic Barred Zone." This combination of Asian and Pacific Islander conflated groups with very different colonial histories and experiences (Jung and Almaguer 2004). Formulated on the cusp of renewed Asian migration in the United States, the two terms represent radically different perspectives on their increasing presence and place: the one acknowledges the precarity of historical racialization to address its legacy and consequence, the other occludes that history to transform its racial legacy into a descriptive metric.

10.2.4   Racial Formation and Dynamics

These differences in terms, perspectives, and historical genealogies are significant because Asian American racialization has always necessarily involved more than Asian Americans. Speaking in favor of Chinese immigration, naturalization, and citizenship in 1867, Frederick Douglass argued against allowing perceived racial differences to subvert the human equality of what he called a "composite nation" (Douglass 1993). "The problem of the twentieth century," W.E.B. DuBois declared several decades later, "is the problem of the color line—the relations of the darker to lighter races of men in Asia and Africa, America and the islands of the sea" (DuBois 1903). While better known for their writings and ideas about African Americans, both Douglass and DuBois not only included Asia and Asians in their thinking, but also, and as significantly, argued to consider their racialization in relation to other racial groups – to what Michael Omi and Howard Winant called "racial formations" (Mullen 2004; Mullen and Watson 2005; Omi and Winant 2016).

These relations, like racial lines themselves, have changed over time and served different purposes. In the immediate aftermath of the Civil War, Douglass connected Chinese labor migration to the abolition of slavery. In the late 19th and early 20th centuries that DuBois observed, an emergent post-emancipation system of racial apartheid included Asian Americans with African American, Latinx, and Indigenous groups. Their exclusion from immigration and naturalization, in this sense, was part of a racial formation whose "color line" preserved White supremacy within domestic labor relations and overseas capitalism and colonialism.

New racialization of Asian Americans as a "model minority" in the latter half of the twentieth century, however, not only observed their "success," it compared and opposed that success to those of other racial groups. Their model was both proof of racial progress in the United States and reproof of others' apparent lack of progress. Significantly, however, the terms of their example shifted as the Asian American population and social conditions and concerns changed. While notions of Asian American success since the 1980s have associated that success with immigrant over-achievement, observers in the 1960s (prior to renewed Asian migration) originally celebrated their exemplary citizenship, not their income or academic accomplishment. Asian Americans, most of whom were native-born children of immigrant families, 1960s' commentators noted, were exceptionally law-abiding (particularly to compared "problem minorities"), and diligent in overcoming obstacles, including poverty, poor housing, and racial discrimination (Petersen 1966).

In this sense, while, on its surface, Asian Americans' status as a model minority acknowledges their accomplishments, its malleability also reveals its deeper ideological purpose. Comparison to other racial groups, whether they are characterized explicitly as "problems" or implicitly as under-achieving, particularly in public discourse, serves not only to regulate, but also to maintain racial order. Opposing Asian American lawfulness and diligence against the problematic behavior of other groups of color paralleled mid- and late 1960s' political discourse arguing social "law and order" against the urban unrest of racial nationalist movements. Similarly, opponents of affirmative action, who see it as "reverse racism" rather than redress for the legacy of historical racism, point to Asian American admissions to elite colleges to argue for its abolition. The comparative logic within model minority discourse explains Asian American citation and critique, particularly among more recent immigrants, of past anti-Asian racism that see it as separate from, and not connected to, racism involving other groups. It is this kind of "anti-racist" thinking that, paradoxically and unfortunately, continues and contributes to anti-blackness.

Such comparison commits a disservice, both to Asian Americans and the groups with which they are compared. Continued attention to their race – to the fact of their racialization – conflates and confuses generalized observation with causation. It minimizes the diverse range of their lived experiences and circumstances that can run counter to over-determined narratives about and comparing racialized groups. Arguments that affirmative action adversely affects Asian Americans, for instance, oversimplify the case. Anti-affirmative action arguments that involve Asian Americans focus on college admissions without mentioning small businesses, employment, and workplace environments where affirmative action programs benefit Asian Americans.[9] In New York City, the demographics of racialized groups reverse the assignment and assumptions of Asian American model minority success: African immigrants, particularly Sub-Saharan immigrants, have high levels of educational attainment while Asians are the immigrants in the lowest income group and the most likely to live in poverty.[10]

More significantly, conceiving and comparing racialized outcomes as discrete and separate outcomes detracts from broader consideration and improvement of conditions within which racialized groups live, many of which are shared across groups. Historical conditions and policies such as "redlining,"[11] restrictive housing covenants, lending discrimination, and selective application of eminent domain in the construction of urbanization projects have denied non-White groups (especially African Americans) access to wealth accumulation while also racializing their growing class differences (Katznelson 2006; Rothstein 2017). Asian American racialization as a model minority does not insulate them from these vulnerabilities; indeed, it contributes to undercounts of their consequences. Food and housing insecurity, and lack of adequate access to health care, including mental health, dispro-

---

[9] Asian Americans, for instance, are included among socially disadvantaged groups eligible for federal contracts under the Small Business Administration's 8(a) Business Development program (13 CFR § 124.103; Sharpe 1997).

[10] On African immigrants, see Kassa 2012; Echeverria-Estrada and Batalova 2019; Partnership for a New American Research Fund 2018. On Asian poverty levels in New York City, 2013–17 (which uses adjusted data of the US Census Bureau's American Community Survey), see Mayor's Office of Economic Opportunity 2019 and Asian American Federation 2018.

[11] "Redlining" refers to the color-coding system federal housing loan agencies developed to appraise the "mortgage security" of residential neighborhoods. Red was assigned to the lowest grade, most "hazardous" areas, often based on the presence and numbers of African Americans, racial minorities, and undesired immigrants. For an interactive historical map, see the University of Richmond's "Mapping Inequality: Redlining in New Deal America," https://dsl.richmond.edu/panorama/redlining

portionately affect Asian Americans as they do other racial groups, but are often under-reported. Medical researchers similarly note lack of coverage when reporting the impact of COVID-19, particularly high mortality rates, among Asian Americans (della Cava 2020; Rozenfeld et al. 2020; Yan et al. 2020a, b).

Racialization, even when constructed positively for certain groups, continues to inform and shape precarity across racial groups, and by extension, conditions for their exploitation and trafficking. The modern "super-immigrant model minority" notion belies the fact that immigration policies continue to exacerbate these existing vulnerabilities even for Asian Americans. While racial associations about labor migration have shifted from Asians to Latinx groups, immigration policies, particularly with regard to the undocumented, continue to inform the conditions of both populations. Senator Richard Durbin cited both a Mexican American, Diana, and a Korean immigrant from Brazil, Tereza, in 2004 as inspirations for his support for the Development, Relief, and Education for Alien Minors Act (DREAM) Act. The DREAM Act sought to protect undocumented migrants who had come to the United States as children from deportation and provide them with a path to permanent residency and citizenship (Durbin 2004).

10.3 Conclusion

The challenge for contemporary policymakers is to be conscious of Asian Americans' historical racialization and that continuing legacy without diminishing the opportunity and achievement that some Asian Americans have realized. This requires attention to particular conditions and circumstances rather than reference to universal principles. To appeal to race-neutral, color-blind policy is to be blind to color and its history. The term "Asian American" is a result of racialization, and Asian American success requires recognition of continued vulnerability.

The arc of Asian American history illustrates the complex ways that racialization informs social precarity and by extension, vulnerabilities to trafficking. Post-emancipation attention to and exclusion of Asian Americans, particularly workers, made explicit the racial concerns of White citizens in a society increasingly based on wage labor and was foundational in the development of race-based anti-immigration policies. Asian American exclusion, moreover, informed the emergent system of federal immigration practices where inspection and enforcement allowed and leaned toward scrutiny and suspicion of immigrant arrivals. Asian American racialization and exclusion meant that they were, by definition, "legally and permanently alien;" their racialization was intended to be a permanent othering.

The legacy of historical Asian racialization and exclusion, moreover, lies beyond the experience and mistreatment of Asians and extends to other groups of color. Contemporary, supposedly color-blind concerns about the deleterious consequences of admitting "public charges" trace their legislative genealogy to the late 19th and early 20th centuries when advocates for immigration restrictions expressed their racist intent even more explicitly (Villazor 2009). Targeting Latinx more than Asian migrants, explicit and increasingly extreme public commentary on the issue, nevertheless, reveals the intent underlying that neutral language. If no longer formal, racial exclusion's historical legacy continues to echo within a federal infrastructure that incarcerates the vulnerable with little to no recourse in the name of border enforcement. Precarity remains, redefined as rightlessness and illegal immigration without considering their contexts, migrations that are the consequence of US foreign policy, "interventions," and global capitalism (Chap. 12). Ignorance of the situations and dynamics that create precarity and facilitate vulnerability to exploitation and trafficking result in a failure to meaningfully address the underlying conditions that produce it.

The roots of human trafficking are social vulnerability and precarity. Whether by intentional design or unintended consequence, policies that result in precarity enable conditions for human trafficking. While the 13th Amendment abolished slavery and involuntary servitude formally and the Supreme Court upheld its authority to eliminate the "badges and incidents of slavery" (Civil Rights Cases 1883), continued desire for inexpensive labor fuels efforts to recruit while also redefining immigrant workers to meet its requirements. Historically, exclusionary immigration policies rooted in racial animus sought explicitly not only to prevent migrant peoples of color from entering the United States, but also to limit their access to full or partial rights if and once they arrived. Racialization rendered migrant workers of color doubly vulnerable to commodification and exploitation; it not only separated them ideologically from the labor they produced, it also denied them claims to social membership. Moreover, and significantly in the post-1965 era of renewed and expansive immigration (particularly of Asians and Latinx migrants), racialization results in commodification and exploitation through different means. Used as social metrics for state purposes, racial categories obscure information about and differences between sub-groups within aggregated data; within broad generalizations, particularly about model success, obscured vulnerability becomes its own form of insecurity. While racial precarity has found various forms historically, its clear consequence for immigrants of color – especially those already most socially vulnerable – has been the persistent denial of rights and access to systems of care and protection. The concomitant labor and gender practices that that denial enables are abusive, exploitative, and very near the line – indeed, sometimes crossing it – that defines modern notions of human trafficking.

10.4 Recommendations

The recommendations below prevent human trafficking in the modern day by addressing broader social inequities – focused on (1) eliminating institutionalized systems creating precarity and (2) increasing access to systems of care and protection. Addressing precarity and advancing social inclusion of previously marginalized populations and communities decreases vulnerabilities to trafficking.

Anti-trafficking strategies and policies should be analyzed through a public health-principled, historical, and race-conscious framework (Kim 2020).

In broad categories, recommendations to address the roots of human trafficking include as follows:

1. *Avoid institutionalizing precarity.* Policies should be analyzed, monitored, and evaluated from a precarity framework; intentional and regular efforts should be made to avoid creating or continuing policies that increase social vulnerabilities.
2. *Resolve the implicit racism entrenched in immigration policies and practices.* Current immigration policies are built around structures that were historically rooted in racial animus. Immigration reform and policies must not be built on negative race-based historical precedents and should instead be crafted to ensure principles of equity and justice.
3. *Disaggregate Asian American and Pacific Islander data to avoid overgeneralizations about Asians.* Avoid masking risk and precarity of different Asian ethnicities and lower income groups in aggregate data.
4. *Develop comprehensive immigration reform policies that enable all classes and categories of non-citizen people residing in the United States to equal access to systems of care and protection.* Delink access to social welfare programs, health care, and criminal justice legal protections from differential immigration documentation status. When people are working and residing within the United States and contributing to the fabric of community, they should be able to access a minimum of social services, health care, and legal protections, regardless of documentation status.
5. *Where precarity already exists in current policies, ensure that corrective social welfare systems can fully address the gaps for vulnerable populations.* Increase safety net programs and eligibility. For example, reduce eligibility restrictions to healthcare exchanges or Medicaid.
6. *Develop stronger worker rights protections, regardless of immigration documentation.* Worker rights and labor protections should be applied equally to US and non-immigrant foreign workers (e.g., temporary agricultural workers under H2A visas).
7. *Anti-trafficking legislation requires substantial funding for prevention efforts.* At the time of this writing, most funding supports anti-trafficking interventions (e.g., law enforcement and investigation, prosecution, shelter homes). Intervention work is important but insufficient to eradicate precarity and trafficking vulnerability. Investments in prevention are necessary to decrease precarity.
8. *"Anti-trafficking" funding earmarked for prevention should be distributed to health centers and educational systems (for example) that serve AA and PI populations.* Prevention of trafficking requires minimizing and mitigating existing vulnerabilities to being trafficked.
9. *Develop a national, public health, historically rooted, race-conscious anti-trafficking framework.* Anti-trafficking initiatives should consider the vulnerabilities of populations of color, due to historical policies across sectors, based on racial

animus, including the history of colonialism in the United States, and the legacy of exclusionary immigration policies. These historical policies affected Indigenous peoples, enslaved Africans, and then African Americans, Asians, and Pacific Islanders and now directly affect Latinx populations in the present day. Any anti-trafficking framework should seek to correct systematic biases. An honest understanding of history puts precarity and vulnerability prevention within reach.

References

American Anthropological Association (AAA). (1998). *Statement on Race.* https://www.americananthro.org/ConnectWithAAA/Content.aspx?ItemNumber=2583.

American Association of Physical Anthropologists (AAPA). (1996). Statement on biological aspects of race. *American Journal of Physical Anthropology, 101*, 569–570.

Aoki, K. (1998). No right to own: The early twentieth-century alien land laws as a prelude to internment symposium: The long shadow of Korematsu. *Boston College Third World Law Journal, 19*, 37–72.

Armstrong, C. (2019). Concepts of slavery in the United States, 1865-1914. In J. Winterdyk & J. Jones (Eds.), *The Palgrave international handbook of human trafficking* (pp. 35–51). New York: Springer International Publishing.

Asian American Federation. (2018). *Hidden in plain sight: Asian poverty in New York City.* New York: Asian American Federation.

Baldoz, R. (2011). *The third Asiatic invasion.* New York: NYU Press.

Banks, D., & Kyckelhahn, T. (2011). *Characteristics of suspected human trafficking incidents, 2008–2010.* Washington, D.C.: Bureau of Justice Statistics, U.S. Department of Justice. http://www.bjs.gov/content/pub/pdf/cshti0810.pdf. Accessed October 12, 2012.

Berger, B. (2016). Birthright Citizenship on Trial: Elk v. Wilkins and United States v. Wong Kim Ark. *Cardozo Law Review, 37*, 1185.

Bonner, S. J. (Ed.). (2014). *Lafcardio Hearn's America: Ethnographic sketches and editorials.* Lexington: University Press of Kentucky.

Bredbenner, C. L. (1998). *A nationality of her own.* Berkeley: University of California Press.

Browne, W. R. (Ed.) (1921). Japanese-American passport agreement. In *What's what in the labor movement: A dictionary of labor affairs and labor terminology* (Vol. 261). New York: B.W. Huebsch.

Bryant-Davis, T., & Tummala-Narra, P. (2018). Cultural oppression and human trafficking: Exploring the role of racism and ethnic bias. In N. M. Sidun & D. L. Hume (Eds.), *A feminist perspective on human trafficking of women and girls* (pp. 146–163). New York: Routledge.

Budiman, A., Cilluffo, A., & Ruiz, N. G. (2019, May 22). *Key facts about Asian origin groups in the U.S.* Washington, DC: Pew Research Center. https://www.pewresearch.org/fact-tank/2019/05/22/key-facts-about-asian-origin-groups-in-the-u-s/. Accessed 2 September 2020.

Bump, B. (2019, October 14). Lawsuit: Albany Med's Filipino nursing program violates human trafficking law. *Times Union.* https://www.timesunion.com/news/article/Lawsuit-Albany-Med-s-Filipino-nursing-program-14521113.php. Accessed 21 June 2020.

Butler, J. (2004). *Precarious life.* New York: Verso.

Butler, J. (2009). *Frames of war.* New York: Verso.

Cacho, L. M. (2012). *Social death.* New York: NYU Press.

Card, C. (2003). Genocide and social death. *Hypatia, 18*(1), 63–79.

Chang, G., & Fishkin, S. F. (Eds.). (2019). *The Chinese and the iron road.* Palo Alto: Stanford University Press.

Cheng, C. I.-F. (2013). *Citizens of Asian America*. New York: NYU Press.

Chin, G. J. (2001). Citizenship and exclusion: Wyoming's anti-Japanese alien land law in context symposium: Heart Mountain. *Wyoming Law Review, 1*, 497–522.

Chin, M. (2020). *Stuck*. New York: NYU Press.

Civil Rights Cases. (1883). 109 U.S. 3.

Code of Federal Regulations. *8(a) business development/small disadvantaged business status determinations ₋ who is socially disadvantaged? 13 CFR § 124.103*. https://www.govinfo. gov/content/pkg/CFR-2020-title13-vol1/xml/CFR-2020-title13-vol1-sec124-103.xml. 63 FR 35739, June 30, 1998, as amended at 74 FR 45753, Sept. 4, 2009; 76 FR 8254, Feb. 11, 2011; 81 FR 48579, July 25, 2016.

Della Cava, M. (2020, October 18). Asian Americans in San Francisco are dying at alarming rates from COVID-19. *USA Today*. https://www.usatoday.com/in-depth/news/nation/2020/10/18/coronavirus-asian-americans-racism-death-rates-san-francisco/5799617002/. Accessed October 18, 2020.

Douglass, F. (1993). The composite nation. In P. S. Foner & D. Rosenberg (Eds.), *Racism, dissent and Asian Americans from 1850 to the present: A documentary history* (pp. 217–230). Westport: Praeger.

DuBois, W. E. B. (1903). *The souls of Black folk*. Chicago: A. C. McClurg &.

Dudziak, M. (2002). *Cold war civil rights*. Princeton: Princeton University Press.

Durbin, R. Dream Act. *Congressional Record* 150 (2004) S8670–71. Text from *Congressional Record Permanent Digital Collection*. Accessed 2 Sept 2020.

Echeverria-Estrada, C., & Batalova, J. (2019). *Sub-Saharan African immigrants in the United States*. Washington, DC: Migration Policy Institute. https://www.migrationpolicy.org/article/sub-saharan-african-immigrants-united-states-2018.

Fong Yue Ting v. United States. (1893). 149 U.S. 698, 707.

Gardiner, H. C. (1981). *Pawns in a triangle of hate*. Seattle: University of Washington Press.

Gardner, M. (2009). *The qualities of a citizen*. Princeton: Princeton University Press.

Geary Act. (1892). 27 Stat. 25.

Hernández, K. L. (2017). *City of inmates*. Chapel Hill: University of North Carolina Press.

Hoeffel, E. M., Rastogi, S., Kim, M. O., & Shahid, H. (2012). *The Asian population 2010: 2010 census briefs*. Washington, DC: Economics and Statistics Administration, U.S. Department of Commerce. https://www.census.gov/prod/cen2010/briefs/c2010br-11.pdf.

Hong, J. (2019). *Opening the gates to Asia*. Chapel Hill: University of North Carolina Press.

Hsu, M. (2000). *Dreaming of gold, dreaming of home*. Palo Alto: Stanford University Press.

Hsu, M. (2015). *The good immigrants*. Princeton: Princeton University Press.

Immigration Act. (1917). 39 Stat. 874.

Immigration Act. (1924). 43 Stat. 153.

Ishimatsu, J. (2013). *Spotlight: Asian American & Pacific Islander Poverty*. Washington, DC: National Coalition for Asian Pacific American Community Development (CAPACD).

Jones, R. (2016). *Violent borders*. New York: Verso.

Jung, M.-H. (2006). *Coolies and cane*. Baltimore: The Johns Hopkins University Press.

Jung, M.-K., & Almaguer, T. (2004). The state and the production of racial categories. In R. D. Coates (Ed.), *Race and ethnicity: Across time, space, and discipline* (pp. 55–72). Leiden: Brill.

Karuka, M. (2019). *Empire's tracks*. Berkeley: University of California Press.

Kassa, A. (2012). *Dimension of the new diaspora: African immigrant communities & organizations in New York, Washington, D.C., and Atlanta*. Oakland: Priority Africa Network.

Katznelson, I. (2006). *When affirmative action was White*. New York: W. W. Norton.

Kim, K. (2020). The thirteenth amendment and human trafficking: Lessons & Limitations. *Georgia State University Law Review, 36*, 1005–1026.

Kochhar, R., & Cilluffo, A. (2018, July 12). *Income inequality in the U.S. is rising most rapidly among Asians*. Washington, DC: Pew Research Center.

Lai, W. L. (1993). *Indentured labor, Caribbean sugar*. Baltimore: The Johns Hopkins University Press.

Lake, M., & Reynolds, H. (2008). *Drawing the global colour line*. Cambridge: Cambridge University Press.

Lazarus, M., III. (1988). An historical analysis of alien land law: Washington territory & state 1853–1889. *University of Puget Sound Law Review, 12*, 197–246.

Lee, E. (2003). *At America's gates*. Chapel Hill: University of North Carolina Press.

Lee, I. C., & Lewis, M. (2003). Human trafficking from a legal advocate's perspective: History, legal framework and current anti-trafficking efforts. *U.C. Davis Journal of International Law & Policy, 10*(1), 169.

Lee, J., & Zhou, M. (2015). *The Asian American achievement paradox*. New York: Russell Sage Foundation.

Lee, J., & Tran, V. C. (2019, February 21). Asian Americans May Have an Educational Advantage, but They Face a 'Bamboo Ceiling' at Work. *Los Angeles Times*. https://www.latimes.com/opinion/op-ed/la-oe-lee-asian-american-attainment-gap-20190221-story.html.

Lew-Williams, B. (2018). *The Chinese must go!* Cambridge: Harvard University Press.

Longo, M. (2018). *The politics of borders*. Cambridge: Cambridge University Press.

Lowe, L. (2015). *Intimacies of four continents*. Durham: Duke University Press.

Lui, M. (2005). *The Chinatown trunk mystery*. Princeton, N.J: Princeton University Press.

Lui, M. T. L. (2005). *The Chinatown trunk mystery*. Princeton: Princeton University Press.

Maeda, D. (2009). *Chains of Babylon*. New York: Routledge.

Maeda, D. (2012). *Rethinking the Asian American movement*. Minneapolis: University of Minnesota Press.

Mak, S. (2009). *America's other internment: World War II and the making of modern human rights*. Ph.D. diss., Northwestern University.

Man, S. (2018). *Soldiering through empire*. Berkeley: University of California Press.

Mayor's Office of Economic Opportunity. (2019). *New York City government poverty measure, 2017*. New York: Office of the Mayor.

Michelen, O. (2019, October 1). 200 Filipino nurses win human trafficking lawsuit against SentosaCare and its owners. *Courtroomstrategy*, https://courtroomstrategy.com/2019/10/200-filipino-nurses-win-human-trafficking-lawsuit-against-sentosacare-and-its-owners/. Accessed 21 June 2020.

Mullen B., & Watson, C. (Eds.). (2005). *W.E.B. DuBois on Asia*. Oxford: University of Mississippi Press.

Mullen, B. (2004). *Afro-Orientalism*. Minneapolis: University of Minnesota.

Ngai, M. (2004). *Impossible subjects*. Princeton: Princeton University Press.

Omi, M., & Winant, H. (2016). *Racial formation in the United States* (3rd. ed.). New York: Routledge.

Ozawa v. United States. (1922). 260 U.S. 178.

Paik, A. N. (2016). *Rightlessness*. Chapel Hill: University of North Carolina Press.

Partnership for a New American Research Fund. (2018). *Power of the purse: How sub-Saharan Africans contribute to the U.S. economy*. Washington, DC: New American Economy.

Pascoe, P. (1990). *Relations of rescue*. New York: Oxford University Press.

Patterson, O. (1982). *Slavery and social death*. Cambridge: Harvard University Press.

Peffer, G. A. (1992). From under the sojourner's shadow: A historiographical study of Chinese female immigration to America, 1852–1882. *Journal of American Ethnic History, 11*(3), 41–67.

Peffer, G. A. (1999). *If they don't bring their women here*. Urbana: University of Illinois Press.

Petersen, W. (1966, January 9). Success Story, Japanese-American Style. *New York Times Magazine*.

Pew Research Center. (2012, June 19). *The rise of Asian Americans*. Washington, DC: Pew Research Center. https://www.pewsocialtrends.org/2012/06/19/chapter-1-portrait-of-asian-americans/.

Price, J. M. (2015). *Prison and social death*. Newark: Rutgers University Press.

Rothstein, R. (2017). *The color of law*. New York: Liveright.

Roy, Y. (2019, October 2). Court: LI nursing home firm violated anti-human trafficking laws. *Newsday*. https://www.newsday.com/long-island/suffolk/sentosa-nursing-home-nurses-1.37091421. Accessed 21 June 2020.

Rozenfeld, Y., Beam, J., Maier, H., et al. (2020). A model of disparities: Risk factors associated with COVID-19 infection. *International Journal of Equity in Health, 19*, 126. https://doi.org/10.1186/s12939-020-01242-z.

Said, E. (1978). *Orientalism*. New York: Pantheon.

Sharpe, R. (1997, Sept 9). Asian-Americans See gains in Affirmative Action Program. *Wall Street Journal*. https://www.wsj.com/articles/SB873753487297501500.

Social Science Research Council (SSRC). *Is race "Real"?* http://raceandgenomics.ssrc.org/.

Sunahara, A. G. (1981). *The politics of racism: The uprooting of Japanese Canadians during the second world war*. Toronto: James Lorimer Limited.

Tatum, B. D. (2000). The complexity of identity: Who am I? In M. Adams, W. J. Blumenfeld, R. Castaneda, H. W. Hackman, M. L. Peters, & X. Zúñiga (Eds.), *Readings for diversity and social justice* (pp. 9–14). New York: Routledge.

Tchen, J. K.-W., & Yates, D. (Eds.). (2014). *Yellow peril! An archive of anti-Asian fear*. New York: NYU Press.

Tran, V. C., Lee, J., & Huang, T. J. (2019). Revisiting the Asian second-generation advantage. *Ethnic and Racial Studies, 42*(13), 2248–2269. https://doi.org/10.1080/01419870.2019.1579920.

United Nations Office on Drugs and Crime. (2008). *An introduction to human trafficking: Vulnerability, impact and action*. https://www.unodc.org/documents/human-trafficking/An_Introduction_to_Human_Trafficking_-_Background_Paper.pdf.

United States v. Bhagat Singh Thind. (1923). 261 U.S. 204.

United States v. Wong Kim Ark. (1898). 169 U.S. 649.

United States Constitution, Amendment XIII. 1865.

Victims of Trafficking and Violence Protection Act (TVPA). (2000). 114 Stat. 1464. Pub. Law 106–386.

Villazor, R. C. (2009). Rediscovering Oyama v. California: At the intersection of property, race, and citizenship. *Washington University Law Review, 87*, 979–1042.

Volpp, L. (2005). Divesting citizenship: On Asian American history and the loss of citizenship through marriage. *UCLA Law Review, 52*, 405–483. UC Berkeley Public Law Research Paper No. 870087. Available at SSRN: https://ssrn.com/abstract=870087.

Wong Wing v. United States. (1896). 163 U.S. 228, 237.

Wu, E. (2015). *The color of success*. Princeton: Princeton University Press.

Yan, B. W., Ng, F., Chu, J., Tsoh, J., & Nguyen, T. (2020a, July 13). Asian Americans Facing High COVID-19 Case Fatality. *Health Affairs*. https://www.healthaffairs.org/do/10.1377/hblog20200708.894552/full.

Yan, B. W., Ng, F., & Nguyen, T. (2020b). *High mortality from COVID-19 among Asian Americans in San Francisco and California*. San Francisco: Asian American Research Center on Health. https://asianarch.org/press_releases/Asian%20COVID-19%20Mortality%20Final.pdf.

Yang, J. L. (2020). *One mighty and irresistible tide*. New York: W.W. Norton.

Yuh, J.-Y. (2002). *Beyond the shadow of camptown*. New York: NYU Press.

Chapter 11
Systemic and Structural Roots of Child Sex Trafficking: The Role of Gender, Race, and Sexual Orientation in Disproportionate Victimization

Erin Williamson and Aria Flood

11.1 Introduction

Efforts to address child sex trafficking have historically taken a criminal justice approach, focusing on the actions of individual perpetrators and promoting criminal justice solutions (Farrell and Kane 2020). However, society cannot arrest its way to a world without trafficking. Despite decades of arrests, traffickers appear undeterred and evidence suggests the scale of human trafficking is on the rise (United Nations Office on Drugs and Crime 2018). In order to eradicate this crime, child sex trafficking must be viewed as a social, political, and public health problem, and policies and programs must address the systems and structures that lead to and sustain children's vulnerabilities.

In the United States, children from every demographic have experienced trafficking; no child is immune. The trafficking of children includes both sex and labor trafficking. This chapter, however, will specifically focus on sex trafficking. Research regarding the labor trafficking of children in the United States and data on the demographic breakdown of this population remain scarce (Walts 2017). Without this research, less is known regarding the role of childhood trauma as a risk factor for labor trafficking, variation in the impact of trauma and oppression in child labor trafficking versus child sex trafficking, or the role of child-serving systems in responding to labor trafficking victimization.

Research on sex trafficking, however, is fairly robust especially in reference to girls. While some research suggests that boys are under-identified as survivors of child sex trafficking and certainly more research is needed regarding this population, the majority of studies to date do show a gender disparity, with girls representing a greater percentage of those recognized as trafficked (e.g., Curtis et al. 2008; Institute of Medicine

E. Williamson (✉) · A. Flood
Love146, New Haven, CT, USA
e-mail: erin@love146.org

© Springer Nature Switzerland AG 2021
M. Chisolm-Straker, K. Chon (eds.), *The Historical Roots of Human Trafficking*,
https://doi.org/10.1007/978-3-030-70675-3_11

and National Research Council 2013; Murphy 2017; Swaner et al. 2016). This gender disparity does not appear to be present among survivors of child labor trafficking (Murphy 2017). Therefore, when examining the impacts of trauma and oppression on survivors of child sex trafficking, it is important to examine those impacts in the context of historical and present-day sexual violence against women, especially women who identify as Black, Indigenous, and people of color (BIPOC) (Chap. 5).

Research has repeatedly shown that girls, children who identify as BIPOC, and children who identify as lesbian, gay, bisexual, transgender, queer/questioning, Two-Spirit, and other (LGBTQ2S+) are overrepresented among the child sex trafficking survivor population (Butler 2015; Choi 2015; Georgia State University 2019; Gibbs et al. 2018b; Martinez and Kelle 2013; Swaner et al. 2016; Twis 2020). While some research suggests that these demographic characteristics are not *predictive* of trafficking victimization (Choi 2015), the overrepresentation of these populations is significant and should not be overlooked or understated. Historically, the anti-trafficking field has referred to the overrepresentation of these populations by identifying gender, race, ethnicity, and sexual orientation as individual risk factors. Less attention, however, has been paid to the identity trauma and historical trauma often experienced by these populations or the role that systemic and internalized oppression (sexism, racism, ethnocentrism, homophobia, and transphobia) plays in these children's vulnerabilities.

This chapter addresses gaps in the current literature by discussing the roles of trauma and oppression as risk factors for child sex trafficking and the disproportionate impact trauma and oppression may have on girls, children who identify as BIPOC, and children who identify as LGBTQ2S+. The chapter probes the role that child-serving systems have historically played in responding to childhood trauma and the manner in which modern responses may further contribute to the oppression of these populations and their overrepresentation among trafficked children. Finally, recommendations are made for how the field and child-serving systems can move forward to address legacies of trauma and oppression, especially among overrepresented populations and provide better foundational prevention so that children are not trafficked in the first place.

11.2 Discussion

The issue of child sex trafficking is often discussed in the context of aftercare, serving children who have already experienced this trauma. If a world without trafficking is to be realized, trafficking must be prevented from happening in the first place. In order to do that, understanding what makes children vulnerable to traffickers, how child-serving systems are addressing these vulnerabilities, and where there are missed opportunities for preventative intervention is vital. Children must be protected and empowered *to prevent* traffickers from exploiting them.

In discussing the role of trauma and oppression in trafficking, terminology is critically important. Table 11.1 provides a list of terminology and definitions used throughout this chapter.

Table 11.1 Terms and definitions

Term	Definition
BIPOC	For the purposes of this chapter, BIPOC specifically refers to Black, Indigenous, and Latinx. Note: Asian Americans are not included in this chapter's definition as research does not show that Asian-American children are overrepresented among child sex trafficking survivors in the United States.
Cisgender	A person whose gender is the same as the gender-assumed-at-birth, which is commonly assumed based on genitals at birth.
Historical trauma	The cumulative trauma experienced across generations by a group of people who share an identity or affiliation, and/or experienced the same traumatic event.
Homophobia (and biphobia)	Fear of, aversion to, prejudice, or discrimination against gay, lesbian, or bisexual people.
Identity trauma	Trauma experienced as a result of a person's identity.
Internalized oppression	Oppression that occurs when groups who are subject to systemic oppression over long periods of time begin to normalize this oppression, and as a result, internalize the discrimination perpetrated against them, and incorporate discriminatory messages and experiences into their understanding of themselves as an "inferior" group.
Latinx	Gender-neutral term for people of Latin-American origin or descent.
Microaggression	Everyday comments or actions that subtly either consciously or unconsciously communicate prejudice or discrimination against a person or people based solely upon their marginalized group membership.
Racism	An organized system used to differentially treat and allocate resources based on socially defined "races." This system is based on the presumption that people of one racial group are biologically or culturally "superior" to others who are "inferior." Racism can persist in institutional structures and policies without racial prejudice at the individual level.
Runaways	Children who leave their homes on "their own accord" but without permission.
Sexism	A system, based on the patriarchal hegemony, which categorizes women and girls (in particular) as "inferior" to men and boys. Sexism can persist in institutional structures and policies without sexist prejudice at the individual level.
Systemic oppression	Oppression resulting from the policies and practices in structures and institutions (e.g., education, health, transportation, housing, economic) that intentionally disadvantage certain groups of people based on their identity, while also providing advantages to members of other identity groups (e.g., race, gender, sexual orientation, language, class, etc.).
Transphobia	Fear of, aversion to, prejudice, or discrimination against transgender, gender-nonconforming, and nonbinary people.
Transgender (and nonbinary)	A person whose gender is different than their cisgender-assumed-at-birth.

11.2.1 Trauma

Significant research exists regarding the correlation between childhood trauma and risk for sex trafficking victimization (Choi 2015). A 2015 statewide study of juvenile offenders in Florida, which allowed children to be charged with prostitution until 2016, found that children who had been arrested for exchanging sex for something of value were more likely than both the general population and other incarcerated children to have had almost all of the Adverse Childhood Experiences (ACE) (Naramore et al. 2015). Sexual abuse in childhood, in particular, has been strongly correlated with sex trafficking victimization, with research showing that children with histories of sexual abuse are 2.5 to 3.23 times more likely than those without to experience sex trafficking (De Vries and Goggin 2020; Ulloa et al. 2016). Research also indicates that there may be a correlation between experiencing multiple types of childhood abuse and increased risk for sex trafficking (Choi 2015; Gibbs et al. 2018b; Reid and Piquero 2014).

It is important to recognize that not all trauma leads to victimization. The majority of people exposed to trauma experience mild to moderate psychological distress after which they return to pretrauma health (Fink and Galea 2015). For some people, trauma can even lead to opportunities for post-traumatic growth, where a person experiences psychological growth as they rebuild and regain control of their lives following the traumatic event (Chap. 17) (Tedeschi and Calhoun 2004). Such growth can occur following childhood trauma as well as the trauma experienced as a result of trafficking (Perry and Pecanha 2017). For some individuals, however, trauma experiences cause substantial distress and have long-lasting impact (Chap. 13) (Van Der Kolk 2015). In an effort to identify opportunities for preventative intervention and address the need and opportunities for systemic and structural change, this chapter will focus on the negative impacts of trauma and the role that childhood trauma plays in increasing risk of sex trafficking.

Trauma and Development

Studies have demonstrated that trauma that occurs during periods of life in which there is rapid development has a more dramatic impact on brain development and psychopathological outcomes than trauma occurring during other periods of life (Andersen et al. 2008; Lupien et al. 2009). In the absence of a supportive adult relationship, in particular, strong, frequent, and/or prolonged childhood trauma can result in *toxic stress*, which can disrupt brain circuitry and other organ and metabolic systems. This disruption can result in anatomic changes and/or physiologic dysregulations and lead to later impairments in learning, behavior, and mental health (Shonkoff et al. 2012). Additionally, caregiver-strain tied to ACEs – arrest, relationship problems, and substance use disorders – which may impede a caregiver's ability to serve as a supportive adult in a child's life, has been linked to children's susceptibility to being sex trafficked (Reid and Piquero 2016). Early trauma can also set off a life cycle of trauma, whereby individuals who experience childhood trauma are substantially more likely to experience additional traumas that continue throughout their life (Fink and Galea 2015). Such trauma is cumulative in nature, and children who have already faced trauma are particularly susceptible to the long-term negative consequences of subsequent trauma (De Bellis and Zisk 2014). Twenty-first century research has demonstrated that trauma can have multigenerational impact resulting in epigenetic changes that can be passed down to descendants across generations (Yao et al. 2014).

Traffickers take advantage of children's vulnerabilities by promising to meet their needs in order to deceive and exploit them. Traffickers may offer false love, pseudo-family, or basic needs to children who have experienced sexual abuse, family dysfunction, or physical neglect. One study that explored recruitment lures based on Maslow's hierarchy of needs, found that traffickers most often used love and belonging to recruit and lure people, followed by lures of safety, including opportunities for secure work and promises of having their basic needs consistently met (Rosenblatt 2014).

Identity and Historical Trauma

It is critical to discuss how *identity trauma* and *historical trauma* (Chap. 13) contribute to the overrepresentation of girls, children who identify as BIPOC, and children who identify as LGBTQ2S+ among sex trafficking survivors.

Identity trauma is trauma experienced as a result of a person's personal identity. Identity trauma can manifest itself at an interpersonal level (e.g., individual microaggressions or discrimination) or on a community or societal level (e.g., discriminatory policies and practices). Regardless of how it is manifested, identity trauma can have long-term health consequences and can result in symptoms that mimic posttraumatic stress disorder (Degruy 2017; Kelleher 2009; Kucharska 2018; Perreira and Ornelas 2013; Solomon et al. 2019). When examining the impact of identity trauma on individuals with intersecting oppressed identities (e.g., individuals who experience racism and homophobia), the long-term health consequences and trauma impact may be cumulative in nature (Balsam et al. 2011; Bostwick et al. 2014; Watson et al. 2016).

Historical trauma refers to the collective trauma experienced over a period of time by a group of people who share an identity, affiliation, or circumstance. The impact of historical trauma is multigenerational, whereby members of the group may experience trauma-related symptoms without having experienced the original traumatic event (Mohatt et al. 2014). For example, historical chattel slavery and the continued passage of racist policies (e.g., discriminatory housing policies) have been linked to modern Black children growing up with a sense of hopelessness and depression, internalized racism, and apparent propensity for anger and violence. These feelings and behaviors have been postulated to be a defense mechanism in response to extreme suspicion of others' motivations (Degruy 2017). Another example of historical trauma is the legacy of the 1860–1978 "Boarding School Era" (Chap. 16). During this period, the federal government removed Indigenous children from their families and communities, and sent the children to government- and church-run boarding schools for the purpose of forced assimilation (Haag 2007). These schools resulted in the long-term loss of parenting knowledge, diminished cultural-based protective factors, exposure to sexual violence, and increased child welfare involvement, all of which continue to negatively impact Indigenous children (Farley et al. 2011; Haag 2007; Pearce et al. 2008). As with separation policies of the past, twenty-first century immigration policies that result in children at the southern border being separated from their parents are expected to result in both immediate and generational trauma (Zero to Thrive Initiative and the Center for Human Growth and Development at the University of Michigan 2018). Parent-child separation can lead to long-term psychological, social, and health problems that are often not mitigated upon reunification (Society for Research in Child Development 2018).

Systemic and Internalized Oppression

Systemic oppression occurs when the policies and practices of structures and institutions (e.g., education, health, transportation, housing, economic) intentionally disadvantage certain groups of people based on their identity, while also providing advantages to members of the privileged identity groups (e.g., race, gender, sexual orientation, language, class, etc.) (National Equity Project n.d.). Many individuals who experience identity trauma and historical trauma have also experienced systemic oppression. Indigenous Americans historically faced systemic oppression through the forced removal and relocation of their communities, and continuing tribal sovereignty disputes (Gonzalez et al. 2014). Black communities historically experienced mass killing through legalized lynching and continue to experience state-sanctioned killing by police and discrimination in the judicial system (David and Derthick 2018). Until 1973, homosexuality was considered a mental health disorder and until 2003, "homosexual acts" were criminalized. Today, LGBTQ2S+ communities continue to endure systemic oppression manifested in the denial of equal rights (e.g., adoption, participation in the military) (David and Derthick 2018). Transgender and nonbinary individuals experience systemic oppression demonstrated by unequal health insurance access to support how they express their gender, and obstruction of obtaining government issued identification that accurately reflects their gender (Grant et al. 2011; Lambda Legal n.d.). Women face systemic oppression in the continued fight for the legal right to make decisions regarding their own bodies or receive equal pay for their work (Center for Reproductive Rights 2006; Rose and Hartmann 2018). Examples of identity and historical trauma, and systemic oppression abound.

Internalized oppression occurs when groups who are subject to systemic oppression over long periods of time normalize the oppression and then internalize the discrimination perpetrated against them (David and Derthick 2014). Internalized oppression among Indigenous Americans, for example, can manifest itself in the adoption of Western standards of beauty (e.g., men cutting their hair short), looking down on peers not educated in Western institutions, and negatively judging peers without material wealth (Gonzalez et al. 2014). Among Latinx communities, internalized oppression can manifest itself in opposing bilingual education, refraining from speaking Spanish due to a belief that English is better, and internalizing the belief that there are too many immigrants in the United States (Padilla 2001). Within the Black community, internalized oppression can manifest itself in negative self-images related to skin complexion, hair texture, and body size and shape based on valuation of White beauty standards (Bailey et al. 2014). Among the LGBTQ2S+ community, internalized oppression can result in rejection or denial of one's sexual orientation or gender identity (David and Derthick 2018; David et al. 2018). Internalized oppression can lead to intergroup and intragroup discrimination and violence; in such interplays, anger at the privileged group (e.g., Whites, men) is misdirected at other intragroup members or other marginalized groups who are viewed as "inferior" (David and Derthick 2014). Examples of this include a Latinx individual, or another person who identifies as BIPOC, ridiculing someone for speaking with an accent, or an individual who identifies as LGBTQ2S+ mocking a masculine lesbian for their nonconformity to gender expectations (David et al. 2018).

Impact of Trauma and Oppression on Children

The impact of identity trauma and historical trauma, systemic oppression, and resulting internalized oppression on children's self-esteem and mental health, school performance, and behavior has yet to be exhaustively studied (Morris 2016). It is clear, however, that the culmination of these systemic traumas and oppression can negatively impact how children view themselves with respect to adversity and resilience (Mohatt et al. 2014). When girls, children who identify as BIPOC, and children who identify as LGBTQ2S+ experience personal trauma, such as sexual abuse, they frequently seek to make sense of these events within the context of the identity and historical traumas they, or their community members, have experienced (Mohatt et al. 2014). For example, the media often portray Black girls as "exotic" and the figure of sexual fetishes. Their bodies are often sexualized by people who say that they "appear older" and they are often treated as if they are older than their chronological age by social systems and people in authority. A study out of Georgetown Law School found that adults from various racial and ethnic backgrounds and different educational levels across the United States, perceived Black girls as more adult than their White peers at almost all stages of childhood, beginning at the age of 5, peaking during the ages of 10–14, and continuing through the ages of 15–19 (Epstein et al. 2017). In their follow-up research, Black women and girls who participated in focus groups across the country, overwhelmingly confirmed that adults hypersexualize Black girls, assuming that Black girls are sexually active at an early age and generally less innocent than their White peers (Blake and Epstein 2019). These experiences are compounded by the knowledge that throughout slavery, Black women and girls were often raped and their bodies viewed as commodities that were sold (Morris 2016); as a result, Black girls may internalize childhood sexual abuse as something that is inevitable, and likely to be repeated in the future.

A study of Indigenous women who experienced trafficking and prostitution found that 62% of those interviewed cited a connection between colonialism, sexism, and their sexual exploitation. These women explained that the rape of Indigenous women by White men during colonization diminished Indigenous women's self-respect and social status within their communities. According to the interviewed women, Indigenous communities were unaware of the concept of prostitution before colonialism, but as Indigenous men saw White men raping and degrading

Indigenous women, they too began to treat women similarly. Additionally, colonialism thrust Indigenous communities into extreme poverty by passing policies that systematically stripped Indigenous communities of their land and assets. As a result, today, the sex trade and trafficking are some of the only options left for some Indigenous women to meet their basic needs and the need of their families (Farley et al. 2011).

For the LGBTQ2S+ communities, the historical criminalization of homosexuality and common conflation of gender identity and sexual orientation, coupled with persistent—and in some cases, government-sanctioned—discrimination and harassment, may result in children who identify as LGBTQ2S+ believing that adults and governmental institutions are not safe places for them to disclose sexual and other forms of child abuse they have experienced (Martinez and Kelle 2013; Peters et al. 2017; Trump 2017). Transgender and nonbinary children, in particular, may come to internalize sexual abuse and the later commodification of their bodies as the only viable option for their survival given the lack of legal protections and economic options they are often afforded (Tomasiewicz 2018). A 2015 survey of transgender and nonbinary folks found that more than a quarter (27%) of respondents who held or applied for a job in the past year reported not being hired, being denied a promotion, or being fired during that same year as a result of their gender identity or expression. Respondents were three times more likely to be unemployed and more than twice as likely to live in poverty as the general population. Almost one in five (19%) reported exchanging sex for money, food, or shelter (James et al. 2016).

11.2.2   System Responses

When people experience danger, their bodies engage in an automatic and natural stress response by which they fight, flee, or freeze (or faint) (Chap. 13). This response causes hormonal and physiological changes and is designed to protect the body. Once the danger passes, the body returns to its normal state. When danger occurs in childhood, however, and resulting trauma is not identified or successfully treated, it can cause permanent disruption to the body's regulatory processes. This in turn can lead to physical manifestations such as headaches, difficulty sleeping, difficulty concentrating, oversensitivity to touch and sound, and unexplained pain. Trauma may also manifest itself as difficulty processing language and challenges engaging in fine-motor coordination, as well as impaired memory, decision making, and conceptual reasoning skills. Without healthy coping skills, children may engage in self-harming (e.g., cutting, hitting themselves, pulling out their hair) or self-soothing (e.g., rocking, excessive masturbation) behaviors. Children may also oscillate between acting out and withdrawing. Without appropriate clinical treatment, these maladaptive coping strategies are likely to continue into adolescence and adulthood (Van Der Kolk 2015).

Educational System

The effects of childhood trauma often first become apparent in school. Children with higher ACE scores are more likely to have language delays, fail grades, require special education, be suspended, and be expelled (Balfanz et al. 2014; Brunzell et al. 2016). Despite the fact that almost half (approximately 45%) of all children experience at least one adverse childhood experience (Child Trends 2019a), most schools do not implement trauma-informed curricula or have sufficient counselors and social workers on staff to appropriately identify and address the trauma present in their student body populations (ACLU 2019). In fact, according to a report by the American Civil Liberties Union (ACLU), 14 million students are in schools with police presence but without a school counselor, nurse, psychologist, or social worker (2019).

The overfunding of law enforcement in the educational system was precipitated by The Gun Free School Act (20 U.S.C. 7151 et seq.) of 1994 and the 1999 Columbine shooting. The resulting laws and policies aimed at curtailing school violence; however, conflated trauma response behaviors with criminal activity, and severely limited schools' discretion in responding. The Gun Free School Act, for example, requires that in order to receive federal funds, schools must have *zero tolerance* policies that mandate expulsion for bringing a weapon to school. These mandates run counter to current research which has shown that children who have experienced trauma often engage in activities and behaviors such as carrying weapons, fighting in defense of self, joining gangs, and self-medicating in order to make themselves feel safer (Burrell 2013).

The presence of law enforcement in schools does *not* increase school safety (ACLU 2019). It does, however, increase the number of arrests for disorderly conduct (Theriot 2009). The negative impact of the laws and policies aimed at curtailing school violence, such as increasing arrests for disorderly conduct, has disproportionately impacted children who identify as BIPOC (ACLU 2019). Students who identify as BIPOC are three times as likely to attend a school with more law enforcement than mental health personnel (Gray and Lewis 2015). In fact, despite data showing that White males are the most common population to initiate school-based shootings, zero tolerance policies, metal detectors, security officers, and other forms of police force have been disproportionately implemented in schools with populations comprised largely of students who identify as BIPOC (Morris 2016).

Without a sufficient quantity of mental health providers, disruptive classroom behaviors (e.g., behaviors perceived to be insubordinate, disrespectful, uncooperative, or uncontrollable) once dealt with within the school system, are now being addressed with school dismissals, suspensions, expulsions, and even arrests (ACLU 2019; Morris 2016). Troublingly, many states and school districts permit children to be suspended for "defiance" and "disruptions;" these determinations are subjective, ambiguous, and can extend to behaviors such as cursing and talking back (ACLU 2019). Again, these policies run counter to current research that demonstrates that adolescents' moodiness, impulsivity, and their inability to regulate distress likely reflects normal brain development (Romer 2010; Sebastian et al. 2010). When taking disciplinary action, children who identify as BIPOC receive harsher punishment than their White counterparts for similar classroom behaviors (Jarvis and Okonofua 2019). For example, Black girls make up 16% of student enrollment but 31% of school-related arrests (US Department of Education [DOE] 2014). From 2011 to 2012, Black girls in public elementary and secondary schools nationwide were suspended at a rate of 12%. This was more than girls of any other race or ethnicity; in comparison, White girls are suspended at a rate of 2% (DOE 2014). Similarly, while Indigenous children make up less than 1% of the student population at the national level, they account for 2% of out-of-school suspensions and 3% of expulsions. Indigenous girls (7%) are suspended at higher rates than White boys (6%) and White girls (2%) (DOE 2014). One study found that, among adolescent participants, self-identified nonheterosexual students (especially girls) had a 1.25–3 times greater odds of experiencing sanctions (e.g., being stopped by police) in comparison to self-identified heterosexual students (Himmelstein and Bruckner 2011).

Metal detectors, higher suspension rates, and perceptions of unfair discipline have been found to negatively impact students' sense of school safety (Bradshaw et al. 2009; Gastic 2010; Lacoe 2015; Movement Advancement Project and Center for American Progress 2016). As children deem schools to be unsafe, many choose to leave the educational system, greatly increasing their risk for running away and experiencing sex trafficking (ACLU 2019; Choi 2015; Gibbs et al. 2018a, Gibbs et al. 2018b; McKinney 2014). Compared to their White peers, during the 2015–2016 school year, Indigenous students were over 50% more likely to experience chronic absenteeism (i.e., loss of three or more weeks of school), Black students were 40% more likely, and Latinx students were 17% more likely (DOE n.d.). In addition, a 2017 school climate survey found over one-third (34.9%) of students who identify as LGBTQ2S+ reported missing at least one full day of school in the past month due to feeling unsafe or uncomfortable, and 10.5% missed four or more days in the past month (Kosciw et al. 2018).

When schools address disruptive classroom behaviors and trauma response-behaviors using punitive measures, they miss critical opportunities for preventative intervention. The public education system interacts with 90% of school age children in the United States (National Center for Education Statistics 2020). This system is poised to play a critical role in identifying the vulnerabilities of children and providing protective interventions that empower children and reduce traffickers' opportunities to groom and recruit them. A survey of 260 youth who had been trafficked found that 55% of children continued to attend school while they were being trafficked; 26% attended irregularly, 15% attended most of the time, and 14% attended the entire time. Several of the survivors in this survey reported that school could have played a larger role in identifying their victimization and intervening on their behalf. These survivors reported that schools should be doing more to prevent child sex trafficking (Thorn 2018). Similar sentiments were echoed by youth survivors who participated in an evaluation of Connecticut's Human Anti-trafficking Response Team (HART). Youth interviewed for this evaluation reported that information and resources about human trafficking should be provided in schools so that children learn to identify red flags before they are trafficked, and school officials and peers are better able to help children that have been trafficked reintegrate back into school (ICF 2019). In order to prevent children from being sex trafficked, the educational system must shift how it views and addresses behavioral issues; schools must provide appropriate preventative interventions, especially to children at high risk for sex trafficking and other forms of sexual violence.

An Abdication of System Responsibility – Running Away

The term "runaway" is used to describe children who leave their homes on "their own accord" but without permission. This term and corresponding definition imply a child left their place of residence willingly without accounting for the fact that research has repeatedly demonstrated that children often run away from or are kicked out of their homes due to various traumas, including sexual abuse, homophobia and transphobia, and poverty (Baker 2018). In addition, some children leave their home as a result of being trafficked by a family member (Covenant House 2013; Romero et al. 2020). Without a definition that recognizes the realities of *why* children "runaway," the term implies that a child is not in imminent danger nor potentially being harmed or exploited. It puts blame on the child and fails to identify any governmental, community, or adult culpability in failing to ensure the child's safety (Moss 2019). In many cases of child sex trafficking, children are often recruited to leave their homes. By misidentifying this behavior as "running away," important opportunities for early intervention are lost.

Despite significant research demonstrating the correlation between running away and child sex trafficking (Choi 2015; Gibbs et al. 2018a, Gibbs et al. 2018b), government safety nets for missing children often have loopholes for "runaways." For example, in most states, in order to issue an AMBER Alert law enforcement must confirm that an abduction has taken place and there is reason to believe that the child is in imminent danger of serious bodily injury or death (US Department of Justice 2019). In many instances when a youth is reported as a "runaway," law enforcement presumes that they do not have enough evidence to issue an AMBER alert because the child "went willingly" and was not "abducted." As a result, "runaways," even those who are potentially being trafficked, often do not receive the same type of coordinated emergency response and media attention that other missing children receive (Moss 2019). In addition, prior to the 2018 AMBER Alert in Indian Country Act, tribal law enforcement on many reservations did not have an AMBER Alert plan to notify the people living in Indigenous communities of missing and abducted Indigenous children. The AMBER Alert in Indian Country Act provided federal funding to collaborate toward the goal of providing all federally recognized tribes access to the AMBER Alert system (US Department of Justice 2019).

Many children who "run away" or are forced to leave their home, end up homeless (Covenant House 2013). According to national estimates, 1 in 30 youth ages 13 to 17 experiences homelessness each year. Black and Latinx children have a respective 83% and 33% higher risk of being homeless, and children who identify as LGBTQ2S+ have a 120% higher risk of being homeless (Morton et al. 2017).

Traffickers often prey on homeless youths' lack of housing and other basic needs. Trafficked youths have reported that traffickers often loiter where homeless youths congregate, telling them shelters are full and offering them a place to stay (Covenant House 2013). Homeless youths who identify as LGBTQ2S+ are particularly vulnerable to trafficking victimization. One ten-city study found 24% of homeless youths who identified as LGBTQ2S+ were trafficked for sex compared to 12% of their heterosexual and cisgender peers (Murphy 2017).

Many homeless youths remain engaged in the educational system offering an important opportunity for preventative and early intervention. During the 2016–2017 school year, state educational agencies reported serving over 1.3million homeless youths (National Center for Homeless Education 2019). Providers working with runaway and homeless youth can also play a critical role in preventing trafficking and supporting the identification of and service provision to children who are being trafficked. Research suggests that the presence of a supportive adult in a homeless youth's life can help mitigate the risk of trafficking victimization (Chisolm-Straker et al. 2019).

Child Welfare System

Children who experience abuse and/or neglect, may come into contact with the child welfare system. The establishment of government sponsored child protective services in the United States was sparked by outcry following the 1962 publication of "The Battered-Child Syndrome" by pediatrician Henry Kempe and his colleagues. That same year, Congress amended the Social Security Act to identify Child Protective Services as part of all public child welfare and required states to make child welfare services available statewide (Myers 2008).

In 1974, Congress passed the Child Abuse Prevention and Treatment Act (CAPTA), which provided federal funding to states for the prevention, identification, and treatment of child abuse and neglect. Despite research dating back to the 1960s and 1970s demonstrating the impact of social determinants on child abuse and neglect, proponents of CAPTA intentionally shifted the paradigm for understanding child abuse and neglect away from racial and social inequality and towards parental mental health (Raz 2017). The inaccurate paradigm that child abuse and neglect are equal-opportunity social ills that equally affect people from all walks of life remains influential. By not addressing the social determinants impacting child abuse and neglect, policy makers have undermined the child welfare system's ability to meet their often conflicting goals of child protection and family preservation. As a result of continued research, there is now general agreement regarding the correlation between poverty, race, and child welfare involvement. The debate, however, continues regarding whether the child welfare system is protecting those who are most vulnerable from maltreatment or exploiting populations that are already oppressed and disenfranchised (Cooper 2013).

After CAPTA, Congress passed numerous other child welfare laws, with some aimed at mitigating racial disparities and the number of children brought into the foster care system. Some of these efforts included: the 1978 Indian Child Welfare Act, which set federal requirements for state child custody proceedings involving Indigenous children; the 1980 Adoption Assistance and Child Welfare Act which focused on family preservation, and required states to make "reasonable efforts" to avoid removing children, and reunite families when removal was necessary; the 1994 Multiethnic Placement Act (MEPA), which prohibited state child welfare agencies from delaying or denying adoptive placements based on race; and the 1997 Adoption and Safe Families Act (ASFA), which establishes timelines for returning children to their parents or terminating parental rights (Myers 2008).

Following a record high of 567,000 in 1999, child welfare systems saw a significant decrease in the number of children involved in the child welfare system, reaching an historic low of 397,000 in 2012. Since then, however, the numbers have steadily increased (Child Trends 2019b). This increase has largely been due to increases in substance and opioid use disorders (Radel et al. 2018). In 2018, Congress responded by passing the Family First Prevention Services Act. This law focuses on reforming the child welfare system by allowing federal money to be used for prevention and services to reduce the number of children entering care. It also limits the amount of federal funding that can be used to house children who do enter care in group and residential placements (Lindell et al. 2020). By focusing on preventing children from entering the child welfare system, the Family First Prevention Services Act recognized that, even when trauma-informed services such as the Child Advocacy Centers are used, system interactions in and of themselves can be traumatizing (American Bar Association 2019).

Historically Contextualizing Child Removal

For Black and Indigenous children, the trauma of removal must be understood within the framework of chattel slavery and the "Boarding School Era" (Chap. 16). In these legal and commonplace paradigms, Black and Indigenous children were forcibly removed from their families and sold as commodities or placed in government- or church-run boarding schools (Farley et al. 2011; Morris 2016). In the 1960s and 1970s, as the "boarding school era" came to an end, states began bringing Indigenous children into their child welfare system at alarming rates. Studies conducted by the Association on American Indian Affairs at that time found that 25%–35% of Indigenous children had been separated from their homes and placed in foster homes, adoptive homes, or institutions; that rate of removal was far greater than that of non-Indigenous children (Jacobs 2013). For Indigenous families and children, this was similar to being placed in White-run boarding schools. The increased rate of entry of Indigenous children into the child welfare system was partly due to the fact that social workers assessed the welfare of Indigenous children's homes from an Anglo-Saxon perspective; these workers were quick to mis-identify differences in culture as "neglect" or "social deprivation" (Haag 2007). In order to address this and reduce the number of Indigenous children in the child welfare system, in 1978 Congress enacted the Indian Child Welfare Act (ICWA), which set federal requirements for all state child custody proceedings involving Indigenous children (Myers 2008).

Still, Black and Indigenous children continue to be removed from their families at disproportionate rates, with their overrepresentation increasing at each major decision point from investigation to placement (Hill 2007). In 2017, 23% of children in foster care were Black, a significant drop from 31% in 2007 (Child Welfare Information Gateway 2019). Comparatively however, Black children only accounted for 14% of all children in the United States in both 2007 and 2017 (Kids Count Data Center 2020). Today, Indigenous children represent 2% of the children in foster care but only 1% of the children in the general population (Child Trends 2019b), with the disproportionate rate of Indigenous children in foster care increasing since 2008 (Woods and Summers 2016).

Children who identify as LGBTQ2S+, especially those who also identify as BIPOC, are also overrepresented in the child welfare system (The Annie E. Casey Foundation 2016). Findings from the 2013 to 2015 California Healthy Kids Survey, which surveyed a total of 895,218 students ages 10–18 years old, found that of those who reported living in foster care, 30.4% identified as LGBTQ2S+. In a national probability-based sample, 11.2% of children ages 12–18 year-olds identified as lesbian, gay, bisexual, or unsure (Baams et al. 2019). Another study using data from The Second National Survey of Child and Adolescent Well-Being (NSCAW-II), found that 15.5% of all children referred to child welfare identified as lesbian, gay, or bisexual. It should be noted, however, that NASCAW-II data only captures prevalence among youth who openly identified as lesbian, gay, or bisexual within the child welfare system (Dettlaff et al. 2018). Both of these studies found that the overrepresentation of children who identify as LGBTQ2S+ in the foster care system is even starker among children who identify as LGBTQ2S+ and BIPOC (Baams et al. 2019; Dettlaff et al. 2018; Dettlaff and Washburn 2016). For children who identify as LGBTQ2S+, their gender identity and/or sexual orientation may be directly tied to their child welfare involvement, as many children in the child welfare system report being physically abused by family members or forced to leave their home after disclosing their gender identity or sexual orientation (Martin et al. 2016).

Once in the system, children who identify as BIPOC and children who identify as LGBTQ2S+ children often do not receive the culturally appropriate housing or services they desperately need to effectively address their trauma. A review of child welfare agencies between 2000 and 2004 found that only 21 states engaged in efforts to recruit foster and adoptive families that reflected the racial and ethnic diversity of children in need of these services; the number of states recruiting reflective homes decreased to 19 between 2007 and 2010 (US Department of Health and Human Services [HHS] 2011; HHS 2012). Children who identify as LGBTQ2S+ are more likely than heterosexual and cisgender children to have multiple placements (Mallon et al. 2002); 19.6% of lesbian, gay, and bisexual children in out-of-home placements are removed from their first placement at the request of their caregiver or foster family (Martin et al. 2016). In comparison, only 8.6% of heterosexual children in out-of-home placements are removed from their first home at the request of the caregiver or foster family (Martin et al. 2016). The large majority of states lack laws and policies to explicitly protect youth who identify as LGBTQ2S+ from discrimination based on sexual orientation and gender within the foster care system (Gill 2015). Lack of culturally appropriate and frequent changes in housing and services increase children's risk of running away and a child who runs away from foster care once is exponentially more likely to run away in the future (Courtney and Zinn 2009). As previously discussed, running away may increase a child's risk for being trafficked. In addition, the correlation between running away and trafficking continues beyond initial the trafficking experience, as children involved in the child welfare system who have been sex trafficked are significantly more likely to runaway than those without prior trafficking histories (O'Brien et al. 2017).

Given the large body of evidence demonstrating the correlation between involvement in child welfare and child sex trafficking (Gibbs et al. 2018b), the child welfare system has a unique and important role to play in the prevention and early intervention of the sex trafficking of children. Recognizing this, Congress passed the Justice for Victims of Trafficking Act (PL 114-22) and the Preventing Sex Trafficking and Strengthening Families Act (PL 113-183). Together, these legislations require state child welfare agencies to develop policies and procedures to identify children at risk for or experiencing sex trafficking, assess their needs, and provide appropriate services. Despite the passage of this legislation, as of 2019, only 41 states and the District of Columbia define child abuse and/or neglect to include sex trafficking (Shared Hope International 2019a). In addition, confusion continues to exist regarding the role of the child welfare system as it relates to addressing sex trafficking in cases where the perpetrator is unknown or not a caregiver or family member. In 2019, only 34 states and the District of Columbia define "caregiver" broadly enough that they are able to provide protection (if necessary) and services to child survivors of nonfamilial sex trafficking (Shared Hope International 2019a). As a result, there is wide variation in how states are responding to nonfamilial child sex trafficking, with child welfare systems investigating and providing services to children in some states but not others. At the time of this writing, no comprehensive data exist regarding states' basic compliance with the federal requirements or the effectiveness of current policies and procedures in providing preventative and early interventions to child sex trafficking survivors.

Juvenile Justice System

The origins of the juvenile justice system date back to the establishment of the New York House of Refuge in 1825 which was developed in order to provide discipline and education to poor children who were labeled "delinquent." Legislation passed around the same time contributed to the formation of the juvenile justice system and allowed children to be held against their will for crimes related to poverty, crimes such as "soliciting charity" (now called "panhandling") (Bell 2016; Pasko 2010). Following reports documenting abusive and exploitative discipline in houses of refuge, these facilities were shut down. They were replaced by juvenile courts, which first opened in 1899 with the focus on providing rehabilitation and protective supervision (Bell 2016).

From the system's inception, immigrants and children who identifies as BIPOC were disproportionately represented among the juvenile justice population (Tedor and Mallott 2018). Black children, for example, were initially not permitted in houses of refuge; however, a decade later when special sections for "colored" children were added, Black children entered at younger ages, suffered higher death rates, and had fewer employment opportunities upon discharge than their White counterparts (Bell 2016). Black Codes allowed the government to incarcerate Black citizens, including children, for behaviors that were only illegal if performed by individuals who identify as Black (Bell 2016). From its earliest days, girls were also treated differently than boys within the juvenile justice system. While the court defined a "delinquent" as someone who violated a city ordinance or law, for girls, this definition included "incorrigibility," associations with "immoral" persons, "vagrancy," frequent attendance at pool halls or saloons, and use of "profane" language. For girls, the focus of juvenile institutions was on sexual morality, and addressing concerns about presumed promiscuity and prostitution (Pasko 2010). As previously discussed, child-serving systems and individuals of authority have a long history of hypersexualizing Black girls; in the case of the juvenile justice system, this hypersexualization can lead to loss of Black girls' liberties and incarceration.

Between 1920 and 1960, there was significant increase in the number of children incarcerated, and the focus shifted away from rehabilitation and more towards punishment. In the 1990s during the "tough on crime" era, there was a renewed focus on juvenile delinquency and incarceration; the media often portrayed children who identify as BIPOC as "super-predators." This occurred despite the fact that starting in 1993, juvenile offender crime decreased by 67% over the next decade. In 1994, Congress passed the Violent Crime Control and Law Enforcement Act and the Gun-Free Schools Act, specifically aimed at curbing youth violence through punitive responses. Subsequently, there has been recognition by a number of lawmakers that this harsh approach has not been effective and interest in a less punitive approach to juvenile offenders has gained traction. Some states have repealed laws requiring transfers to adult court; other states have raised the age of juvenile court jurisdiction. Efforts at the state level to reduce the number of incarcerated children have been supported by US Supreme Court decisions (e.g., *Roper vs. Simmons*, *Graham vs. Florida*) which have repeatedly recognized that adolescents are developmentally different from adults and as a result should not be held to the same legal standards or consequences (Tedor and Mallott 2018).

As with the child welfare system, there is a strong correlation between involvement in the juvenile justice system and child sex trafficking (Connor 2016; Gruber et al. 2016; Naramore et al. 2015; Swaner et al. 2016). In fact, as of 2019, only 30 states prohibit the criminalization of minors for prostitution (i.e., 20 states continue to allow children to be incarcerated for their experience(s) of being sex trafficked). In addition, only 18 states extend noncriminalization protections to child sex trafficking survivors for offenses beyond prostitution (legal offenses children commit as a result of sex trafficking, e.g., shoplifting) (Shared Hope International 2019b).

In states that continue to allow children to be arrested for prostitution, transgirls (37%) are significantly more likely than cis-boys (12%) or cis-girls (17%) to be arrested on prostitution charges (Swaner et al. 2016). A national study of child sex trafficking survivors found 65% of participants reported having been arrested at some point (Swaner et al. 2016). Of these, 82% were arrested for nonviolent offenses including status offenses (e.g., running away, truancy, violating curfew), which are noncriminal acts that are only violations of the law because the child is under the age of 18 (Swaner et al. 2016).

As with the educational and child welfare response to trauma, the juvenile justice response to trauma is disproportionately harmful to girls, children who identify as BIPOC, and children who identify as LGBTQ2S+. For example, 32% of Latinx children, 30% of Black children, and 26% of Indigenous children with delinquency cases are detained, compared to only 21% of White children (Sawyer 2019). While only 14% of children in the United States are Black, 42% of boys, and 35% of girls in juvenile facilities are Black (Sawyer 2019). In another report, Indigenous youths are three times more likely to be held in juvenile detention than White youth (Rovner 2014). Indigenous youth make up approximately 1% of the general population of youth but 3% of girls and 1.5% of boys in juvenile facilities (Sawyer 2019). The rate of girls' involvement in the juvenile justice system is growing disproportionately, especially among Black and Indigenous children (Saar et al. 2015). The increased arrests and incarceration are not a result of girls engaging in higher rates of criminal activity; rather, it is a result of more aggressive law enforcement approaches to addressing nonserious and status offenses (e.g., running away, truancy) (Morris 2016; Saar et al. 2015). While girls make up only 25% of those in the juvenile justice system, they account for 40% of children taken to court for status offenses, and 55% of children taken to court for running away (Rosenthal 2018). Lesbian, gay, and bisexual children are also detained for running away at higher rates than their heterosexual counterparts. In one study, 28% of gay and bisexual boys were detained for running away compared to only 12% of their heterosexual counterparts; this disproportionate representation was even more pronounced for lesbian and bisexual girls (Irvine 2011). The disproportionate rate of girls, children who identify as BIPOC, and children who identify as LGBTQ2S+ being arrested for running away is compounded by the fact that children adjudicated for running away are more likely to be ordered to an out-of-home placement than children adjudicated for any other status offense (Puzzanchera and Hockenberry 2013).

Unlike the child welfare system, the juvenile justice system was not established to address trauma or care for the safety and well-being of children; it was meant to punish and rehabilitate juvenile offenders. Many of the policies and practices used in juvenile facilities can be traumatizing, especially for children who have prior histories of trauma. Solitary confinement, for example, is routinely used in juvenile institutions and results in extreme mental health harm. Children in juvenile institutions may also be subjected to intrusive searches (e.g., cross-gender searches, strip searches, body cavity searches), placed in unsafe settings (e.g., with gang members they are trying to avoid), and experience excessive discipline for minor infractions (Burrell 2013). Children may also experience new victimization, including sexual abuse and harassment (Saar et al. 2015). *In many respects, the juvenile justice system treats survivors of child sex trafficking in the same manner as those children's traffickers and buyers by incarcerating survivor children and mandating program participation.* Even when the juvenile justice system takes a more rehabilitative approach through the use of residential treatment centers, such approaches remove children from their families and begin the escalation of youth involvement in the judicial system. When involvement in the juvenile justice system is necessary, community-based supervision has been found to be an effective and less costly alternative to confinement, be it a group home, residential treatment facility, or an institution (Ryon et al. 2013).

Instead of viewing sex trafficking as a social, political, and public health problem, and consequently developing policies and programs focused on prevention and early intervention, the overemphasis of the criminal justice response has resulted in prosecuting victims in the name of "protecting them" (Chap. 12). Today, many states claim to have enacted "Safe Harbor" legislation, a catch-all phrase widely used to convey any attempt to reduce the criminalization of minors for prostitution (Raino and Roeck 2017). Safe Harbor legislation, however, may actually lead to an increase in the number of trafficked youth arrested, as law enforcement arrests them for offenses resulting from their victimization (e.g., loitering, curfew violations, nonviolent misdemeanors), and extends the length and restrictive conditions of involuntary commitment in an effort to "protect them" (Chap. 12) (Connor 2016). As part of their Safe Harbor, some states have introduced trafficking courts. Despite the name, which implies the offer of a safe haven to victims and focuse on the prosecution of traffickers, these courts, in fact, prosecute potential victims, including children, for prostitution and then "offer" mandated services in lieu of a criminal conviction and jail time. While some laude these courts as models, in reality, they continue the criminalization of victims and enforce "penal welfare" – the practice of using criminal courts to mandate social services and "benefits" (Gruber et al. 2016).

11.3 Conclusion

In order to end child sex trafficking, sustainable and effective solutions must work at the intersections of marginalized identities, early trauma, and trafficking, and address the historical ways systems and structures have led to and sustain children's vulnerabilities.

11.4 Recommendations

Despite the existing challenges across systems, research suggests there are potentially effective solutions that will decrease the likelihood that girls, children who identify as BIPOC, and children who identify as LGBTQ2S+ will continue to experience trafficking at disparate rates. The below recommendations aim to shift the prevention and intervention paradigm to understand child sex trafficking as a social, political, and public health problem. They focus on changing child-serving systems so that they are better equipped to address childhood trauma, provide preventative and early interventions, and protect and empower children before traffickers have the opportunity to exploit them.

1. *Require initial and ongoing training on childhood trauma, historical trauma, systemic oppression, and human trafficking* for all school, child welfare, and juvenile and family justice personnel.
2. *Provide universal prevention education on human trafficking and other related subject matters (e.g., internet safety) to all middle and high school age children*, and specialized content to children involved in the child welfare and juvenile justice systems.
3. *Further refine the codes in the Gun Free School Act* to ensure that categorical offenses are addressed in proportionate measure.
4. *Remove "zero tolerance" policies and enable school administrators to impose disciplinary consequences proportional to the infraction*, with consideration of mitigating circumstances and the unique situations that may have contributed to the incident.
5. *Mandate and provide funding to support at least one counselor and one social worker for every 250 students, and at least one nurse and one psychologist for every 750 students and every 700 students, respectively* (ACLU 2019).
6. *Remove law enforcement from all publicly funded schools.*
7. *Remove loopholes for "runaways" in the government's safety nets for missing children*, so that all children away from home receive the same type of coordinated emergency response and media attention that other missing children receive.
8. *Train law enforcement officers to assess missing children, including "runaways," for human trafficking victimization.*
9. *Mandate that child welfare agencies proactively engage in efforts to recruit staff, and foster and adoptive families that reflect the racial and ethnic diversity of children in need of these services.*
10. *Enact laws and policies explicitly protecting LGBTQ2S+ youth from discrimination* based on sexual orientation and gender identity within the foster care system.
11. *Ensure all states prohibit the criminalization of minors for prostitution.*
12. *Remove the Valid Court Order (VCO) Exception from the Juvenile Justice and Delinquency Prevention Act* so that no youth can be committed to detention simply for violating a status offense (e.g., truancy, curfew violations).
13. *Provide sufficient funding for research regarding the labor trafficking of children* in the United States and data on the demographic breakdown of this population.

References

American Bar Association. (2019). *Trauma caused by separation of children from parents: A tool to help lawyers.* Retrieved from https://www.americanbar.org/content/dam/aba/publications/litigation_committees/childrights/child-separation-memo/parent-child-separation-trauma-memo.pdf

American Civil Liberties Union. (2019). *Cops and no counselors: How the lack of school mental health staff is harming students.* Retrieved from https://www.aclu.org/sites/default/files/field_document/030419-acluschooldisciplinereport.pdf

Andersen, S., Tomada, A., Vincow, E., Valente, E., Polcari, A., & Teicher, M. (2008). Preliminary evidence for sensitive periods in the effect of childhood sexual abuse on regional brain development. *The Journal of Neuropsychiatry and Clinical Neurosciences, 20*(3), 292–301.

Baams, L., Wilson, B. D. M., & Russell, S. T. (2019). LGBTQ youth in unstable housing and foster care. *Pediatrics, 143*(3), e20174211.

Bailey, T.-K. M., Williams, W. S., & Favors, B. (2014). Internalized racial oppression in the African-American community. In E. J. R. David (Ed.), *Internalized oppression: The psychology of marginalized groups* (pp. 137–162). New York: Springer Publishing.

Baker, C. N. (2018). *Fighting the US youth sex trade: Gender, race, and politics.* Cambridge, UK: Cambridge University Press.

Balfanz, R., Byrnes, V., & Fox, J. (2014). Sent home and put off-track: The antecedents, disproportionalities, and consequences of being suspended in the ninth grade. *Journal of Applied Research on Children, 5*(2), Article 13.

Balsam, K. F., Molina, Y., Beadnell, B., Simoni, J., & Walters, K. (2011). Measuring multiple minority stress: The LGBT people of color microaggressions scale. *Cultural Diversity and Ethnic Minority Psychology, 17*(2), 163–174.

Bell, J. (2016). *Repairing the breach: A brief history of youth of color in the justice system.* Oakland: W. Haywood Burns Institute for Youth Justice Fairness and Equity.

Blake, J. J., & Epstein, R. (2019). *Listening to Black women and girls: Lived experiences of adultification bias.* Washington, DC: Georgetown Law, Center on Poverty and Inequality. https://endadultificationbias.org/wp-content/uploads/2019/05/Listening-to-Black-Women-and-Girls-v7.pdf.

Bostwick, W. B., Meyer, I., Aranda, F., Russell, S., Hughes, T., Birkett, M., & Mustanski, B. (2014). Mental health and suicidality among racially/ethnically diverse sexual minority youths. *American Journal of Public Health, 104*(6), 1129–1136.

Bradshaw, C. P., Sawyer, A. L., & O'Brennan, L. M. (2009). A social disorganization perspective on bullying-related attitudes and behaviors: The influence of school context. *American Journal of Community Psychology, 43*(3–4), 204–220.

Brunzell, T., Stokes, H., & Waters, L. (2016). Trauma-informed flexible learning: Classrooms that strengthen regulatory abilities. *International Journal of Child, Youth and Family Studies, 7*(2), 218–239.

Burrell, S. (2013). *Trauma and the environment of care in juvenile institutions.* Los Angeles: The National Traumatic Stress Network. Retrieved from https://www.nctsn.org/sites/default/files/resources/trauma_and_environment_of_care_in_juvenile_institutions.pdf

Butler, C. N. (2015). The racial roots of human trafficking. *UCLA Law Review, 62,* 1464–1514.

Center for Reproductive Rights. (2006). *Women's reproductive rights in the United States: A shadow report.* Retrieved from https://www2.ohchr.org/english/bodies/hrc/docs/ngos/crr.pdf

Child Trends. (2019a). *Adverse childhood experiences.* Retrieved from https://www.childtrends.org/?indicators=adverse-experiences

Child Trends. (2019b). *Foster care.* Retrieved from https://www.childtrends.org/indicators/foster-care

Child Welfare Information Gateway. (2019). *Foster care statistics 2017.* Washington, DC: U.S. Department of Health and Human Services, Children's Bureau.

Chisolm-Straker, M., Sze, J., Einbond, J., White, J., & Stoklosa, H. (2019). A supportive adult may be the difference in homeless youth not being trafficked. *Children and Youth Services Review, 91*, 115–120.

Choi, K. R. (2015). Risk factors for domestic minor sex trafficking in the United States: A literature review. *Journal of Forensic Nursing, 11*(2), 66–76.

Connor, B. M. (2016). In loco Aequitatis: The dangers of "Safe Harbor" Laws for youth in the sex trades. *Stanford Journal of Civil Rights & Civil Liberties, 12*(43), 45–116.

Cooper, T. A. (2013). Racial bias in American foster care: The national debate. *Marquette Law Review, 97*(2), 215–277.

Courtney, M. E., & Zinn, A. (2009). Predictors of running away from out-of-home care. *Children and Youth Services Review, 31*(2), 1298–1306.

Covenant House. (2013). *Homelessness, survival sex and human trafficking: As experienced by the youth of Covenant House New York.* Retrieved from https://humantraffickinghotline. org/sites/default/files/Homelessness%2C%20Survival%20Sex%2C%20and%20Human%20 Trafficking%20-%20Covenant%20House%20NY.pdf

Curtis, R., Terry, K., Dank, M., Dombrowski, K., & Khan, B. (2008). *Commercial sexual exploitation of children in New York City, volume one: The CSEC population in New York City: Size, characteristics, and needs.* New York: Center for Court Innovation.

David, E. J. R., & Derthick, A. O. (2014). What is internalized oppression, and so what? In E. J. R. David (Ed.), *Internalized oppression: The psychology of marginalized groups* (pp. 1–31). New York: Springer Publishing.

David, E. J. R., & Derthick, A. O. (2018). *The psychology of oppression.* New York: Springer Publishing.

David, E. J. R., Petalio, J., & Crouch, M. (2018). Microaggressions and internalized oppression. In C. M. Capodilupo, K. L. Nadal, D. P. Rivera, D. W. Sue, & G. C. Torino (Eds.), *Microaggressions theory: Influence and implications.* Hoboken: Wiley.

De Bellis, M. D., & Zisk, A. A. B. (2014). The biological effects of childhood trauma. *Child Adolescent Psychiatric Clinics of North America, 23*(2), 185–222.

De Vries, I., & Goggin, K. E. (2020). The impact of childhood abuse on the commercial sexual exploitation of youth: A systematic review and meta-analysis. *Trauma, Violence, & Abuse, 21*(5), 886–903.

Degruy, J. (2017). *Post-traumatic slave syndrome: America's legacy of enduring injury and healing.* Portland: Joy Degruy Publications.

Dettlaff, A. J., & Washburn, M. (2016). *Sexual minority youth in the child welfare system: Prevalence, characteristics and risk.* Houston: University of Houston, Graduate College of Social Work. Retrieved from https://cssp.org/wp-content/uploads/2018/08/Sexual-Minority-Youth-in-Child-Welfare_providers_final.pdf

Dettlaff, A. J., Washburn, M., Carr, L. C., & Vogel, A. N. (2018). Lesbian, gay, and bisexual (LGB) youth within in welfare: Prevalence, risk and outcomes. *Child Abuse and Neglect, 80*, 183–193.

Epstein, R., Blake, J. J., & Gonzolez, T. (2017). *Girlhood interrupted: The erasure of Black girls' childhood.* Washington, DC: Georgetown Law, Center on Poverty and Inequality. https:// endadultificationbias.org/wp-content/uploads/2019/05/girlhood-interrupted.pdf.

Farley, M., Matthews, N., Deer, S., Lopez, G., Stark, C., & Hudson, E. (2011). *Garden of truth: The prostitution and trafficking of Indigenous women in Minnesota.* St. Paul: William Mitchell College of Law.

Farrell, A., & Kane, B. (2020). Criminal justice system responses to human trafficking. In J. A. Winterdyk & J. Jones (Eds.), *The Palgrave international handbook of human trafficking.* Switzerland: Springer International Publishing AG.

Fink, D. S., & Galea, S. (2015). Life course epidemiology of trauma and related psychopathology in civilian populations. *Current Psychiatry Reports, 17*(5), 566.

Gastic, B. (2010). Metal detectors and feeling safe at school. *Education and Urban Society, 43*, 486–498.

Georgia State University. (2019). *Atlanta youth count 2018 community report: The prevalence of sex and labor trafficking among homeless youth in metro Atlanta*. Retrieved from https://atlantayouthcount.weebly.com/

Gibbs, D. A., Feinberg, R. K., Dolan, M., Latzman, N. E., Misra, S., & Domanico, R. (2018a). *Report to congress: The child welfare system response to sex trafficking of children.* Washington, DC: U.S. Department of Health and Human Services, Administration for Children and Families. Retrieved from https://www.acf.hhs.gov/sites/default/files/cb/report_congress_child_trafficking.pdf.

Gibbs, D. A., Henninger, A. M., Tueller, S. J., & Kluckman, M. N. (2018b). Human trafficking and the child welfare population in Florida. *Children and Youth Services Review, 88*, 1–10.

Gill, A. M. (2015). *2014 state equality index*. Washington, DC: Human Rights Campaign Foundation.

Gonzalez, J., Simard, E., Baker-Demaray, T., & Iron Eyes, C. (2014). The internalized oppression of North American Indigenous peoples. In E. J. R. David (Ed.), *Internalized oppression: The psychology of marginalized groups* (pp. 31–56). New York: Springer Publishing.

Grant, J. M., Mottet, L. A., Tanis, J., Harrison, J., Herman, J. L., & Keisling, M. (2011). *Injustice at every turn: A report of the National Transgender Discrimination Survey*. Washington, DC: National Center for Transgender Equality and National Gay and Lesbian Task Force.

Gray, L., & Lewis, L. (2015). *Public school safety and discipline: 2013–14 (NCES 2015-051)*. U.S. Department of Education. Washington, DC: National Center for Education Statistics. Retrieved from http://nces.ed.gov/pubsearch

Gruber, A., Cohen, A. J., & Mogulescu, K. (2016). Penal welfare and the new human trafficking intervention courts. *Florida Law Review, 68*(5), 133–1402.

Haag, A. (2007). The Indian boarding school era and its continuing impact on tribal families and the provision of government services. *Tulsa Law Review, 43*(1), 149–168.

Hill, R. B. (2007). *An analysis of racial/ethnic disproportionality and disparity at the national, state, and county levels*. Seattle: Casey Family Programs.

Himmelstein, K. E. W., & Bruckner, H. (2011). Criminal-justice and school sanctions against non-heterosexual youth: A national longitudinal study. *Pediatrics, 127*(1), 49–57.

ICF. (2019). *Connecticut's human antitrafficking response team (HART): Final report*. Fairfax: ICF.

Institute of Medicine and National Research Council. (2013). *Confronting commercial sexual exploitation and sex trafficking of minors in the United States*. Washington, DC: The National Academies Press.

Irvine, A. (2011). *LGBT kids in the prison pipeline*. The Public Intellectual. Retrieved from https://thepublicintellectual.org/2011/05/02/lgbt-kids-in-the-school-to-prison-pipeline/.

Jacobs, M. D. (2013). Remembering the "forgotten child": The American Indian child welfare crisis of the 1960s and 1970s. *American Indian Quarterly, 37*(1–2), 136–159.

James, S. E., Herman, J. L., Rankin, S., Keisling, M., Mottet, L., & Anafi, M. (2016). *The report of the 2015 U.S. transgender survey*. Washington, DC: National Center for Transgender Equality.

Jarvis, S. N., & Okonofua, J. A. (2019). School deferred: When Bias affects school leaders. *Journal of Social Psychology and Personality Science, 11*, 492–498.

Kelleher, C. (2009). Minority stress on health: Implications for lesbian, gay, bisexual, transgender, and questioning (LGBTQ) young people. *Counselling Psychology Quarterly, 22*(4), 373–379.

Kids Count Data Center. (2020). *Child population by race in the United States: 2007 and 2017.* https://datacenter.kidscount.org/data/tables/103-child-population-by-race#detailed/1/any/false/871,18/68,69,67,12,70,66,71,72/423,424

Kosciw, J. G., Greytak, E. A., Zongrone, A. D., Clark, C. M., & Truong, N. L. (2018). *The 2017 national school climate survey: The experiences of lesbian, gay, bisexual, transgender, and queer youth in our nation's schools*. New York: GLSEN. https://www.glsen.org/sites/default/files/2019-10/GLSEN-2017-National-School-Climate-Survey-NSCS-Full-Report.pdf.

Kucharska, J. (2018). Cumulative trauma, gender discrimination and mental health in women: Mediating role of self-esteem. *Journal of Mental Health, 27*(5), 416–423.

Lacoe, J. R. (2015). Unequally safe: The race gap in school safety. *Youth Violence and Juvenile Justice, 13*(2), 143–168.

Lambda Legal. (n.d.). FAQ: *Equal access to health care.* Retrieved from https://www.lambdalegal. org/know-your-rights/article/trans-related-care-faq

Lindell, K. U., Sorenson, C. K., & Mangold, S. V. (2020). The family first prevention services act: A new era of child welfare reform. *Public Health Reports, 135*(2), 282–286.

Lupien, S. J., McEwen, B. S., Gunnar, M. R., & Heim, C. (2009). Effects of stress throughout the lifespan on the brain, behavior and cognition. *Nature Reviews Neuroscience, 10*(6), 434–445.

Mallon, G. P., Aledort, N., & Ferrera, M. (2002). There's no place like home: Achieving safety, permanency, and well-being for lesbian and gay adolescents in out-of- home care settings. *Child Welfare, 81*(2), 407–439.

Martin, M., Down, L., & Erney, R. (2016). *Out of the shadows: Supporting LGBTQ+ youth in child welfare through cross-system collaboration.* Washington, DC: Center for the Study of Social Policy. Retrieved from https://cssp.org/wp-content/uploads/2018/08/Out-of-the-Shadows-Supporting-LGBTQ-youth-in-child-welfare-through-cross-system-collaboration-web.pdf.

Martinez, O., & Kelle, G. (2013). Sex trafficking of LGBT individuals: A call for service provision, research and action. *The International Law News, 42*(4), 21–24.

McKinney, S. (2014). *Runaway youth: A research brief.* Status Offense Reform Center. Retrieved from http://www.modelsforchange.net/publications/624

Mohatt, N. V., Thompson, A. B., Thai, N. D., & Tebes, J. K. (2014). Historical trauma as public narrative: A conceptual review of how history impacts present day health. *Social Science Medicine, 106*, 128–136.

Morris, M. W. (2016). *Pushout.* New York: The New Press.

Morton, M. H., Dworsky, A., & Samuels, G. M. (2017). *Missed opportunities: Youth homelessness in America. National estimates.* Chicago: Chapin Hall at the University of Chicago.

Moss, J. L. (2019). The forgotten victims of missing White woman syndrome: An examination of legal measures that contribute to the lack of search and recovery of missing Black girls and women. *William & Mary Journal of Race, Gender, and Social Justice, 25*(3), 737–762.

Movement Advancement Project and Center for American Progress. (2016). *Unjust: How the broken criminal justice system fails LGBT people of color.* Retrieved from https://www.lgbtmap. org/file/lgbt-criminal-justice-poc.pdf

Murphy, L. T. (2017). *Labor and sex trafficking among homeless youth: A ten-city study.* New Orleans: Modern Slavery Research Project, Loyola University New Orleans.

Myers, J. E. B. (2008). A history of child protection in America. *Family Law Quarterly, 42*(3), 449–463.

Naramore, R., Bright, M. A., Epps, N., & Hardt, N. S. (2015). Youth arrested for trading sex have the highest rates of childhood adversity: A statewide study of juvenile offenders. *Sexual Abuse, 29*(4), 396–410.

National Center for Education Statistics. (2020). *Fast facts: Back to school statistics.* Retrieved from https://nces.ed.gov/fastfacts/display.asp?id=372

National Center for Homeless Education. (2019). *Federal data summary school years 2014–15 to 2016–17: Education for homeless children and youth.* Retrieved from.

National Equity Project. (n.d.). *The lens of systemic oppression.* Retrieved from https://nationalequityproject.org/wp-content/uploads/Lens-of-Systemic-Oppression.pdf

O'Brien, J. E., White, K., & Rizo, C. F. (2017). Domestic minor sex trafficking among child welfare-involved youth: An exploratory study of correlations. *Child Maltreatment, 22*(3), 265–274.

Padilla, L. M. (2001). But you're not dirty Mexican: Internalized oppression, Latinos & law. *Texas Hispanic Journal of Law & Policy, 7*, 59–114.

Pasko, L. (2010). Damaged daughters: The history of girls' sexuality and the juvenile justice system. *Journal of Criminal Law and Criminology, 100*(3), 1099–1130.

Pearce, M. E., Christian, W. M., Patterson, K., Norris, K., & Moniruzzaman, A. K. M. (2008). The cedar project: Historical trauma, sexual abuse and HIV vulnerability among young Aboriginal people who use injection and non-injection drugs in two Canadian cities. *Social Science & Medicine, 66*, 2185–2194.

Perreira, K. M., & Ornelas, I. (2013). Painful passages: Traumatic experiences and post-traumatic stress among U.S. immigrant Latino adolescents and their primary caregivers. *International Migration Review, 47*(4), 976–1005.

Perry, C. L., & Pecanha, V. C. (2017). Sex-trafficked survivors: The relation between post-traumatic growth and quality of life. *Journal of Human Trafficking, 3*(4), 271–284.

Peters, J. W., Becher, J., & Hirschfeld, D. J. (2017, February 22). Trump rescinds rules on bathrooms for transgender students. *The New York Times*. Retrieved from https://www.nytimes.com/2017/02/22/us/politics/devos-sessions-transgender-students-rights.html

Puzzanchera, C., & Hockenberry, S. (2013). *Juvenile court statistics 2010*. Pittsburgh: National Center for Juvenile Justice. Retrieved from https://www.ncjrs.gov/pdffiles1/ojjdp/grants/244080.pdf.

Radel, L., Baldwin, M., Crouse, G., Ghertner, R., & Waters, A. (2018). *Substance use, the opioid epidemic, and the child welfare system: Key findings from a mixed methods study*. Washington, DC: U.S. Department of Health and Human Services, Office of the Assistant Secretary for Planning and Evaluation.

Raino, C., & Roeck, E. (2017). *What's in a name? Lack of consistency in child sex trafficking laws may hurt our children*. Retrieved from https://sharedhope.org/2017/02/21/whats-in-a-name/

Raz, M. (2017). Lessons from history: Parents anonymous and child abuse prevention policy. *Pediatrics, 140*(6), e20170340.

Reid, J. A., & Piquero, A. R. (2014). Age-graded risks for commercial sexual exploitation of male and female youth. *Journal of Interpersonal Violence, 29*(9), 1747–1777.

Reid, J. A., & Piquero, A. R. (2016). Applying general strain theory to youth commercial sexual exploitation. *Crime and Delinquency, 62*(3), 341–367.

Romer, D. (2010). Adolescent risk taking, impulsivity, and brain development: Implications for prevention. *Developmental Psychobiology, 52*(3), 263–276.

Romero, A. P., Goldberg, S. K., & Vasquez, L. A. (2020). *LGBT people and housing affordability, discrimination, and homelessness*. Los Angeles: UCLA School of Law, Williams Institute.

Rose, S. J., & Hartmann, H. (2018). *Still a man's labor market: The slowly narrowing gender wage gap*. Washington, DC: Institute for Women's Policy Research.

Rosenblatt, K. (2014). Determining the vulnerability factors, lures and recruitment methods used to entrap American children into sex trafficking. *Sociology and Criminology, 2*(108), https://doi.org/10.4172/2375-4435.1000108.

Rosenthal, L. (2018). *Girls matter: Centering gender in status offense reform efforts*. Washington, DC: Vera.

Rovner, J. (2014). *Disproportionate minority contact in the juvenile justice system*. Washington, DC: The Sentencing Project.

Ryon, S. B., Early, K. W., Hand, G., & Chapman, S. (2013). Juvenile justice interventions: System escalation and effective alternative to residential placement. *Journal of Offender Rehabilitation, 52*(5), 358–375.

Saar, M. S., Epstein, R., Rosenthal, L., & Vafa, Y. (2015). *The sexual abuse to prison pipeline: The girls' story*. Washington, DC: Human Rights Project for Girls, Georgetown Law Center on Poverty and Inequality, & Ms. Foundation for Women. Retrieved from https://www.law.georgetown.edu/poverty-inequality-center/wp-content/uploads/sites/14/2019/02/The-Sexual-Abuse-To-Prison-Pipeline-The-Girls%E2%80%99-Story.pdf.

Sawyer, W. (2019). *Youth confinement: The whole pie 2019*. Northampton: Prison Policy Initiative. Retrieved from https://www.prisonpolicy.org/reports/youth2019.html.

Sebastian, C., Viding, E., Williams, K. D., & Blakemore, S. (2010). Social brain development and the affective consequences of ostracism in adolescence. *Brain and Cognition, 72*, 134–145.

Shared Hope International. (2019a). National state law survey: Barriers to child welfare involvement. *Protect Innocence Challenge*. Retrieved from https://sharedhope.org/PICframe9/state-surveycharts/NSL_Survey_BarrierstoChildWelfareInvolvement.pdf.

Shared Hope International. (2019b). National state law survey: Non-criminalization of juvenile sex trafficking victims. *Protect Innocence Challenge*. Retrieved from https://sharedhope.org/PICframe9/statesurveycharts/NSL_Survey_Non-CriminalizationofJuvenileSexTraffickingVictims.pdf.

Shonkoff, J. P., Garner, A. S., Siegel, B. S., Dobbins, M. I., Earls, M. F., McGuinn, L., et al. (2012). The lifelong effects of early childhood adversity and toxic stress. *Pediatrics, 129*(1), 232–246.

Society for Research in Child Development. (2018). *The science is clear: Separating families has long-term damaging psychological and health consequences for children, families, and communities*. Retrieved from https://www.srcd.org/sites/default/files/resources/FINAL_The%20Science%20is%20Clear_0.pdf

Solomon, D. T., Combs, E. M., Allen, K., Roles, S., DiCarlo, S., Reed, O., & Klaver, S. J. (2019). The impact of minority stress and gender identity on PTSD outcomes in sexual minority survivors of interpersonal trauma. *Psychology and Sexuality,* https://doi.org/10.1080/19419899.2019.1690033.

Swaner, R., Labriola, M., Rempel, M., Walker, A., & Spadafore, J. (2016). *Youth involvement in the sex trade: A national study*. New York: Center for Court Innovation. Retrieved from https://www.courtinnovation.org/sites/default/files/documents/Youth%20Involvement%20in%20the%20Sex%20Trade_3.pdf.

Tedeschi, R. G., & Calhoun, L. G. (2004). The foundation of post-traumatic growth: New considerations. *Psychological Inquiry, 15*(1), 93–102.

Tedor, M. F., & Mallott, C. A. (2018). *Juvenile delinquency: Pathways and prevention*. New York: SAGE Publications.

The Annie E. Casey Foundation. (2016). *LGBTQ in child welfare: A systematic review of the literature*. Retrieved from https://www.aecf.org/resources/lgbtq-in-child-welfare/

Theriot, M. T. (2009). School resource officers and the criminalization of student behavior. *Journal of Criminal Justice, 37*, 280–287.

Thorn. (2018). *Survivor insights: The role of technology in domestic minor sex trafficking*. Retrieved from https://www.thorn.org/wp-content/uploads/2019/12/Thorn_Survivor_Insights_090519.pdf

Tomasiewicz, M. L. (2018). *Sex trafficking of transgender and gender nonconforming youth in the United States*. Chicago: Loyola University School of Law Center for the Human Rights of Children. Retrieved from https://ecommons.luc.edu/cgi/viewcontent.cgi?article=1017&context=chrc.

Trump, D. (2017, August 25). *Military service by transgender individuals* [Memorandum]. National Security and Defense. Retrieved from https://www.whitehouse.gov/presidential-actions/presidential-memorandum-secretary-defense-secretary-homeland-security/

Twis, M. K. (2020). Risk factor patterns in domestic minor sex trafficking relationships. *Journal of Human Trafficking, 6*(3), 309–326.

U.S. Department of Education (n.d.). *Chronic absenteeism in the nation's schools: A hidden educational crisis*. https://www2.ed.gov/datastory/chronicabsenteeism.html?src=pr

U.S. Department of Education, Office for Civil Rights. (2014). *Data snapshot: School discipline*. Retrieved from https://ocrdata.ed.gov/Downloads/CRDC-School-Discipline-Snapshot.pdf

U.S. Department of Health and Human Services, Administration for Children and Families, Children's Bureau. (2011). *Federal Child and Family Services Reviews aggregate report: Round 2: Fiscal years 2007–2010*.

U.S. Department of Health and Human Services, Administration for Children and Families, Children's Bureau. (2012). *General findings from the Federal Child and Family Services Review*.

U.S. Department of Justice, Office of Juvenile Justice and Delinquency Prevention. (2019). *Implementation of the Ashlynne Mike AMBER Alert in Indian Country Act of 2018: A report to Congress*.

Ulloa, E., Salazar, M., & Monjaras, L. (2016). Prevalence and correlates of sex exchange among a nationally representative sample of adolescents and young adults. *Journal of Child Sexual Abuse, 25*(5), 524–537.

United Nations Office on Drugs and Crime. (2018). *Global report on trafficking in persons 2018* (United Nations publication, Sales No. E.19.IV.2). Retrieved from https://www.unodc.org/documents/data-and-analysis/glotip/2018/GLOTiP_2018_BOOK_web_small.pdf

Van Der Kolk, B. (2015). *The body keeps the score: Brain, mind, and body in the healing of trauma*. New York: Penguin.

Walts, K. K. (2017). Child labor trafficking in the United States: A hidden crime. *Social Inclusion, 5*(2), 59–68.

Watson, L. B., DeBlaere, C., Langrehr, K. J., Zelaya, D. G., & Flores, M. J. (2016). The influence of multiple oppressions on women of color's experiences with insidious trauma. *Journal of Counseling Psychology, 63*(6), 656–667.

Woods, S., & Summers, A. (2016). *Technical assistance bulletin: Disproportionality rates for children of color in foster care (fiscal year 2014)*. Reno: National Council of Juvenile and Family Court Judges.

Yao, Y., Robinson, A. M., Zucchi, F. C., Robbins, J. C., Babenko, O., Kovalchuk, O., Kovalchuk, I., Olson, D. M., & Metz, G. A. (2014). Ancestral exposure to stress epigenetically programs preterm birth risk and adverse maternal and newborn outcomes. *BMC Medicine, 12*, 121.

Zero to Thrive Initiative and the Center for Human Growth and Development at the University of Michigan. (2018). *Research and policy perspectives on separating (and reconnecting) children and parents: Implications for families on the border*. Retrieved from https://medicine.umich.edu/sites/default/files/content/downloads/Rapid%20Response%20Talk_Research%20and%20Policy%20Perspectives%20on%20Separating%20Children%20and%20Parents.pdf

Chapter 12
The Long History of Child Saving as Nation Building in the USA: An Argument for Privileging Children's Perspectives on Recovery

Anna Mae Duane

12.1 Introduction

In April 2018, after months of quiet discussion in the Trump administration, Attorney General Jeff Sessions declared a "zero-tolerance policy" be enforced on the southern border of the USA. Under this new policy, every instance of the misdemeanor offense of crossing the border into the USA without documentation would be referred for federal prosecution. This would place thousands of parents in detention, which made it impossible for families to remain together (Kandel 2018; US Government Accountability Office 2018; Office of Attorney General 2018; Todres and Fink 2020). The Flores Settlement Agreement, consequent to the 1993 Supreme Court case of *Reno v. Flores*, was designed to limit child detention; the agreement stipulates that border crossing detained children must be "released" into the care of parents or other adults or licensed care programs within 20 days (Stracqualursi et al. 2019). Thus, citing this legal stipulation, the Trump administration operationalized "zero tolerance" by summarily separating parents from the children who were traveling with them, even when those children were under 5 years old (Roth et al. 2018).

When faced with public outcry against his administration's harmful family separation policy, Donald Trump argued that such draconian measures were a necessary weapon in the battle against human trafficking. In a 2019 *Meet the Press* interview, Trump insisted that family separation and subsequent child detention were required because cartels were using the children in ways that were analogous to modern-day slavery (Rubin 2019). On other occasions, Trump and his administration framed the need to separate children from their parents (and thus subject them to all the abuses associated with detention or congregate care) as a "humanitarian issue." Such drastic actions are, according to the administration, "a moral obligation," required to

A. M. Duane (✉)
University of Connecticut, Storrs, CT, USA
e-mail: anna.duane@uconn.edu

© Springer Nature Switzerland AG 2021
M. Chisolm-Straker, K. Chon (eds.), *The Historical Roots of Human Trafficking*,
https://doi.org/10.1007/978-3-030-70675-3_12

confront the threat of "traffickers" and their "heinous crimes" (WhiteHouse.gov 2019). While Trump's Executive Order of 2019 supposedly ended the practice, there is ample evidence that family separation continued, and that little has been done to address the trauma imposed on the thousands of children already affected, and who have been subject to mental and physical abuse as a result of this policy (Haag 2019; Hernández 2019; Honarvar 2018; Jordan 2019; Neuman 2018).

Current scholars of trafficking have noted that public discussions of the problem often rely on tropes such as the ones Trump deploys: images of passive children who need to be rescued by legal and governmental authorities (Chuang 2010; Williams 2008). The USA has a long history of using the specter of a helpless child victim to justify state coercion with the language of care (Duane 2011). This chapter provides a historical perspective of accounts in which children were exploited, trafficked, and enslaved by legal authorities in order to delineate the ideological threads which have long tied national sovereignty to the sanctioned abuse and coercion of children of color. From English colonial appropriation of Indigenous children in the 16th and 17th centuries, to the childrearing practices of slavers through the nineteenth century, to the promotion of Indian boarding schools in the twentieth, official narratives of "rescue" have provided cover for a process in which the state first victimizes children in the name of nation building, often separating them from their families, and then uses the children's vulnerability as a justification for exerting state authority over them.

This chapter does not seek to exculpate or minimize the harms caused by criminal trafficking, which undoubtedly inflicts trauma and creates conflicting loyalties. Rather, it looks to history to trace how wholly legal state intervention have also inflicted levels of trauma, while casting that trauma as a necessary form of rescue. More specifically, this chapter interrogates the fantasy—most recently espoused by the Trump administration, but echoed in centuries of harsh and racist treatment of Black, Indigenous, and immigrant children—that the good of the nation, and the children themselves, requires their separation from their families of origin. This work provides context for modern public health policymakers and practitioners on three levels. First, engagement with this history interrogates current narratives that reduce child trafficking to a narrow set of criminal acts, rather than addressing larger structural forces that lead to the widespread abuse of migrant and marginalized children (Chuang 2010). Second, drawing from the words and experiences of enslaved trafficked and exploited children in the past, this chapter dispels the false narrative that children's innocence prevents them from realizing their oppression. Instead, these accounts often reveal that even young children found canny ways to ameliorate and resist their subjugation. In short, history demonstrates that children have long been savvy critics of abusive treatment at the hands of authority and have been active agents in navigating the most viable paths to liberation. Third, this history of harmful "helpers" serves to dislodge the reductive narrative of care that suggests that children's innocence requires they are excluding from informing the state-sanctioned decisions about their lives. It has long been argued that paternalism does not serve vulnerable adults. The complex history of US children who have been trafficked, enslaved, and abused by state-sanctioned actors suggests that paternalism is equally dangerous when aimed at children, especially when neglecting the best interests of the child. Ideally, reckoning with the resilience of children of the past creates space for a partnership model in the present that would render children's accounts of their own experiences and aspirations vital components in assessing trafficking's harms. Thus, this chapter is a historically inflected addition to the ample and growing work in both the social sciences and humanities that have argued for engaging children as agents of culture and collaborators in their own well-being.

12.2   Discussion

12.2.1   A History of Children Abducted for Their Own Good

The romance of a kidnapped child animates one of the USA's most cherished origin stories. An oft-retold narrative of early American contact imagines Indigenous teenager Pocahontas and Englishman John Smith as star-crossed lovers. That amorous fiction has obscured the historical reality that one of the nation's founding narratives is based on the trauma of an abducted teenager. When John Smith first encountered Pocahontas, he described meeting a "childe of tenne yeares old." When Smith wrote Queen Anne in anticipation of Pocahontas's visit to England, Smith remembers her as a "childe of twelve or thirteene yeeres of age," and writes of her "compassionate and pitifull heart" (Smith 1608). Whatever admiration the English might have had for the young girl's "heart," they soon took her prisoner, hoping to leverage her separation from family and tribe into a military and economic advantage. During Pocahontas's forced stay with the British, she was baptized into Christianity and married to John Rolfe at the young age of seventeen.[1] Her coerced absorption into British culture was heralded as a sign of good things to come for the nascent British Empire. Returning colonists assured authorities that the pliability of this Native girl was a harbinger that "America"—and Native Americans—would happily relinquish initial resistance and embrace Britain's "civilized" culture. Ever since the marriage, a British colonist related in a missive to the mother country, "we have had friendly commerce and trade, not onely with Powhatan himselfe, but also with his subjects about us; so now I see no reason why the Colllonie should not thrive a pace" (Hamor 1615; Kupperman 2019). Perhaps more important for this chapter's concerns, Pocahontas's familial loss was narrated as an imperialist gain: The British congratulated themselves on introducing the girl to Christianity and to the wonders of the English monarchy. Pocahontas's grief at her disconnection from her home culture, and even her early death at the age of twenty, was acceptable collateral damage for the greater good of the British empire, mirrored later in the USA. For more than

---

[1] In England at this time, the average age of a newly married woman hovered slightly above twenty-five.

three centuries after Pocahontas' kidnapping, the nation's sense of identity—not to mention its economic prosperity—has been propagated by controlling the movements, the familial connections, the labor, and the loyalty of children who were considered outside the parameters of "true" US identity, all the while insisting that such control was for the children's own good.

12.2.2   Black Children as Child Slaves

The state-sanctioned trafficking of children and wide-scale familial disruption was central to the US slave régime, an institution upon which the nation's prosperity relied for centuries (Schwartz 2009; Sánchez-Eppler 2017). US census data indicate that from 1830 (when census questions on age first appeared) through 1860, over 30 percent of the enslaved population of the USA were less than 10 years old (King 2011; Sánchez-Eppler 2017). To better exploit the work of children and to reduce their resistance, slavers routinely separated children from their parents. Frederick Douglass, perhaps one of slavery's most famous survivors, wrote that family separation was a key element to the slave system's success. In 1845, he wrote, "It is a common custom, in the part of Maryland from which I ran away, to part children from their mothers at a very early age," often before the child was 1 year old. Douglass surmised that such actions were taken to "hinder the development of the child's affection toward its mother, and to blunt and destroy the natural affection of the mother for the child" (Douglass 1845). Such detached children, slavers imagined, would make more pliable laborers. Under the legal structures of slavery, even children who might have been lucky enough to be near their family of origin would have no legal evidence to testify to the value, or even the existence, of those bonds. Enslaved people could not legally marry, which rendered all enslaved children "illegitimate," and thus cut off from patrilineal connection in the eyes of the law. Enslaved people were denied surnames or were called by their enslaver's surname, a practice that made it difficult for families to reunite after emancipation (Regosin 2002). Modern ethnographic studies of trafficked children find echoes of Douglass's trauma, as children indicated that they were harmed most severely, not by the type of labor forced upon them, but by their isolation from family, from their exposure to physical and sexual abuse, and by the lack of control over their movements (Blagbrough and Craig 2017).

Yet, even under such dire circumstances, the young Frederick Douglass was able to recognize the injustice of his situation. As a young child, he actively disobeyed legal injunctions against learning to read and attained literacy by the age of ten. By sixteen, he was physically resisting his enslaver and plotting his escape (Douglass 1845). He was not alone. Other narratives by formerly enslaved people testify to their ability as young children to identify their situation as oppressive and to deftly identify actions that could improve their lot, even in the midst of dire constraints. Venture Smith, kidnapped and brought to the USA in the eighteenth century, was 8 years old when he resisted adult demands to hand over property (Smith and Horton

1798). Olaudah Equiano, who described being abducted from his homeland as a young child, was still a teenager when he deployed his skills as a sailor and as an accountant to begin accumulating his own money; this allowed him to eventually purchase his own freedom (Equiano 2001). Harriet Jacobs, born into slavery in the nineteenth century, was fourteen when she resisted her enslaver's sexual advances and only a few years older when she defied him by forging a romantic alliance with a powerful White neighbor (Jacobs 1861). Indeed, the bulk of the accounts of enslavement in the USA is in many ways, testimony to the resilience and intelligence of minors. The largest repository of US slave narratives, generally known as the WPA (Works Progress Administration) Narratives, was predominantly collected from informants who were 15 years old or younger when the Civil War began; hence, the bulk of knowledge of US slavery comes from the perspective of children who had managed to survive the system (Blassingame 1975; Sánchez-Eppler 2017).

12.2.3 Child Separation as "Education"

Throughout the 19th century and into the 20th, US government responses toward Indigenous children echoed the tactics of familial separation employed in chattel slavery. In this case, the state relied on paternalistic metaphors of care and cultivation to obscure the fact that these children had been harmed by the government in order to advance the nation's financial and political interests. Their traumatic "education" would ultimately serve to further state interests. The violent removal of Native tribes from the southern USA had enabled the expanse of slaveholder landholdings (Chap. 2), which were, of course, dependent on the violently coerced labor of Black adults and children to turn a profit (Baptist 2016). Those profits, in turn, benefited both Southern slavers and Northern bankers and factory owners (Baptist 2016; Johnson 2013). After years of warfare and forcible land appropriation that had rendered Native people particularly vulnerable, the USA imagined entire Native tribes as wayward wards who needed to be assimilated into White US culture. An 1831 Supreme Court case justified the government's choice to overrule the rights and wishes of Native people by comparing them to children. Because Indigenous people occupied "a territory to which we [the US government] assert a title independent of their will...they are in a state of pupilage," the Court declared. "[T]heir relations to the United States resemble that of a ward to his guardian. They look to our Government for protection, rely upon its kindness and its power, appeal to it for relief to their wants, and address the President as their Great Father" (Cherokee Nation 1831). In short, after leaving tribes bereft by appropriating their land "against their will," the nation congratulated itself for its "kindness" as a "Great Father" who provided "relief" for the very "wants" it had created without regard for those affected.

The figurative language describing the need to disregard the wishes of Native "pupils" became literal policy through the work of residential schools (Chap. 16), which violently separated Native children from their families for the alleged greater good. The Carlisle Indian Industrial School is perhaps the most famous of the residential schools in which generations of Indian youth were physically and psychologically traumatized through family separation, physical and sexual abuse, and forced labor (Adams 1995; American Eagle 1994). Captain Richard H. Pratt, the school's founder, looked to the abduction and exploitation of enslaved Black children as a worthy model to follow: "Left in Africa," Pratt wrote, "seven millions of industrious black fellow-citizens would still be savages." But because Africans had been trafficked into slavery, which Pratt euphemized as "new surroundings and experiences," enslaved people became "English-speaking and civilized." According to Pratt, enslaved people's salvation was all "because [they were] forced into association with English-speaking and civilized people" (Pratt 1892). In Pratt's formulation, inflicting trauma on enslaved children was necessary. Thus, taking the children's assessment of the situation into account would have been a foolish act of sentimentalism. Pratt and other boarding school administrators followed this model and inflicted trauma on generations of Indigenous children, all under the auspices of saving them. Children were forcibly taken from their homes and placed in boarding schools, often far from all they had known (Adams 1995; American Eagle 1994; Grinde 2004; Glancy 2014). At the schools, they were subject to sexual and physical exploitation and were forced to work, both at the school and in private homes, for no remuneration (Grinde 2004, Glancy 2014). The feelings of Native children taken from their parents and placed in abusive boarding schools were of no account to the adults in charge. If anything, their grief over losing their family and their culture was an indication of their misguided attachment to an "uncivilized" and "un-American" past. As educators sought to "Kill the Indian, Save the Man," they systematically dismantled attachment to students' native language, traditions, and family ties (Grinde 2004; Indian Education 1969; Pratt 1892; Woolford 2015).

As a Congressional Report later indicated, the USA benefited both culturally and financially from the exploitation of Native children (Indian Education 1969). Certainly, the boarding school system served to reinforce the idea that White middle-class culture was the epitome of civilization. The system also, the report indicated, was designed upon "the implicit hope that a 'civilized Indian' would settle down on his 160 acres and become a gentleman farmer, thus freeing large amounts of land for the white man." Thus, the report concluded that it "is clear that the 'assimilation by education' policy was primarily a function of the 'Indian land policy'" which systematically appropriated Indigenous property for profit (Indian Education 1969).

12.2.4   State Intervention as Child Exploitation: The Pattern Continues

The current crisis on the USA–Mexico border offers a particularly salient example of the historic pattern in which vulnerable children are first rendered victims by the state and then become unwilling subjects to a host of state-sponsored abuses packaged as necessary responses to that same victimhood. For decades, US foreign policy has significantly weakened the economies and thus the quality of life of the Central American Northern Triangle (CANT). In 1954, the USA helped to stage a *coup* against the government of Guatemala and then supported the new military government for years despite the military government's well-documented human rights abuses (Baker-Jordan 2018; Bracken 2016). In the 1980s, the Reagan administration used El Salvador as a staging ground for the Contras, a group the USA backed in neighboring Nicaragua's civil war. Decades of consequent destabilization subjected generations to poverty and set the stage for the chaos and violence that plagues the region today. More recently, failed "drug war" policies have created a regimé of criminality that operates under a sort of "structural impunity." There is a tacit guarantee from the USA that there will be no interference as long as US governmental interests are not threatened (Thornton et al. 2016).

Even as US policies of destabilization and the drug war have created incentives for families to migrate north to escape violence and chaos, harsh border policies render it more likely that vulnerable people will have to rely on criminals to make the journey. In other words, the militarized USA–Mexico border policy creates the conditions for a vibrant market for traffickers and increases the chances that traffickers will be able to inflict slavery-like abuses with little interference (Baker-Jordan 2018; Gendle and Mónico 2017). The prevalence of such abuse in turn provides moral and legal cover for still further draconian US action, which inflicts upon children many of the most egregious harms associated with the very trafficking that the Trump administration ostensibly seeks to combat. Numerous reports have detailed the trauma that detained children are experiencing because of the violent separation from their families at the border; reports also indicate both the high likelihood and actual experiences of physical and sexual abuse while in detention (Haag 2019; Honarvar 2018; Wood 2018).

12.2.5   Conceptions of Childhood and Consent that Enable the Rescue Narrative

In both historical and contemporary cases of child enslavement and trafficking, the insistence that children's unique status makes their consent to and collaboration with their own care unnecessary has effectively made it easier for trafficking and exploitation to take place. Indeed, muting children's capacity for legal dissent has made it more likely for exploitation to occur with the sanction of legal authority. The USA's legal conception of consent creates a sharp dividing line excluding nearly all people under 18 years from having legally recognizable veto power over their treatment. Overall, children are deemed too innocent and too incompetent to be asked to participate in their own care or to have their objections to mismanaged care considered legally viable (Appell 2009; Woodhouse 2010). Being disallowed from giving consent does not only mean that a child cannot legally say "yes" to exploitative arrangements. As demonstrated by exploitative, racist, US-sanctioned "apprenticeship" and schooling regimes, the logic of child protection also neutralizes the child's ability to say "no" to adults vested with state-sanctioned authority. In other words, the law's insistence on a minor's inability to consent, often touted as a means to guard children from a host of dangers, has often served as cover for coercion (Brewer 2012; Meiners 2016).

For example, the "common sense" belief that young people's wishes need not be addressed or heeded was so ingrained in the nineteenth century that even national legislators agreed that children were excluded from the protections against slavery and involuntary servitude enshrined in the Thirteenth Amendment (Duane 2018). During the congressional debate over ratifying the amendment, Senator Edgar Cowen rhetorically asked "Will anybody…undertake to say that it [the 13th Amendment] was to prevent the involuntary servitude of my child to me…?" Quickly, he answered his own question, "Certainly not" (Cong Globe 1866; Duane 2018). While involuntary servitude was deemed unacceptable for all adults (except those convicted of a crime) (Chap. 9), all seemed to agree that children—simply by virtue of their age—had no right to refuse labor, especially if the person demanding that labor held the position of legal guardian. This stipulation immediately provided legal cover to ignore children's objections to family separation, forced labor, and other forms of exploitation.

Indeed, after the Thirteenth Amendment, family separation and child trafficking continued, now under the guise of providing protection and guardianship. Slavers were now simply renamed as guardians, and the enslaved became "apprentices." For example, 2500 African American children were apprenticed to their former owners in Maryland shortly after emancipation in 1865, under the auspices of guardianship (Woodhouse 2010; Davis 1998). The 1865 Mississippi Black Code allowed for the apprenticeship of all Black or mixed-race children under 18 years whose parents were deemed by the state "unable to provide for or support" them. Throughout the South, there were financial and cultural incentives to remove such children from Black homes and place them as unpaid labor in White businesses and households. In Mississippi, the Code even stipulated that "the former owner of said minors shall have the preference" in acquiring them for apprenticeship, thus placing formerly enslaved children with the very same people who had enslaved them (Mississippi 1865; Mitchell 2008). The USA was far from alone in its practice of calling on "protection" to keep children subject to adults who viewed them as property. Post-abolition, English and French colonists in Africa summarily dispatched children as the wards of those who had been their former owners (Diptee 2017; Moitt 2011).

The nineteenth-century belief that children should—in a legal sense—be neither seen, nor heard, was reinforced by the legal apparatus designed in the twentieth century to address human trafficking. The "White slavery scare" at the turn of the twentieth century was largely defined through the image of an innocent, noncon-senting child, creating legal precedent that continues to shape contemporary defini-tions and responses to human trafficking to this day (Allain 2017). The influential 1902 International Conference "On the White Slave Traffic" carved out particular exceptions for minors that made their own experience irrelevant to the assessment of crime (Allain 2017). The language of the conference proceedings made it clear that if a person was under 21 years, and thus, a legal minor, their consent, or even their own perception of harm, was irrelevant to determining whether or not they had been trafficked. Even if the young person was willingly engaging in activities to support themselves or their family, their intentions and choices about economic survival were superseded by one factor alone: their age. "A minor does not have complete exercise over her free will," was one of the conclusions of the 1902 legislative report. "Rather," the report indicated, a young girl "is *res sacra* [a sacred thing]; the law must defend her, even against her own weakness" (Allain 2017).[2]

The report's pivotal phrase—which states that defending children demands disregarding their own will—weds the historical assumptions of the past to the legal structures of the present. What a minor articulates as a necessity for survival, or even as a choice, is legally constructed as irrelevant (Appell 2009; Woodhouse 2010). A minor's will, in this context, is nothing more than a weakness to be corrected by the expertise of outsiders. Any objections to that correction are beneath legal notice and arguably viewed as evidence that children simply do not know what is best for them. More recent statutes, like the US Trafficking Victims Protection Act (TVPA) of 2000 concurs with the general agreement in the international community that, in the case of minors, sex trafficking charges apply regardless of whether that young person was taken forcibly or agreed voluntarily (Miko 2004a, b). Then and now, it is the intentions of the adult, not the youth, that matters, both in the commission of the crime and in the interventions designed to address that crime. Failure to prioritize the child's perspective and agency not only cuts off a valuable source of information about their circumstances, but also forecloses a valuable form of healing. A recent study determined that including young people in their own treatment plan improved their outcomes (The Annie E. Casey Foundation 2019). To take just one contemporary example, Ravi, a child who had been forced into commercial sex, related his simple desire to be heard: "I hope that by sharing my story, my life will finally have meaning and can help prevent others from the deep sadness of my life" (Bales and Trodd 2008; Goździak 2016).

12.2.6 Rather than Perfect Innocence, Imperfect Partnerships

Of course, there are valid objections to rendering minors, especially younger children, as partners in their own legal or medical journeys. Children's perspectives can be clouded or compromised by misguided allegiances to abusers or by an inability to fully grasp their situation and ramifications of certain choices. This, however, can also be true of trafficked adults as well. Children, like adults, are faced with limited options, but this does not mean that they are incapable of knowing which option offers the best chance of survival and eventual recovery. When it comes to Black and Brown children, the language of child saving and protectionism is particularly

---

[2] According to Ballentine's legal dictionary, "res sacra" is commonly translated in the law to mean: "A sacred thing does not admit of valuation." Ballentine's Law Dictionary (1916). The Bobbs-Merrill Company.

pernicious, as it invokes the idea of innocence to excuse overriding the objections of children and families already vulnerable to the nation's economic and expansionist goals.

Collaborating with vulnerable children will require a recalibration of many "common sense" assumptions about what children are capable of, and realizing that their interpretations and choices may clash with middle-class expectations. As history demonstrates, children are often savvy negotiators of the difficult choices presented to them. By refusing to recognize the ambivalence attending child agency, authorities can revictimize children by rendering their choices a crime. Scholars of mass incarceration have documented how the legal structures designed to protect minors from exploitation often inflict grievous harms on youth by criminalizing their (admittedly constrained) involvement in commercial sex and work (Meiners 2016: Pliley 2017; Wagner 2010). Similarly, youth identified as "child soldiers" have, at times, found that taking up arms was their best option to defend their community and their families (Rosen 2017). To return to the situation at the USA–Mexico border, well-meaning adults in the media and nongovernmental organizations (NGO), horrified by the thought of young people faced with the trials and traumas of migration often mistakenly conflate all forms of youth migration with trafficking (Ensor 2010; Goździak 2016). In truth, for many people under the age of 18, migration may be their best option in a constrained set of choices. Recognizing that reality would allow responses better calibrated to truly improve these children's circumstances (Goździak 2016).

Ideally, all young people would be protected from dangerous or exploitative work and from commercial sex abuse. But the narrative which reduces children in difficult circumstances to a static role in a tale of villainous criminals and helpless victims actually obscures the structural analysis necessary to change the conditions in which young people find themselves. Without addressing the poverty, political strife, and discrimination that drive young people to such circumstances, criminalizing their place in the global marketplace can do more harm than good, and often in ways that benefit the state (Bernstein 2010; Pliley 2017; Rosen 2017).

12.3 Conclusion

The long history of state-sponsored exploitation of Black and Brown children, often couched as caretaking or rescue, offers an important framework for understanding and addressing the plight of trafficked children in the twenty-first century. The legal and cultural emphasis on children's incompetence and "innocence" has too often been deployed as a reason why the state need not take their perspectives seriously. Overturning professional and cultural biases against allowing children to advocate for their own best interests will require sustained effort and considerable humility. However, the historical evidence of the harms perpetrated by those who refused to consider children collaborators in their own care renders it ethically necessary and clinically efficacious to understand a vulnerable child's perspective as a prerequisite to any interventions designed to help them.

12.4   Recommendations

1. As studies have indicated, *privileging the perspective of young people and incorporating their insights into policy and treatment plans* raise the likelihood of successful outcomes (Goździak 2016; The Annie E. Casey Foundation 2019).
2. *Anti-trafficking and immigration policies should draw on both historical and ethnographic research* that indicates that children find family separation to be among the most painful aspects of trafficking. One concrete outcome of privileging children's perspectives would change current policies in order to sustain family and community ties if at all possible, an outcome supported by evidence on the trauma caused by such policies (Blagbrough and Craig 2017; Physicians for Human Rights 2020).
3. To enact this collaborative, *health practitioners can partner with child advocates* (and possibly engage in court proceedings) *to better enable the child to represent their own perspectives* as a prerequisite to designing interventions (Malina 2019).
4. *A shift away from the narrow definitions of what constitutes trafficking and toward responding primarily to what children themselves consider harmful* would further create possibilities for expanding the parameters of treatment for vulnerable children, particularly children harmed by legal authorities.

References

Adams, D. W. (1995). *Education for extinction*. Topeka: University of Kansas Press.
Allain, J. (2017). White slave traffic in international law. *Journal of Trafficking and Human Exploitation, 1*(1), 1–40.
American Eagle. (1994). Goodbye BIA, Hello New Federalism. *American Eagle, 2*(19).
Appell, A. R. (2009). The pre-political child of child-centered jurisprudence. *Houston Law Review, 46*, 703.
Baker-Jordan, Skylar. (2018, October 23). The US' actions in Central America are to blame for the migrant caravan leaving Honduras—Trump has to let them in. *Independent*.
Bales, K., & Trodd, Z. (2008). *To plead our own cause: Personal stories by today's slaves*. Ithaca: Cornell University Press.
Ballentine's Law Dictionary. (1916). The Bobbs-Merrill Company.
Baptist, E. (2016). *The half has never been told: Slavery and the making of American capitalism*. New York: Basic Books.
Bernstein, E. (2010). Militarized humanitarianism meets Carceral feminism: The politics of sex, rights, and freedom in contemporary antitrafficking campaigns. *Signs: Journal of Women in Culture and Society, 36*(1), 45–71.
Blagbrough, J., & Craig, G. (2017). When I play with the master's children, I must always let them win: Child domestic labor. In A. Duane (Ed.), *Child slavery before and after emancipation: An argument for child-centered slavery studies* (pp. 251–269). New York: Cambridge University Press.

Blassingame, J. W. (1975). Using the testimony of ex-slaves: Approaches and problems. *Journal of Southern History, 41*, 490.

Bracken, A. (2016). Why you need to know about Guatemala's civil war. *The World*.

Brewer, H. (2012). *By birth or consent: Children, law, and the Anglo-American revolution in authority*. Chapel Hill: UNC Press.

Cherokee Nation v. Georgia, 30 U.S. 1. (1831).

Chuang, J. A. (2010). Rescuing trafficking from ideological capture: Prostitution reform and anti-trafficking law and policy. *University of Pennsylvania Law Review, 158*(6), 1655–1728.

Cong Globe. (1866). *39th congress 1st session 499 (remarks of Senator Cowen)*.

Davis, P. C. (1998). *Neglected stories: The constitution and family values*. New York: Macmillan.

Diptee, A. (2017). Notions of African childhood in abolitionist discourses: Colonial and postcolonial humanitarianism in the fight against child slavery. In A. M. Duane (Ed.), *Child slavery before and after emancipation: An argument for child-centered slavery studies* (pp. 208–230). New York: Cambridge University Press.

Douglass, F. (1845). *Narrative of the life of Frederick Douglass, an American slave: Written by himself*. Boston: Antislavery Office.

Duane, A. M. (2011). *Suffering childhood in early America: Violence, race and the making of the child*. Victim: University of Georgia Press.

Duane, A. M. (2018). All boys are bound to someone. In E. Swanson & J. Stewart (Eds.), *Human bondage and abolition: New histories of past and present slaveries* (pp. 173–189). Cambridge: Cambridge University Press.

Ensor, M. O., and Goździak, E. (2010). *Children and migration: At the crossroads of resiliency and vulnerability*. London, Palgrave Macmillan.

Equiano, O. (2001). *The interesting narrative of the life of Olaudah Equiano*. Peterborough, Canada: Broadview Press.

Gendle, M. H., & Mónico, C. C. (2017). The balloon effect: The role of US drug policy in the displacement of unaccompanied minors from the Central American Northern Triangle. *Journal of Trafficking, Organized Crime and Security, 3*(1–2), 12–20.

Glancy, D. (2014). *Fort Marion prisoners and the trauma of native education*. Lincoln: University of Nebraska Press.

Goździak, E. M. (2016). Forced victims or willing migrants? Contesting assumptions about child trafficking. In M. Seeberg & E. Goździak (Eds.), *Contested childhoods: Growing up in migrancy. IMISCOE research series*. Cham: Springer.

Grinde, D. A. (2004). Taking the Indian out of the Indian: US policies of ethnocide through education. *Wicazo Sa Review, 19*(2), 25–32.

Haag, M. (2019, February 27). Thousands of immigrant children said they were sexually abused in U.S. Detention Centers, report says. *New York Times*.

Hamor, R. (1615). *A true discourse of the present estate of Virginia*. Repr. *Jamestown Narratives* (1850) J. Munsell.

Hernández, L. H. (2019). Feminist approaches to border studies and gender violence: Family separation as reproductive injustice. *Women's Studies in Communication, 42*(2), 130–134.

Honarvar, A. (2018, July 27). A 6-year-old girl was sexually abused in an Immigrant-Detention Center. *The Nation*.

Indian Education: A National Tragedy – A National Challenge (Kennedy Report). (1969). Report of the Committee on Labor and Public Welfare, United States Senate made by its Special Subcommittee on Indian Education Pursuant to S. Res. 80 p 9.

Jacobs, H. A. (1861). *Incidents in the life of a slave girl: Written by herself*. Jean Fagan Yellin (Ed.) (2009). Harvard University Press.

Johnson, W. (2013). *River of dark dreams: Slavery and empire in the cotton kingdom*. Cambridge, MA: The Belknap Press of Harvard University Press.

Jordan, M. (2019, January 17). Family separation may have hit thousands more migrant children than. *New York Times*.

Kandel, W. A. (2018). *The trump administration's "zero tolerance" immigration enforcement policy*. Congressional Research Service. Accessed at https://fas.org/sgp/crs/homesec/R45266.pdf

King, W. (2011). *Stolen childhood: Slave youth in nineteenth-century America*. Bloomington: Indiana University Press.

Kupperman, K. O. (2019). *Pocahontas and the English boys: Caught between cultures in early Virginia*. New York: NYU Press.

Malina, G. (2019). How should unaccompanied minors in immigration detention be protected from coercive medical practices? *AMA Journal of Ethics, 21*(7), E603–E610.

Meiners, E. (2016). *For the children?: Protecting innocence in a carceral state*. Minneapolis: University of Minnesota Press.

Miko, F. T. (2004a, March 26). *Trafficking in women and children: The US and international response-updated*. Washington, DC: Congressional Research Service

Miko, F. T. (2004b). *Trafficking in women and children: The U.S. and international response*. CRS Report to Congress, The Library of Congress.

Mississippi Black Codes. (1865). *In Laws of Mississippi*.

Mitchell, M. N. (2008). *Raising freedom's child: Black children and visions of the future after slavery*. New York: NYU Press.

Moitt, B. (2011). Slavery and guardianship in postemancipation Senegal. In G. Campbell, S. Miers, & J. C. Miller (Eds.), *Child slaves in the modern world*. Athens: Ohio University Press.

Neuman, S. (2018, August 3). Allegations of sexual abuse surface at Arizona shelters for migrant children. *NPR*. Accessed at https://www.npr.org/2018/08/03/635203037/allegations-of-sexual-abuse-surface-at-arizona-shelters-for-migrant-children

Office of the Attorney General. (2018). Memorandum, supra note 7.

Physicians for Human Rights. (2020). *"You will never see your child again:" The persistent psychological effects of family separation*. Accessed at: https://phr.org/wp-content/uploads/2020/02/PHR-Report-2020-Family-Separation-Full-Report.pdf

Pliley, J. (2017). 'Protecting the young and the innocent': Age and consent in the enforcement of the White slave traffic act. In A. Duane (Ed.), *Child slavery before and after emancipation: An argument for child-centered slavery studies* (pp. 156–176). New York: Cambridge University Press.

Pratt, R. H. (1892). Official report of the nineteenth annual conference of charities and correction. Reprinted in Richard H. Pratt, (1973) "The advantages of mingling Indians with Whites," *Americanizing the American Indians: Writings by the "Friends of the Indian" 1880–1900*. Harvard University Press.

Regosin, E. (2002). *Freedom's promise: Ex-slave families and citizenship in the age of emancipation*. Charlottesville: University of Virginia Press.

Rosen, D. (2017). In A. Duane (Ed.), *Child slavery before and after emancipation: An argument for child-centered slavery studies* (pp. 156–176). New York: Cambridge University Press.

Roth, B. J., Crea, T. M., Jani, J., Underwood, D., Hasson, R. G., III, Evans, K., Zuch, M., & Hornung, E. (2018). Detached and afraid: U.S. immigration policy and the practice of forcibly separating parents and young children at the border. *Child Welfare, 96*(5), 29–49.

Rubin, J. (2019, June 24) Trump's lies need to be exposed in real time. *Washington Post*.

Sánchez-Eppler, K. (2017). 'Remember Dear, when the Yankees came through here, I was only ten years old': Valuing the enslaved child of the WPA slave narratives. In A. Duane (Ed.), *Child slavery before and after emancipation: An argument for child-centered slavery studies* (pp. 156–176). New York: Cambridge University Press.

Schwartz, M. J. (2009). *Born in bondage: Growing up enslaved in the antebellum South*. Cambridge, MA: Harvard University Press.

Smith, J. (1608). A true relation. In P. Barbour (Ed.) (1986), *Complete works of captain John Smith* (Vol. I). Chapel Hill: University of North Carolina Press.

Smith, V., & Horton, G. M. (1798). *A narrative of the life and adventures of venture: A native of Africa, but resident above sixty years in the United States of America, related by himself. With poems by a Slave*. Lulu.com

Stracqualursi, V., Snads, G., Elkin, E. L., & Rocha, V. (2019, August 23). *What is the Flores settlement that the Trump administration has moved to end?* CNN.com. Available at: https://www.cnn.com/2019/08/21/politics/what-is-flores-settlement/index.html

The Annie E. Casey Foundation. (2019). *In-depth case studies of authentic youth engagement in Jim Casey youth opportunities initiative sites.* Baltimore, MD: Washington State University Vancouver.

Thornton, C., Robinson, W. I., Gibler, J., Tzul Tzul, G., & Paley, D. (2016). Violence, displacement, and death. *NACLA Report on the Americas, 48*(2), 130–143.

Todres, J., & Fink, D. V. (2020). The trauma of Trump's family separation and child detention actions: A children's rights perspective. *Washington Law Review, 95*(1), 377.

United States Government Accountability Office. (2018). *Unaccompanied children: Agency efforts to reunify children separated from parents at the border 14–15.* GAO-19-163. Accessed at: https://www.gao.gov/assets/700/694918.pdf; https://perma.cc/YX38-9Q6V

Wagner, C. (2010). The good left undone: How to stop sex offender laws from causing unnecessary harm at the expense of effectiveness. *American Journal of Criminal Law, 38*, 263.

WhiteHouse.gov. Issued February 1, 2019. Accessed at: https://www.whitehouse.gov/briefings-statements/president-donald-j-trump-fighting-prevent-human-trafficking-southern-border/

Williams, P. (2008). Trafficking in women: The role of transnational organized crime. In S. Cameron & E. Newman (Eds.), *Trafficking in humans.* New York: United Nations University Press.

Wood, L. (2018). Impact of punitive immigration policies, parent-child separation and child detention on the mental health and development of children. *BMJ Paediatr Open, 2*(1), e000338.

Woodhouse, B. B. (2010). *Hidden in plain sight: The tragedy of children's rights from ben Franklin to Lionel Tate.* Princeton: Princeton University Press.

Woolford, A. (2015). *This benevolent experiment: Indigenous boarding schools, genocide, and redress in Canada and the United States.* Lincoln: University of Nebraska Press.

Chapter 13
The Complexities of Complex Trauma: An Historical and Contemporary Review of Healing in the Aftermath of Commercialized Violence

Kate Keisel

13.1 Introduction: Contextualizing Human Trafficking through a Complex Trauma Framework

Trauma is often thought of as a highly disturbing event(s) that happened in the past. Trauma, however, includes the legacy or imprint of these adverse life events that cause distress and fear that manifest in emotions, thoughts, and even physical sensations in the present (van der Kolk 2014). Trauma can be characterized by the sense of loss in the aftermath of an event(s) that leaves an individual feeling that they have fundamentally been changed by the experience. This loss can be as tangible as a bodily wound from physical abuse that leaves the body forever changed. The loss also includes more abstract applications such as the way in which one newly relates to and perceives the world around them (Herman 1992a). Throughout the life course, most individuals experience at least one event that could be considered traumatic (Ozer et al. 2003). These events activate a neurobiological survival response that triggers an automatic flight, fight, or freeze reaction in an attempt to keep an individual safe. In the aftermath of the event, these same responses can be triggered by experiences or sensory stimuli that remind an individual of the initial trauma. These are often known as flashbacks. These can elicit the same survival responses in the present moment that occurred at the time of the initial traumatic event (Levine 2010). Later in the chapter, a more thorough outline of trauma responses will be explored.

While a nearly universal human experience, the impact of trauma and the responses that develop after adverse life events is uniquely individual; it varies in severity, frequency, and intensity for each person. How one responds in the wake of traumatic events, including commercialized violence, is influenced by a variety of

K. Keisel (✉)
Sanar Institute, Newark, NJ, USA
e-mail: kate@sanar-institute.org

© Springer Nature Switzerland AG 2021
M. Chisolm-Straker, K. Chon (eds.), *The Historical Roots of Human Trafficking*,
https://doi.org/10.1007/978-3-030-70675-3_13

individual, environmental, and intergenerational factors (Courtois 2004; Rinker and Lawler 2018). These factors can include a history of the following:

- *Complex Trauma*: The experience of more than one traumatic event in one's life course is called complex trauma (Cook et al. 2005). Complex trauma frequently begins in early childhood which can subsequently impact key development of protective factors that leave individuals vulnerable to ongoing and escalating abuse, such as commercialized violence (Kisiel et al. 2014). Individuals that have experienced complex trauma commonly face increased trauma responses due to the frequency with which the neurobiological survival responses are triggered.
- Commercialized violence in both modern and historical contexts is often characterized by a traumatic event or, more commonly, a series of traumatic events that occur over time. Complex trauma can occur within a singular trafficking situation. For example, coercive tactics that threaten the life or well-being of an individual over a period of hours, days, months, or years can be labeled as complex trauma. Many individuals that have exited trafficking situations have reported complex trauma histories of violence and abuse prior to the exploitation (Thompson and Haley 2018). A number of studies have highlighted the prevalence of traumatic events prior to trafficking situations (Chappel and Crawford 2019; Hossain et al. 2010; Ottisova et al. 2012; Sprang and Cole 2018; Zimmerman et al. 2008).
- *Poly-Victimization*: The phenomenon of experiencing more than one kind of violence during one's life course is referred to as poly-victimization (Courtois 2004). Individuals that have experienced commercialized violence have often survived other types of traumatic events prior to trafficking. Often, this abuse has taken place across the life course, for example, an individual might experience physical abuse as a child and labor trafficking in early adulthood. Individuals that have experienced trafficking often report varied and escalating forms of violence and oppression throughout their life (Kisiel et al. 2014). Marginalized groups are disproportionately impacted by poly-victimization such as sexual and physical violence that frequently precedes commercialized violence (De Vries and Farrell 2018). A number of studies have also found that children and youth involved in child protective services (CPS) have experienced complex trauma and polyvictimization (Chap. 11) (Greeson et al. 2011; Griffin et al. 2011; Jonson-Reid et al. 2004; Kisiel et al. 2009, Kisiel et al. 2014; Oswald et al. 2013). Many of these same CPS-involved young people are then exploited through trafficking situations (O'Brien et al. 2017; Wolfe et al. 2018).
- *Intergenerational Trauma Transmission and Multigenerational Trauma Histories*: The long-term impact of oppression and marginalization that is intrinsically tied to trafficking frequently results in multigenerational patterns of traumatic events and intergenerational transmission of trauma (Chap. 11); this occurs when families and communities have been continually victimized by violence and exploitation across generations (Straussner and Calnan 2014). Violence and

exploitation are subsequently normalized by society, allowed to continue with minimal consequences, and are often internally and externally perpetrated (Zeynel and Uzer 2019). For example, the institution of slavery in the USA can be clearly traced to historically racially focused violence. Contemporary institutions maintain this through the ongoing oppression of Black communities.

- A trauma legacy that has an intergenerational transmission becomes part of the fabric of the collective identity of oppressed communities. The ongoing exposure to individual and collective violence, scarcity of resources, and ongoing systemic oppression that implicitly, and at times explicitly, designates communities as disposable (Chap. 14) contributes to trauma transmission between generations (Rinker and Lawler 2018). Native communities in the USA have similarly experienced ongoing traumatic events perpetrated through colonization, boarding schools designed to eliminate culture and identity (Chap. 16), and ongoing oppression and marginalization (Evans-Campbell 2008; Whitbeck et al. 2004). Historic violence against LGBTQ+[1] communities has also created well-documented vulnerabilities at the individual and community level.

- In addition to the intergenerational transmission of trauma within communities, there is also the repeated experience of certain kinds of violence within a family unit across the generations. For example, intimate partner violence might be experienced or witnessed by an individual in childhood. The normalization of this violence exposure, and the neurobiological survival response, can result in survivors of violence later surviving or perpetrating similar actions (Flemke et al. 2014). This may also include one's children experiencing violence at the hands of others. For example, there are a number of studies that have highlighted a linkage in the increased vulnerability to sexual or physical abuse of a child when a parent or caregiver has a history of sexual abuse (Baker 2001; Kim et al. 2010; Leifer et al. 2004; Noll et al. 2008). Both intergenerational and multigenerational trauma histories increase vulnerability to human trafficking as well as many other forms of interpersonal violence (Zeynel and Uzer 2019). Understanding the impact of intergenerational and multigenerational trauma is a critical aspect in addressing and healing complex trauma.

Neurobiological Implications of Traumatic Events
Complex traumatic events have significant impacts on the way in which the human brain and body functions during the event(s) and after the brain is hardwired for survival. When its emergency system detects a perceived threat, it is thrust into a reactionary mode that is commonly called the "human stress response." This response prepares the body to: (1) go to battle with the perceived threat (fight); (2) flee from the immediate danger (flight); or (3) remain painstakingly still until the threat passes (freeze) (Levine 2010). During a stress response, how the brain functions, including how memory is encoded, is temporarily changed to increase chances of survival. The more frequently an individual is faced with traumatic events (or

---

[1] Lesbian, gay, bisexual, transgender, queer/questioning, and other nonheterosexual, non-cis identities and experiences.

perceived traumatic events), the faster the human stress response is triggered. Individuals that have experienced complex trauma are more quickly activated into the survival mode with increased frequency and intensity of trauma responses (Kisiel et al. 2017).

Trauma Responses

After an individual experiences a traumatic event(s), the way one thinks, feels, behaves, and even experiences reflexive physical symptoms is known as trauma responses. Commonly, more intense and ongoing traumatic events result in heightened trauma responses (Helsel 2015). Individuals that have experienced complex trauma have a diverse range of responses that may occur in the days, months, and years after the traumatic event. How one perceives trauma, and the consequent responses, is a completely individual experience; that is to say, there is not a required or a singular set of responses. No two individuals will experience trauma in the same manner. This is true even in cases where multiple people were exploited by the same trafficker(s).

Thoroughly exploring the diverse spectrum of neurobiological trauma responses forms the groundwork to understanding how traumatic events impact individuals and communities. Furthermore, it is vital to contextualize the ways in which trauma responses have both helped individuals and communities to cope and/or have continued to create harm in the wake of poly-victimization, multigenerational trauma legacies, and complex trauma histories. Individuals and communities often experience many different trauma-related responses, not just one, and these responses may change over time. Common trauma responses may include:

Dissociation is when the individual feels disconnected from the present moment, as if a person is not really in their body. It is often thought of as "spacing out" or "losing track of time" (Ross et al. 2004). Many people experience dissociation, but trauma can often intensify this in such a way that an individual feels totally disconnected from what is happening around them in the present moment. It is important to note that when an individual is in a traumatic situation, dissociation can be an important coping mechanism that allows that person to survive the atrocities of commercialized violence. This trauma response, however, can continue to be activated once an individual has exited a situation of exploitation but is exposed to a trigger or sensory-based reminder of a traumatic event. This can result in an individual feeling lost in a perpetual or temporary state of disconnection (Jepsen et al. 2013). For example, once an individual has exited a situation of commercial sexual exploitation, a smell that reminds them of the trafficking situation can trigger a disconnection in the present moment.

Trauma Bonding, formally known as "Stockholm Syndrome," is the developed bond or sense of connection and resulted loyalty to an abuser or exploiter. This is a coping mechanism that individuals may develop to survive the violence they experience during trafficking. Trauma bonds are part of a neurobiological response to keep an individual safe in a situation of danger. Trauma bonds are formed when abuse and perceived kindness are alternated by a perpetrator. For example, a trafficker might physically abuse someone but then send money back to their family. This alternating between acts of abuse and perceived kindness creates an environment of fear with competing feelings of affection or positive regard in the exploited person. This is a tactic that many traffickers use to control the people they victimize. This can lead to an individual having hope that things can get better or believe that the perpetrator does in fact care about or love them (Graham 1994). It is important to note that these bonds may have kept a person alive in a life-threatening situation. However, due to these bonds, the individual, as well as untrained stakeholders including behavioral health systems, law enforcement, and service providers, may have a hard time understanding the victimization that occurred (Chap. 5). In circumstances where individuals do not build traumatic bonds, exploitation is often clearer and more visible to the person because only fear is used as the mechanism of control used by perpetrators (Hossain et al. 2010).

Somatization is the physical symptom within the body such as muscle aches, nausea, rashes, or exacerbations of medical diagnoses that are a manifestation of the psychological and emotional distress of trauma survived (Tagay et al. 2010). Individuals with somatic symptoms often do not realize the connection between their physical and emotional symptoms. An individual might have physical symptoms that a clinician cannot explain using laboratory testing or imaging. For example, an individual exiting a trafficking situation might be experiencing chronic stomach pain. Despite seeking ongoing medical treatment, the pain might persist. Somatic complaints are frequently the first thing to be addressed in the aftermath of trauma because they do not carry the same stigma as accessing mental health care (Engel 2004).

Reenactment is the recreation of the traumatic event (or parts of the event) in the present life of an individual. This is the brain's way of trying to understand why an event or experience might have happened and/or regain a sense of control in a situation in which a person felt powerless (Trippany et al. 2006). Reenactments may also address the body's somatic experience by attempting to complete the trauma response that did not occur during the original trauma. For example, an individual that has experienced continued sexual abuse and commercial sexual exploitation might continue hypersexualized behavior after exiting a situation of exploitation. Moreover, an individual who experienced physical abuse during commercialized violence might also use physical violence in the future as a reenacted behavior of exploitation.

Self-blame and Internalization of Abuse are when individuals that have experienced complex trauma frequently find reasons to hold themselves responsible for the event or some part of the violence as this allows for an artificial sense of control (Johnson 2012). Often traffickers will rationalize the perpetration of abuse and state that the individual is to blame. For example, a trafficker may harm the child of an individual in a domestic servitude trafficking situation as punishment for speaking to a neighbor while outside. The goal for the trafficker is to assert control and isolate the individual through ongoing psychological manipulation. This is done in a way to make the individual believe that it is their mistakes that led to the abuse, when in reality this was a calculated plan and tactic by the trafficker to maintain control. This phenomenon of "gaslighting" is when a perpetrator intentionally makes someone question reality and can lead to deep feelings of confusion and self-blame. In this example, the internalization of harm to the child can lead to feelings of self-blame and shame that impact an individual's self-concept and self-esteem.

In addition, survivors of commercialized violence are frequently asked by law enforcement, service providers, and even family members why they did not leave the situation earlier. The complexities of trauma bonds, neurobiological responses, and layers of barriers might be difficult for an individual to articulate or even understand. This can lead to ongoing feelings of self-blame, responsibility, and even a sense of self-hatred (Chap. 17). These thoughts and beliefs often leave individuals vulnerable to revictimization, and they may utilize substances to cope with their trauma or to numb these difficult emotions (Johnson 2012).

Numbing is when emotions become detached from thoughts, memories, and behaviors that can result in feeling a limited range of emotions (van der Kolk and Saporta 1991). The numbing response can hide what an individual is feeling because the overwhelming emotions are not yet something that are (often subconsciously) perceived to be safe to express. This can often result in behavioral health systems and other stakeholders believing that the impact of the traumatic event is less severe for an individual as they are not actively displaying symptoms typically associated with trauma. Numbing can manifest as shock, denial, or disbelief; feeling disconnected from others; and substance misuse. For example, an individual might use alcohol or other drugs to find some reprieve from the overwhelming emotional, physical, and cognitive responses they are experiencing in the aftermath of traumatic events. The use of drugs can act as a strong coping mechanism and often increases in the wake of trauma triggers (Garland et al. 2013).

Hyperarousal is the increased set of physical responses that make it difficult for individuals to feel calm and safe in their body and within their thoughts and feelings. Hyperarousal can often cause individuals to feel like they are in a state of constant activation with an ongoing "fight" or "flight" response. Individuals might appear to be "very speedy" in all of their interactions. Hyperarousal can manifest in the form of insomnia or nightmares; being easily startled; having a racing heartbeat; sweating; feeling "on edge," difficulty sitting still, moving quickly; speaking rapidly; the trembling of hands; and/or having disorganized thoughts (Corrigan et al. 2011). For example, an individual experiencing hyperarousal might feel their heart beating very quickly when they are asked to recount the details of a traumatic situation. This might be accompanied by a nonlinear account of events in a rapid speech pattern that is difficult to follow or understand.

Hypoarousal is the decreased set of physical responses in which individuals report or appear to be totally shut down with respect to their body, thoughts, and feelings (Helsel 2015). Hypoarousal can often look like and feel like an individual is stuck in the "freeze" response of trauma. Hypoarousal can manifest in the form of long durations of sleep; decreased speech; self-isolation; dissociation; difficulty remembering details; inability to pay attention in the present moment; and/

or excessive quietness. Individuals may also have a difficult time recognizing or being aware of any sensations in their body (Corrigan et al. 2011). For example, a person might be on a train home after a meeting where they were asked to recount their trauma history. Slowly, they become unaware of what is happening around them; they do not even notice that they have passed the stop where they need to exit the train. When asked a question by a fellow passenger, they respond with confusion and slowness because they did not process the information asked in the question.

Trauma responses are often adaptive reactions to initial traumatic events (Greenbaum 2017). These trauma responses may be the very methods that mitigated harm to the individual in their trafficking situation and may even be the reason they survived prior incidents of abuse. In the aftermath of trauma, these responses may no longer serve their original purpose and may now be harmful to the individual (Flemke et al. 2014). These responses, however, need to be replaced with coping mechanisms that now serve that individual. Mechanism replacement can only take place once the individual is in a safe situation and should not be viewed as simply removing a previous coping mechanism. In absence of trauma-specific care, individuals are left without a road map to make connections between current and prior violence, understand and normalize the neurobiological impacts, and recognize and manage the ongoing trauma responses. The trauma of their past becomes the terror of their present. The feelings and trauma responses frequently continue to amplify throughout the life course and are used as a tool of reexploitation by traffickers and other perpetrators.

Trafficking methods: exploiting and perpetuating traumatic events in trafficking and exploitation as a means of control.

Perpetration of Overt Violence in Trafficking Situations

The perpetration of intentional and strategic violent acts with the goal of traumatization is a frequently used tactic to gain and maintain control over individuals in trafficking situations. The use of violence and the subsequent outcomes of asserting dominance are often a central tenet of exploitation. Physical, sexual, and/or psychological violence are used to traumatize individuals in order to ensure they adhere to the rules set by perpetrators (Hossain et al. 2010). These rules are often intentionally arbitrary in nature and lack of adherence results in consequences that further perpetuate traumatic events. In addition, abuse can be perpetrated in a completely randomized manner that is designed to continuously keep an individual in a state of uncertainty and fear.

Traumatic events are not just those that would be considered extraordinary but instead are the result of "a thousand tiny cuts" designed to immobilize individuals' cognitive perception of freedom. These violent acts are calculated to systematically breakdown the psyches of individuals in trafficking situations and, at times, create a bond with the trafficker (Straussner and Calnan 2014). Those bonds can support feelings of well-being, financial compensation, or other perceived acts of kindness when the individual is in good standing with the trafficker; when the individual is not following the rules set out by the trafficker, explicit physical, psychological, and/or sexual violence is perpetrated (Greenbaum 2017). For example, a trafficker exploiting individuals in the commercial sex industry often sets a minimum monetary amount (quota) that must be earned through commercial sex acts by someone they are victimizing. If the individual does not meet the quota, the trafficker may then use violence as a punishment to create fear of not "following the rules." Moreover, a trafficker exploiting foreign national individuals will frequently use psychological abuse, including threats of reporting individuals to immigration officials for deportation. For example, a foreign national exploited through domestic servitude might experience physical violence when they have not completed cleaning tasks as desired in a home. This may be followed by threats by the trafficker of calling immigration officials if the individual attempts to contact law enforcement to report the abuse.

Use of Psychological and Emotional Manipulation
While physical, sexual, and psychological violence are regularly present in trafficking situations, countless other forms of traumatic events can occur to allow the trafficker to exercise control. These are often mechanisms of instilling fear that are difficult for individuals exiting trafficking situations to identify and thus recount (Mehlman-Orozco 2017). For example, a trafficker may tell an individual that if they are to speak with an attorney or a law enforcement official they will be arrested because they have broken the law; traffickers often cite examples of illicit activities the survivor has been coerced to participate in or make up illegal activities that they threaten to report, such as stealing from the trafficker. Traffickers use this form of psychological manipulation to maintain control over individuals.

Psychological manipulation and abuse are often a daily occurrence in trafficking situations that can completely transform an individual's perception of reality in a way that benefits the trafficker. Moreover, a trafficker might tell an individual, who is being exploited in the commercial sex industry, that they are building a better life with their trafficker and making more money than they ever could in any other situation. They may now be exposed to more material wealth, with access to clothing and other items that are purchased by the trafficker. However, the individual is required to give the trafficker all of (or much of) the money from commercial sex acts. Thus, the manipulation creates an illusion that life has improved and that the individual has choice. In reality, it is the trafficker who controls the money, access, and choices. While the psychological manipulation may be less visible than the cases of overt physical, sexual, or psychological abuse, they are often more powerful in maintaining control and altering the perception of reality for individuals in trafficking situations.

Moreover, for some individuals, the abuse perpetrated by the trafficker is less severe than violence experienced in previous situations. The trafficker strategically uses that history of abuse to maintain control. This can make it more difficult to identify the abuse perpetrated by the trafficker both for the individual and for stakeholders such as law enforcement or behavioral health systems. It is important to note that many individuals report that the trafficking situation is not the most traumatic experience they have faced over their life course.

Exploitation of Prior Violence

Traffickers capitalize on prior trauma experiences and traumatic responses of individuals and communities that have historically been oppressed and marginalized (Chap. 14) (Thompson and Haley 2018; Reid 2014). These groups may be without the means, opportunities, or resources to process past trauma and its consequences. This takes place at the individual, familial, and community level within systems of exploitation. Traumatic memories, experiences, and trauma-related responses are used by traffickers during recruitment as a means to assert ongoing power and control while simultaneously creating a scenario in which individuals in trafficking situations do not have meaningful paths to exit (Judge et al. 2018). Here, traffickers do not actively create, but instead can profit from the historical legacy of institutionalized trauma. Research has shown that both male and female "pimps" in the USA actively look to exploit young people with a history of abuse and turbulent home environments (Raphael and Myers-Powell 2010; Roe-Sepowitz et al. 2014). A study conducted by DePaul University, through a series of interviews with ex-"pimps," sheds light on this method of exploitation. One ex-"pimp" stated he looked for "neighborhood girls who were not doing well and had low self-esteem"; several others interviewed expressed similar tactics (Raphael and Myers-Powell 2009, p. 4). It is important to note that many of these same individuals that perpetrated trafficking and exploitation reported a history of unaddressed complex trauma, poly-victimization, and multigenerational trauma, which will be addressed later in the chapter (Raphael and Myers-Powell, 2010).

The diversity of trafficking situations makes it challenging to capture the impact of complex trauma in a fully reflective state, but complex trauma includes aspects illuminated in the following case:

Case Study[2]

Daniella and her parent's community of origin in Central America have experienced a legacy of collective trauma and systemic oppression. The roots of the historically traumatic events included a civil war and active institutions of slavery and racism against Indigenous communities. These events are a part of how her community conceptualized the world around them. They experienced lack of opportunities and severe consequences for speaking out against authority figures. The acts of terror that were carried out by the government and organized criminal groups resulted in familial practices designed to keep individuals safe in the context of collective trauma.

Daniella's parents were raised in a marginalized community where close family members and friends experienced violence at the hands of the government and individuals involved with organized criminal activities. Daniella's father was murdered after he was perceived as having reported a crime to law enforcement. His death left the family in fear and economic despair. Daniella's mother felt no choice but to find work in the USA and send money back to her children. Leaving Daniella and her siblings with their paternal grandmother, her mother told the family she was

---

[2] Names and details in the case study have been changed to protect privacy.

working in a factory. Daniella's grandmother was mourning the death of her son and the countless other losses experienced throughout her life course and through intergenerational trauma.

Daniella experienced physical abuse when she questioned her grandmother's authority. Consequently, from a young age Daniella became afraid to ask questions and found herself increasingly withdrawn. Migration for work was normalized by her mother which was positively perceived as a path out of an impossible situation. Thus, Daniella was optimistic when she was approached by a recruiter to work in the USA in the agricultural industry. The quiet 16 year old was a prime target for the recruiter. When she arrived to work on the farm, Daniella was fearful of asking any questions regarding rights to compensation or a contract. She complied with any of the employer's demands. The farm leadership, often referred to as "the grower," enforced countless requirements upon the workers and dictated every detail of their lives. Men with guns would often patrol the perimeter and Daniella frequently heard sounds of sexual violence in the work camp at night. Daniella found herself frozen with fear as the trauma response of hypoarousal from her past was triggered by the events taking place around her. Daniella was told that she owed a debt to the initial recruiter who brought her to the farm which would be automatically deducted from her wages. She was too afraid to ask when she would be compensated in full for her work. Several years passed with minimal payment. Her fear increased as she witnessed other workers requesting compensation and experiencing violence as a result. She would frequently find herself dissociating which allowed her to feel numb to the overwhelming memories of abuse from her childhood, the turmoil of growing up in a community filled with violence, and the hopelessness of her current situation.

13.2   Discussion: Historical and Contemporary Responses to Human Trafficking and Complex Trauma in Behavioral Health Systems

In contemporary times, behavioral health systems have looked to "treat" trauma and its health consequences using a primarily medical model. Although studies have recognized promising paths toward healing for individuals impacted by human trafficking, the structures of behavioral health systems have not adequately met the wide-ranging needs that result from intergenerational trauma legacies and individual experiences of complex trauma (Snowden 2003). An exploration of the development of today's behavioral health systems can provide greater context in understanding historical and contemporary limitations (and at some points harm) of addressing the mental and behavioral health needs of individuals experiencing commercialized violence.

Contextualizing engagement with individuals that have experienced commercialized violence within behavioral health systems requires an exploration of the origins of diagnostic criteria and the medical diagnostic model. These models have focused on the identification and alleviation of symptoms perceived as suffering. Where they fall short is in striving to identify pathways to reliance, post-traumatic growth, and studies of how individuals can live full, meaningful, and self-actualized lives (Joseph 2011). Examining the impact, evolution, and approaches to classifying and resolving trauma responses can provide important insight into the ways in which historical systems have caused further harm to individuals that have experienced human trafficking and distrust within many marginalized communities. With this foundation, the chapter explores the advancements in evidence-based models that support post-traumatic growth, resilience, and the promising paths forward for contemporary engagement with individuals that have experienced complex trauma, including human trafficking.

Historical Conceptualizations of the Impact and Aftermath of Traumatic Events

Behavioral health institutions in the USA have been predominantly guided by diagnostic criteria outlined in the American Psychiatric Association's Diagnostic and Statistical Manual (DSM) since its first publication in 1952 (American Psychiatric Association 1952). International diagnostic criteria included through the International Statistical Classification of Disease and Health-Related Problems (ICD) first introduced the inclusion of mental health-related disorders in the sixth edition. Endorsed in 1948, the ICD had some influence on the DSM development criteria (World Health Organization 2012). Prior to this time, an understanding of trauma-related responses and the impact of traumatic events was virtually nonexistent (Ozer et al. 2003). Behavioral health systems of the past were focused on placing individuals in institutional settings that often were themselves sources of further trauma (Gallop et al. 1999). Individuals with access to resources were treated privately, thus continuing the long history of exclusionary practices that disregard marginalized communities' right to access meaningful care (Alegría et al. 2016). As in other systems and services of care, marginalized groups have access to one kind of behavioral health care while those with wealth receive fundamentally different, and almost always better, treatment (Chap. 14). This history created valid fear for oppressed communities in accessing care due to the abuses that have occurred in behavioral health institutions. This is the architecture that has contributed to the present-day barriers for marginalized communities in engaging with these systems.

The abuses that took place in the USA behavioral health institutions and asylums are well documented in the nineteenth and twentieth centuries (Grob 1973; Grob 1991; Lamb and Weinberger 2005). Once individuals were committed to institutions and asylums, nearly all personal freedoms were dissolved. Widespread abuses such as physical and sexual abuse, torture, and unconsented experimental treatment occurred in these facilities (Nibert et al. 1989). Individuals that were committed to institutions and asylums were frequently from oppressed and marginalized groups including women, individuals with low socioeconomic status, LGBTQ+ groups, and communities of color (Hill and Laugharne 2003; Lynch 2019; Pouba and Tianen 2006). These are the same groups that are disproportionately impacted by commercialized violence and complex trauma histories. The legacy of systemic abuse surrounding behavioral health institutions has significantly contributed to historic and contemporary fear and stigma of present-day behavioral health care for individuals within communities impacted by commercialized violence, oppression, and marginalization (Snowden 2003; Wilkins et al. 2013).

Partially in response to documented abuses, the move to deinstitutionalize mental health treatment and shift to outpatient settings started in the 1950s (Yohannan 2013). Over the next few decades, mental asylums and institutions closed, often resulting in the release of individuals that had been housed in these settings for years (Community Mental Health Centers Construction Act 1963; Social Security Amendments 1965). Individuals exiting these facilities were virtually invisible to the privileged, White, heteronormative individuals in positions of power. Thus, as institutions shut down, the people within them were once again discarded. Individuals were released without any aftercare services in place, leaving already marginalized and vulnerable individuals from disenfranchised communities chronically homeless or frequently incarcerated (Lamb and Weinberger 2005).

Shortly before and during the movement to deinstitutionalized mental health treatment, and in the wake of World War II, the idea of trauma was becoming visible in behavioral health systems. Both the DSM and the ICD were heavily influenced by the US Veteran Association's effort to address the mental health presentations of combat veterans (Suris 2016). Post-traumatic Stress Disorder (PTSD), often mistakenly conflated with "trauma responses," was not introduced to the DSM until its 1980 third edition (American Psychiatric Association 1980). This edition was a further attempt to characterize and validate the experiences of veterans after the Vietnam War. The diagnostic criteria were heavily associated with war-related traumatic events that impacted cisgender,[3] predominantly White, males faced with traumatic exposure to violence in combat. This gave way to a narrow understanding of trauma impact that was predominately based on the experience of the most privileged demographic in society. As such, behavioral health systems' conceptualization of trauma has not been representative of the traumatic experiences resulting from historical and contemporary slavery, intergenerational transmission of trauma, and complex trauma related to interpersonal violence (Courtois 2004; Herman 1992a, b; Hollar 2001). As a result, much of the understanding of the impacts of traumatic events, diagnostic criteria, research, and treatment modalities have not adequately identified trauma responses, acknowledged the role of resilience and post-traumatic growth, or identified treatments that are applicable for individuals impacted by commercialized violence (Chap. 17) (Joseph 2011; Judge et al. 2018).

Standards for successful behavioral health outcomes for survivors of complex trauma have historically been defined as the absence of diagnostically significant criteria related to PTSD. This pathologically based criterion presumes that traumatic events cause mental health disorders and are something from which people

---

[3] Cisgender: An adjective used to describe a person whose gender identity and gender expression align with sex assumed/gender assigned at birth (American Psychological Association 2015).

need to "recover." This limited "recovery" narrative has dominated behavioral health systems and academic institutions (Bonanno 2004). There are distinct limitations of the pathologized framework which ignore the role of resilience and the importance of healing-based contexts that recognize and contextualized trauma responses as normal reactions to an abnormal or adverse event(s) (Bonanno et al. 2002).

Historical Engagement of Individuals and Communities Impacted by Commercialized Violence in Behavioral Health Institutions

It was not until the late 1980s and early 1990s that further research began to emerge on the unique features associated with complex trauma (Courtois 2004). During this period, human trafficking was not yet characterized as a crime nor studied as a field in the USA or internationally. With the introduction of the Palermo Protocol (United Nations 2000) and the Trafficking Victim's Protection Act of 2000 (H.R. 3244. 2000), human trafficking-specific dialog entered public discourse. Given the relatively recent emergence of studies that specifically address the impacts of trauma on individuals victimized through human trafficking, many previous behavioral health studies may have unknowingly already engaged individuals and communities impacted by commercialized violence.

Historical and Contemporary Responses to Commercialized Violence in Behavioral Health Systems

Early conceptualizations and representations of individuals who were victimized by human trafficking were particularly limited in scope and understanding (Ottisova et al. 2018). Sensationalized narratives that focused on young girls who were sold and purchased by older men dominated the public narrative. As a result, the magnitude and extent of trafficking and the understanding of those impacted and what trafficking entailed were limited. Historically, members of marginalized groups were not recognized as victimized, and thus, the requisite behavioral health engagement was not provided. These marginalized communities have included communities of color, individuals identifying on the LGBTQ+ spectrum, immigrant communities, communities living in poverty, and gender minorities.

Much of the research that has guided behavioral health interventions with individuals impacted by commercialized violence has focused on a narrow category of survivors: young adult, cisgender women that have experienced commercialized sexual violence from men (Thompson and Haley 2018). The impact of traumatic events in diverse labor industries has been largely unaddressed and understudied. Hence, the identified mental health disorders that have typically been associated with human trafficking are reflective of the specific subset of individuals impacted by a specific kind of exploitation which frequently excludes non-White racial and ethnic and non-cis experiences (Lynch 2019).

A handful of studies have identified PTSD, anxiety-related disorders, and depression as predominant mental health disorders associated with trafficking histories (Chappel and Crawford 2019). These disorders have often been treated in isolation as opposed to viewing anxiety and depressive features in the context of traumatic responses resulting from the neurobiological stress response to traumatic events.

Historically, Cognitive Behavioral Therapy (CBT) has been used in treatment, but this is a modality that does not address the fundamental underpinnings of trauma (Courtois 2004).

Limited Understanding Results in Poor System Responses

There has been a slow evolution in the public discourse about the true diversity and scope of human trafficking. Many of the outcomes of this limited understanding of what constitutes trafficking has resulted in a narrow perception of potentially traumatizing events, and challenges in the treatment of individuals with complex trauma experiences. Some of the most notably harmful outcomes have included the following:

Criminalizing Trauma Responses: Individuals and communities that have been left out of the mainstream conception of who is considered a human trafficking "victim" have frequently been criminalized for offenses committed as part of their trafficking and/or criminalized for their mental health conditions related to the trauma responses from commercialized violence (Lamb and Weinberger 2005). This includes criminalization of substance use and/or perceived distribution. As mentioned previously in the chapter, substance use is frequently used as a coping response to numb the intense thoughts, feelings, and physical sensations that can result from complex trauma histories and intergenerational trauma transmission. Additional behaviors associated with traumatic bonding, such as assisting a perpetrator in carrying out illicit activities, have been criminalized (Mehlman-Orozco 2017). Other examples include situations where victims of prior traumatic events perpetrate violence and/or trafficking, such as the experience of people that have been charged with "pimping" (Raphael and Myers-Powell). In addition, there has been a long history of criminalization of the trafficking acts themselves and the labor which individuals are forced into commercial sex, theft, and forced drug trafficking. This highlights the blurry line of who is characterized as a "victim" and who is seen as a "perpetrator" of trafficking. In addition, individuals that have assaulted or killed their traffickers in self-defense have frequently been charged with assault or murder, ignoring their history of trauma at the individual and community level.

Overdiagnosing and Misdiagnosing: Many individuals with a commercialized violence history have engaged with behavioral health systems in a limited manner. Those who are able to access care frequently do so only in the confines of meeting the diagnostic criteria that were previously discussed in the chapter. Frequently, individuals who are identified as "victims" (most with a marginalized life experience are not) received inappropriate and/or excessive diagnoses (if they are diagnosed at all). This has predominantly happened in two ways: (1) Individuals receive an inappropriate diagnosis from a mental health professional who lacks specialized training in complex trauma and commercialized violence or (2) individuals, particularly those who have been incarcerated, detained in immigration detention centers, and those who have been placed in child protective services frequently receive an array of predictable, pathologized, and inappropriate diagnoses (e.g., personality disorders). In the former, the incorrect diagnosis and subsequent treatment fail to address the underlying history of poly-victimization and intergenerational trauma (Kawaii-Bogue et al. 2017). This is particularly common with cismen and boys seeking treatment who are assumed to be perpetrators of commercialized violence; they are consequently given incorrect behavioral- or cognitive-based diagnoses, as opposed to identifying and healing past trauma (Kawaii-Bogue et al. 2017). In the case of misdiagnosis, individuals' criminalization and/or mental health profession-als' dismissive responses are seen as justified, as there is a presumed limit to the progress that stereotyped individuals can make with behavioral health interventions.

Contemporary Responses to Complex Trauma

In the 1990s, the advancement of brain imaging techniques and the burgeoning field of neuroscience provided significant advancements in contemporary under-standing of both the impact of and interventions used to treat complex trauma responses (Levine et al. 1999). This period of time and study yielded significant insights into how traumatic events are stored in the body. Research shows that inter-ventions need to address trauma in a holistic manner by recognizing both the bodily and cognitive impacts (van der Kolk 2014). New ways of understanding interper-sonal traumatic features highlighted the nonlinear process of healing after a trauma (Herman 1992a). These advancements acknowledged the neurobiological reper-cussions of trauma and how individuals heal; new knowledge created a novel path-way for contemporary behavioral health interventions, many of which have application for individuals and communities impacted by commercialized violence. This reframing from the "recovery-based" frameworks for traumatized individuals has been critical. Shifting from a strictly pathological approach, systems now con-textualized the impact of complex trauma in a broad scope of resilience, post-trau-matic growth, and healing (Denham 2008; Rothschild 2000).

Advances in Evidence-Based Trauma Interventions: Best Practices and Promising Research in Trauma Healing and Resiliency

Interventions that historically siloed behavioral health treatment based on diagnos-tic criteria, such as PTSD or anxiety, have now taken more inclusive approaches (Helsel 2015). A new narrative of trauma healing and the ability for both the body and mind to heal have paved the way for more meaningful approaches to addressing trauma histories (Levine et al. 1999). For example, Eye Movement Desensitization and Reprocessing (EMDR) has demonstrated promising responses. This includes the building of new neuronetworks that promote Adaptive Information Processing (AIP) which allows trauma survivors to process, contextualize, and heal from trau-matic events (Shapiro 2014; Shapiro and Laliotis 2011). This can lead to survivors moving past traumatic events *and* experiencing personal growth that exceeds the individual baseline functioning prior to the trauma (Chap. 17) (Moran et al. 2013). In addition, evidence-based modalities in trauma care now include the application of body-based processing through applications such as Somatic Experiencing (SE) (Levine et al. 1999). SE supports individuals, and those from communities, impacted by complex trauma in significantly decreasing trauma-related responses by using a body-based model to address somatic responses (Payne et al. 2015).

Moreover, trauma processing modalities such as Narrative Therapy, Dialectical Behavioral Therapy (DBT), and Trauma-Focused Cognitive Behavioral Therapy (TF-CBT) have yoked body and brain research to yield knowledge about ways to heal from complex trauma. Cutting-edge research shows that neuroplasticity facilitates significant repair and growth using such systems. Other promising techniques have been integrated into healing practices including Art and Music Therapy; Trauma-Sensitive Yoga; Mindfulness-Based Stress Reduction; and the integration of systems of traditional medicine and healers (Heilbron and Guttman 2000; Quinn 2007; van der Kolk 2014).

Furthermore, the study of post-traumatic growth has reframed the narrative: Not only is it possible for individuals to respond resiliently in the aftermath of trauma but humans in fact have positive psychological growth as a result of healing from traumatic events (Ulloa et al. 2016). Post-traumatic Growth discussion has moved away from a stigmatized lens, so frequently associated with PTSD. Instead, the discussion honors the unique wisdom and growth that that is born out of lived experience (Joseph 2011). The post-traumatic growth narrative has defined areas in which individuals with complex trauma histories can experience enhanced personal relationships and personal strength and fostered the ability to create meaning from traumatic events that enhances connectivity and life possibilities (Elderton et al. 2015).

Contemporary Behavioral Health Institutions Engaging with Individuals with Commercialized Violence Histories

In more recent years, human trafficking-specific studies, examining the impacts of trauma and the success of treatment modalities, have acknowledged the need for more inclusive research (Hossain et al. 2010). Slowly, human trafficking is being seen as a kind of violence experienced by individuals who have been impacted by complex trauma. Additionally, mental health professionals—particularly professionals in human trafficking-specific mental health treatment programs—are becoming more familiar with the nuances of commercialized violence (Thompson and Haley 2018). Evidence-based approaches to support individuals and communities who have experienced commercialized violence are also increasing within public and nonprofit behavioral health systems.

Limitations of Contemporary Behavioral Health Interventions

While significant improvements have been made in contemporary approaches to address complex trauma, there are still substantive access barriers at the individual and community level. Legacies of asylum-based facilities and institutional abuses are still memorialized in the collective memory of many communities. In addition, mental health treatment is still tied in some circumstances to the criminal justice system (Wilkins et al. 2013). Furthermore, complex trauma is still predominantly perceived as an *effect* of commercialized violence and not understood as a root *vulnerability* to both experiencing and perpetrating trafficking (Domoney et al. 2015).

- *Access Points: Public vs. Private Behavioral Health Care*: While evidence-based treatment modalities have been identified for complex trauma histories, these services remain difficult to access. The evidence-based trauma therapy modalities, such as EMDR and SE, require specialized postgraduate training for mental health professionals. Often, mental health practitioners' professional trajectories involve working in the public sphere while starting out in lower-paying positions that do not require certification in specialized, evidence-based modalities. Often, individuals working in the public sphere also have limited cultural competency, do not reflect the individuals and populations they are serving, and are predominantly English language speakers. These jobs are often at nonprofit or government institutions that interface with marginalized and oppressed populations that do not have the financial resources to pay for specialized mental health care. After practitioners complete further training and postgraduate certificates in complex trauma-specific treatment modalities, many exit the public sector and launch or join a more lucrative private practice. Private behavioral health care is typically reserved for the wealthy, situated in locations that are difficult to access via public transportation, and practitioners often participate in very limited, if any, insurance networks. Thus, the inability to heal from traumatic events is not because of the damage it has caused to the individual. Rather, the struggle to heal is due to lack of access to appropriate care. Despite advances in knowledge, healing from complex trauma largely remains available to the privileged and is frequently impossible for marginalized and oppressed communities (Kawaii-Bogue et al. 2017).
- *Mandated Mental Health Treatment*: Federal laws pertaining to human trafficking afford general protections for individuals impacted by commercialized violence. But early state legislative frameworks on human trafficking were incorporated into local vice statutes which interpreted crimes involving commercial sex as, at best, a "victimless crime" (Chap. 5). At worst, these state statutes did not differentiate between the role of individuals forced or coerced into commercial sexual activity, and controllers or purchasers of such activities. That is to say, survivors of trafficking were criminalized for their involvement in the commercial sex industry. Subsequently, "Safe Harbor" laws were put into place in some states to theoretically ensure that minors arrested for commercial sex would not be charged as criminals and would be connected to resources. Still, the reality of Safe Harbor laws is more complex and marginally successful (Connor 2016) but is beyond the scope of this chapter. As states began to pass "Safe Harbor" laws to provide victim assistance protections for survivors of trafficking, state statutes also began establishing other criminal justice solutions to address commercial sexual violence in the USA.

  For example, some local innovations included the creation of human trafficking courts. Such courts began in New York City and were designed to provide an alternative to incarceration for individuals that were arrested for prostitution-related charges. These courts frequently mandate individuals in the commercial sex industry to a defined number of counseling sessions. These sessions are required to avoid criminal charges; such mandates void personal agency and often do not take into account the impact on work schedules or child care needs.

In addition, child protection services and family courts will frequently mandate parents and children to mental health treatment as part of the process to regain parental rights. The linkages of behavioral health and criminal justice systems have led to further distrust in mental health services. In addition, as mentioned in the prior section, community-based mental health practitioners often lack specialized training in trauma-specific modalities that would ultimately benefit individuals mandated to participate in sessions.

Unfortunately, many individuals mandated to this "care" report further fragmentation, hardship, and disempowerment as a result of court-mandated mental health linkages. Operationalized in these ways, mandated behavioral health sessions can become sources of trauma, rather than spaces for healing. Some activists have recommended that behavioral healthcare professionals should identify and intervene with individuals impacted by commercialized violence in the commercialized sex industry before arrests are made, reducing the trauma associated with arrests and mandated interventions (Russell 2019).

- *Inclusive Healing Led by Individuals with Lived Experience*: Frequently, it is the very individuals and communities directly impacted by commercialized violence who are excluded from the identification of solutions. Individuals with lived experiences including those who have experienced commercialized violence are critical architects in the pathways of healing. It is through a collaborative, meaningful, and non-tokenized effort that behavioral health systems can repair the damage done of the past, (re)build trust, and ensure inclusive, person-centered care that addresses complex trauma, poly-victimization, and intergenerational trauma transmission. Presently, this inclusion of lived experiences has at best been ornamental and, at worst, exploitive, sensationalized, and traumatizing.

- *Addressing Individual and Collective Trauma Histories as a Human Trafficking Prevention Effort*: Behavioral health approaches have yet to be earnestly viewed as a critical component in trafficking prevention efforts; rather, they are seen as components of aftercare. It is important to note that many perpetrators of violence, including trafficking, have a history of complex trauma themselves. Thus, anti-trafficking leaders cannot oversimplify the complexities of trafficking situations as simply "victim-and-perpetrator." This false paradigm must be challenged to properly understand commercialized violence and other forms of violence, using the context of intergenerational transmission of trauma when relevant. In addition, addressing unresolved early childhood trauma is critical in mitigating the vulnerabilities of individuals frequently recruited into trafficking situations. While violence prevention methods are paramount, anti-trafficking leaders cannot fail to account for the individuals and communities that have already been chronically victimized. Until trauma-specific services are no longer characterized as ancillary services but are understood to be a fundamental part of prevention, the revolving door of violence for disenfranchised communities of color and low socioeconomic status will continue.

13.3   Conclusion

The legacy of trauma histories for individuals and communities impacted by commercialized violence is layered with complexity. Behavioral health systems are in a unique position to actively repair the fractures of practices that have frequently harmed individuals and communities while simultaneously creating a dedicated space to elevate resilience and provide paths to healing. Such paths would require honest conversations about the deep wounds created through Indigenous and Black slavery, and the oppression of many groups impacted by commercialized violence not only in the arena of behavioral health but as a society at large. To do so in a meaningful way requires leadership and representation by the communities and individuals directly impacted by human trafficking to create a new definition of what "success" entails in trauma healing (Chap. 17). It also requires accountability for systems, institutions, and individuals that have maintained and benefited from oppressive conditions that lead to exploitation. Such a foundation fully recognizes and supports the human capacity to resiliently respond in the aftermath of trauma.

Recommendations

1. *Increase access to evidence-based mental health services.*
   Access to trauma-specific, evidence-based mental health services should not be reserved for those with access to resources; it should not predominantly exclude marginalized and oppressed communities. There is a fundamental need to increase the quality, quantity, and access to evidence-based mental health services that specifically address complex trauma for communities disproportionately and historically impacted by commercialized violence. Furthermore, access is not simply about the available resources, location, and prevalence but also the *trust* required for an individual to engage with behavioral health systems (Chaps. 14 and 15). Collaborative, community-based approaches to mental health that reduce stigma in accessing services and use of a person-centered and culturally relevant lens of care are necessary to create meaningful paths of healing. Such approaches acknowledge the strength and resilience of and honors individuals living with traumatic histories. Critical to this are mental health service options that are led by the communities that are impacted by human trafficking. A focus on culturally relevant and reflective services led by individuals within the communities that foster positive racial, gender, ethnic identities, and/or identities around sexuality is key to increasing access and competencies.
2. *Integrate complex trauma solutions into the broader anti-trafficking movement.*
   Understanding and responding to the impact of complex trauma in a meaningful and prioritized manner, both within behavioral health systems and broader anti-trafficking efforts, are critical to reducing the occurrence of commercialized violence. Addressing complex trauma histories before commercialized violence reduces vulnerability to human trafficking; addressing it after commercialized violence reduces vulnerability to reexploitation and other forms of violence.

3. *Define "success" through diverse, lived experience and community-led initiatives.*
Building trusted and accessible behavioral health systems within an inclusive anti-trafficking movement must be led by diverse communities that have historically been impacted by slavery and that are presently effected by commercialized violence. To foster trust and ensure actions and policies are aligned with the needs and goals of the individuals and communities impacted by commercialized violence, there must be a fundamental pivot in how systemic goals and definitions of clinical success are developed, especially in systematically marginalized populations. Those with lived experiences must be the architects in the plans of justice set forth by the anti-trafficking field.

4. *Community leadership will properly center historically oppressed groups in the anti-trafficking movement.*
Community support and involvement is critical in the healing of survivors of trafficking (Judge et al. 2018). The current narrative that defines human trafficking in the USA has been monopolized by academic, government, and public institutions. These are often people who have had limited lived experience or minimal deep work with individuals and communities impacted by trafficking. The voices of these institutions must be balanced with and rooted in community leadership to properly calibrate the anti-trafficking movement's goals. Community-led anti-trafficking work must be grounded in dignity, healing, justice, and meaningful change of socioeconomic systems that, at present, keep communities disenfranchised.

References

Alegría, M., Alvarez, K., Ishikawa, R. Z., DiMarzio, K., & McPeck, S. (2016). Removing obstacles to eliminating racial and ethnic disparities in behavioral health care. *Health Affairs, 35*(6), 991–999. https://doi.org/10.1377/hlthaff.2016.0029.

American Psychiatric Association. (1952). Diagnostic and Statistical Manual of Mental Disorders, First Edition. Washington DC: American Psychiatric Association.

American Psychiatric Association. (1980). *Diagnostic and statistical manual of mental disorders* (3rd ed.). Washington, DC: American Psychiatric Association.

American Psychological Association. (2015). Guidelines for psychological practice with transgender and gender nonconforming people. *American Psychologist, 70*(9), 832–864. https://doi.org/10.1037/a0039906.

Baker, J. L. (2001). Multigenerational sexual abuse: A cognitive developmental approach to understanding mothers in treatment. *Journal of Adult Development, 28*(2), 51–59. https://doi.org/1 0.1080/10538712.2011.607753.

Bonanno, G. A. (2004). Loss, trauma, and human resilience: Have we underestimated the human capacity to thrive after extremely aversive events? *American Psychologist, 59*(1), 20–28. https://doi.org/10.1037/0003-066X.59.1.20.

Bonanno, A. G., B, W., Lehman, R. D., Tweed, G. R., Haring, M., & Sonnega, J. (2002). Resilience to loss and chronic grief: A prospective study from pre-loss to 18 months postloss. *Journal of Personality and Social Psychology, 83*(5), 1150–1164. https://doi.org/10.1037/0022-3514.83.5.1150.

Chappel, C., & Crawford, B. (2019). Mental health diagnoses of youth commercial sex exploitation victims: An analysis within an adjudicated delinquent sample. *Journal of Family Violence, 25*(1), 723–732. https://doi.org/10.1016/j.chc.2015.08.007.

Community Mental Health Act of 1963, Pub. L 106-386, 77 Stat. 282, codified as amended at 42 U.S.C. §§2661–2666

Connor, B. M. (2016). In Loco Aequitatis: The dangers of "Safe Harbor" laws for youth in the sex trades. *Stanford Journal of Civil Rights & Civil Liberties, 12*(43), 45–116. https://scholarship.law.wm.edu/facpubs/1934.

Cook, A., Spinazzola, J., Ford, J., Lanktree, C., Blaustein, M., Cloitre, M., & van der Kolk, B. (2005). Complex trauma in children and adolescents. *Psychiatric Annals, 35*, 390–398.

Corrigan, F., Fisher, J., & Nutt, D. (2011). Autonomic dysregulation and the Window of Tolerance model of the effects of complex emotional trauma emotional trauma. *Journal of Psychopharmacology, 25*(*1*), 17–25. https://doi.org/10.1007/s40653-020-00310-4.

Courtois, C. (2004). Complex trauma, complex reactions: Assessment and treatment. *Psychotherapy: Theory, Research, Practice, Training, 41*(4), 86–100. https://doi.org/10.1037/1942-9681.S.1.86.

De Vries, I., & Farrell, A. (2018). Labor trafficking victimizations: Repeat victimization and polyvictimization. *Psychology of Violence, 8*(5), 630–638. https://doi.org/10.1037/vio0000149.

Denham, A. (2008). Rethinking historical trauma: Narratives of resilience. *Transcultural Psychiatry, 45*(3), 391–414. https://doi.org/10.1177/1363461508094673.

Domoney, J., Howard, L. M., Abas, M., Broadbent, M., & Oram, S. (2015). Mental health service responses to human trafficking: A qualitative study of professionals' experiences of providing care. *BMC Psychiatry, 15*, 289–297. https://doi.org/10.1186/s12888-015-0679-3.

Elderton, A., Berry, A., & Chan, C. (2015). A systematic review of posttraumatic growth in survivors of interpersonal violence in adulthood. *Trauma, Violence and Abuse, 18*(2), 223–236. https://doi.org/10.1177/1524838015611672.

Engel, C. C. (2004). Somatization and multiple idiopathic physical symptoms: Relationship to traumatic events and posttraumatic stress disorder. In B. L. Green & P. P. Schnurr (Eds.), *Trauma and health: Physical health consequences of exposure to extreme stress* (pp. 191–215). Washington, DC: American Psychological Association. https://doi.org/10.1037/10723-008.

Evans-Campbell, T. (2008). Historical trauma in American Indian/native alaska communities: a multilevel framework for exploring impacts on individuals, families, and communities. *Journal of Interpersonal Violence, 23*(3), 316–338. https://doi.org/10.1177/0886260507312290.

Flemke, K., Underwood, J., & Allen, K. (2014). Childhood abuse and Women's use of intimate partner violence: Exploring the role of complex trauma. *Partner Abuse, 25*(2), 98–112. https://doi.org/10.1177/1077801218766628.

Gallop, R., McCay, E., Guha, M., & P, K. (1999). The experience of hospitalization and restraint of women who have a history of childhood sexual abuse. *Health Care for Women International, 41*(4), 401–416. https://doi.org/10.1080/073993399245683.

Garland, E. L., Pettus-Davis, C., & Howard, M. O. (2013). Self-medication among traumatized youth: Structural equation modeling of pathways between trauma history, substance misuse, and psychological distress. *Journal of Behavioral Medicine, 36*(2), 175–185. https://doi.org/10.1007/s10865-012-9413-5.

Graham, D. (1994). *Loving to survive*. New York: New York University Press.

Greenbaum, J. V. (2017). Child sex trafficking in the United States: Challenges for the healthcare provider. *PLoS Medicine, 14*(11), e1002439. https://doi.org/10.1371/journal.pmed.1002439.

Greeson, J., Briggs, E., Kisiel, C., Layne, C., Ake, G., Ko, S., Gerrity, E., Steinberg, A., Howard, M., Pynoos, R., & Fairbank, J. (2011). Complex trauma and mental health in children and adolescents placed in Foster Care: Findings from the National Child Traumatic Stress Network. *Child Welfare, 90*, 91–108.

Griffin, G., Mcclelland, G., Holzberg, M., Stolbach, B., Maj, N., & Kisiel, C. (2011). Addressing the impact of trauma before diagnosing mental illness in child welfare. *Child Welfare, 90*, 69–89.

Grob, G. (1973). *Mental Institutions in America: Social Policy to 1875*. New York: The Free Press.

Grob, G. (1991). *From asylum to community: Mental health policy in modern America*. Princeton: Princeton University Press.

Heilbron, L. C., & Guttman, J. A. (2000). Traditional healing methods with First Nations women in group counseling. *Canadian Journal of Counselling, 34*(1), 3–13. ISSN-0828-3893.

Helsel, B. P. (2015). Witnessing the Body's response to trauma: Resistance, ritual, and nervous system activation. *Pastoral Psychology, 64*(5), 681–693. https://doi.org/10.1007/s11089-014-0628-y.

Herman, J. (1992a). Complex PTSD: A syndrome in survivors of prolonged and repeated trauma. *Journal of Traumatic Stress, 5*(3), 377–391. https://doi.org/10.1002/jts.2490050305.

Herman, J. (1992b). *Trauma and recovery*. New York: Basic Books.

Hill, S., & Laugharne, R. (2003). Mania, dementia and melancholia in the 1870s: Admissions to a Cornwall asylum. *Journal of the Royal Society of Medicine, 96*(7), 361–363. https://doi.org/10.1258/jrsm.96.7.361.

Hollar, M. (2001). The impact of racism on the delivery of health care and mental health services. *The Psychiatric Quarterly. 72*, 337–45. https://doi.org/10.1023/A:1010341332036.

Hossain, M., Zimmerman, C., Abas, M., Light, M., & Watts, C. (2010). The relationship of trauma to mental disorders among trafficked and sexually exploited girls and women. *American Journal of Public Health, 100*(12), 2442–2449. https://doi.org/10.2105/AJPH.2009.173229.

Jepsen, E. K., Langeland, W., & Heir, T. (2013). Impact of dissociation and interpersonal functioning on inpatient treatment for early sexually abused adults. *European Journal of Psychotraumatology, 4*(1), 22825. https://doi.org/10.3402/ejpt.v4i0.22825.

Johnson, C. B. (2012). Aftercare for survivors of human trafficking. *Social Work and Christianity, 39*(4), 370–389.

Jonson-Reid, M., Drake, B., Kim, J., Porterfield, S., & Han, L. (2004). A prospective analysis of the relationship between reported child maltreatment and special education eligibility among poor children. *Child Maltreatment, 9*(4), 382–394. https://doi.org/10.1177/1077559504269192.

Joseph, S. (2011). *What doesn't kill us: The new psychology of posttraumatic growth*. New York: Basic Books.

Judge, M. A., Murphy, A. J., Hidalgo, J., & Macias-Konstantopoulos, W. (2018). Engaging survivors of human trafficking: Complex health care needs and scarce resources. *Annals of Internal Medicine, 168*(9), 658–663. https://doi.org/10.7326/M17-2605.

Kawaii-Bogue, B., Williams, N. J., & MacNear, K. (2017). Mental health care access and treatment utilization in African American communities: An integrative care framework. *Best Practices in Mental Health: An International Journal*, 13(2), 11–29.

Kim, K., Trickett, P. K., & Putnam, F. W. (2010). Childhood experiences of sexual abuse and later parenting practices among non-offending mothers of sexually abused and comparison girls. *Child Abuse & Neglect, 34*(8), 610–622. https://doi.org/10.1016/j.chiabu.2010.01.007.

Kisiel, C., Conradi, L., Fehrenbach, T., Torgersen, E., & Briggs, E. C. (2014). Assessing the effects of trauma in children and adolescents in practice settings. *Child and Adolescent Psychiatric Clinics of North America, 23*(2), 223–242. https://doi.org/10.1016/j.chc.2013.12.007.

Kisiel, C. Fehrenbach, T., Small, L., &. Lyons, J. (2009). Assessment of complex trauma exposure, responses, and service needs among children and adolescents in child welfare. *Journal of Child & Adolescent Trauma, 2*(3), 143–160. https://doi.org/10.1080/19361520903120467.

Kisiel, C., Summersett-Ringgold, F., Weil, L., & Mcclelland, G. (2017). Understanding strengths in relation to complex trauma and mental health symptoms within child welfare. *Journal of Child and Family Studies, 26*, 437–451. https://doi.org/10.1007/s10826-016-0569-4.

Lamb, R. H., & Weinberger, W. E. (2005). The shift of psychiatric inpatient care from hospitals to jails and prisons. *Journal of American Academy of Psychiatry Law, 33*(4), 529–534. http://hdl.handle.net/10822/985676.

Leifer, M., Kilbane, T., Jacobsen, T., & Grossman, G. (2004). A three-generational study of transmission of risk for sexual abuse. *Journal of Clinical Child & Adolescent Psychology, 33*(4), 662–672. https://doi.org/10.1207/s15374424jccp3304_2.

Levine, P., Lazrove, S., & van der Kolk, B. (1999). What psychological testing and neuroimaging tell us about the treatment of posttraumatic stress disorder (PTSD) by eye movement desensitization and reprocessing (EMDR). *Journal of Anxiety Disorders, 13*(1–2), 159–172. https://doi.org/10.1016/S0887-6185(98)00045-01.

Levine, P. A. (2010). *In an unspoken voice: How the body releases trauma and restores goodness.* Berkley: North Atlantic Books.

Lynch, H. (2019). Involuntary hospitalization and Bias against marginalized groups. *The Stanford Undergraduate Research Journal of Humanities and Social Sciences, 18*(1), 40–45.

Mehlman-Orozco, K. (2017). Projected heroes and self-perceived manipulators: Understanding the duplicitous identities of human traffickers. *Trends in Organized Crime, 23*, 1–20. https://doi.org/10.1007/s12117-017-9325-4.

Moran, S., Burker, E. E., & Schmidt, J. (2013). Posttraumatic growth and posttraumatic stress disorder in veterans. *Journal of Rehabilitation, 79*(2), 34–43.

Nibert, D., Cooper, S., & Crossmaker, M. (1989). Assaults against residents of a psychiatric institution: Residents' history of abuse. *Journal of Interpersonal Violence, 4*(3), 342–349. https://doi.org/10.1177/088626089004003007.

Noll, J. G., Trickett, P. K., Harris, W. W., & Putnam, F. W. (2008). The cumulative burden borne by offspring whose mothers were sexually abused as children: Descriptive results from a multigenerational study. *The Journal of Interpersonal Violence, 24*(3), 424–449. https://doi.org/10.1177/0886260508317194.

O'Brien, J. E., White, K., & Rizo, C. F. (2017). Domestic Minor Sex Trafficking Among Child Welfare–Involved Youth: An Exploratory Study of Correlates. *Child Maltreatment, 22*(3), 265–274. https://doi.org/10.1177/1077559517709995

Oswald, F., Mitchell, G., Blanton, H., Jaccard, J., & Tetlock, P. (2013). Predicting Ethnic and Racial Discrimination: A Meta-Analysis o IAT Criterion Studies. *Journal of Personality and Social Psychology.* 105. https://doi.org/10.1037/a0032734.

Ottisova, L., Hemmings, S., Howard, M. L., Zimmerman, C., & Oram, S. (2012). Prevalence and risk of violence and the mental, physical and sexual health problems associated with human trafficking: An updated systematic review. *PLoS Medicine, 9*(5), e1001224. https://doi.org/10.1371/journal.pmed.1001224.

Ottisova, L., Smith, P., Shetty, H., Stahl, D., Downs, J., & Oram, S. (2018). Psychological consequences of child trafficking: An historical cohort study of trafficked children in contact with secondary mental health services. *PLoS One, 13*(3), e0192321. https://doi.org/10.1371/journal.pone.0192321.

Ozer, E. J., Best, S. R., Lipsey, T. L., & Weiss, D. S. (2003). Predictors of posttraumatic stress disorder and symptoms in adults: A meta-analysis. *Psychological Bulletin, 129*(1), 52–71. https://doi.org/10.1037/0033-2909.129.1.52.

Payne, P., Levine, P., & Crane-Godreau, M. (2015). Somatic experiencing: Using interoception and proprioception as core elements of trauma therapy. *Frontiers in Psychology, 6*(93), 1–18. https://doi.org/10.3389/fpsyg.2015.00093.

Pouba, K., & Tianen, A. (2006). *Lunacy in the 19th century: Women's admission to asylums in United States of America.* University of Wisconsin Oshkosh, 95–103.

Quinn, A. (2007). Reflections on intergenerational trauma: Healing as a critical intervention. *First People Child & Family Review, 3*(4), 73–82. Retrieved from https://fpcfr.com/index.php/FPCFR/article/view/62.

Raphael, J., & Myers-Powell, B. (2009). *Five ex-pimps in Chicago.* DePaul University.

Raphael, J., Myers-Powell, B., (2010). From Victims to Victimizers: Interviews with 25 Ex-Pimps in Chicago. Chicago. DePaul University, Schiller DuCanto & Fleck Family Law Center.

Reid, J. A. (2014). Risk and resiliency factors influencing onset and adolescence-limited commercial sexual exploitation of disadvantaged girls. *Criminal Behavior and Mental Health, 24*(5), 332–344. https://doi.org/10.1002/cbm.1903.

Rinker, J., & Lawler, J. (2018). Trauma as a collective disease and root cause of protracted social conflict. *Peace and Conflict: Journal of Peace Psychology, 24*(2), 150–164. https://doi.org/10.1037/pac0000311.

Roe-Sepowitz, D., Gallagher, J., Risinger, M., & Hickle, K. (2014). The sexual exploitation of girls in the United States: The role of female pimps. *Journal of Interpersonal Violence, 30*(16), 2814–2830. https://doi.org/10.1177/0886260514554292.

Ross, C., Farley, M., & Schwartz, H. (2004). Dissociation among women in prostitution. *Journal of Trauma Practice, 20*(2), 199–212. https://doi.org/10.1300/J189v02n03_11.

Rothschild, B. (2000). *The body remembers: The psychophysiology of trauma and trauma treatment*. New York: W. W. Norton.

Russell, A. (2019). Finding a Safer Harbor: Mandating health care clinics to intervene in child sex trafficking by amending the Safe Harbor Act. *Family Court Review, 57*, 136–150. https://doi.org/10.1111/fcre.12401.

Shapiro, F. (2014). The role of eye movement desensitization and reprocessing (EMDR) therapy in medicine: Addressing the psychological and physical symptoms stemming from adverse life experiences. *The Permanente Journal, 18*(1), 71–77. https://doi.org/10.7812/TPP/13-098.

Shapiro, F., & Laliotis, D. (2011). EMDR and the adaptive information processing model: Integrative treatment and case conceptualization. *Clinical Social Work Journal volume, 39*, 191–200. https://doi.org/10.1007/s10615-010-0300-7.

Snowden, L. R. (2003). Bias in mental health assessment and intervention: Theory and evidence. *American Journal of Public Health, 93*(2), 239–243. https://doi.org/10.2105/ajph.93.2.239.

Social Security Amendments of 1965 Pub. L 89-97, 79 Stat. 268, 422 U.S.C. §1818

Sprang, G., & Cole, J. (2018). Familial sex trafficking of minors: Trafficking conditions, clinical presentation, and system involvement. *Journal of Family Violence, 33*, 185–195. https://doi.org/10.1007/s10896-018-9950-y.

Straussner, S. L. A., & Calnan, A. J. (2014). Trauma through the life cycle: A review of current literature. *Clinical Social Work Journal, 42*(4), 323–335. https://doi.org/10.1007/s10615-014-0496-z.

Suris, A. H. (2016). The evolution of the classification of psychiatric disorders. *Behavioral Sciences (Basel, Switzerland), 6*(1), 5. https://doi.org/10.3390/bs6010005.

Tagay, S., Schlegl, S., & Senf, W. (2010). Traumatic events, posttraumatic stress symptomatology and somatoform symptoms in eating disorder patients. *European Eating Disorders Review, 18*(2), 124–132. https://doi.org/10.1002/erv.972.

Thompson, J., & Haley, M. (2018). Human trafficking: Preparing counselors to work with survivors. *International Journal for the Advancement of Counselling, 40*(3), 298–309. https://doi.org/10.1007/s10447-018-9327-1.

Trippany, L. R., Helm, H., & Simpson, L. (2006). Trauma reenactment: Rethinking borderline personality disorder when diagnosing sexual abuse survivors. *Journal of Mental Health, 28*(2), 95–110. https://doi.org/10.17744/mehc.28.2.ef384lm8ykfujum5.

Ulloa, E., Guzman, M., Salazar, m., & Cala, C. (2016). Posttraumatic growth and sexual violence: A literature review. *Journal of Aggression, Maltreatment & Trauma, 25*(3), 286–304. https://doi.org/10.1080/10926771.2015.1079286.

United Nations General Assembly. (2000). *Protocol to prevent, suppress and punish trafficking in persons especially women and children*. Supplementing the United Nations Convention against Transnational Organized Crime.

van der Kolk, B. (2014). *The body keeps the score*. New York: Viking.

van der Kolk, B., & Saporta, J. (1991). The biological response to psychic trauma: Mechanisms and treatment of intrusion and numbing. *Anxiety Research, 4*(3), 199–212. https://doi.org/10.1080/08917779108248774.

Victims of Trafficking and Violence Protection Act of 2000 Pub. L 106-386, 141 Stat. 1464, 422 U.S.C. §7101

Whitbeck, L. B., Adams, G. W., Hoyt, D. R., & Chen, X. (2004). Conceptualizing and measuring historical trauma among American Indian people. *American Journal of Community Psychology, 33*(3–4), 119–130. https://doi.org/10.1023/B:AJCP.0000027000.77357.31.

Wolfe, D. S., Greeson, J. K. P., Wasch, S., & Treglia, D. (2018). Human trafficking prevalence and child welfare risk factors among homeless youth: A multi-city study. Philadelphia: University of Pennsylvania, Field Center for Children's Policy, Practice & Research.

World Health Organization. (2012). History of the Development of the ICD. Geneva, Switzerland

Wilkins, E., Whiting, J., Watson, M., Russon, J., & Moncrief, A. (2013). Residual effects of slavery: What clinicians need to know. *Contemporary Family Therapy: An International Journal, 35*, 14–28. https://doi.org/10.1007/s10591-012-9219-1.

Yohannan, D. (2013). Deinstitutionalization of people with mental illness: Causes and consequences. *AMA Journal of Ethics, 15*(10), 886–891. https://doi.org/10.1001/virtualmentor.2013.15.10.mhst1-1310.

Zeynel, Z., & Uzer, T. (2019). Adverse childhood experiences Lead to trans-generational transmission of early maladaptive schemas. *Child Abuse and Neglect, 99*, 104253. https://doi.org/10.1016/j.chiabu.2019.104235.

Zimmerman, C., Hossain, M., Yun, K., Gajdadziev, V., Guzun, N., Tchomarova, M., Ciarrocchi, R. A., Johansson, A., Kefurtova, A., Scodanibbio, S., Motus, M. N., Roche, B., Morison, L., & Watts, C. (2008). The health of trafficked women: A survey of women entering posttrafficking services in Europe. *American Journal of Public Health, 98*(1), 55–59.

Chapter 14
Historical Context Matters: Health Research, Health Care, and Bodies of Color in the United States

Makini Chisolm-Straker

14.1 Introduction

The origin story of the United States is often portrayed as a virtuous one of identity protection: A small group of English people came to a "new land" to pursue religious freedom. The well-documented truth is less glorious and noble. A settler–colonial nation, the USA was founded on the often-violent theft of land and labor. Various Indigenous tribes protected and cultivated the land that is now called the "US;" White colonists and settlers repeatedly and forcibly took that land and then poorly tended it. Furthermore, colonial Europeans (and their descendants) stole the labor of Indigenous, African, and African-descended peoples and forced them to develop the foundation of the US economy. In this way, the bodies of Indigenous and Black peoples had value only insomuch as they could be translated into fiscal profit for White colonists and settlers. For example, slave owners raised slave children as an investment: These children could be used as labor for decades (starting in childhood), and because of this, they could also be used as a source of collateral and credit when applying for loans (Isenberg 2016). To be clear, people were commonly used and recognized as capital (Chap. 2). When those bodies were no longer economically valuable, they were discarded. And when the people, to whom those bodies belonged, meaningfully threatened (or were perceived to threaten) the White supremacist and classist hegemony, acts of genocide via brute force and medical manipulation were employed.

M. Chisolm-Straker (✉)
Institute for Health Equity Research, Department of Emergency Medicine,
Icahn School of Medicine at Mount Sinai, New York, NY, USA
e-mail: Makini.Chisolm-Straker@mountsinai.org

14.1.1   Poor Whites and Abolition

Race-based slavery was the bedrock of the US economy (Chap. 2). Indigenous people in North America were the first to be enslaved here by Europeans, on the basis of race (Etheridge and Shuck-Hall 2009; Gallay 2002; Gallay 2009; Rushforth 2012; Synder 2010). It is more commonly known that chattel slavery, specifically of Black people in North America, endured for centuries. In elementary, junior/middle, and high schools across the US, children are taught that the Civil War ended such slavery; they are taught that Abraham Lincoln magnanimously led the US in the fight to end race-based slavery in the USA. The truth is more complex.

In the mid-1800s, there were a few objections to race-based slavery. One objection was that it was immoral to enslave people, on the basis of race or otherwise. The Free Soil Party of 1848 (starting in 1854, the Republican Party) held that the existence of poor Whites, particularly those in the US South, proved that slavery had a negative impact on free labor. That is to say, because slavery was legally allowed, poor Whites (who did not own land and could not afford slaves) were unable or unwilling to find work. White slave owners who had the economic wherewithal also pushed poor Whites off their land (never mind that this land was originally the home of Indigenous peoples). The Free Soil Party offered a solution to the problem of poverty among Whites: Slavery should be outlawed in Western territories. In doing this, Southern slavery might die out and with abolition former slaves should be moved out of the US (e.g., to the Caribbean islands or the continent of Africa). On the other hand, the pro-slavery South argued that it is the natural order for a few people to be in power and have privilege; in fact, poor Whites were of "corrupt pedigree and cursed lineage" and did not deserve better in life (Isenberg 2016). Besides, they argued, slavery was more effective than free labor because it eliminated the struggle between labor and capital (Isenberg 2016). For many Whites, the controversy of abolition was about the merits of class mobility and even whether poor Whites deserved better at all.

14.2   Discussion

The ratification of the Emancipation Proclamation in 1865 technically ended slavery as a legal practice in the US (Chap. 9). But Blacks were not excommunicated *a la* the Free Soil Party proposition, nor were they suddenly or meaningfully given the freedoms afforded landowning Whites. Whites continued to exclude Blacks from public institutions, including hospitals and other health services. The Freedmen's Bureau was established in 1865 to support the newly freed slaves and impoverished Whites (National Archives 2016). After the war, these groups in particular were, unsurprisingly, economically destitute. Many had no homes, no job opportunities, and little to no access to food; basic survival was unlikely without support. The Freedmen's Bureau was intended to serve as a relief effort and to help with social reconstruction. The Bureau helped its target population with family reunification, offered food and clothing, and set up and operated hospitals and temporary housing (camps); the Bureau helped get Blacks settled on "abandoned" (formerly Native) or confiscated land and helped Black soldiers and sailors obtain back pay, bounty payments, and pensions (National Archives 2016). The Bureau, with the US Army, forced Southern White leadership to provide Blacks with the public services that Whites could access. In practice though, Southern Whites were not willing to share spaces or resources with Blacks.

In the setting of extreme poverty, appalling living conditions, and exclusion, Blacks experienced higher morbidity and mortality but remained barred from hospitals. Hence, a "separate but equal" paradigm was created due to the Bureau's efforts (Rabinowitz 1974), and apartheid was instituted to support Black survival and protect White comfort. During the war, hospitals had separate quarters for Blacks and Whites. To meet the obvious need and protect White "sensibilities," the Freedmen's Bureau borrowed a move from the Army hospital playbook and created separate spaces for Blacks needing health (medical and mental health[1]) care. Akin to the COVID-19 pandemic manifest in the USA, major gaps in needed services remained despite federal help, and charitable organizations like Black churches and benevolent societies attempted to fill in. Predating the advent of the Blue Cross health insurance–employment paradigm of the 1930s, Black churches and benevolent societies offered sick benefits to dues-paying members. As time passed, Black communities amassed some wealth and developed philanthropic societies which also provided needed services that were not publicly available to Blacks. But despite charitable efforts (and again, as in the COVID-19 pandemic), in the absence of meaningful systems and efforts to eliminate institutional marginalization, Black health disproportionately suffered.

The concept of "separate but equal" was actually rooted in the White assumption that Blacks were inherently inferior; this "...led to an inequitable administration of separate facilities" (Rabinowitz 1974). Where there were not physically separate healthcare buildings, for example, there were separate wards: one for Whites, one for Blacks. Whether a separate edifice or a segregated area, the space, services, and resources allocated to Blacks were less, and so was their quality; examples of this were innumerable (Atlanta 1885; Atlanta 1889; Georgia 1890; Nashville Banner 1884; Tennessee 1889-90; Tennessee 1889-91; Virginia 1875-76; Virginia 1877). This was true of almost all Black facilities, regardless of Blacks' ability to pay. For example, in Tennessee and Alabama, while there were three separate tiers of health care for Whites ("paying," "indigent," "criminal"), only the latter two tiers were available to Blacks (Alabama 1888-90; Tennessee 1875). At an 1896 convention to examine the problem of disproportionate Black mortality, one participant observed:

---

[1] Of note, "mental health" was not the term of the time. "Insane asylums" and "lunatic asylums" were warehouses of individuals who were particularly ill, did not have family willing or able to support them at home, and/or did not conform to societal standards of decorum. Many were from chronically oppressed groups; see Chap. 13 for more.

"There is no decent hospital where colored people can be cared for. At the Grady Hospital...is a small wooden annex down by the kitchen, in which may be crowded fifty or sixty beds, and that is all the hospital advantages 40,000 colored citizens have. But, on the other hand, our White friends, with a population of 70,000, have all the wards and private rooms in the entire brick building at this hospital, together with a very fine hospital here, known as St. Joseph's Infirmary" (Gibson and Crogman 1902).

Grady Hospital, which opened in 1892, remains today. Over a century later, it is technically a hospital for all comers and its facilities have certainly improved, yet Grady still predominantly serves patients of color and particularly people with a lower socioeconomic status (Harvey et al. 2004). It is considered a "safety net" hospital.[2] Today, Emory St. Joseph's Hospital is also open to all but serves a comparatively White and well-off population. The hospitals have overlapping catchment areas and are only 6 miles apart. Similar US hospital origin mythologies abound.

In addition to facilities and resources, clinicians willing and able to staff Black-designated and segregated healthcare settings were in short supply. There was a small cadre of Black physicians who were trained—some in Northern medical schools—prior to the 13th Amendment. Born in 1762 and thought to be the first Black physician born in the US, James Durham (Derham) was trained via apprenticeship by two physician slave masters (Cobb 1948; Curtis 1971). He practiced in New Orleans, Louisiana, though his practice was limited by the city because "he did not have a formal degree" (Harley 2006). After Emancipation, Black medical schools were either church-related or proprietary (Savitt 1992); they were underfunded with limited faculty and facilities and did not have access to many patients for educational purposes (Charlotte Observer 1990; Savitt 1992). That some of the proprietary schools were merely commercial endeavors meant the graduates had little qualifications for patient care. Medical education reforms were implemented in an effort to eliminate poorly trained medical school graduates (Black or White), and only two of the Black medical schools survived: Howard University College of Medicine and Meharry Medical College (Harley 2006). Still, the schools remained comparatively underfunded and struggled to produce enough physicians who could genuinely serve Black communities.

14.2.1 Medical and "Research" Use of Bodies of Color

During legal slavery, White physicians "caring" for Black slaves were invested in serving the fiscal interests of slave owners. In other words, the health of Black slaves was only important insomuch as Black bodies could be used for unpaid labor

---

[2]According to the Institute of Medicine, a safety net hospital "...organize[s] and deliver[s] a significant level of both health care and other health-related services to the uninsured, Medicaid, and other vulnerable populations..." (IOM 2000). The US Department of Health & Human Services notes that this definition "includes most—if not all—public hospitals that are often the providers of last resort in their community..." (US Dept of HHS 2013).

or to produce more bodies for unpaid labor (including through the rape of Black women). Healthy slaves were more profitable than sick ones. Even after legal slavery, Black bodies were considered a means to an end, be that end an increase in Whites' capital gains and comfort, or the advancement of medical science for the benefit of White patients. The advancement of health care occurred in part because of physician training reforms (Duffy 2011; Flexner 1910) and in part because of organized scientific inquiry. And some "scientific inquiry" relied upon the abuse of vulnerable populations (Krugman 1986; Langer 1964; Weindling 2004).

It is well documented that White physicians forcibly used Black slaves for medical experimentation (Kenny 2010; Unknown Author 1890; Washington 2006; West and Irvine 2015). A commonly cited example, during the 1830s through 1880s, Marion J. Sims, historically called the "Father of Gynecology," invented the Sims speculum (among other tools, procedures, and techniques), which is still used for pelvic exams today. During slavery, Sims purchased enslaved Black women and performed numerous surgeries—sometimes twenty to thirty times per "patient"— without anesthesia (though it was available at the time) to correct vesicovaginal fistulae[3] (Warren et al. 2020a). Sims was not unique in his use of Black bodies; it was socially acceptable (among Whites) at the time, as boasted by the South Carolina Medical College:

> "No place in the United States offers as great opportunities for the acquisition of anatomical knowledge, subjects being obtained from among the colored population in sufficient number for any purpose, and proper dissections carried on without offending any individuals in the community!!" (Curry and Cowden 1972).

White physicians used slaves (and later, free Blacks) for a variety of health research and medical experiments, including testing vaccines for smallpox and typhoid, resection of ovarian tumors; the list goes on and on (Randall 1996). Anesthesia for surgery was not developed until the 1840s, and the experiments were not humane; for example, to test for a cure for typhoid pneumonia, Walter F. Jones poured boiling water onto the backs of Black slaves (Randall 1996). Slaves' bodies were human enough to use for experimentation, but their lives did not have value beyond that of improving the lives of Whites. Suffice it to say, the benefits of the research (if any) were not extended to the "study participant" communities.

The abuse of bodies of color was by no means restricted to Blacks. Whites also abused Indigenous bodies in slavery and desecrated them during and after violent encounters with White squatters (Dunbar-Ortiz 2014; Isenberg 2016; Reséndez 2016). For example, in 1862, President Abraham Lincoln approved the largest mass execution in US history: 38 Dakota warriors were publicly hanged, in Mankato, Minnesota, for their retaliatory acts against White settlers. Physician William Mayo took—without permission or consequence—the body of Marpiya Okinajin (common name, Cut Nose). Mayo dissected Cut Nose's body and then used the skeleton

---

[3] Abnormal communications between the vagina and the bladder; in the 1800s, they may have been caused by surgery, obstetric injury (e.g., obstructed labor during childbirth), or severe pathology of the pelvis. They can result in urinary leakage from the vagina (Garely and Mann 2020).

for medical study and his children's play. Mayo founded the famous Mayo Clinic and displayed the skull of Cut Nose there. The Santee Dakota and Cut Nose's family have long known this historical truth, but it is not mainstream knowledge. The Mayo Clinic is lauded for its clinical care and innovation. The associated desecration of a Native American body—of a man who was killed with the sanction of the US government—has largely been untold. The Mayo family only returned Cut Nose's violated remains to his family in the late 1990s. In 2018, 156 years later, Mayo leadership created a medical school scholarship to honor Cut Nose and to fully support one Native student, in perpetuity (Hansen 2018).

Medical science owes a great debt to Henrietta Lacks. Ms. Lacks was a Black woman who contributed one of the cell lines still considered among the most important in medical research. In 1951, her cervical cancer cells were biopsied at Johns Hopkins Hospital, another bastion of US clinical care. White physicians did not seek her consent nor did they compensate her or her family for the extraction of her cells or their use (they were cultured into the HeLa cell line). Ms. Lacks' cells are still used in a wide range of medical research, including research examining the impacts of radiation and testing life-saving vaccines. Ms. Lacks died at 31 years old. Her story was publicized 60 years after her cancer cells were biopsied, in 2011 with the book, *The Immortal Life of Henrietta Lacks* by Rebecca Skloot. Only in 2013 did Johns Hopkins Hospital work with her family and the National Institutes of Health (NIH) to develop a protocol requiring scientists to obtain permission to use HeLa cells or Ms. Lacks' genetic blueprint in NIH-funded research (Johns Hopkins Medicine n.d.).

Even more commonly known is the unethical treatment of the 399 Black men who were infected with syphilis[4] but remained untreated. The goal of the study was to examine the "natural course" of the infection to justify treatment programs for Blacks. In the 1932–1972 US Public Health Service Study called the "Tuskegee Study of Untreated Syphilis in the Negro Male," researchers did not consent the impoverished, Black sharecroppers of Macon County, Alabama for study inclusion. The men were not even told they had syphilis, which became treatable with penicillin in the late 1940s. They were told they were being treated for "bad blood" (a local term to describe any number of problems, including fatigue and anemia), but in fact they never received any syphilis treatment at all. Syphilis complications can eventually be fatal, and a person with untreated syphilis may spread the infection to sexual partners (via active lesions) or a pregnant parent may infect their fetus (via the placenta). The Associated Press exposed and reported about this federal study ultimately leading to its conclusion (CDC 2013). An out-of-court settlement of $10 million USD was reached in 1974, and the US government committed to lifetime medical benefits and burial services to remaining living participants via the Tuskegee Health Benefit Program. A year later, the wives, widows, and children of study "participants" were included in this programming (CDC 2013).

---

[4] They were not infected for the study. Their infection status is why they were targeted for study inclusion.

In another federal bioethical violation from 1989 to 1991 and as part of a Centers for Disease Control and Prevention (CDC) study, 900 mostly Black and Latinx infants in Los Angeles, California, were experimentally vaccinated against the measles. The groups were targeted for the trial because they lived in the communities with the highest rates of measles infections. But their guardians did not provide informed consent (Cimons 1996). According to the CDC, none of the children were harmed. But it was because of similar trials in Haiti, Senegal, and Guinea-Bissau, which raised concerns about safety for female infants who received a more potent dose of the vaccine,[5] that the US study ended in 1991 (Cimons 1996). In both federal studies, the medical researchers report the intent was to help, but their actions yielded further harm: In the Tuskegee Study, the physical health and mental health of Blacks were injured. In the measles study, the trust of communities of color in the US healthcare system was, yet again, battered.

That distrust has been well-earned. The US medical society has repeatedly perpetuated institutional abuse and violations of bodies of color for the purposes of "progress" and has sometimes even purported those violations to be health care. Eugenics was an acceptable, mainstream policy paradigm for progress in Europe and settler–colonial nations like Canada and the US until the 1940s with the rise of the Nazis. Eugenics supporters (including Theodore Roosevelt) believed that humanity could be improved by "breeding out" "undesirable" characteristics. Plainly put, those in power determined what types of people and characteristics were "undesirable" and who should procreate. In line with racist eugenics principles, the sterilization of people of color is well documented and still within living memory at the time of this writing (Gurr 2012; Hernandez 1976; Price and Darity Jr 2010).

Indian Health Services is responsible for the coercive sterilization of Native women in the 1960s and 1970s; this continued at least into the 1990s (Gurr 2012; Johansen 2001; Langston 2003; Lawrence 2000; Smith 2005; Torpy 2000). Similarly, the University of Southern California, Los Angeles Medical Center, coerced and forced Chicana women into sterilization; cases from the 1970s are documented in the 1975 lawsuit *Madrigal v. Quilligan* (Madrigal 1975). Long-term chemical contraceptives were used in Native communities for almost two decades before use approval by the Food and Drug Administration in 1992 (Smith 2005), and many Native patients were not informed of possible medication side effects (Ralston-Lewis 2005; Smith 2005). The institutionally sanctioned policing of reproduction in communities of color is in line with the principles of eugenics, constitutes acts of genocide (Price and Darity Jr 2010; United Nations 1948), and continues today. In September 2020, news broke of the unauthorized sterilization (via hysterectomy) of people in immigration detention (Latinas from Latin American countries). One physician was named as responsible for the surgeries that took place over years (Project South 2020; Ramirez 2020; Vasquez 2020). At the time of this

---

[5] No causal association between the more potent vaccine dose and death were found, and other factors like malnourishment and inadequate access to health care may have contributed to the death of those children.

writing, the legal case is still pending, but many perspectives have been publicly aired. Some argue that, if true, this is the action of one person. A clear rebuttal to such a claim is that surgeons do not act alone, but with the sanction of an institution and with the support of a clinical team.

It is no wonder that many people of color are skeptical of medical research and health care. The two fields are deeply entwined, and for centuries, their interactions with people of color have been anything but noble. Initially, the two acted within legal bounds and without shame, as bodies of color were not meaningfully recognized as belonging to people and informed consent was not yet a research or healthcare principle. But even after the ratification of the 13th Amendment, the advent of the Nuremberg Code of 1947, and with the Belmont Report of 1979, the fields of medical research and health care have continued to harm communities of color. Communities pass on knowledge of historical experiences, truths, and traumas to new generations (Chap. 16) and continued institutionalized perpetration leaves little space for expectations of better.

14.2.2   The Living Legacy of Racism in Contemporary US Health Care

Deep-rooted patterns of healthcare injustices and disparities are the legacy of continued structural racism. In 1985, the "Report of the Secretary's Task Force on Black & Minority Health" described "excess death" as the age- and sex-adjusted difference in death among "minority" populations (people of color) in comparison to the "nonminority" population (Whites) (US Department of Health and Human Services 1985). In comparison to the White population, the average annual excess deaths in the Black population from 1979 to 1981 were over 58,000 (US Department of Health and Human Services 1985). In 2002, the reported number of excess Black deaths *rose* to more than 83,000 (Satcher et al. 2005). During the 2020 COVID-19 pandemic, available data for New York City (among the hardest hit with respect to total COVID-19 mortality) identified death rates among Blacks at 92.3 per 100,000 population, while White deaths were at 45.2 per 100,000 (CDC 2020). The disparity of excess deaths based upon race continues and extends beyond the oversimplified Black–White dichotomy.

Native people die at higher rates than *all other* people in the US in many illness and injury categories, including diabetes, unintentional injuries, and chronic liver disease and cirrhosis (IHS 2019). Asian Americans are more likely to die of an acute myocardial infarction (heart attack) than White counterparts (Kim et al. 2018). In 2017, 10.5% of Hispanic[6] girls in high school attempted suicide, compared to 7% of same-aged White girls—that is a 40% higher suicide attempt rate for Hispanic girls

---

[6] The term "Hispanic" is used here, rather than the non-Eurocentric and more gender-inclusive "Latinx" to reflect the term used by the cited source, the Centers for Disease Control and Prevention.

(CDC 2019). "Social" factors may contribute to these health disparities, but those factors are rooted in structural racism and ethnocentrism and ultimately contribute to poor health and health outcomes in communities of color.

In addition to collective and intergenerational knowledge of harm (Chap. 13), persistent race- and/or ethnicity-based disparities in health resource allocations and outcomes reinforce a skepticism about Western medical intervention settings. The context-free use of race and ethnicity in medical guidelines may contribute to such disparities. For example, multiple professional medical societies have created or endorse algorithms that use race and/or ethnicity to determine risk or allocate healthcare resources (Eneanya et al. 2019; Grobman et al. 2007; Kowalsky et al. 2020; Levey et al. 2009; Moore et al. 2014; Rao et al. 2009; Shahian et al. 2018; Shaikh et al. 2018). Algorithms and protocols are meant to standardize care and help clinicians make evidence-based decisions. Theoretically, these guidelines should help facilitate equitable resource allocation by decreasing practitioners' cognitive load and implicit bias to help patients get what they need. But when the "evidence" is based in poor science and not considered in sociohistorical context, the fruits of racism may be borne—regardless of individual clinician intent (Vyas et al. 2020). For example, the American Heart Association Heart Failure Risk Score assigns additional points to non-Black patients (Peterson et al. 2010). This means that Black patients may inherently be assigned a lower score, implying less risk of a bad outcome, and thus guideline-compliant clinicians may systematically assign fewer resources (e.g., connection to cardiology specialists) to Black patients (Eberly et al. 2019). What is the scientific reason for Blacks being assigned a lower score for heart failure?[7] Modern science is clear that race and ethnicity are social constructions[8] (AAPA 2019; Maglo et al. 2016). It is vital to systematically collect race and ethnicity data in medical research, as it helps demonstrate when, where, and how disparities are present. But researchers and clinicians must also interrogate the nuanced and complex impact of race- and/or ethnicity-based risk determination and resource allocation (Chap. 15), else miss the truth: Race and ethnicity may function as proxies for the root variables of racism and ethnocentrism. If the research methods are not sound and underlying risk is overlooked, clinicians can perpetuate disparity.

---

[7] This does not mean that race and ethnicity data should not be collected. It means that when a difference appears to be related to race and/or ethnicity, the responsible and critical researcher and/or clinician should examine the implications and investigate–with an accurate sociohistorical context–what undergirds that apparent association. Moreover, singular studies that demonstrate race- and/or ethnicity-based outcomes should be replicated and findings need to be externally validated prior to widespread adoption. Good science demands this.

[8] To be clear, this does not mean that "race" is not real. Social constructs, like gender and race, are real and deeply impact lived experiences. These constructs intermingle with the physical body to impact health. Behaviors, including institutionalized systems like racism, can be changed to cease inequitable impacts on bodies.

14.2.3 Contemporary Health Care and People of Color with a Trafficking Experience

Affordability Access to health care is an important factor in the health, well-being, and ability of people to heal and recover. The ability to access health care has multiple driving factors, including "affordability." Because the US system of access is based on health insurance, and health insurance is not yet universal here, those with limited health insurance or lacking it completely may go without. Health insurance is often tied to employment status, but many who are employed still lack health insurance. This limits such persons' ability to meaningfully engage with preventative medicine and increases their risk of catastrophic illness and medical bankruptcy.

People of color are disproportionately impacted by this paradigm of healthcare "access" and hence are disproportionately among those who are under- or uninsured, limiting their ability to afford health care (Racial 2017). For example, Black and Brown[9] bodies disproportionately comprise inmates in prisons (Racial 2016); many are incarcerated for nonviolent crimes like drug possession, and sentencing is well documented as privileging White defendants (Spohn & Cederblom 1991; Crawford et al. 1998). Obtaining a job after prison release or on parole can be difficult (Pager 2003), and many jobs available to people with criminal records do not offer health insurance. The Affordable Care Act (ACA) of 2010 made some steps to increase the number of those covered by insurance (about 20 million more people), but the subsequent executive administration chipped away at the content of ACA legislation. Among those not covered are people in states that decline to fully participate in health insurance coverage expansion and persons without immigration documentation; in 2017, most of the uninsured were people of color and lived in the South (Berchik 2018).

People of color are also disproportionately recognized among those with a trafficking experience (Banks and Kyckelhahn 2011). Given that the general population struggles to afford health care, it is not surprising that cost is a barrier to healthcare access for people with a trafficking experience (Chisolm-Straker et al. 2016; Chisolm-Straker et al. 2019). Still, the literature indicates that people with a trafficking experience do access healthcare services while in their trafficking situation, and many visit emergency departments and primary care settings for a variety of acute or chronic conditions (Baldwin et al. 2011; Chisolm-Straker et al. 2016; Chisolm-Straker et al. 2019; Lederer and Wetzel 2014). And while there is little prevalence data available on human trafficking-related mortality rates, empiric data related to health indicate that factors such as unsafe working conditions and infectious diseases are associated with labor and sex trafficking (Zimmerman and Kiss 2017).

Acceptability In light of the historical atrocities committed against people of color in the name of medical research, healthcare advancement, and "progress," and in

---

[9] Here refers to Latinx folks.

light of continued health disparities along racial and ethnic lines, anti-trafficking workers and healthcare specialists must consider how acceptable the healthcare field is to persons of color with a trafficking experience. Given their vulnerabilities in xenophobic and racist systems, many people of color (including immigrants of color) regardless of trafficking experience have a tenuous relationship with the field of Western health care. At the individual level, present-day patients still struggle to find exceptions to the historical reality. For example, health facilities do not uniformly and consistently adhere to the National Standards for Culturally and Linguistically Appropriate Services in Health and Health Care. They are not reliably linguistically or culturally relevant, respectful, competent, or humble. Why and how should a patient trust a clinician with whom they cannot even communicate?

Furthermore, implicit bias, as a by-product of systemic racism and pervasive racist ideology, can negatively impact the care of patients. The majority of US hospitals' leadership (e.g., chief executive officers, board members, managers) is White (Livingston 2018). And White doctors, who make up 75% of the physician workforce (AMA 2010), commonly hold an anti-Black bias[10] (Blair et al. 2014; Green et al. 2007; Nosek et al. 2007; Penner et al. 2010; Sabin et al. 2009), which can impact patient satisfaction and patient–practitioner communication (Cooper et al. 2012; Hagiwara et al. 2013). While more and better research is needed to determine if and how these outcomes equate to tangible health outcomes for patients of color (Chisolm-Straker and Straker 2017), if patients avoid clinicians to avoid experiencing discrimination in health care, existing health conditions can be exacerbated. This phenomenon of avoiding health care even when needed has been demonstrated in transgender and nonbinary populations, for example. Based on stories or experiences of previous negative experiences (e.g., verbal harassment, mocking, assault) with healthcare practitioners (Chisolm-Straker et al. 2017; Samuels et al. 2018), 23% of trans and nonbinary people surveyed in 2015 reported avoiding healthcare settings (James et al. 2016). But avoidance of care does not mean health care is not needed: For example, 0.3% of the general population lives with HIV. Among the trans and nonbinary people surveyed, 1.4% live with HIV; oppressed intersecting identities and experiences compound risk such that 19% of Black trans women reported living with HIV (James et al. 2016). Finding health care to be an historical and continued place of harm, it is logical that many people of color present inconsistently, late or not at all for needed health care.

Exacerbating a person's experience of complex trauma with trafficking is their experience as a body of color in the US. Beyond the instilled fear of authority figures, including healthcare practitioners, traffickers of people of color benefit from the US's long history of racist structures to aid in control of their "workers" (Chap. 13). History has demonstrated that health care is not and has never been a uniformly safe space for people of color. Patients of color may not enter healthcare spaces with a trusting spirit—they may have more reasons to expect poor treatment and

---

[10] Much of the implicit bias research only explores the Black–White relationship, so the data on implicit bias are limited.

worsened health conditions than evidence to the contrary. Price et al. (2019) found that some patients with a trafficking experience (regardless of race) may exhibit a "distrustful" attitude; clinical care teams may struggle to "reach" these patients and connect them to useful services and provide relevant care (Shandro et al. 2016). The archetype of a docile, subservient, grateful "victim" may not be many trafficking survivors' clinical presentations. Trafficking-untrained and US-history naïve clinicians may not appreciate that apparent "distrust" of the care team does not rule out a patient's survival of exploitation, abuse, or trafficking.

14.2.4 Health Care Today as an Exploitative Workplace

Health care is not simply a potentially complicated avenue or conduit to services for trafficked persons. It is also the trafficker or exploiter for many. From 2007 to 2017, the National Human Trafficking Hotline received information about 64 potential labor trafficking cases (and 70 labor exploitation cases[11]) in the field of health care (National Human Trafficking Hotline, 2018). Specifically, concerns were expressed about, for, or by workers in residential nursing homes, occupational health facilities, and home care workers (Polaris 2018). The exploitation of workers in health care is also highlighted by the "Ain't I a Woman?" (AIW) campaign. Named for the famous question posed by Sojourner Truth at an 1851 Women's Rights Convention, the AIW campaign was started by a group of garment workers fighting for their rights while working for DKNY. These women were mostly immigrants of color, were paid less than minimum wage, and worked 70–100 hours a week—more than twice what is traditionally called "full time" in the USA—without overtime pay (AIW n.d.; Ahn 2020). The campaign now includes other industries. In New York, home health aides (HHA) work 24 consecutive hours, providing care for elderly and infirm persons, but only receive 13 hours of pay. The aides are mostly immigrant women and women of color (AIW n.d.; Ahn 2020). The workers fought back in court and were winning. In response, the New York State Department of Labor issued an emergency order to allow the practice of unpaid labor to continue. AIW fought the order in the New York Supreme Court and won again; still, the practice is rampant, and home care agencies and insurance companies continue to only pay. HHA for 13 of their 24 consecutive hours worked. AIW is now fighting to prohibit the 24-hour workday altogether (Ahn 2020; see Fig. 14.1).

The home care workers of New York are not unique in their experience of institutionally sanctioned exploitation; until 2015 and across the US, home care

---

[11] "Polaris was not able to provide demographic or detailed information on the individual potential victims of trafficking related to these cases. Cases reference situations of trafficking which may involve one or more potential victims, and data collection on uniquely identifiable likely victims of trafficking was not conducted until January 2015." Electronic communication from Elizabeth Gerrior, Associate Director of Data Quality, Learning, Innovation, and Data Systems Program of Polaris. December 7, 2020.

Fig. 14.1 Sabina Lino and other home health aides protest unjust labor and compensation at a rally near Wall Street in New York City, December 11, 2019. (Photograph by Makini Chisolm-Straker)

workers—who are disproportionately Black, immigrants, women (Chap. 4), and older than the general population—were *explicitly* excluded from federal wage and hour protections (Paraprofessional Healthcare Institute 2017; US Census Bureau 2016; American Public Health Association, 2020). Their exclusion from the Fair Labor Standards Act of 1935 was based in an effort to maintain Jim Crow employment practices, which facilitated economic control over workers of color (Chap. 9). They are not allowed to form unions in many states, and in 2014, almost a quarter of home care workers were uninsured, even though they were providing healthcare service themselves (Rowe et al. 2016; Zoeckler et al. 2020).

In another example of healthcare workers' exploitation (specifically trafficking), 577 Filipino nurses and 13 Filipino medical technicians reported being forced to work at an upstate New York hospital under threat of debt owed ($20,000 for each nurse) and possible deportation (Bump 2019). A similar suit was tried and found in favor of 200 Filipino nurses working at Sentosa nursing homes in New York (Michelen 2019; Roy 2019). In the late 1800s, the USA colonized the Philippines (previously colonized by Spain) and established nursing schools there (Bump 2019). For many, nursing school represents a way out of poverty, even if it ultimately means moving to the US. There is a clear power differential when a worker's immigration status is tied to their employer (Chaps. 3 and 9) (Littenberg and Baldwin 2017). With the Philippines being a leading "exporter" of nurses to the US, how many other healthcare workers are being exploited or trafficked?

14.3   Conclusion

For centuries, bodies of color in the USA have been used as commodities for consumption. People trafficked for labor or sex today are similarly used for the profit of others. While US health care in the 21st century is often billed as a safe space for people to seek help, the field's historical reality has yielded the distrust of communities of color;[12] clinicians were as flawed as their contemporaries. That truth has continued in more nuanced ways, and racial disparities in health persist with the endurance of racist structures. US health care has a long legacy of earned distrust and has cultivated well-founded fear of medical researchers and clinicians among communities of color.

Recommendations
1. *US historical truth-telling must start in primary education to begin to unravel systemic and systematic racism.* Telling the truth is the root of a meaningful apology and the beginning of just action.
2. *Collectively planned, evidence-based, historically rooted public health measures, that comprehensively include diverse systems such as the educational and criminal "justice" systems, can be enacted to eliminate functional apart-*

---

[12] For more reading on medical and research abuses of Blacks, see Prather et al. (2018).

heid in the US. Health disparities based on race and ethnicity demonstrate that apartheid, though not legally enforced, continues today. Overall, the health of one group (Whites) remains privileged above all others.

3. *More clinicians of color are needed to diminish the impact of practitioners' implicit bias and centuries of medical abuse of people of color; more support (fiscal and otherwise) of historically Black medical schools, and medical, physician assistant, and nursing students of color is overdue.* This, in and of itself, will not resolve health disparities, but it may make healthcare spaces more welcoming to patients of color, including those with a trafficking experience. Patients cannot benefit from health care that they do not access.

4. *More sociohistorically aware researchers need to engage communities of color in ethical medical research.* Much of the "evidence" used to guide clinical action is rooted in studies that did not include people of color, included only one group of color, or one sub-group of color (Chap. 10). Inclusive, ethical, and historically conscious medical research is a necessary step in earning the trust of people of color,[13] so that the "evidence-based" care they receive can be relevant to them.

5. *All clinicians need to be taught, in professional school, about the long history of commonplace, legal, and normalized abuse of bodies of color by medical research and healthcare professionals.* Clinicians need to understand that their "good intentions" now do not outweigh the failure of the field for centuries; such knowledge can help contextualize racially and/or ethnically discordant patient–practitioner experiences in particular.

6. *Medical and pharmaceutical research and care teams (regardless of "not-for-profit" status) benefitting from the use of ill-gotten knowledge or resources, gained via the abuse of people of color, should pay a "tax."* For example, researchers using the HeLa cell line could contribute to a scholarship fund for the education of Black female medical students. Minnesota Mayo Clinic care could be free for the descendants of the original keepers of the land (e.g., the Santee and Southern Anishinaabe), as it is founded on their stolen homeland.

7. *Guaranteeing health care for all who live in the US can decrease the racial and ethnic disparities around the affordability of, and thus access to, care.* Improving access is an important step toward decreasing bad health outcomes in groups of oppressed peoples.

8. *Healthcare facilities should offer free language interpreters (in-person, video, and/or telephonic) for patients, and partner with local community-based organizations to best serve their patient population.* This can improve patients' willingness and ability to approach healthcare practitioners and better access health (medical and psychiatric) professionals' knowledge and skills.

9. *Medical guidelines that include race/ethnicity to determine risk and resource allocation should be based in rigorous, reproducible investigative science; responsible guideline implementation requires contextual comprehension and*

---

[13] See Warren et al. (2020), for more on earning trust in communities of color.

reevaluation. Race and ethnicity data must be systematically collected in an effort to understand when, where, and how disparities exist and persist. Until justice and equity prevail, race in medicine will remain a proxy for the consequences of racism and ethnicity a proxy for the consequences of ethnocentrism.

10. *Health facilities' board and corporation members should reflect the racial and ethnic makeup of the patient population served.* In this way, healthcare leadership may be more attuned to the clinical concerns and needs, and social milieu of the community served to improve care delivered.

11. *All healthcare workers should be fairly compensated for the time they work;* as in many other industries, healthcare workers whose shifts are at least 8 hours should have a scheduled, paid break. The people who take care of other people deserve to be well-rested and fed.

12. *More work and research are needed to understand the dangerous, modern push–pull factors that facilitate trafficking scenarios in health care*, including in former and current US colonies and territories. Labor-based immigration should not be bound to a single employer. This may endow workers with more confidence to speak up about abuses and exploitation and deter employers from engaging in such behaviors.

Acknowledgments   Special thanks to Iris Chung and Cynthia Pong for reviewing this chapter.

References

Ahn, S. (2020). *Electronic communication*.

Ain't I a Woman (AIW) Campaign. (n.d.). https://www.aintiawoman.org/. Accessed 21 June 2020.

Alabama. (1888-90). *Report of the Alabama Insane Hospital, 1888–90*. p. 11.

American Association of Physical Anthropologists. (2019). *AAPA statement on race & racism*

American Public Health Association. (2020). Supporting and Sustaining the Home Care Workforce to Meet the Growing Need for Long-Term Care. Policy Statement Number:202011. https://apha. org/Policies-and-Advocacy/Public-Health-Policy-Statements/Policy-Database/2021/01/13/ Supporting-and-Sustaining-the-Home-Care-Workforce Accessed on 13 March 2021.

Association of American Medical Colleges. (2010). *Diversity in the physician workforce: Facts & figures 2010* (p. 11). Washington, DC: Association of American Medical Colleges.

Atlanta. (1885). *Annual Reports, 1885*, p. 54.

Atlanta Constitution. (1889).

Baldwin, S. B., Eisenman, D. P., Sayles, J. N., et al. (2011). Identification of human trafficking victims in health care settings. *Health and Human Rights, 13*(1), E36–E49. PMid: 22772961.

Berchik, E. (2018). *Most uninsured were working-age adults*. United States Census Bureau. Retrieved 18 October 2020, from https://www.census.gov/library/stories/2018/09/who-are-the-uninsured.html

Blair, I. V., Steiner, J. F., Hanratty, R., Price, D. W., Fairclough, D. L., Daughtery, S. L., Bronsert, M., Magid, D. J., & Havranek, E. P. (2014). An investigation of associations between clinicians' ethnic or racial bias and hypertension treatment, medication adherence and blood pressure control. *Journal of General Internal Medicine, 29*(7), 987–96.

Bump, B. (2019). Lawsuit: Albany Med's Filipino nursing program violates human trafficking law. *Times Union*. Available at: https://www.timesunion.com/news/article/Lawsuit-Albany-Med-s-Filipino-nursing-program-14521113.php. Accessed 21 June 2020.

Centers for Disease Control and Prevention (CDC). (2013). *U.S. public health service syphilis study at Tuskegee*.

Centers for Disease Control and Prevention (CDC). (2019). *High school youth risk behavior survey data*. Available at https://nccd.cdc.gov/youthonline.

Centers for Disease Control and Prevention (CDC). (2020). *COVID-19 in racial and ethnic minority groups*. 2020. Available at: https://www.cdc.gov/coronavirus/2019-ncov/need-extra-precautions/racial-ethnic-minorities.html. Accessed 20 June 20, 2020.

Charlotte Observer. (1990). Monday, February 12, 1990.

Chisolm-Straker, M., Baldwin, S., Gaïgbé-Togbé, B., Ndukwe, N., Johnson, P., & Richardson, L. (2016). Health care and human trafficking: We are seeing the unseen. *Journal of Health Care for the Poor and Underserved, 27*(3), 1220–1233.

Chisolm-Straker, M., Jardine, L., Bennouna, C., Morency-Brassard, N., Coy, L., Egemba, M. O., & Shearer, P. L. (2017). Transgender and gender nonconforming in emergency departments: A qualitative report of patient experiences. *Transgender Health, 2*(1), 8–16. https://doi.org/10.1089/trgh.2016.0026.

Chisolm-Straker, M., Miller, C. L., Duke, G., & Stoklosa, H. (2019). A framework for the development of healthcare provider education programs on human trafficking part two: Survivors. *Journal of Human Trafficking, 6*(4), 410–424. https://doi.org/10.1080/23322705.2019.1635333.

Chisolm-Straker M, Straker H. (2017). Implicit bias in US medicine: complex findings and incomplete conclusions. *International Journal of Human Rights in Healthcare*, 10(1), 43–55.

Cimons, M. (1996, June 17). CDC says it erred in measles study, *Los Angeles Times*, available at: http://articles.latimes.com/1996-06-17/news/mn-15871_1_measles-vaccine. Accessed 21 Nov 2015.

Cobb, W. M. (1948). *Progress and portents for the Negro in medicine*. New York: National Association for the Advancement of Colored People.

Cooper, L. A., Roter, D. L., Carson, K. A., Beach, M. C., Sabin, J. A., Greenwald, A. G., & Inui, T. S. (2012). The associations of clinicians' implicit attitudes about race with medical visit communication and patient ratings of interpersonal care. *American Journal of Public Health, 102*(5), 979–987. https://doi.org/10.2105/AJPH.2011.300558.

Crawford, C., Chiricos, T., & Kleck, G. (1998). Race, racial threat, and sentencing of habitual offenders. *Criminology, 36*, 481–511.

Curry, R. O., & Cowden, J. D. (1972). *Slavery in America: Theodore Weld's American Slavery As It Is*. Itasca: F. E. Peacock. OCLC 699102217.

Curtis, J. L. (1971). *Blacks, medical schools, and society*. Ann Arbor: The University of Michigan Press.

Duffy, T. P. (2011). The Flexner Report–100 years later. *The Yale Journal of Biology and Medicine, 84*(3), 269–276.

Dunbar-Ortiz, R. (2014). *An Indigenous people's history of the United States*. Boston: Beacon Press.

Duren Banks and Tracey Kyckelhahn. (2011). *Characteristics of suspected human trafficking incidents, 2008–2010, 1*. Washington, DC: Bureau of Justice Statistics, U.S. Department of Justice, 2011, 1, accessed October 12, 2012, http://www.bjs.gov/content/pub/pdf/cshti0810.pdf.

Eberly, L. A., Richterman, A., Beckett, A. G., et al. (2019). Identification of racial inequities in access to specialized inpatient heart failure care at an academic medical center. *Circulation. Heart Failure, 12*(11), e006214–e006214.

Eneanya, N. D., Yang, W., & Reese, P. P. (2019). Reconsidering the consequences of using race to estimate kidney function. *JAMA, 322*, 113–114.

Etheridge, R., & Shuck-Hall, S. M. (Eds.). (2009). *Mapping the Mississippian shatter zone: The colonial Indian slave trade and regional instability in the American South*. Lincoln: University of Nebraska Press.

Flexner, A. (1910). *Medical education in the United States and Canada: Report carnegie to the foundation for the advancement of science*. Bulletin Number Four 1910, New York, NY

Gallay, A. (2002). *The Indian slave trade: The rise of the English empire in the American South, 1670–1717*. New Haven: Yale University Press.

Gallay, A. (Ed.). (2009). *Indian slavery in colonial America*. Lincoln: University of Nebraska Press.

Garely, A. D., & Mann, W. J. (2020). Urogenital tract fistulas in women. In L. Brubaker & K. Eckler (Eds.), *UpToDate*. Waltham: UpToDate. Accessed 19 Jun 2020.

Georgia. (1890). *Report of the Institution for the Deaf and Dumb, 1890*, 20–21.

Gibson, J. W., & Crogman, W. H. (1902). Quoting Mrs. Hale. In *Progress of a race or the remarkable advancement of the American Negro* (rev ed., pp. 480–481). Atlanta: JL Nichols & Co.

Green, A. R., Carney, D. R., Pallin, D. J., Ngo, L. H., Raymond, K. L., Iezzoni, L. I., & Banaji, M. R. (2007). Implicit bias among physicians and its prediction of thrombolysis decisions for Black and White patients. *Journal of General Internal Medicine, 22*(9), 1231–1238.

Grobman, W. A., Lai, Y., Landon, M. B., et al. (2007). Development of a nomogram for prediction of vaginal birth after cesarean delivery. *Obstetrics and Gynecology, 109*, 806–812.

Gurr, B. (2012). The failures and possibilities of a human rights approach to secure Native American women's reproductive justice. *Societies Without Borders, 7*(1), 1–28.

Hagiwara, N., Penner, L. A., Gonzalez, R., Eggly, S., Dovidio, J. F., Gaertner, S. L., West, T., & Albrecht, T. L. (2013). Racial attitudes, physician-patient talk time ratio, and adherence in racially discordant medical interactions. *Social Science & Medicine, 87*, 123–131. https://doi.org/10.1016/j.socscimed.2013.03.016.

Hansen, M. (2018). Hansen: After more than 150 years, the Mayo Clinic finally apologizes to a Nebraska tribe. *Live Well Nebraska*. Available at: https://www.omaha.com/livewellnebraska/hansen-after-more-than-150-years-the-mayo-clinic-finally-apologizes-to-a-nebraska-tribe/article_9adcf8e0-334b-5c6a-92ca-2c40d9602372.html. Accessed 7 Jul 2020.

Harley, E. H. (2006). The forgotten history of defunct Black medical schools in the 19th and 20th centuries and the impact of the Flexner Report. *Journal of the National Medical Association, 98*(9), 1425–1429.

Harvey, J., Regenstein, M, & Jones, K. (2004). An assessment of the safety net in Atlanta, Georgia. *Urgent Matters*. Safety net assessment team, The George Washington University Medical Center, School of Public Health and Health Services, Department of Health Policy. Retrieved 28 October 2020 from https://publichealth.gwu.edu/departments/healthpolicy/DHP_Publications/pub_uploads/dhpPublication_3BA2E82E-5056-9D20-3DA098C4AD847F57.pdf

Hernandez, A. (1976). Chicanas and the issue of involuntary sterilization: Reforms needed to protect informed consent. *Chicana/o Latina/o Law Review, 3*(3), 1–35.

Indian Health Services. (2019, October 2019). *Disparities*. Available at: https://www.ihs.gov/newsroom/factsheets/disparities/. Accessed 20 Jun 2020.

Institute of Medicine (IOM). (2000). *America's health care safety net: Intact but endangered*. Washington, DC: National Academies Press.

Isenberg, N. (2016). *White Trash. The 400-year untold history of class in America*. New York: Penguin Books.

James, S. E., Herman, J. L., Rankin, S., Keisling, M., Mottet, L., & Anafi, M. (2016). *The Report of the 2015 U.S. Transgender Survey*. Washington, DC: National Center for Transgender Equality.

Johansen, B. (2001). Reprise/forced sterilizations: Native Americans and the "Last Gasp of Eugenics". In R. Lobo & S. Talbot (Eds.), *Native American voices: A reader* (2nd ed., pp. 212–217). Upper Saddle: Prentice Hall.

Johns Hopkins Medicine. (n.d.). Upholding the highest bioethical standards. In: *The Legacy of Henrietta Lacks*. Retrieved 28 October 2020 from: https://www.hopkinsmedicine.org/henriettalacks/upholding-the-highest-bioethical-standards.html

Kenny, S. C. (2010). 'A dictate of both interest and mercy'? Slave hospitals in the Antebellum South. *Journal of the History of Medicine and Allied Sciences, 65*(1), 1–47.

Kim, E. J., Kressin, N. R., Paasache-Orlow, M. K., Lopez, L., Rosen, J. E., Lin, M., & Hanchate, A. D. (2018). Racial/ethnic disparities among Asian Americans in inpatient acute myocardial infarction mortality in the United States. *BMC Health Services Research, 18*, 370.

Kowalsky, R. H., Rondini, A. C., & Platt, S. L. (2020). The case for removing race from the American Academy of Pediatrics clinical practice guideline for urinary tract infection in infants and young children with fever. *JAMA Pediatrics, 174*, 229–230.

Krugman, S. (1986). The Willowbrook hepatitis studies revisited: Ethical aspects. *Reviews of Infectious Diseases, 8*(1), 157–162. https://doi.org/10.1093/clinids/8.1.157.

Langer, E. (1964). Human experimentation: Cancer studies at Sloan-Kettering stir public debate on medical ethics. *Science, 143*(3606), 551–553. https://doi.org/10.1126/science.143.3606.551.

Langston, D. H. (2003). American Indian Women's activism in the 1960s and 1970s. *Hypatia, 18*(2), 114–132.

Lawrence, J. (2000). The Indian health service and the sterilization of Native American women. *American Indian Quarterly, 24*(3), 400–419.

Lederer, L., & Wetzel, C. (2014). The health consequences of sex trafficking and their implications for identifying victims in healthcare facilities. *Annals of Health Law, 23*(1), 61–91.

Levey, A. S., Stevens, L. A., Schmid, C. H., et al. (2009). A new equation to estimate glomerular filtration rate. *Annals of Internal Medicine, 150*, 604–612.

Littenberg, N., & Baldwin, S. (2017). The ignored exploitation: Labor trafficking in the United States. In S. Chisolm-Straker (Ed.), *Human trafficking is a public health issue, a paradigm expansion* (pp. 67–92). Cham: Springer.

Livingston, S. (2018). Racism still a problem in healthcare's C-suite. *Modern Healthcare*. Retrieved 28 October 2020 from: https://www.modernhealthcare.com/article/20180224/NEWS/180229948/racism-still-a-problem-in-healthcare-s-c-suite#:~:text=Hospital%20C%2Dsuites%20and%20boards,part%20of%20the%20patient%20population.&text=-Minorities%20represent%2011%25%20of%20executive,chief%20diversity%20officers%20are%20minorities

Madrigal v. Quilligan, No. 75-2057 (C.D. Cal., filed June 18, 1975)

Maglo, K. N., Mersha, T. B., & Martin, L. J. (2016). Population genomics and the statistical values of race: An interdisciplinary perspective on the biological classification of human populations and implications for clinical genetic epidemiological research. *Frontiers in Genetics, 7*, 22–22.

Michelen O. (2019). *200 Filipino Nurses Win Human Trafficking Lawsuit Against SentosaCare and its Owners*. Courtroomstrategy.com. Available at: https://courtroomstrategy.com/2019/10/200-filipino-nurses-win-human-trafficking-lawsuit-against-sentosacare-and-its-owners/. Accessed 21 Jun 2020.

Moore, C. L., Bomann, S., Daniels, B., et al. (2014). Derivation and validation of a clinical prediction rule for uncomplicated ureteral stone — The STONE score: Retrospective and prospective observational cohort studies. *BMJ, 348*, g2191–g2191.

National Archives. (2016). *African American records: Freedmen's bureau*. Available at: https://www.archives.gov/research/african-americans/freedmens-bureau. Accessed 21 Jun 2020.

National Human Trafficking Hotline. (2018). *Texas. [Online] national human trafficking hotline*. Available at: https://humantraffickinghotline.org/state/texas. Accessed 23 Dec 2019.

Nosek, B. A., Smyth, F. L., Devos, T., Lindner, N. M., Ranganath, K. A., Smith, C. T., et al. (2007). Pervasiveness and correlates of implicit attitudes and stereotypes. *European Review of Social Psychology, 18*, 36–88.

Pager, D. (2003). The mark of a criminal record. *American Sociological Review, 103*(March), 937–975. https://doi.org/10.1086/374403.

Paraprofessional Healthcare Institute. (2017). *U.S. home care workers: Key facts*. New York; 29 2017. Retrieved 21 October 2020 from https://phinational.org/resource/u-s-home-care-workers-key-facts/

Penner, L. A., Dovidio, J. F., West, T. V., Baertner, S. L., Albrecht, T. L., Dailey, R. K., & Markvoa, T. (2010). Aversive racism and medical interactions with Black patients: A field study. *Journal of Experimental Social Psychology, 46*(2), 436–440.

Peterson, P. N., Rumsfeld, J. S., Liang, L., et al. (2010). A validated risk score for in-hospital mortality in patients with heart failure from the American Heart Association Get with the Guidelines program. *Circulation. Cardiovascular Quality and Outcomes, 3*, 25–32.

Polaris. (2018). *On-ramps, intersections, and exit routes: A roadmap for systems and industries to prevent and disrupt human trafficking.* Available at: https://polarisproject.org/wp-content/uploads/2018/08/A-Roadmap-for-Systems-and-Industries-to-Prevent-and-Disrupt-Human-Trafficking-Health-Care.pdf Accessed 21 June 2020.

Prather, C., Fuller, T. R., Jeffries, W. L., IV, Marshall, K. J., Howell, A. V., Belyue-Umole, A., & King, W. (2018). Racism, African American women, and their sexual and reproductive health: A review of historical and contemporary evidence and implications for health equity. *Health Equity, 2,* 1. https://doi.org/10.1089/heq.2017.0045.

Price, G. N., & Darity, W. A., Jr. (2010). The economics of race and eugenic sterilization in North Carolina: 1958–1968. *Economics & Human Biology, 8*(2), 261–272.

Price, K., Nelson, B., & Macias-Konstantopoulos, W. (2019). Understanding health care access disparities among human trafficking survivors: Profiles of health care experiences, access, and engagement. *Journal of Interpersonal Violence, 28*(9), 1859–1885.

Project South. (2020). *Re: lack of medical care, unsafe work practices, and absence of adequate protection against COVID-19 for detained immigrants and employees alike at the Irwin county detention center.* Available at: https://projectsouth.org/wp-content/uploads/2020/09/OIG-ICDC-Complaint-1.pdf. Accessed 6 Oct 2020.

Rabinowitz, H. (1974). From exclusion to segregation: Health and welfare services for southern Blacks, 1865–1890. *Social Service Review, 48*(3), 327–354. Retrieved June 21, 2020, from www.jstor.org/stable/30015123.

Racial, S. H. (2017). Ethnic disparities in health insurance coverage: Dynamics of gaining and losing coverage over the life-course. *Population Research and Policy Review, 36*(2), 181–201.

Racial, N. A., & Ethnic Disparity in State Prisons. (2016). *The sentencing project.* Available at: https://www.sentencingproject.org/publications/color-of-justice-racial-and-ethnic-disparity-in-state-prisons/. Accessed 21 Jun 2020.

Ralston-Lewis, M. (2005). The continuing struggle against genocide: Indigenous Women's reproductive rights. *Wicazo Sa Review, 20*(1), 71–95.

Ramirez, I. (2020). *An ICE nurse revealed that a Georgia detention center is performing mass hysterectomies.* Refinery 29. Available at: https://www.refinery29.com/en-us/2020/09/10024657/ice-hysterectomies-immigration-whistleblower-project-south. Accessed 6 Oct 2020.

Randall, V. (1996). *Slavery, segregation and racism: Trusting the health care system ain't always easy! An African American perspective on bioethics.* St. Louis University: Public Law Review. Retrieved 21 October 2020 from http://academic.udayton.edu/health/05bioethics/slavery02.

Rao, P. S., Schaubel, D. E., Guidinger, M. K., et al. (2009). A comprehensive risk quantification score for deceased donor kidneys: The kidney donor risk index. *Transplantation, 88,* 231–236.

Report of the Commissioners of the Asylum to the County Court, reprinted in *Nashville Banner,* July 7, 1884.

Reséndez, A. (2016). *The other slavery: The uncovered story of Indian enslavement in America.* New York: First Mariner Books.

Rowe, J. W., Berkman, L., Fried, L., Fulmer, T., Jackson, J., Naylor, M., Novelli, W., Olshansky, J., & Stone, R. (2016). Preparing for better health and health care for an aging population: a vital 4 direction for health and health care. *NAM Perspectives.* Discussion Paper, National 5 Academy of Medicine, Washington, DC, https://doi.org/10.31478/201609n.

Roy, Y. (2019). Court: LI nursing home firm violated anti-human trafficking laws. *Newsday. com.* Available at: https://www.newsday.com/long-island/suffolk/sentosa-nursing-home-nurses-1.37091421. Accessed 21 June 2020.

Rushforth, B. (2012). *Bonds of alliance: Indigenous and atlantic slaveries in New France.* Chapel Hill: University of North Carolina Press.

Sabin, J. A., Nosek, B. A., Greenwald, A. G., & Rivara, F. P. (2009). Physicians' implicit and explicit attitudes about race by MD race, ethnicity, and gender. *Journal of Health Care for the Poor and Underserved, 20*(3), 896–913. https://doi.org/10.1353/hpu.0.0185.

Samuels, E. A., Tape, C., Garber, N., Bowman, S., & Choo, E. K. (2018). "Sometimes you feel like the freak show": A qualitative assessment of emergency care experiences among transgender and gender-nonconforming patients. *Ann Emerg Med, 71*(2), 170–182. https://doi.org/10.1016/j.annemergmed.2017.05.002. PMID: 28712604.

Satcher, D., Fryer, G. E. Jr., McCann, J., Troutman, A., Woolf, S. H., & Rust, G. (2005). What if we were equal? A comparison of the Black-White mortality gap in 1960 and 2000. *Health Affairs*, 242, 459–464.

Savitt, T. L. (1992). Abraham Flexner and the Black medical schools. In B. Baransky & N. Gevitz (Eds.), *Beyond Flexner: Medical education in the 20th century* (pp. 5–218). New York: Greenwood Press.

Shahian, D. M., Jacobs, J. P., Badhwar, V., et al. (2018). The Society of Thoracic Surgeons 2018 adult cardiac surgery risk models. 1. Background, design considerations, and model development. *The Annals of Thoracic Surgery, 105*, 1411–1418.

Shaikh, N., Hoberman, A., Hum, S. W., et al. (2018). Development and validation of a calculator for estimating the probability of urinary tract infection in young febrile children. *JAMA Pediatrics, 172*, 550–556.

Shandro, J., Chisolm-Straker, M., Duber, H. C., Findlay, S. L., Muñoz, J., Schmitz, G., Stanzer, M., Stoklosa, H., Wiener, D. E., & Wingkun, N. (2016). Human trafficking: a guide to identification and approach for the emergency physician. *Annals of Emergency Medicine, 68*(4), P501–P508.

Skloot, R. (2011). *The immortal life of Henrietta lacks*. Broadway Books. ISBN-10: 9781400052189.

Smith, A. (2005). *Conquest: Sexual violence and American Indian Genocide*. Cambridge, MA: South End Press.

Spohn, C., & Cederblom, J. (1991). Race and disparities in sentencing: A test of the liberation hypothesis. *Justice Quarterly, 8*, 305–327.

Synder, C. (2010). *Slavery in Indian Country: The changing face of captivity in early America*. Cambridge, MA: Harvard University Press.

Tennessee. (1875). *Report of the central Tennessee hospital for the insane for the two years ending January 1, 1875, p. 19.*

Tennessee. (1889-90). *Report of the Tennessee Industrial School, 1889–90, p. 26.*

Tennessee. (1889-91). *Report of the central Tennessee hospital for the insane, 1889–91, p. 14.*

Torpy, S. (2000). Native American women and coerced sterilization: On the trail of tears in the 1970s. *American Indian Culture and Research Journal, 24*(2), 1–22.

U.S. Department of Health and Human Services. (1985). *Report of the secretary's task force on Black and minority health.* Washington, DC: Government Print Office.

U.S. Department of Health and Human Services. (2013). *Environmental scan to identify the major research questions and metrics for monitoring the effects of the affordable care act on safety net hospitals.* Retrieved 28 October 2020 from: https://aspe.hhs.gov/report/environmental-scan-identify-major-research-questions-and-metrics-monitoring-effects-affordable-care-act-safety-net-hospitals/c-definition-safety-net-hospitals

United Nations. (1948). *Convention on the prevention and punishment of the crime of genocide.* Available at: https://www.un.org/en/genocideprevention/documents/atrocity-crimes/Doc.1_Convention%20on%20the%20Prevention%20and%20Punishment%20of%20the%20Crime%20of%20Genocide.pdf. Accessed 12 July 2020.

United States Census Bureau. (2016). *American community survey (ACS), sex by age by employment status for the population 16 years and over (White alone, not Hispanic or Latino).* https://factfinder.census.gov/bkmk/table/1.0/en/ACS/15_1YR/B23002H; analysis by PHI (July 19, 2017).

Unknown Author. (1890). Concerning negro sorcery in the United States. *Journal of American Folklore, 3*, 210.

Vasquez, T. (2020). Georgia doctor who forcibly sterilized detained women has been identified. *Prism.* Available at: https://www.prismreports.org/article/2020/9/15/exclusive-georgia-doctor-who-forcibly-sterilized-detained-women-has-been-identified?fbclid=IwAR3YaaaDDnlzQ0ouAsQhtKyxJltAydc_rXrEA4V7XVwsoRQb38PSI4_2PBo. Accessed 6 Oct 2020.

Virginia. (1875-76). *Report of the Central Lunatic Asylum, 1875–76, p. 8.*

Virginia. (1877). *Annual report of the Virginia eastern lunatic asylum for the year ending September 30, 1877*, p. 17.

Vyas, D. A., Eisenstein, L. G., & Jones, D. S. (2020). Hidden in plain sight—Reconsidering the use of race correction in clinical algorithms. *The New England Journal of Medicine, 383*(9), 874–882. https://doi.org/10.1056/NEJMms2004740.

Warren, R. C., Lachlan, F., Hodge, D. A., & Truog, R. D. (2020). Trustworthiness before Trust – COVID-19 vaccine trials and the Black community. *The New England Journal of Medicine, 383*(22), e121.

Warren, R. C., Clare, C. A., Villanueva, R., & Pinn, V. W. (2020a). In the interest of science or humanity: J. Marion Sims was wrong then and now! *Journal of the National Medical Association, 112*(2), 233–236. https://doi.org/10.1016/j.jnma.2020.01.002.

Washington, H. A. (2006). *Medical apartheid: The dark history of medical experimentation on Black Americans from colonial times to the present* (1st ed.). New York: Doubleday.

Weindling, P. J. (2004). *Nazi medicine and the Nuremberg trials: From medical war crimes to informed consent*. London: Palgrave Macmillan. https://doi.org/10.1057/9780230506053.

West, M. J., & Irvine, L. M. (2015). The eponymous Dr James Marion Sims MD, LLD (1813–1883). *Journal of Medical Biography, 23*(1), 35–45.

Zimmerman, C., & Kiss, L. (2017). Human trafficking and exploitation: A global health concern. *PLoS Medicine, 14*(11), e1002437. https://doi.org/10.1371/journal.pmed.1002437.

Zoeckler, J., Sokas, R. K., Hagopian, A., Morrissey, M. B., Coto-Batres, R., Tsui, E. K., & Muramatsu, N. (2020). Supporting and sustaining the home care workforce to meet the growing need for long-term care. *American Public Health Association Policy Proposal.*

Chapter 15
Health Care as a Right for the Human Trafficked

Rueben C. Warren

15.1 Introduction

The 13th Amendment to the US Constitution prohibits slavery, yet in many ways, modern-day enslavement remains. In the twenty-first century, one form of modern-day slavery is human trafficking (National Human Trafficking Hotline 2018).The Trafficking Victims Protection Act of 2000 (TVPA), as amended (22 U.S.C. § 7102), defines "severe forms of trafficking in persons" as:

- *Sex trafficking*: the recruitment, harboring, transportation, provision, obtaining, patronizing, or soliciting of a person for the purpose of a commercial sex act, in which the commercial sex act is induced by force, fraud, or coercion, or in which the person induced to perform such act has not attained 18 years of age; (or)
- *Labor trafficking*: the recruitment, harboring, transportation, provision, or obtaining of a person for labor or services, with force, fraud, or coercion for the purpose of subjection to involuntary servitude, peonage, debt bondage, or slavery.

This chapter discusses the disparity in health care for the "privileged," or those who have financial and geographic access to available health care and find that health care acceptable, and the "trafficked," a specific subset of those who do not. *Available* simply means that health care exists. *Accessible* means that health care is physically and financially within reach. *Acceptable* refers to health care being pleasing, satisfactory, agreeable, welcomed, and/or meeting minimal needs (Warren 1999). The "trafficked" are those persons directly impacted by labor and/or sex trafficking; these impacts may compromise their ability to receive high-quality health care that is available, accessible, and acceptable, or their ability to receive health care at all.

R. C. Warren (✉)
National Center for Bioethics in Research and Health Care at Tuskegee University,
Tuskegee, AL, USA
e-mail: rwarren@tuskegee.edu

© Springer Nature Switzerland AG 2021   279
M. Chisolm-Straker, K. Chon (eds.), *The Historical Roots of Human Trafficking*,
https://doi.org/10.1007/978-3-030-70675-3_15

"Health" and "health care" are terms interchangeably used, but they are very different constructs. According to the World Health Organization (WHO) health is, "a state of complete physical, mental and social well-being and not merely the absence of disease or infirmity" (WHO 2021) (Chap. 17). Health can also be described as "a dynamic relationship, a synergistic interplay between physical, social, psychological and spiritual elements that create the well-being of individuals and/or groups in their physical and social environment" (Warren 1999). Using a description rather than a definition of health allows for a broader array of considerations in determining outcome measures to quantify and improve individual and population health. Health care is an umbrella term that encompasses health services, procedures, and/or interventions. Health care combines health services and health education, which may go beyond specific health concerns, and can be conducted by nonclinicians. *Health disparities* are a term used to describe population-based health differences (Braveman 2006). Braveman defines health disparities as "systematic, potentially avoidable differences in health—or in the major socially determined influences on health—between groups of people who have different relative positions in social hierarchies according to wealth, power, or prestige" (Braveman 2006).

15.2   Discussion

15.2.1   Health Disparities of the United States

The US Is Worse off, Overall

The health status of people in the United States falls far behind other industrialized countries, even though the United States spends more money on medical care than any other peer country. For example, in 2013, the US infant mortality rate (IMR) ranked 51st internationally, comparable to Croatia, despite an almost three-fold difference in GDP per capita (the United States has the higher per capita GDP). Another way to conceptualize the magnitude of the infant mortality disadvantage is to consider that the US IMR is about 3 deaths per 1000 greater than in Scandinavian countries. Aggregating 4 million annual US births and taking a standard value of life estimate of $7 million USD (Viscusi and Aldy 2003) suggests that reducing the US IMR to that of Scandinavian countries would cost about $84 billion USD annually. By this metric, it would cost up to $21,000 per live birth to lower the US IMR to the IMR in Scandinavia (Chen et al. 2016).

Disparities in Healthcare Affordability

Within the United States, some groups have less access to health care, due to cost. Depending on legislation and federal leadership, that access decreases or increases. For example, the Affordable Care Act (ACA) of 2010 increased healthcare coverage for approximately 20 million people through a variety of mechanisms, though in 2015, more than 25 million US residents still were not covered (Serakos and Wolfe 2016). Until 2017, the United States had been decreasing the number of uninsured children since 2008 (Alker and Pham 2018). In a recent survey, the number of uninsured children in the United States increased almost immediately with a change in federal government leadership: According to the US Census Bureau American Community Survey, in 2017 children's uninsured rate in the United States significantly increased from 4.7 percent in 2016 to 5 percent in 2017—a 0.3 percent increase in only one year. That means the number of uninsured children increased by approximately 276,000. For children in states that declined to expand Medicaid to parents and other low-income adults, uninsured rates of children increased at nearly triple the rate than that of states that did expand Medicaid (Alker and Pham 2018). Overall, most of the uninsured in 2017 were people of color, and the uninsured were concentrated in the South (Berchik 2018).

Race-Based Disparities

The United States' deep-rooted patterns of inequities and disparities (Chap. 14) are exemplified in the commodification of enslaved Black women's childbearing and physicians' investment in serving the interests of slave-owners. Even certain medical specialties, such as obstetrics and gynecology, owe a debt to enslaved Black women. The abuse of the bodies of Black women, in particular, enabled the advancement of science, biomedical research, and the technology of health care. For example, during the 1830s through 1880s, Marion J. Sims, often referred to as the "Father of Gynecology," *purchased* enslaved Black women and performed numerous surgeries without anesthesia, sometimes twenty to thirty times, to correct vesicovaginal fistulae[1] (Warren et al. 2020). It is disappointing to learn that in the twenty-first century, there remain persons who justify Sims' barbaric behavior under the guise of improving surgical innovation (Warren et al. 2020). The legacies of the acceptability of Black enslavement are embedded in structural racism that accounts, in part, for the continuation of Black-White health disparities. For example, in 2017, African Americans had over twice the sudden infant death syndrome mortality rate as non-Hispanic[2] Whites. Also, in 2017, African American mothers were 2.3 times more likely, than non-Hispanic Whites, to receive late or no prenatal care (Greenwood et al. 2020). African Americans have 2.3 times the infant mortality rate as non-Hispanic Whites and African-American infants are 3.8 times as likely to die from complications related to low birthweight as compared to non-Hispanic White infants (Chen et al. 2016). The examples abound.

---

[1] This is an abnormal communication between the bladder and the vagina.

[2] Where the term "Hispanic" is used, rather than the non-Eurocentric and more inclusive "Latinx," it reflects the term used by the cited source.

Health Disparities Are Rooted in the Hierarchy of Valued Lives

As Braveman points out that health disparities are based on hierarchies, the question is raised, is health care a right or a privilege? In 1985, in the Report of the Secretary's Task Force on Black and Minority Health, then Secretary of the U.S Department of Health and Human Services, Margret Heckler wrote,

> [T]here was a continuing disparity in the burden of death and illness experienced by African American and other minority Americans as compared with our nation as a whole. That disparity has existed ever since accurate Federal recordkeeping began more than a generation ago, and although our health charts do itemize steady gains in the health of minority Americans, the stubborn disparity remained … an affront to both our ideals and to the ongoing genius of American medicine (US Department of Health and Human Services 1985).

That report also coined the term *excess deaths*, which are the number of plausibly preventable deaths that occur in the Black population, if using the death rate of non-Hispanic White counterparts as a baseline. In 1985, there were almost 60,000 excess deaths reported in the Black population. These excess deaths were calculated using the sex- and age-adjusted death rate of non-Hispanic White counterparts. In 2005, the reported number of excess deaths *rose* to 83,000 (Satcher 2005). If Black lives were valued, these health disparities would be positively correlated with access to health care; ironically, they are not.

15.2.2 Early Black Experiences with Western "Health Care"

Western health care evolved from an apprenticeship trade to an evidence-based profession during the twentieth century (Flexner 1910; Duffy 2011). Population health improvements and advancement of health care occurred because of human subjects' research and scientific discovery. However, some of the most horrific and inhuman treatments of people have been due to human subjects research targeting vulnerable populations. Unethical research traces back to the African enslavement in North America when devaluing and abusing Black bodies were the norms (Jones 1993; Reverby 2009; Katz and Warren 2011). Three major occurrences set forth the context for abuse and enslavement in the U.S: (1) the Middle Passage, (2) chattel slavery, and (3) the Eugenics Movement:

1. The Middle Passage involved the transport of captured Africans, who were primarily from West Africa, West Central Africa, and Southeastern Africa to the Americas (including the Caribbean). The European countries of Portugal, England, Spain, France, the Netherlands, Denmark–Norway, Sweden, and Brandenburg, as well as White traders from Brazil and North America, participated in the trading of human cargo, which diminished the humanity of people of African descent. Even before the sea voyage, large numbers of Africans died during the process of capture and transport from the land to the ships. And then, approximately 15% of enslaved Africans died at sea. The total number of African

deaths directly attributable to the Middle Passage voyage has been estimated at up to two million (Appian and Gates 1999).

2. Chattel slavery (Chap. 9) was the (legal) owning of human beings as property to be bought, sold, given, and inherited. In this context, the enslaved persons had no personal freedom nor recognized rights to decide the direction of their own lives. While chattel slavery may have developed before the Middle Passage and enslavement in the Americas, its expansion, based on race, is unique to the Western hemisphere with Whites as the slavers.

    Labor, as punishment, was also used to pay for a crime. In his book, "Slavery by Another Name," Blackmon documents how thousands of African Americans were forced back (after Emancipation) into exploitative labor, called the chain gangs. These were sanctioned by the judicial and legislative system for fabricated crimes such as loitering or vagrancy. This form of forced labor was driven by the loss of Black slave labor after the Civil War which ended US chattel slavery (Blackmon 2008). Similar exploitation continues due to the 13th Amendment loophole that allows for unpaid (Chap. 9) labor as a form of punishment.

3. Eugenics is a scientific and social movement that ascribes human behavior to genetic makeup, which supported social policies to maintain racial "hygiene." This bigoted philosophy originated in the 1880s and is rooted in the biological determinist ideas of Sir Francis Galton. Galton studied the "inheritence of intelligence," (Bramwell 1948) which he concluded was biologically determined (Galton 1869; Galton 1883). Early proponents of eugenics believed that, through selective breeding, the human species should direct its own evolution. The eugenicist tended to believe in the genetic superiority of Nordic, Germanic, and Anglo-Saxon peoples and supported strict immigration laws and anti-miscegenation laws (Chap. 9). Eugenics was widely accepted in the US academic community, including the field of health care. In fact, by the early 1900s, eugenics was taught in institutions of higher education including medical schools (Lombardo & Dorr 2006). Some (White) lives held more value than others (people of color).

15.2.3   Historical Slavery's Echoes

Writers of the United States Constitution neither include nor address the rights of people of color, particularly Black people. The 13th Amendment abolished slavery by declaring it illegal, "except as a punishment for crime where of the party shall have been duly convicted" (enabling later forced labor through convict leasing and leading to present-day mass incarceration). But in the twenty-first century, the legacies of the historic Middle Passage, chattel slavery, and the Eugenics Movement, manifest in human trafficking. Human trafficking is a symptom of long-ago forged systems that promoted racism, sexism, xenophobia, classism, and other forms of bigotry. These are the root vulnerabilities of many of those trafficked in the United States. Identifying and dismantling these institutionalized barriers are essential if meeting the needs (including health care) of trafficked persons is to be achieved, and ultimately trafficking is to be finally abolished. An historical understanding is a necessary first step.

Twenty-first century human trafficking mirrors historic Black enslavement in the United States with, "the recruitment, transportation, transfer, harboring or receipt of persons, by means of threat or use of force" (TVPA 2000). Trafficked persons are coerced, defrauded, and/or deceived. Commonly employed, coercion may include threats of serious harm or physical restraint, psychological manipulation, document confiscation, and shame- and fear-inducing threats to share information or pictures with others, or report to authorities (Chap. 9). Historically, chattel slavery was of Blacks; centuries later and though illegal, trafficking disproportionately continues to impact people of color (Banks and Kyckelhahn 2011; Martin and Pierce 2014). Then, health care was used as another form of control of slaves; today, *if* health care is conceptualized as a right for all and society seeks to meaningfully address race-based health disparities, health care can be a point of opportunity for people directly impacted by trafficking, but only if it is affordable (Chap. 14), accessible, and acceptable.

15.2.4 Health Care in Historical Slavery

Healthcare services have been provided at varying levels of availability and accessibility for varying reasons. During the Middle Passage, captured Africans died from diseases due to crowding, poor sanitation, poor hygiene, and/or limited or no food; all these things contributed to diminished health during the voyage to North America. On the longer trips, more people died, because there was less food and water, and bad conditions during the journey were exacerbated. Diseases such as dysentery and scurvy were common. Many of the abducted were too depressed to eat. Beyond the deaths due to illnesses, many experienced physical harm and died from beatings if they did not follow the sailors' orders or if they seemed disobedient. Chattel slavery was the most inhuman treatment recorded in history. However, healthy slaves were more profitable than sick ones. Efforts were made to keep this human cargo alive and "healthy looking" to command the highest price at the slave auctions (Whelchel 2011). Still, the recovery down times from work and the cost for health care, however minimal, were not profitable for slaveholders. The profit motive of Whites slavers undergirded health care for enslaved people (Milano 2019).

The economy of the southern parts of the United States was largely agriculture based and enslaved Black people were the economic foundation for Southern growth and wealth. In theory, the Civil War ended unpaid Black labor in the South and Reconstruction attempted to align the country with the Constitution. During this period in US history, there was great expectation for a rebuilt country based on principles of social justice embedded in the US Constitution. Health care was provided, in large part, for Black people so that they could continue to work (Du Bois 1935). However, Black people had difficulty in accessing medical care, and when they did, the care was suboptimal. In fact, during the middle 1800s, 12 Black medi-cal schools were established to increase health care for Black people (Harley 2006). The Flexner Report of 1910, reviewed medical education for all medical schools, found them significantly wanting, and most of the schools—for Blacks and Whites—closed. The two Black medical schools that remained opened were Howard College of Medicine in Washington D.C. and Meharry Medical College in Nashville, Tennessee. For African Americans, many of the Flexner Report's proposed medical education improvements were never fully realized (Gasman and Sullivan 2012). The Civil Rights Movement, the War on Poverty, and other movements attempted to address many of the social injustices in the United States. And through legal slavery and all of these periods, human trafficking continued (though unnamed) and the healthcare needs of trafficked persons continued to go unmet, including the chance for resolution of their underlying trauma of being trafficked.

15.2.5   Somewhat Accessible but Still Unacceptable

The literature base about health care for trafficked persons is growing, and there is sufficient data to state that trafficked persons today are accessing healthcare ser-vices (Baldwin et al 2011; Lederer and Wetzel 2014; Chisolm-Straker et al. 2016). Based upon patient recall, most clinicians do not recognize patients as having a trafficking experience. So even though patients present for care, an important social history element (their trafficking experience) goes unaddressed. It is not yet stan-dard to screen or assess for a labor and/or sex trafficking experience in health care (Dols et al. 2019). Healthcare providers have little formal training in identifying and treating patients with a trafficking experience (Chisolm-Straker et al. 2012). Validated comprehensive screening tools do not yet exist for healthcare settings (Chisolm-Straker 2020), and screening may not even be the best way for clinicians to recognize exploitation. As a result, the health care provided is limited to treating a specific illness or condition, bypassing the greater problem of the inhumanity of human trafficking. Consequently, the opportunity to provide comprehensive health care is lost. Thus, episodic care and symptom-based treatment, rather than root-cause treatment, will necessarily continue. Such incomplete care may make it dif-ficult for some patients with a trafficking experience to trust that health care is a safe setting. Moreover, given previous negative experiences, knowledge of peers' nega-tive experiences, and/or historical awareness, many trafficked people may not find the healthcare setting trustworthy.

Price, Nelson, and Macias-Konstantopoulos, examined the disparities in health-care access and engagement related to trafficking survivors' experiences and per-ceptions of medical care. The investigators identified three patient profiles: avoidant, distrustful, and constrained. Of note, distrustful profiles were characterized as not believing healthcare providers listened, cared, or tried to help them (Price et al. 2019). The study did not examine the impact of race in these profiles. But in light of the function of US health care in historical slavery, it is not hard to imagine that

US health care might be difficult for trafficked persons of color to access or accept, even when it is technically available. In fact, in a 2016 study, Black women, who had survived commercial sexual exploitation, reported experiencing racism in therapeutic (social service and substance use disorder) settings; their White peers received preferential treatment regardless of the provider's race (Gerassi 2019).

15.3 Conclusion

Understanding the multifactorial causes of human trafficking today requires dissecting the systems that allow and promote abuse of vulnerable and historically oppressed populations. The historical devaluation of Black lives as means to an economic end (White prosperity) explains early and contextualizes current Black patient interactions with healthcare providers. Its legacy is alive in the Black-White health disparities that continue to communicate that US health care is a right for the privileged, though disproportionately it is people of color who have been oppressed and thus experience increased morbidity and mortality.

John T. Chissell, MD, conceptualized *optimal health* in response to a failing US healthcare system. Dr. Chissell defines optimal health as "the best possible, emotional, intellectual, physical, spiritual, and socio-economic *aliveness* [emphasis added] that we can attain" (Chissell 1993). He conceptualized optimal health for African Americans in response to a failed healthcare system, which since its inception has privileged Whites over people of color. Optimal health has tremendous potential to promote and protect the health of trafficked persons, harmed by the same healthcare system that may have failed them as well. The two groups—people of color and trafficked people—continue to overlap. One of the richest and most influential countries in the world, the United States can and must do better to promote optimal health for the people that built and continue to fuel it.

15.4 Recommendations

1. *Develop healthcare educational modules for selected health professional school faculty and all health professional school students.* When people with a trafficking experience do not trust their clinicians, an opportunity at relevant service provision is missed.
2. *Clinical competency training should be required for all clinicians employed in federally qualified community health centers (FQCHC*; commonly called federally qualified health centers, FQHC). FQCHCs largely serve communities of color, that may be disproportionately impacted by labor and/or sex trafficking. If clinical sites are considered more trustworthy (Warren et al. 2020, trafficked patients may believe it useful to share about their trafficking experience(s).

3. *Universal health insurance should be provided to remove the financial barrier to health care.* Accessibility and acceptability may take more time to achieve, but affordability of US health care is more rapidly achievable.
4. *Health care resources should focus on the health and healthcare needs of people of color*, particularly African Americans who continue to carry the disproportionate burden of morbidity and mortality in the United States.
5. *Bioethics and public health ethics consideration should be included in all public health and healthcare initiatives focused on trafficked persons to avoid past mistakes* in providing health care to underserved and unserved populations.

References

Alker, J., & Pham, O. (2018). *Nation's progress on children's health coverage reverses course.* Georgetown University Health Policy Institute, Center for Children and Families. Retrieved from https://ccf.georgetown.edu/wp-content/uploads/2018/11/UninsuredKids2018_Final_asof1128743pm.pdf. On 27 Dec 2020.

Appian, K. A., & Gates, H. L. (1999). *The encyclopedia of the African and African American experience.* Oxford: Oxford University Press.

Baldwin, S. B., Eisenman, D. P., Sayles, J. N., et al. (2011). Identification of human trafficking victims in health care settings. *Health Hum Rights, 13*(1):E36–49. PMid:22772961.

Banks, D., & Kyckelhahn, T. (2011). *Characteristics of suspected human trafficking incidents, 2008–2010,* 1. Washington, DC: Bureau of Justice Statistics, U.S. Department of Justice. http://www.bjs.gov/content/pub/pdf/cshti0810.pdf.

Berchik, E. (2018, September 12). *Most uninsured were working-age adults.* United States Census Bureau. Retrieved 18 October 2020, from https://www.census.gov/library/stories/2018/09/who-are-the-uninsured.html

Blackmon, D. A. (2008). Slavery by Another name: The Re-enslavement of Black Americans from the Civil War to World War II. Doubleday. ISBN-10 : 0385506252

Bramwell, B. S. (1948, January). Galton's hereditary genius and the three following generations since 1869. *The Eugenics Review, 39*(4), 146–153. PMC 2986459. PMID 18903832.

Braveman, P. (2006). Health disparities and health equity: Concepts and measurement. *Annual Review of Public Health, 27,* 167–194.

Chen, A., Oster, E., & Williams, H. (2016). Why is infant mortality higher in the United States than in Europe? *American Economic Journal: Economic Policy, 8*(2), 89–124. Retrieved April 18, 2020, from www.jstor.org/stable/24739218.

Chisolm-Straker, M. (2020). By the right name: Screening and assessing for trafficking in the clinical setting. In J. H. Coverdale, M. R. Gordon, & P. T. Nguyen (Eds.), *Human trafficking: A Treatment guide for mental health professionals* (pp. 31–48). Washington, DC: American Psychiatric Association Publishing.

Chisolm-Straker, M., Baldwin, S., Gaïgbé-Togbé, B., Ndukwe, N., Johnson, P., & Richardson, L. (2016). Health care and human trafficking: We are seeing the unseen. *Journal of Health Care for the Poor and Underserved, 27*(3), 1220–1233.

Chisolm-Straker, M., Richardson, L. D, & Cossio, T. (2012). Combating slavery in the 21st century: The role of emergency medicine. *Journal of Health Care for the Poor and Underserved, 23*(3), 980–987.

Chissell, J. (1993). *Pyramids of power: An ancient African centered approach to optimal health.* Baltimore: Positive Perceptions.

Dols, J. D., Beckmann-Mendez, D., McDow, J., Walker, K., & Moon, M. D. (2019). Human trafficking victim identification, assessment, and intervention strategies in South Texas emergency departments. *Journal of Emergency Nursing, 45*(6), 622–633.

Du Bois, W. E. B. (1935). *Black Reconstruction in America*. Oxford: Oxford University Press. ISBN: 9780199385652.

Duffy, T. P. (2011). The Flexner Report–100 years later. *The Yale Journal of Biology and Medicine, 84*(3), 269–276.

Flexner, A. (1910). *Medical education in the United States and Canada: Report Carnegie to the foundation for the advancement of science: Bulletin Number Four 1910*. New York.

Galton, F. (1883). *Inquiries into human faculty and its development*. London: Macmillan.

Galton, F. (1869). *Hereditary genius: An inquiry into its laws and consequences*. London: Macmillan and Co. https://doi.org/10.1037/13474-000

Gasman, M. B., & Sullivan, L. (2012). *The Morehouse Mystic: Becoming a Black doctor at the newest medical school*. Baltimore: Johns Hopkins University Press.

Gerassi, L. B. (2019). Experiences of racism and racial tensions among African American women impacted by commercial sexual exploitation in practice: A qualitative study. *Violence Against Women*. https://doi.org/10.1177/1077801219835057, (107780121983505).

Greenwood, B. N., Hardeman, R. R., Huang, L., & Sojourner, A. (2020). Physician–patient racial concordance and disparitiesin birthing mortality for newborns. *Proceedings of the National Academy of Sciences, 117*(35), 21194–21200; https://doi.org/10.1073/pnas.1913405117.

Harley, E. H. (2006). The forgotten history of defunct Black medical schools in the 19th and 20th centuries and the impact of the Flexner Report. *Journal of the National Medical Association, 98*(9), 1425–9.

Jones J. (1993). Bad Blood: The Tuskegee Experiment (New Expanded Edition) New York: Free Press

Katz, R., & Warren, R. C. (eds). (2011). *The search for the legacy of the USPHS Syphilis study at Tuskegee: Reflective essays based upon findings from the Tuskegee Legacy Project*. Lexington Books, Inc.

Lederer, L., & Wetzel, C. (2014). The health consequences of sex trafficking and their implications for identifying victims in healthcare facilities. *Annals of Health Law, 23*(1), 61–91.

Lombardo, P. A., & Dorr, G. M. (2006). Eugenics, medical education, and the public health service: Another perspective on the Tuskegee Syphilis experiment. *Bulletin of the History of Medicine, 80*(2), 291–316.

Martin, L., & Pierce, A. (2014). *Mapping the market for sex with trafficked minor girls in Minneapolis: Structures, functions, and patterns*. Urban Research and Outreach-Engagement Center. Retrieved from https://uroc.umn.edu/sites/uroc.umn.edu/files/MTM_SexTraf_Summ.pdf

Milano, B. (2019). How slavery still shadows healthcare. *The Harvard Gazette*. https://news.harvard.edu/gazette/story/2019/10/

National Human Trafficking Hotline. (2018). Texas. [Online] National Human Trafficking Hotline. Available at: https://humantraffickinghotline.org/state/texas. Accessed 23 Dec 2019.

Price, K., Nelson, B., & Macias-Konstantopoulos, W. (2019). Understanding health care access disparities among human trafficking survivors: Profiles of health care experiences, access, and engagement. *Journal of Interpersonal Violence*. 088626051988993.

Reverby, S. (2009). *Examining Tuskegee: The Infamous Syphilis Study and its legacy*. Chapel Hill: The University of North Carolina Press.

Satcher, D., Fryer, G. E. Jr., McCann, J., et al. (2005). What if we were equal? A comparison of the Black-non-Hispanic White mortality gap in 1960 and 2000. *Health Affairs (Millwood), 24*(2), 459–64.

Serakos, M., & Wolfe, B. (2016). The ACA: Impacts on health, access, and employment. *Forum for Health Economics & Policy, 19*(2), 201–259. https://doi.org/10.1515/fhep-2015-0027.

US Department of Health and Human Services. (1985). *Report of the secretary's task force on Black and minority health*. [Executive summary]. Washington, DC: Government Print Office.

Victims of Trafficking and Violence Protection Act of 2000 (P.L. 106–386), reauthorized by the Trafficking Victims Protection Reauthorization Act (TVPRA) of 2003 (P.L. 108–193), the TVPRA of 2005 (P.L. 109 164), and the William Wilberforce Trafficking Victims Protection Reauthorization Act (WW-TVPA) of 2008 (P.L. 110–457) and the TVPRA of 2013 (P.L. 113–4).

Viscusi, W. K., & Aldy, J. E. (2003, August). The value of a statistical life: a critical review of market estimates throughout the world. *Journal of Risk and Uncertainty* (Springer), *27*(1), 5–76.

Warren, R. C. (1999). *Oral health for all: Policy for available, accessible, and acceptable care policy paper*. Washington, DC: Center for Policy Alternatives.

Warren, R. C., Clare, C. A, & Villanueva, Pinn V. W. (2020). In the interest of science or humanity: J. Marion Sims was wrong then and now!. *Journal of the National Medical Association*, *112*(2), 233–236.

Whelchel, L. K. (2011). *The history and heritage of African American churches: A way out of no way*. St. Paul: Paragon Press.

World Health Organization. (2021). https://www.who.int/about/who-we-are/constitution, accessed 24 March 2021.

Chapter 16
Mother Tongues and Community Well-Being: Survivance, Decolonization, and the Wôpanâak Language Reclamation Project

Nitana Hicks Greendeer and Jennifer Weston

16.1 Introduction

Only in the twenty-first century, has detailed macrolevel scholarship emerged to enumerate the magnitude of Indian slavery in the Americas—estimated at 2.5–5 million individuals. Indian slavery remains a largely hidden chapter in US history, and especially so in the northeastern region of the United States (Reséndez 2016; Calloway 2013; Database of Indigenous Slavery in the Americas, indigenousslavery.org 2020). Often considered a bastion of abolitionism and resistance, the New England states have ignored and concealed their own participation in slavery, slavery's impacts on people of color, and among the Indigenous Peoples who have called the region home for more than 10,000 years. But the historical record is clear. Indian slavery in what would become the United States began early in the Plymouth and Massachusetts Bay colonies. In fact, exacting scholarship details the numbers: " …New England armies, courts, and magistrates enslaved more than 1200 Indian men, women, and children in the seventeenth century alone, and bound many others into finite terms of servitude" (Newell 2003). One especially chilling document from the island of Martha's Vineyard, seals the fate of Native children in the region for generations to come, and portends the systematically enforced militarized subjugation and severing of cultural and linguistic ties that colonial courts would use to wrest Indigenous children from their homes across a continent: "Ordered that whereas many of the Indians… warre against our nation… that such as are young may be put out as Servants to such English as may give them a good education… children to serve to the age of 24 years" (Dukes County Deed 1676).

Native American tribes and tribal governments like those among the Wampanoag Nation have persisted on pockets of once vast traditional homelands. Families today

N. H. Greendeer · J. Weston (✉)
Wôpanâak Language Reclamation Project, Mashpee, MA, USA
e-mail: jweston@wlrp.org

© Springer Nature Switzerland AG 2021   291
M. Chisolm-Straker, K. Chon (eds.), *The Historical Roots of Human Trafficking*,
https://doi.org/10.1007/978-3-030-70675-3_16

continue to share oral and written histories of ancestors' struggles against seventeenth century dispossession and widespread enslavement, followed throughout the eighteenth century by a rise in court-mandated colonial indentured servitude practices akin to slavery. The fall of 2020 marked 400th anniversary of the arrival of the famed settler-colonial vessel the *Mayflower* in Wampanoag territory. Many Wampanoag families assert that these carefully preserved stories must be shared more widely than ever before – through exhibits, lectures, performances, publications, and partnerships with cultural organizations like the *Plymouth 400*, The Mayflower Society, libraries, museums, theatre, and arts groups. A traveling exhibit created and filmed by Wampanoag families, "Our Story: 400 Years of Wampanoag History" (Mashpee Wampanoag Tribe 2019), opens with an in-depth chapter entitled "Captured: 1614," complete with victim statements and re-enactments of the horrors of separation and enslavement endured by 27 Wampanoag men and boys trafficked from Patuxet—modern day Plymouth, MA, and Nauset—to Malaga, Spain. Only Tisquantum—popularly known as Squanto—returned from this traumatic journey in 1619, to find his home village Patuxet in ruins and his family victim to a sweeping epidemic that tragically killed 60 to 90% of the Wampanoag Nation in southeastern Massachusetts (Salisbury 1982).

Tisquantum and his 26 enslaved relatives were not the first Wampanoag to experience sudden, violent trans-Atlantic trafficking. The earliest well-documented abduction and subsequent return of a Wampanoag occurred between the years 1611–1614 when Epenow, was kidnapped from the north Atlantic coast on an English ship. Piloted by Captain Edward Harlow, the vessel eventually delivered Epenow into the custody of the ominous Sir Fernando Gorges, "a prime mover in England's first colonization efforts and collector of Indians" (Silverman 2005). Like Tisquantum, Epenow also made his way home to a territory forever altered by settler-colonial courts, epidemics, and a new economic order.

In his groundbreaking 2016 book, "The Other Slavery: The Uncovered Story of Indian Enslavement in America," historian Andrés Reséndez demonstrates "the other slavery that affected Indians throughout the Western Hemisphere was never a single institution, but instead a set of kaleidoscopic practices suited to different markets and regions…. that were extremely difficult to track, let alone eradicate" (Reséndez 2016). Throughout New England, historians have explored these varied forms of coerced labor through the centuries since that first 1611 trafficking event in Wampanoag territory. Scholars Ruth Wallis Herndon and Ella Wilcox Sekatau have produced detailed regional histories of Indian slavery and indenture in Rhode Island and Massachusetts. They often incorporate Narragansett oral traditions alongside written documentary evidence while exploring the role of colonial courts in regulating and imposing "order" on poor communities, people of color, and especially Native mothers who bore children while in servitude to White masters (Wallis Herndon and Wilcox Sekatau 2009). Ojibwe historian Jean O'Brien has also richly documented the extensive social and cultural controls imposed on Native families by the "social order" of colonial Massachusetts (O'Brien 1997). These controls included missionaries and governors working hand in hand to convert and regulate the daily lives of Native families. They particularly focused on those in the network of "praying towns" which were created to undermine and replace traditional Native leaders. Simultaneously, they imposed colonial practices governing religion, compulsory schooling, and everything from hair cutting to regendered planting practices that misaligned with Wampanoag cultural norms (O'Brien 1997; Tears of Repentance 1653).

Notably, Wallis Herndon and Wilcox Sekatau highlight the significant overrepresentation of Native children in the records of child indenture in Narragansett and Wampanoag territory in contemporary Rhode Island (Wallis Herndon and Wilcox Sekatau 2009). Native Peoples comprised scarcely 10% of the population, but Native American and African- American children made up fully one quarter of 1200 writs of indenture spanning the years 1680–1880. Nearby, in the Wampanoag territories around modern day Little Compton, RI and Westport, MA, a more recent study by the local historical society details a hidden history. There were 250 "forcibly enslaved and indentured" Native Americans and African Americans—many of them children—identified in 1674–1816 local records. These records were from the sleepy agricultural hamlets located in close proximity to New England's anchor in the infamous trans-Atlantic triangle trade, the wealthy slaving port of Newport, RI (Gomez O'Toole 2016). In "The Changing Nature of Indian Slavery, 1670–1720," scholar Margaret Newell describes the racialized legal codes encompassing criminal, civil, and tax laws combined with a sharp rise in the practice of judicial enslavement (Chap. 9)—"the sentencing of Native Americans to long periods of involuntary service to settle debts, as well as civil and criminal penalties" (Newell 2003). Slavery thus persisted in the "kaleidoscopic practices" cataloged regionally throughout early America by Reséndez. Native women and children were more likely to suffer "de facto" slavery (Wallis Herndon and Wilcox Sekatau 2009; Newell 2003), and the removal of the younger generations from family and community settings until they reached age 24—as referenced in the opening document excerpt—were doubtless among the first-ever colonial-era legal documents referencing "Indian education."

Some 350 years later, Native American families are still seeking a return to control over their children's education, and a place in curricula for the histories of the Black and Indigenous peoples whose stolen labor and land formed the foundation for the United States.

16.2   Discussion

Four tribes among the Wampanoag nation today operate three immersion school classrooms and provide weekly language education to over 100 tribal children weekly in a powerful expression of educational sovereignty[1] while shaping a new

---

[1] Educational sovereignty is the inherent right to self-govern and control tribal educational institutions.

curricular approach. In this novel educational methodology, immersion in Wôpanâak language is melded with Montessori pedagogy and formalized teacher training. As a growing community school, The Weetumuw School revolves around a curriculum framework informed and shaped by generations of Wampanoag people. The framework relies on tribal land, language and spiritual practice, and a true accounting of Wampanoag and Indigenous Peoples histories for its young students, 2–8 years in age.

The language revitalization journey of the Wampanoag tribes was catalyzed through the visionary leadership of Mashpee Wampanoag mother and tribal leader jessie little doe baird. In 1993, baird cofounded the Wôpanâak Language Reclamation Project (WLRP) with Aquinnah Wampanoag elder and retired educator Helen Manning. Baird's recurring dreams in the long-silent Wôpanâak language inspired her to seek the guidance of Wampanoag elders and are recounted in "WE STILL LIVE HERE: Âs Nutayuneân." A 2012 Makepeace Productions film, "Âs Nutayuneân" aired nationally on PBS's Independent Lens series and internationally on the Independent Television Service. Numerous language teachers, students, and other supporters of the Wampanoag nation's Wôpanâak Language Reclamation Project appear in the documentary which was filmed over 3 years in the tribal communities of Aquinnah, Assonet, Herring Pond, and Mashpee on Cape Cod and Martha's Vineyard, and in Cambridge and Boston, Massachusetts.

In addition to many Wampanoag voices, "Âs Nutayuneân" also employs simple animation sequences to convey especially troubling aspects at the root of Indigenous language loss in early New England. Due to massive and previously unknown epidemics throughout the early seventeenth century and as many Indian families were sold into slavery, communities were separated and intergenerational language transmission was cut off. Colonial courts also mandated widespread indentured servitude for Indian children in seventeenth and eighteenth century New England, placing them in English households "as may give them a good Education" (Dukes County Deed 1676). Original documents, from local public records repositories in New England and the writings of seventeenth century missionaries Daniel Gookin and John Eliot, help tell the complex story of the first American- Indian communities to use an alphabetic writing system, and to adapt to English conventions of recording land transfers, deeds, will, petitions, and letters—but in their Native language.

By the mid-1800s, the language shift to English had overtaken Indigenous languages throughout much of New England, but tightly-knit communities and intertribal social, political, and family networks persevered, as well as local institutions of tribal governance and traditional leadership positions. And since 1993, through the efforts of WLRP, the Wampanoag language is being revived in the home of Mashpee Wampanoag Tribal Vice Chairwoman baird, and through WLRP's language school and programs. The programming includes after school programs and classes at area public schools, community-based classes, summer youth camps, elders' classes, and language immersion camps for tribal families. Based primarily on the Mashpee Wampanoag Indian reservation, but offering community classes to its four member tribes throughout the Cape and Islands region of Massachusetts, WLRP operates on tribal lands still contested with the federal government in 2020.

Mashpee's place as one of 69 original Wampanoag villages among the Wampanoag nation was followed by establishment of a praying town, then an Indian district, and then individual land allotments in the mid-1800s. Many families lost their land due to non-payment of property taxes to the Commonwealth.

16.2.1 Historical Trauma in "Education": The Colonial Mission of Erasure and Assimilation

In the late 1800s, following the Indian Removal Act of 1830 which forced Native people to leave their homelands so that the land would be available to White US citizens and their slaves, came the introduction of the boarding school era. Once Native people were removed from their lands, the government oversaw an effort to "educate" Native people living outside of their homelands; the purpose of the boarding schools was assimilation and erasure of Native cultures (Grande 2004). Other schools were initially established by churches as "manual labor schools." Students there were expected to do hard labor under the guise of "civilizing" them by "allowing" them to learn a trade (Reyhner and Eder 1992). When these schools were no longer in operation, the federal government took up the charge and established—using this and the original boarding school model—its own Indian education system. The church's use of the day school model was dismissed as allowing Native students too much access to their families and homes; the model was "deemed detrimental to the overall project of deculturization" (Grande 2004, citing Noriega, p. 13). Native children were brought to the schools by force and under duress.

The emphasis in boarding schools was conformity and subservience. These schools relied on methods based on military regimentation and discipline, including the requirement that children wear government-issued military uniforms. Military tactics were used to treat what was viewed as the students' deficiencies. For example, while in boarding school captivity, students were beaten for speaking their native languages—the only language they knew in many cases. Boys had their long hair cut short and children were separated from their siblings and friends in order to assist the process of assimilation. When children did not conform, sometimes they were denied food, sometimes they were isolated entirely from other children, and sometimes they were severely beaten. Many children also experienced sexual abuse, both as a means to manipulate behavior or in exchange for less physical abuse (Lomawaima 1999).

For some students, boarding schools accomplished what they set out to do: to completely eliminate the Native culture. Some children were scarred by their experiences in boarding school to such a degree that they were ashamed to be who they were before their "educational" experience began. So indoctrinated by the institutionalized racism they experienced at the boarding schools, many Native people who survived the schools removed themselves from their families' homes. They built lives outside of their culture in mainstream society, leaving behind their former identities as Indigenous people. Some left their culture behind because they could not face their families and communities after the humiliation they experienced at the hands of the institution. Some survivors felt resentment toward those who were not forced to go to these schools, or toward their families for not stopping abduction or for not coming to bring them home. Other boarding school survivors chose capitalism and Christianity over their own cultures and remained separate from their Native communities as a result. Many were unequipped to survive in an unfamiliar world. For example, Commissioner Hiram Price advocated for Native people receiving allotments that they would have to cultivate, care for, and upon which they would pay taxes (Grande 2004). Enticed by the promise of owning their own land from which they would not be removed, many Native people received their allotments only to lose it for money owed in taxes. As private land ownership and taxation on said land was a previously unknown concept to a great many Natives at that time, they were unaware of the process and therefore were unprepared for the financial burden of land ownership. This explicit assimilation and erasure effort continued into the middle of the twentieth century (Lomawaima 1999; UMN 2010).

Many boarding school survivors, who emerged with as much of their Native culture and identity intact as possible, understandably came away with a fear and distrust of the educational system. This distrust has been passed down from parents and grandparents to children, and still exists among many Native youth today (Chap. 11). As Grande (2004) explains, "the miseducation of American Indians precedes the 'birth' of this nation" (p. 11). The tenets of colonial era and continued government education throughout the centuries are deeply rooted as truths in the minds of US learners today (Lomawaima 1999). The characteristics of European education from centuries past include: (1) teachers having the final word in their classrooms without the ability of students to question them; (2) students being punished for not strictly conforming to teachers' expectations; and (3) students are not allowed to bring their own experiences and identities into the classroom. These tenets facilitate the ease of moving the class through colonially-framed material quickly and without imagination; these tenets facilitate indoctrination, rather than critical thinking. Creativity and curiosity are still not truly desirable qualities of a mainstream education in this country and therefore US classrooms are indeed often still structured in these ways.

16.2.2   The Settler-Colonial Project Legacy

In accord with the settler-colonial project of removing the Indigenous people from their homelands, the above-described educational model remains to this day—one that is by and large, in competition with a Wampanoag worldview. In a Wampanoag way of being, people learn by observation and by practice, as opposed to being told information. The Wampanoag people believe in a socialist societal organization for the collective success of the group rather than a competitive, meritocratic, capitalist structure. There is a clear mismatch between the traditional Wampanoag teachings and the preferred pedagogy of US society. The US pedagogy marginalizes

Wampanoag (and in general, Native) people, further removing them from control of their lives on their own homeland. In order to compete in a way that will win them academic success and acceptance from the non-Native mainstream group, success has meant finding a way for Wampanoag learners to conform to the colonizer's prescribed framework. This often means leaving behind some pieces of one's Indigenous identity; this is a win for the settler colonial project because the colonized mind is less likely to protest the theft of its rightful resources (Fanon 1967). The negative consequences experienced by young Wampanoag people in the 1600s continue to be felt by the young Wampanoag people of today. This is in part because the practices have not drastically changed, but also because the miseducation experienced by the ancestors of today's Native youth is still present as a form of historical trauma. Historical trauma allows settler colonialism to continue to affect the lives of Indigenous people.

Historical trauma is defined by Dr. Maria Yellow Horse Brave Heart as "a constellation of characteristics associated with massive cumulative group trauma across generations" (Michaels 2010). Dr. Brave Heart further explains that "the traumatic event is shared by a collective group of people who experience the consequences of the event, as well as the fact that the impact of the trauma is held personally and can be transmitted over generations," (Michaels 2010). In this case, generations of Native people being forced into praying towns and boarding schools, being disallowed their language and their traditions, and forced to live within the US "whitestream" society – a term which Sandy Grande (2004) uses to describe a society where the norm is based on a White, European experience – have caused the historical trauma in education.

Because of these "educational" acts of cultural genocide, Native people nationwide are cautious of the US education system imposed on their children. As a result of generations of Native people who have been exposed to a system that devalues their traditional cultural norms, punishes the use of their language, and forces a way of life that has felt unnatural and difficult, many Tribal citizens have come to view the US educational system as the enemy. Rooted in experience, Native understanding of formal education as a form of oppression (Chap. 11) has been handed down from generation to generation; whitestream education continues to manifest itself as a contributor to the historical cultural traumas felt by Indigenous people.

The Racist Success of the "Common Core"

Curriculum content created to meet "Common Core" or other national standards include histories and teachings that are contrary to the knowledge Native students bring to the classroom. Public and whitestream schools use the month of November to speak superficially about Native people in terms of their interaction with colonizers (e.g., Pilgrims) and then claim that they have covered Native history in their curriculum. However, the story told in schools is contrary to the story Native children understood from their family histories. These students are left with the futile task of attempting to correct their teacher, or must remain silent as their educator silences the truth of their people. Despite the presence of living Native students in the classroom, school, and community, school systems use Thanksgiving to frame lessons about Native people; these lessons relegate Native people and their stories and cultures through their curriculum to objects of the past.

The curriculum Native students are forced to endure, both as it relates to the skewed perspective of Native people as well as the content of general education requirements, has led to limited Native success as compared to their peers of other racial and ethnic groups. In *Indian Nations as Risk*, Demmert and Bell (1991) described the discouraging truths of Indian students' educational experiences:

- Native students have limited opportunities to develop their basic skills such as language through preschool education;
- Family or home-life barriers (which result from the historical traumas previously described, as well as social and political factors, such as institutionalized racism and government-sanctioned violence toward Tribal people) such as poverty, single-parent homes, substance use disorders, violence, suicide, and physical or psychological inability inhibit students' academic achievement;
- Schools do not provide culturally sensitive or relevant education. They teach about Native people as if they are relics of the past when in fact there are students of those still-existing communities sitting in their classrooms. This lack of sensitivity and recognition do not facilitate Indigenous students' spiritual growth or academic engagement. Students are unable to maintain proper language and cultural knowledge in school. Unequipped teachers lack the ability to effectively teach Native students;
- The curriculum is presented through a settler-colonial perspective;
- Students experience racism in their school environments;
- Low expectations are placed upon Native students resulting in their poor academic achievement;
- As much as 35% of Native students drop out of high school (in some places this number is as high as 50–60%);
- Native students score lower on SAT and ACT exams making them technically less qualified for college than other student groups of color;
- Funding at all levels of schooling is insufficient for Native students.

The statistics support the claim that repercussions of these traumas continue to be experienced in myriad formal educational settings by young Native people. In a 1990 survey of American Indians over the age of 25, 66% had completed high school as compared to 75% of the total US population; 9% had a bachelor's degree compared to 20% of the US population; and 3% of American Indians held graduate or professional degrees compared to 7% of the total US population (UMN 2010). In their 2017 report, the National Center for Education Statistics' stated that Native students make up approximately 1% of all students in the United States at the elementary and secondary level. Of those students, American Indian/Alaska Native (AIAN) students represent the highest high school drop-out rate (12%) across all racial groups. Conversely only 82% of AIAN students complete high school, the lowest rate among racial/ethnic groups (Musu-Gillette et al. 2017). While the statistics have improved in the 27 years between reports, AIAN students are still among the lowest achieving groups in the country. In 2015, among 18–24 year olds, AIANs had the lowest instance (23%) of enrollment in degree granting institutions. From 2010 to 2014, all ethnic groups showed an increase in enrollment in post baccalaureate programs, *except* for AIAN students who *decreased* over the same period (Musu-Gillette et al. 2017).

Compounding the historical trauma is the lack of teachers who reflect the students' race and ethnicity. Less than 1% of teachers in the United States self-identify as American Indian or Alaska Native, including in areas where the concentration of Native students is higher. Even some reservation schools lack Native teachers (Hicks 2014; Clarren 2017). Seeing no reflection of themselves in prominent positions in their school environment reinforces for Native students the idea that school is not for them.

These factors combine for an overall negative experience for Native students in school. Children learn from their parental figures how to respond to their teachers and what kind of attitude to have toward learning and the lesson content. With past experiences overwhelmingly ranging from negative to traumatic, Native families are often at best, skeptical, if not afraid of teachers and the system, regardless of the educational environment. Familial skepticism and fear paired with teachers' preconceived biases and expectations often result in non-communication, which in turn results in misunderstanding. Parents' and students' actions are often perceived by non-Native instructors as manifestations of malice or apathy; these interpretations renew the cycle, creating more generations of Native families whose educational experiences are at best, subpar.

16.2.3 Decolonization on Native Land

Culture-based education (CBE) grounds high-quality instructional practices in Native values, in culturally and linguistically relevant contexts. CBE is more than teaching language and culture as individual subjects, but rather a systematic approach that promotes educational sovereignty, use and support of traditional ways of thinking, learning, problem-solving, and teaching as the foundation for education (niea.org), and recognizing students' families and communities as their first and primary teachers.

For Native students, these approaches include recognizing and utilizing Native languages as a first or second language, pedagogy that incorporates traditional cultural characteristics, and involves teaching strategies that are harmonious with Native culture knowledge and contemporary ways of knowing and learning (Hicks 2014).

As a community, the Wampanoag Nation has worked hard through the Aquinnah and Mashpee Education Departments, and the Wôpanâak Language Reclamation Project (WLRP) to decolonize Wampanoag communities through culturally based education. WLRP's mission is to "return language fluency to the Wampanoag

Nation as a principal means of expression," (Wôpanâak Language Reclamation Project, wlrp.org n.d.). Among the most notable and successful of the endeavors made toward decolonizing education is WLRP's immersion school. The year 2020 marked WLRP's fourth year operating a Wôpanâak Language immersion school, for preschool and lower elementary aged children, called *Weetumuw Katnuhtôhtâkamuq*. The school's mission is to:

> [prepare] students ages 3–9 for academic excellence and community leadership by instilling traditional Wampanoag values through Wôpanâaklanguage immersion and culture-based education for decolonization[2] using a Montessori pedagogy. Weetumuw Katnuhtôhtâkamuq students are immersed in Wampanoag language and culture in a safe, healthy, and loving environment, with the goal of fostering academic excellence, leadership skills, and a strong sense of personal, community, and cultural pride (Wôpanâak Language Reclamation Project, wlrp.org n.d.).

Weetumuw Katnuhtôhtâkamuq currently serves 27 children in 22 different households. Each day children arrive and are greeted, by their teachers, in Wôpanâôt8âôk (Wampanoag language) from the moment they walk into the school space; all the teachers are Wampanoag citizens and Wôpanâak language speakers. The adults model the desired behavior so that the children learn proper actions and how to behave, from putting away their belongings, to interacting with their peers and teachers, to completing classroom work. In this way students can learn by observation, just as they learn at home. Work time is in large blocks, allowing children time to get lessons from their teachers individually or as part of a group, work with their materials, and interact socially with their peers. Children are free to move around their classroom, and are not confined to desks; they are allowed to make choices about the work they want to accomplish. This gives them the confidence to choose their work, the ability to learn their strengths, and self-regulation as they move independently around the classroom.

Modeling the classroom pedagogy after the home is not only reflected in how the teachers set expectations for behavior, but also in the content of the lessons. Often family and community members come in to give lessons that mirror the cultural lessons learned at home. Example lessons include hunters bringing freshly harvested ducks for the children to help pluck and clean; a parent and other community members bringing in a wampum belt allowing the children to work on it and learn the history of wampum belts; and frequent trips to the woods to get to know their homelands, both with their teachers, as well as with the guidance of other community members.

---

[2]The traditional use of "decolonization" revolved around the formal process of returning the instruments of government to a people, nation, or organization. Modern use of the term alludes to the complex process of divesting of colonial power; in particular it restores an Indigenous world-view, restores Indigenous culture and traditional ways, and replaces White and Western interpretations of history with Indigenous historical perspectives. (Working Effectively with Indigenous Peoples. 2017. A Brief Definition of Decolonization and Indigenization. Retrieved 22 October 2020 from https://www.ictinc.ca/blog/a-brief-definition-of-decolonization-and-indigenization)

Being educated within the walls of the Mashpee Wampanoag tribal building also helps to reinforce the children's pride in themselves as part of their Tribal community. Every day they see their family coming to the same building where they go to school: a security guard keeping them safe, a judge on the way to Tribal court; the dentist coming from the clinic to give a lesson on oral hygiene; the grounds keepers mowing the field for them to play outside; the drivers dropping off a busload of elders for their language lesson and lunch. This daily occurrence at their school allows Wampanoag children to see Tribal people reflected honorably in their daily lives, outside of their homes. Similarly, the activities inside of the classroom increase children's understanding of and pride in their own culture. They see that Wampanoag culture is worthy of being part of their education. For most Native students, walking into school means leaving their culture, their language, and so much of their identity as Native people at the door. Weetumuw Katnuhtôhtâkamuq students do not know what it is like to have to be anyone other than their Wampanoag selves at school.

16.3   Conclusion

The United States is built on stolen land, stolen labor, and less often discussed, stolen stories, and stolen language. The truth of the violence of English imperialism, settler-colonialism, capitalism, and Christian hegemony goes largely untold in US educational settings. The determined efforts at Native erasure from US mythology and the misuse of education as a tool of assimilation and genocidal efforts have fueled the historical and intergenerational trauma that harm Native youth today. Colonizing Whites knew that controlling education was a means of shaping identity development and severing community connections; they knew it could be used to destroy the social fabric of Native nations as treaty rights were violated and land was and continues to be taken for US economic gain. Children trapped in schools designed for assimilation often leave or are pushed out by the system, only to then struggle with poverty and all its negative physical and mental health sequelae. Lacking connection to self and community, and continually impacted by centuries of institutionalized racism, they are more vulnerable (as children and adults) to abuse and exploitation, including trafficking. WLRP uses language as the foundation for the connection that culturally relevant education provides; language is a protective factor and a social determinate of health for today's 574 federally recognized American-Indian Tribes in the United States.

16.4   Recommendations

1. *Implement Public Law 101–477, the federal Native American Languages Act of* 1990, which recognized that "the status of the cultures and languages of Native Americans is unique and the United States has the responsibility to act together

with Native Americans to ensure [their] survival." Fulfill the legislation's promise to "preserve, protect, and promote" Native rights to widely use Indigenous languages, including "as a medium of instruction" in schools.

2. *Expand modern Indigenous-controlled education systems and culture-based education practices* to restore intergenerational language transmission and traditional ecological knowledge (TEK). Tribal Colleges and Universities (TCUs), and Native American and Indigenous studies in academia warrant increased resources and support (including federal and state funding).

3. *Non-Indigenous-controlled educational systems need to be honest about US history, and correct the content of the "Common Core."* Whitestream education tells incomplete historical truths, at best; for many students of color, the lies told about them and to them, continue historical trauma, perpetuate racist ideologies, and are manifestations of institutionalized racism.

4. *Non-Native educators of Native students need to learn the history of the land where they work and genuinely cultivate relationships with the communities of their Native students.* Until the work required for entire system change is engaged, sincere educators can become trustworthy by meaningfully partnering with their students and the students' elders to provide culturally relevant and historically accurate learning in their classrooms.

References

Calloway, C. (2013). *New worlds for all: Indians, Europeans, and the re-making of early America*. Baltimore: Johns Hopkins University Press.

Clarren, R. (2017). How America is failing Native American students: Punitive discipline, inadequate federal funding created an educational crisis. *The Nation, 2017*(33). https://www.the-nation.com/article/archive/left-behind/

Database of Indigenous Slavery in the Americas. (2020). Retrieved from https://indige-nousslavery.org

Demmert, W. G., Jr., Bell, T. H. (1991). *Indian nations at risk: An educational strategy for action*. Final report of the Indian Nations at Risk Task Force. U.S. Department of Education.

Dukes County Deed. (1676). 1:3, Edgartown, MA.

Fanon, F. (1967). *Black skin, White masks*. New York: Grove Press.

Gomez O'Toole, M. (2016). *If Jane should want to be sold, stories of enslavement, indenture and freedom in Little Compton* (1st ed.). Rhode Island: Little Compton Historical Society.

Grande, S. (2004). *Red pedagogy: Native American social and political thought*. Lanham: Rowman & Littlefield Publishers.

Hicks, N. (2014). *Nuweetanuhkôs8ânuhshômun numukayuhsunônak: 'We are working together for our youth': Securing educational success for Mashpee Wampanoag youth through community collaboration* (Thesis Ph.D.). Boston College.

Lomawaima, K. T. (1999). The unnatural history of American Indian education. Chapter 1. In K. G. Swisher & J. W. Tippeconnic III (Eds.), *Next steps: Research and practice to advance Indian education* (pp. 3–31). Charleston: ERIC Clearinghouse on Rural Education and Small Schools.

Mashpee Wampanoag Tribe. (2019, December). *Nashauonk Mittark. 'Our Story' Wampanoag history exhibit unveils new chapter: The return of Tisquantum*. Retrieved from https://mashpeewampanoagtribe-nsn.gov/december-2019-mittark-blog/2019/12/1/ourstorywampanoag-history-exhibit-unveils-new-chapter-the-return-of-tisquantum#:~:text=%E2%80%9COur%E2%80%9DStory%20is%20an%20 interactive,that%20shaped%20America's%20earliest%20beginnings

Michaels, C. (2010). *Historical trauma and microaggressions: A framework for culturally-based practice.* Retrieved from https://conservancy.umn.edu/bitstream/handle/11299/120667/ cmhereviewOct10.pdf?sequence=1&isAllowed=y

Musu-Gillette, L., de Brey, C., McFarland, J., Hussar, W., Sonnenberg, W., & Wilkinson-Flicker, S. (2017). *Status and trends in the education of racial and ethnic groups 2017 (NCES 2017-051).* Washington, DC: U.S. Department of Education, National Center for Education Statistics. Retrieved from http://nces.ed.gov/pubsearch.

Newell, M. (2003). The changing nature of Indian slavery in New England, 1670–1730. In C. Calloway & N. Salisbury (Eds.), *Reinterpreting New England Indians: The colonial experience.* Charlottesville: University of Virginia Press.

O'Brien, J. (1997). *Dispossession by degrees: Indian land and identity in Natick, Massachusetts, 1650–1790.* Cambridge, UK: Cambridge University Press.

Public Law 101–477. (1990). *Native American Languages Act, S. 2167 (101st).* Retrieved from https://www.govtrack.us/congress/bills/101/s2167/text

Reséndez, A. (2016). *The other slavery: The uncovered story of Indian enslavement in America.* Boston: Houghton Mifflin Harcourt.

Reyhner, J., & Eder, J. (1992). A history of Indian education. In J. Reyhner (Ed.), *Teaching American Indian students.* Norman: University of Oklahoma Press.

Salisbury, N. (1982). *Manitou and providence: Indians, Europeans, and the making of New England, 1500–1643.* New York: Oxford University Press.

Silverman, D. (2005). *Faith and boundaries: Colonists, Christianity, and community among the Wampanoag Indians of Martha's Vineyard, 1600–1871.* Cambridge, UK: Cambridge University Press.

Tears of repentance: or, A further narrative of the progress of the Gospel amongst the Indians in New-England: setting forth, not only their present state and condition, but sundry confessions of sin by diverse of the said Indians, wrought upon by the saving power of the Gospel; together with the manifestation of their faith and hope in Jesus Christ, and the work of grace upon their hearts. Related by Mr. Eliot and Mr. Mayhew, two faithful laborers in that work of the Lord. Published by the corporation for propagating the Gospel there, for the satisfaction and comfort of such as wish well thereunto. Eliot, John, 1604–1690. Mayhew, Thomas., Mather, Richard, 1596–1669. London: Printed by Peter Cole in Leaden-Hall, and are to sold [sic] at his shop, at the sign of the Printing-Press in Cornhil, near the Royal Exchange., 1653.

University of Minnesota. (2010). *Brief history of American Indian education.* Retrieved from http://etc.umn.edu/resources/briefhistory.htm

US Department of Education. (2017). *Status and trends in the education of racial and ethnic groups 2017.* Retrieved from https://nces.ed.gov/pubs2017/2017051.pdf

Wallis Herndon, R., & Wilcox Sekatau, E. (2009, July 2). *Colonizing the children: Indian youngsters in servitude in early Rhode Island, in reinterpreting New England Indians and the colonial experience,* Calloway, C. Salisbury, N. Colonial Society of Massachusetts: Unabridged edition.

WE STILL LIVE HERE: Âs Nutayuneân. (2012). Makepeace Productions.

Wôpanâak Language Reclamation Project. (n.d.). Retrieved from wlrp.org

Chapter 17
Psychological Well-Being for Survivors: Creating a New Legacy

Minh Dang and Sharon Hawkins Leyden

17.1 Introduction

The common understanding of "leaving a legacy" is to have influenced or affected the world and people in a significant way. Typically reserved for conversations about deceased individuals or past events, legacies can be positive, negative, or mixed in valence. There are legacies left by families and legacies left by war. Leaving a legacy can also be a personal endeavor, each person seeking to be remembered for something after they die. Legacy is defined as the long-term impact of something that has occurred, or something that is passed down or left behind by a person who has come before us (Oxford English Dictionary n.d.). Although this chapter focuses on the trauma of human trafficking, the long-lasting effects left by human trafficking are common across other traumatic experiences, such as adverse childhood experiences (Anda et al. 2006) and torture (McDonnell et al. 2013). The focus of this chapter is on two different legacies. First is the legacy of trauma that is forced upon people who are subjected to human trafficking.[1] In this chapter, the legacy of trauma will be referred to as the "old trauma;" it is something that has happened in the past to an individual but has effects in the present and future. Second is the "new legacy;" it refers to a self-determined legacy that survivors of human trafficking (hereafter "survivors") may decide to pursue after exiting exploitation.

---

[1] There is no international consensus on the legal and operational definitions of human trafficking. This chapter aligns with the definition of "severe forms of human trafficking" outlined in the Trafficking Victims Protection Act 2000. However, not all articles cited use this definition.

M. Dang (✉)
University of Nottingham, Nottingham, UK
e-mail: minh.dang@nottingham.ac.uk

S. H. Leyden
Survivor Alliance, Berkeley, CA, USA

© Springer Nature Switzerland AG 2021
M. Chisolm-Straker, K. Chon (eds.), *The Historical Roots of Human Trafficking*,
https://doi.org/10.1007/978-3-030-70675-3_17

This chapter examines the possibility that when survivors pursue a new legacy, they may also experience greater psychological well-being. Currently in academic literature, there are zero studies that examine the overall well-being or the psychological well-being of survivors of human trafficking (Dang et al. n.d.). Survivors are primarily documented as exhibiting Post–Traumatic Stress Disorder (PTSD), anxiety, depression, and suicidal ideation (see, for example, Oram et al. 2012; Ottisova et al. 2016; Hemmings et al. 2016; Zimmerman and Kiss 2017). The conclusions from these studies indicate that the focus of medical, mental health, and social service intervention should be to decrease the incidence and frequency of deleterious psychological symptoms. The tacit assumption is that the absence of psychological diagnosis equates to mental health, even though decades of research demonstrate that health is more than the absence of illness and diagnosis (Slade 2010). Mitigation of distress and incidence is important; however, current literature about survivors does not examine positive mental health outcomes of survivors, nor seek to measure them (Sanchez and Pacquiao 2018; Dang et al. n.d.).

Positive mental health outcomes include concepts of *well-being, recovery, empowerment,* and *post-traumatic growth* (Seligman and Csikszentmihalyi 2000; Charlton 1998; Calhoun and Tedeschi 2006). Although it is beyond the scope of this chapter to explore these concepts in depth, each of them rejects the idea that the focus of mental health care should be on negative psychological sequelae and that health is merely the absence of illness. The Disability Rights Movement of the 1970s and 1980s pushed the mental healthcare field to view people beyond their role of patient or inpatient, and confronted discrimination against those with mental illness diagnoses (Pelka 2012). This led to a shift away from a mental healthcare system that only valued illness-based outcomes and that perceived people with mental health diagnoses as outcast (Pelka 2012). The shift was toward a model that focused on people living independently of formal institutions, and one that accepted service users' self-defined health outcomes, such as recovery, empowerment, and subjective well-being (McLean 2003; Diener 2000). Academic literature on the mental health of survivors of human trafficking has yet to embrace these outcomes and continues to solely describe survivors as people who are encumbered by illness. Evidence of pathologizing survivors is already displayed in the antitrafficking movement, resulting in survivors leading counter messaging campaigns such as "More than a Survivor" (Girls Educational and Mentoring Services 2013) to remind people that survivors have identities outside of their lived experience of human trafficking. Without exploring positive mental health outcomes, practitioners and researchers may overlook the existence of these outcomes within survivors and miss the opportunity to describe survivors through a less disheartening lens.

Before going much further, it is important to highlight that academic literature does not maintain consistency in its use of terms or definitions for various concepts. Literature regarding the health of survivors of human trafficking often uses the term "psychological well-being" interchangeably with the term "mental health," and simultaneously defines mental health as the absence of mental illness (Dang et al. n.d.). Many professionals in the antitrafficking sector emphasize the importance of psychological recovery (e.g., Katona et al. 2015; Sanchez and Pacquiao 2018). Despite this, there is also a lack of research on survivors' that utilizes well-established concepts and measures for recovery (Dang et al. n.d.). The World Health Organization also defines health as "A state of complete physical, mental and social well-being and not merely the absence of disease or infirmity" (1948, 16). This definition indicates that health requires the presence of well-being. In order to maintain consistency, this chapter will use the term "psychological well-being." Other terms will only be used when referencing the work of other authors.

The following pages provide a framework for understanding psychological trauma and psychological well-being for survivors of human trafficking. In order to begin assessing survivors' psychological well-being, it is important to establish a shared baseline of understanding. In other words, before creating an operational definition of *psychological well-being*, this chapter first interrogates and clarifies the theoretical assumptions that inform the understanding of psychological well-being and psychological trauma. The first section of the Discussion provides this interrogation and uncovers the illness-based origins of existing theoretical assumptions. The second section provides alternative theories for psychological trauma and well-being, paving the way for understanding how creating a "new legacy" can be an effective psychological intervention for survivors of human trafficking. Finally, this chapter describes the Legacy-Building Approach to Healing that allows survivors to build personal legacies and promote psychological well-being.

17.2 Discussion

17.2.1 Understanding Psychological Well-Being

The study of well-being is relatively new in the history of psychological research. Positive psychology was established as a field in 2000 to study the presence of positive aspects of functioning (Seligman 2000), whereas the study of psychological dysfunction dates back to the 1800s (Open Textbook Library 2015). There is no universally accepted definition of psychological well-being and the components of well-being are actively contested in academia (Schrank et al. 2013). It is commonly perceived that psychological well-being is the opposite of psychological illness. The general understanding is that a human is not well if they suffer from illness. However, as the WHO definition of health establishes, someone who is healthy must have the presence of well-being, not merely the absence of illness. The WHO does not provide guidance on what a "complete state" of mental well-being might look like but others have expanded on the Complete State Model (Schrank et al. 2013).

Several approaches to well-being exist, including medical, psychological, economic, and integrated well-being (Schrank et al. 2013). There are subfields for every dimension of well-being addressed in the WHO definition, as well as additional dimensions such as economic well-being. The integrated well-being approach recognizes that mental health is a core component of well-being (Schrank et al. 2013). The work of Carol Ryff (1995) was among the first Westernized definitions of psychological well-being and outlines six dimensions of psychological well-being: self-acceptance, positive relationships with other people, autonomy, environmental mastery, purpose in life, and personal growth. These dimensions focus on the presence of positive attributes that apply to all human beings and serves as an example for individual, subjective well-being.

Individual psychological well-being is a useful step in relating to people beyond their psychological symptoms. However, it still removes the larger context of society and the sociopolitical history of people's lives. Social determinant theories of well-being do give credence to the effect of structural factors, such as poverty, on individual well-being (Finlay et al. 2010; Clifton et al. 2020), but the unit of analysis remains the individual. Collective well-being remains an understudied area, even though studies of well-being in collectivist cultures exist. These studies focus on the impact of collectivism on individual well-being (e.g., Swami et al. 2009; Steele and Lynch 2013) rather than measuring collective well-being. Although some nation-states are beginning to report on national well-being, these are typically aggregations of individual happiness measures rather than collective measures (Knifton 2015; Weijers and Jarden 2017). Western medicine and health sciences do not have great models for studying collective psychological health.

Other cultures have offered alternatives to the traditional Western mental health model (e.g., Martin-Baro 1996; D'Amato 2020), addressing the specific areas of critique leveled at Western mental illness and health standards. A strong theory and practice for collective well-being can be found in Ignacio Martin-Baro's liberation social psychology (LSP), developed in Latin America in the 1970s. The approach takes a collectivist approach to addressing psychological issues within a populace. Based on Paulo Freire's liberation theory and the pedagogy of the oppressed, LSP emphasizes the need for *conscientizado*, the process by which people understand their social status in the context of larger institutional structures and begin to take steps to change their situations (Burton and Kagan 2004). This process of *conscientizado* is a collective practice rather than individual. It is through group reflection and dialogue about lived experience, and the space to begin to question existing self-blaming stories, which allows people to see that their lives are interconnected – to each other, but also to larger social structures. In the LSP model, individuals do not just heal themselves; they heal and change the social conditions that created the traumatic experiences. LSP recognizes that even if individuals heal the effects of trauma on their own lives, they will return to, or remain, embedded in social environments that still produce the trauma(s) they suffered. Documentation of the centrality of collective well-being is also prominent within studies of Indigenous communities around the world (D'Amato 2020; Loera-Gonzales 2014). Indigenous communities have argued for greater attention to be paid to the long-term effects of colonialization and genocide, and to ensure that Indigenous peoples are active participants in research about their well-being (Prout 2012; D'Amato 2020; Loera-Gonzales 2014).

The general body of research on psychological well-being and general well-being has not yet been applied to survivors of human trafficking. Survivors are addressed primarily as victims of crime, which is rooted in the criminal justice and law enforcement approach to antihuman trafficking efforts (Choi-Fitzpatrick 2015). Recently, professionals in the United States and United Kingdom have begun to frame human trafficking as a public health concern (APHA 2015; Zimmerman and Kiss 2017; Rothman et al. 2017), but this is not the central approach to engaging with survivors after they have exited exploitation. The pervasive approach in addition to the law enforcement approach is one of psychopathology, where survivors are viewed only through the lens of trauma symptoms.

17.2.2 Understanding Psychological Functioning: Contextualizing Illness-Based Assumptions Rooted in White Supremacy

Most research about the psychological needs of survivors has focused on psychological illness, primarily through the use of mental illness diagnoses from the Diagnostic and Statistical Manual of Mental Disorders (DSM). The DSM was first published after World War II by the American Psychiatric Association (APA) and its intended goal was to assemble a manual that could provide an "authoritative guide to diagnosis of mental disorders" (APA n.d.). Similar to diagnostic manuals for medical diseases, the DSM aimed to provide a comprehensive system of classification of mental illness that would allow practitioners worldwide to operate from a common list of diagnoses and provide effective treatment and symptom reduction (van Heugten-van der Kloet and van Heugten 2015). One of the most highlighted benefits of the DSM throughout its long history is that it has made great strides in providing a common vocabulary for defining mental illness and standardizing diagnostic criteria (van Heugten-van der Kloet and van Heugten 2015).

Nearly 70 years after publication of its first edition in 1952, the DSM faces ongoing criticism from practitioners, scholars, and mental health service users. There are two main critiques of the DSM. The first is that it perpetuates the "medicalization of normality" (Pickersgill 2014, 522), which removes a person's social context from the diagnostic criteria. Assessing individuals without giving attention to the person's socio-cultural and political context is problematic because it can lead to pathologizing people. Rather than viewing particular symptoms as normal human responses within a social context, symptom clusters may become inaccurately interpreted as problematic. If individuals are not able to heal from trauma, it can be perceived as a personal rather than a societal failing. This can be especially true when clinicians from the dominant culture are assessing people who are *not* from the dominant culture.

Durlauf and Bloom, (as cited in World Health Organization 2009), describe how social and cultural norms "offer standards for appropriate and inappropriate behavior, governing what is (and is not) acceptable in interactions among people." Dominant cultures in any geography have the most influence on establishing social norms, including norms regarding emotional expressions and behavioral responses to life events. Anything deemed alternative to these social norms can be labeled abnormal, or pathological, rather than a difference in cultural norms of expression (Loera-Gonzalez 2014). For example, the recent DSM-V removed the exception of bereavement from the diagnosis of depression. This means that prior to the DSM-V, a person who was grieving the loss of a loved one and exhibiting symptoms of depression, might *not* receive a diagnosis of depression unless the symptoms were severe or lasted for longer than 2 weeks (Pies 2014). Now that this exception is removed, there is concern that a natural bereavement process will become pathologized *or* severe conditions that result from natural bereavement may become under-diagnosed (Shear et al. 2012). The very act of defining a standard time period for grieving a loved one and what constitutes severe grief, is an act of creating an acceptable norm and an unacceptable abnormal reaction that will be labeled a medical illness. The question becomes, who defines normal and abnormal? The researchers and practitioners responsible for constructing and validating the DSM are people who exist in a social world that is subject to social inequities. This means that the most marginalized populations will not be the authors of standard diagnoses and are more vulnerable to having their lived experiences pathologized.

This leads to the second major critique of the DSM: it purports to be an indisputable classification of disorders and ignores its own role in the social construction of reality. While the first critique is about the neglect of social context when diagnosing an individual, this second critique is about the neglect of social context *in the process* of creating a diagnostic manual itself. Mental disorders are "not an immutable standard, but rather, may be variable across time and culture, and in this way contingent upon changes in dominant schools of thought" (Kawa and Giordano 2012, 7). It is extremely difficult to define what mental illness is and even more difficult to separate the mental health diagnosis from the social and cultural context in which it exists. For example, the DSM once defined homosexuality as pathological until people who identified as gay and lesbian took social action to challenge the APA (Forstein 2002). The absence of a social and cultural analysis in the DSM leads to patients from the nondominant culture being disproportionately diagnosed with mental disorders (Loera-Gonzalez 2014; Caldwell-Harris and Ayçiçegi 2006).

The DSM-V has tried to address this concern by providing explanations for why culture matters for psychiatric interpretation in its introduction, a separate chapter, and in the glossary (Bredström 2019; Ecks 2016). Although this reference to cultural interpretation is laudable, there is no prerequisite for mental health practitioners to participate in cultural interpretation training prior to using the DSM-V. Diagnostic power remains in the hands of people who have received professional credentials from mainstream (read: dominant culture) training institutions.

This is the nature of mental health diagnosis: the diagnosis itself is validated by the dominant culture, given by a person trained through dominant culture institutions, and provided to an individual person who may or may not be a part of the dominant culture. This approach is not only directed at survivors of human trafficking; it is the standard Western healthcare approach towards anyone who suffers from mental distress. In the United States, diagnosis and treatment is individualized. Insurance companies use diagnoses outlined in the DSM as the barometer for legitimate treatment of mental distress (Halpin 2016).

Authors and practitioners have described additional limitations of the DSM, including stigmatization (Hinshaw 2005; Gambrill 2014), misdiagnosis and overdiagnosis (PLOS Medicine Editors 2013), and overmedicating (Levinson 2011; Gambrill 2014). The key concern about using diagnoses is that it can allow clinicians to lose sight of people as whole human beings and reduce the complexity of human experience. For example, someone with schizophrenia becomes "a schizophrenic." Recent "person-centered" approaches to counseling have promoted the use of "person first" language that emphasizes the human being who is facing a situation of mental illness, rather than becoming equated with the illness (Jensen et al. 2013). Once a person has become reduced to a specific diagnosis, it becomes easier to label and associate all of their behaviors as part and parcel of their diagnosis. Gambrill (2014) argues that the DSM dehumanizes people, "obscuring the role of environmental factors such as poverty and related political, social, moral, and economic factors such as the interest of the state in controlling deviant behavior and maintaining the status quo" (13).

The illness-based assumption of psychological functioning has its roots in White supremacy and was part of the disastrous effects of colonialism on Indigenous people and enslavement of people from Africa (Harvey 2016). White supremacy is defined as, "The idea (ideology) [sic] that White people and the ideas, thoughts, beliefs, and actions of White people are superior to People of Color and their ideas, thoughts, beliefs, and actions" (Jones and Okun 2001). This ideology is supported by social and political institutions of society, which seek to maintain the dominance of White people. Although Europeans had not previously defined themselves as a homogenous group, they invented the concept of race in order to rationalize why they were better equipped to assume the role of the dominant group (Wilkerson 2020). To engage in colonialization, they had to separate themselves as a distinct "White" race from the Indigenous populations they were seeking to rule and labeled Indigenous ways of living as "heathen" (Harvey 2016). Using race to distinguish difference proved to be an effective tool of social control (Wilkerson 2020) and "White people" used racial superiority to justify and invest heavily in establishing and maintaining the institution of slavery.

Because whiteness was often centralized, there was often a dismissal of other, collectivist understandings of trauma and trauma-informed responses (McGoldrick and Hardy 2008). The professionalization of treatments in mental health were historically developed by White men, such as Freud, Jung, and Adler (Open Textbook Library 2015). This has led to unrealistically high standards of normal functioning being classified in narrow White supremacy terms. The standards include: perfectionism, a sense of urgency, defensiveness, quantity over quality, worship of the written word, only one right way, paternalism, either/or thinking, power hoarding, fear of open conflict, individualism, objectivity, and the right to comfort (Jones and Okun 2001). Anyone outside of this standard is labeled as psychologically unhealthy. Gambrill (2014) emphasizes that "Acceptance of the statistically normal condition as equivalent to the psychologically healthy one results in pathologizing people who vary from the statistical norm" (16). Without the contextual understanding of dominant cultural norms, mental health professionals across all sectors may inadvertently pathologize clients who are exhibiting symptoms outside of what they consider a normal range of behavior.

The intended and unintended consequence of these standards, applied by the dominant cultural norm, is to place the sole responsibility of healing on the individual. Individual responsibility for one's life is not itself problematic; rather, decontextualizing individuals from socio-political history is problematic because it leads to pathologizing people. Challenges with healing from trauma may become perceived as personal failings rather than a societal failing to provide adequate resources and care. Survivors of the transatlantic slave trade as well as survivors of contemporary human trafficking both share negative consequences of a decontextualized response to psychological treatment. In Joy De Gruy's Post-Traumatic Slave Syndrome (2005), she describes how African Americans in "post-slavery" United States were treated as if they had "moral deficits." Rather than recognizing the long-term and continued impact of systematic state violence upon people who were forced into slavery and their descendants, White mainstream society attributed the challenges that emancipated Africans and African Americans faced to personal failings. White society made a structural problem (that they created), an individual problem (of African Americans).

As Joy DeGruy (2005) highlights, many African Americans retain behaviors and beliefs that are residual from the traumatizing effects of having to survive slavery, such as "a belief about one's [little or no] worth, not a measure of one's actual worth" (109). This belief, which DeGruy calls "vacant esteem" (2005, 108), is residual from the hundreds of years of dehumanizing practices enacted against Africans brought to the US to be enslaved, and subsequent African-American generations. A behavior example that DeGruy (2005) offers is when an African-American parent receives a compliment about her child. She accepts the compliment, but also says the child was poorly behaved today. The denigration is a learned and passed on behavior, useful when enslaved parents tried to make their children less appealing to Whites who might rape or sell their child (Wolper 2015). These behaviors have been passed down through multiple generations as coping mechanisms against White supremacy. As these coping practices are culturally prevalent across the US in people of African descent, the individual African American presenting for individual therapy will more than likely be seen using both the individual framework and the pathological framework. They will be viewed as someone who needs help in swapping current nonfunctioning behaviors for new functional ones. The understanding of from where these behaviors materialized, the collective wisdom inherent in them, and how the uses of these practices have sustained generations of African Americans will often be hidden. Restorative healing might come with the collective realizations that behaviors originating in "old legacy" of trauma would not be necessary if there was collective dominant culture accountability for oppressive practices that would lead to collective changes in dominant cultural behavior.

17.2.3 Parallels to Psychological Frameworks Applied to Survivors of Human Trafficking

In less obvious ways, this is also true within the anti-trafficking movement. The United States' Trafficking Victims Protection Act (TVPA) of 2000 defines human trafficking as a crime of individual bad actors upon other innocent individual actors. Thus, anti-trafficking efforts have primarily focused on prosecuting criminals, and to some extent supporting individual victims to heal. This individualistic framing leads to a harmful absence of an analysis of the structural causes of human trafficking. As such, the emphasis has been on stopping and punishing the perpetrators, and on helping people who are seen as victims of crime to address the impact of the crime. As a result, the study of the psychological impact has been restricted and allowed only for narrow measurements of psychological illness and ignores concepts of well-being. Consequently, survivors of human trafficking are described primarily in academic literature as traumatized people and viewed through the lens of psychological function or dysfunction (e.g., Oram et al. 2012; Hemmings et al. 2016; Zimmerman and Kiss 2017). There is insufficient and incomplete discussion of survivors as former victims of capitalism's drive for cheap and free labor (Chap. 2), refugees of war and conflict (Chap. 12), displaced citizens of climate change, and/or victims of housing shortages.

Increased attention to the structural causes of human trafficking and other traumas does not require the anti-trafficking field to ignore the individualized impact of structural violence. Structural violence absolutely has impact at the individual level, and it is important to support individuals in addressing those impacts. Many anti-trafficking organizations are providing this support, such as My Life, My Choice in Boston, API Legal Outreach in San Francisco, and Sanar Wellness Institute and You are More Than in New Jersey, to name very few. Federal and private dollars are appropriately being directed to these efforts (e.g., Office on Trafficking in Persons 2019; Office for Victims of Crime 2020; Freedom Fund n.d.). However, to solely focus on individuals and not on changing the structural causes of the impact are to place the burden of healing on individuals (see "Preface"). If people are able to heal from the traumatic consequences, they will still return to a structural environment that is capable of causing (and repeating) the same violence the person already suffered. Individual healing from human trafficking, just like the healing process of African Americans postslavery, must be placed in a structural context. The context is no longer directly supported by nation-states such as the transatlantic slave trade. However, the context is highly facilitated by nation-states through widespread support of corporate greed (Chap. 7), continued racism, child abuse, on-going wars, lack of enforcement of labor regulations (Chap. 6), anti-immigration policies (Chap. 10), impunity for sexual violence (Chap. 5), homophobia (Chap. 11), and so much more.

It is extremely important and therapeutic to address individual distress while holding a structural analysis. The first step in doing this is to move beyond an illness-based model of psychological trauma and to recognize the roots of the illness-based model in colonialism and imperialism. Therapeutic interventions can ensure that survivors are given this alternative explanation for the cause of their trauma and for their trauma reactions. By doing so, survivors can depersonalize the trauma and open up to new meaning-making about their narratives.

17.2.4 Alternatives to Pathology

If we do not accept the Eurocentric model that a functioning person is one who can contribute to economic production without emotional distress, then what do we take as a baseline for a healthy and well human being? The answer to this question is philosophical, culturally defined, and value laden. As discussed, the illness-based model defines a psychologically well human as someone who can consciously control their functioning and adapt behaviors to improve economic productivity. If someone cannot control and adapt their behaviors, this is seen as pathological. This ideal is counter to modern understandings of the impact of trauma, which recognizes that trauma reactions cannot be controlled.

A *trauma-informed* perspective is a useful alternative to the illness model of psychological functioning. Theories of trauma recognize that *all* responses to trauma are biological responses to extraordinary events (American Psychiatric Association n.d.). Across all types of trauma, there are many common traumatic stress reactions. The effects of trauma have been described in many domains: emotional, cognitive, physical, and interpersonal, and neurobiological (e.g., Herman 1992; Siegel 2012; van der Kolk 2005; Briere and Runtz 2002). Emotional effects of trauma are often expressed as blame, anger, guilt, grief, and numbness. Cognitive effects include impaired concentration, memory impairment, confusion, nightmares, and self-blame. Physical effects include fatigue, insomnia, hyperarousal, and startle responses. Finally, interpersonal effects such as increased relational conflict, social withdrawal, distrust, and reduced relational intimacy can be prevalent. Exhibition of any of these types of symptoms are indicators of the severity of the trauma experienced and can be useful in determining the type of supports that would be most conducive to healing.

17.2.5 Individualized Trauma Responses

Antitrafficking professionals must be careful to remember that each person who experiences trauma, whether as a single occurrence or as an ongoing series of experiences, has their own responses. Despite the commonality of responses, individuals always have a subjective experience that ultimately determines how traumatic the event(s) is to them. These unique responses are not a result of inherent weaknesses in people or characterological failings. Rather, they are a result of the ways each person uniquely adapts to the cumulative experiences of their lives – experiences that include biology, human development, environment, geography, social relationships, and early childhood experiences. A trauma-informed approach to psychological functioning recognizes that structural conditions within society (such as racism, sexism, and homophobia) will influence how individuals experience their trauma.

People are not blank slates when trauma, such as human trafficking, meets their life. Before any trauma occurs, a person has lived a life based on a set of values that they have learned from the culture in which they are embedded. Unless born into a traumatic environment—which is not uncommon—people have been taught values based on a collective understanding that are based in culture and subcultures of the society in which they live. How they respond to a traumatic event will be based on the values they hold dear. The more violation of these dearly held values, the more traumatic the event. As such, not all people experiencing trauma will express traumatic symptoms, nor do all suffer from diagnosable mental illness. Many that have symptoms are able to return to the level of functioning they experienced prior to human trafficking. This does not negate the fact that when a person experiences repeated loss of control, violations of safety, betrayal of trust, intense loss of self-autonomy, and a loss of community over a prolonged period of time, that the chances of incurring psychological harm do in fact increase. Recognizing the variety of individual and structural factors that impact psychological functioning allows for an understanding of why each person manifests trauma responses in different ways.

In her groundbreaking book *Trauma and Recovery,* Judith Lewis Herman (1992) defines psychological trauma as:

> …An affiliation of the powerless. At the moment of trauma, the victim is rendered helpless by overwhelming force. When the force is that of nature, we speak of disasters. When the force is that of other human beings, we speak of atrocities.
>
> Traumatic events overwhelm the ordinary systems of care that give people a sense of control, connection, and meaning. *Traumatic events are extraordinary, not because they occur rarely, but rather because they overwhelm the ordinary human adaptations to life* [emphasis added].
>
> Unlike commonplace misfortunes, traumatic events generally involve threats to life or bodily integrity, or a close personal encounter with violence and death. They confront human beings with the extremities of helplessness and terror, and evoke the responses of catastrophe (33).

Survivors of trauma are faced with an inability to make sense of senseless situations. As a result, individuals will often make meaning of trauma by engaging in shaming and blaming practices that make them responsible for the trauma (Chap. 13). The only way that people may be able to make sense of being in such a helpless situation is to blame themselves. Taking responsibility for the trauma allows a survivor to distance themselves from the overwhelming and painful experience of helplessness. It creates a sense of control over something that is uncontrollable, and that can no longer be rectified. The behaviors that manifest from the self-blaming might appear to others as irrational and pathological.

17.2.6   Narrative Therapy Approaches and Complex Trauma

Labeling survivors' coping mechanisms as irrational leads to a calamitous though subtle acceptance of victim blaming. Victim blaming practices increase the effects of the trauma for the survivors and result in the reaffirmation that normal, common, and accepted coping mechanisms should be seen as pathological. *Narrative therapy* approaches are complimentary to Herman's definition of psychological trauma, as they focus on an individual's meaning-making and storytelling of the events. In narrative approaches, the problem is the problem, rather than the person being the problem (Epston 1990). Narrative approaches also place the stories within a larger sociohistorical context. There is no victim blaming. When natural disasters such as hurricanes occur, the collective narrative of the trauma is that the event relates to chance and the randomness of nature. The cause of the trauma is depersonalized; that is to say, individual victims are not blamed by the collective for the event's occurrence. Some individuals might still blame themselves, for not sufficiently preparing for the disaster, but there is an abundance of counter narratives, evidenced by the outpouring of help offered. Large sums of money are often raised quickly as ordinary people donate what they can to help people recover from their losses. These communal responses often lead to a lessened stressor response by individuals and a quicker return to their functioning levels prior to the traumatic event.

A single intrapersonal traumatic event like a robbery can also heighten stressor responses in some people. The person's response would depend on the severity of the event, the age of the victim, the amount of loss, and the quickness of the recovery process and on the well-being of the person before the trauma occurred. Although single events do result in traumatic effects, the most painful and severe mental illness symptoms result from repeated, on-going, traumatic experiences that can last many years. These are now commonly called *complex traumas* (van der Kolk 2005). It is the repeated nature of violence inflicted on someone by another fellow human being that makes interpersonal trauma more difficult to deal with than natural disasters (Herman 1992). There is no narrative that explains the actions of abuse and oppression that makes any sense to the victim and even worse are experiences of trauma that are intentional acts of violence by someone who is a trusted caregiver, especially in a parent-child relationship (Perry 1994; Siegel 2012). These violations are inexplicable and can cause breaches in development, attachment, and security. As a survivor's sense of themselves and their place in the world is violated over and over again the person is left with little ability to make sense of the situation.

As trauma is occurring, people respond to these great hardships with strategies of coping. "No one is a passive recipient of trauma" (White 2004). Everyone utilizes a form of resistance that involves great acts of bravery. Each person who experiences a traumatic event goes on to make meaning of that event. When choice is taken away by enacting violence on another person, the person receiving the violence must make meaning of the situation in order for it to make sense. Trauma, by definition, overwhelms the psychological systems for meaning-making (Herman 1992). As a consequence, people create negative meaning from the traumatic events and apply self-blame to themselves, leading to internalized trauma. From this position, post-traumatic behaviors and narratives are often expressed negatively. Seen without a lens of understanding of how trauma reactions coopt behavior, the person often becomes pathologized as their behaviors clash with dominant social norms. What was once a functional coping mechanism during prolonged trauma appears after trauma as potential maladaptive behavior.

As people try to make meaning of their situation, they rely on their values. They did not learn their values in isolation but from the culture in which they live. Therefore, a key element of how a person responds to trauma is determined by dominant cultural values—which include oppressive practices—which the person internalizes and assumes are their individual responsibility. The meaning a label has is often reflective of the level of blame attributed to the victim. This is most clearly demonstrated in physical diseases where the narrative has been set up as a war against a specific disease and the victim is a heroic blameless survivor; for example, the narrative of the "war on cancer." But identity statements, such as "I am a child sexual abuse survivor," or "I am a victim of human trafficking," if used with an attaching of shame and blame to the victim (by suggesting the victim had a role in being violated), can lead to pathology and disempowerment. But if reclaimed and reappropriated by survivors, these statements can lead to empowerment and healing and often that is a part of the recovery process.

In the case of human trafficking, coping responses might take the form of hyper-vigilance, dissociation, numbing, compliance, and so on. These coping mechanisms are deployed to lessen the harm that is occurring and are used to survive. These strategies both increase one's ability to maintain a sense of self and adjust to a situation that is potentially life threatening. In many instances, these coping mechanisms are the very foundations of making it through the traumatic experiences. They are practices of resistance to trauma. The coping mechanisms deployed during the traumatic events may no longer be useful and may now be harmful as the person moves from surviving to thriving. Although hypervigilance is a protective coping mechanism for someone living in a dangerous situation where at any moment they can be harmed, the response of paying close attention to every little detail and staying on high alert might not serve the person in their new life. They might make relationships difficult, work routines disruptive, and cause physical illness. The body and mind, having adapted to reacting with specific survival coping mechanisms, may now have trouble readapting to safer environments. They may continue to have raised cortical levels, and a hyperaroused sympathetic nervous system such that their behavioral and emotional coping mechanisms that are quickly activated at the slightest hint of danger. These are often categorized in a mental health setting as symptoms of disease. The treatment goal of Western medicine is then symptom reduction rather than understanding. As discussed above, trauma-informed and narrative approaches seek to allow survivors to tell a story about their trauma and their responses, that allows them to make meaning and understand their experiences.

17.2.7   Advocacy as Method for Legacy Building
with Survivors of Human Trafficking

Creating a Personal Legacy

Survivors of any type of trauma are faced with the coexistence of the effects of the trauma and the reality of a new day-to-day life. After the trauma, the next step is to figure out how to go beyond surviving and move to thriving. Now that the reality of danger is over, how does a person cope in the present, imagine a future, and deal with the past? Surviving trauma involves connecting with what a person gives meaning to and the values that they hold dear. If survivors move beyond making sense of the trauma by blaming themselves, they need to find alternative meaning to experience well-being. Making meaning—or in other words, making sense of senseless violence—is a difficult, if not impossible, task. Some survivors make meaning for their present and future lives by using their experiences of trauma to benefit others. Surviving trauma often invokes the desire to create a new legacy, in an attempt to ensure others do not suffer the same trauma (White 1995; Epston 1990).

Building a new legacy is important because it returns control over the meaning of life to the survivors themselves. Survivors can decide for what reason they might live. Because the old legacy of trauma cannot be changed, the ability to create a new legacy gives survivors power. One example of this is Mothers Against Drunk Driving (MADD). A few months after the death of her 13-year-old daughter Cari, Candy Lightner formed MADD to prevent other families from suffering the loss of a child to a drunk driving. She did this explicitly to "try to make sense of the sense-less act and turn her pain into purpose" (MADD 2020) and built an organization that advocates for supporting families and seeks to change social conditions that enable drunk driving. Survivors of many different types of trauma have started their own advocacy organizations including Rise (for rape and sexual assault survivors), Freedom from Torture (for survivors of torture), and March for our Lives 2020 (for survivors of gun violence in Parkland, Florida, USA), to name a few.

Advocacy is a legacy-building activity because it is about changing conditions in the future. For the purpose of this chapter, advocacy is defined as engagement in self-determined social justice work which connects personal issues to larger social problems. These activities integrate: (1) addressing current psychological distress, (2) building positive well-being, and (3) creating a lasting impact for the future. Although advocacy activities are not necessarily pursued by people to "create a legacy," this effect is a key reason why it is beneficial for survivors to be engaged in advocacy. Advocacy gets to the heart of all aspects of Ryff's psychological well-being, particularly the dimension of purpose of life. Advocacy for one's self and others can become a purpose in life. As demonstrated by Candy Lightner, advocacy allows people to utilize their lived experience to motivate and direct their engagement in activities that seek to change a larger social problem. For survivors of human trafficking, many of whom faced near death experiences, life after trafficking involves questioning the purpose of being alive at all. Advocacy allows people to explore how a purpose in life might be created from within oneself. Additionally, survivors can take action to prevent others from being exploited and/or to improve the lives of fellow survivors, which leaves a lasting, positive impact in the world.

These activities also address Ryff's well-being dimensions of autonomy, positive relationships with others, personal growth, and personal acceptance. In order to engage in advocacy, survivors of trauma must get in touch with their own needs and desires and learn to speak on their own behalf. The act of having a need or personal desire can be transformative, especially when trauma requires people to suppress desires and focus on survival. Expressing these needs and/or desired changes to society allows survivors of trauma to experience the potential power of their own voice. Having learned through surviving trauma that many of their actions are futile, the ability to witness their own actions having impact in the external world is vital to well-being.

Community-based and group-based advocacy efforts also help survivors understand their experience in a wider context. They can begin to depersonalize the trauma and see that their responses to trauma are normal. When people can come together to tell collective stories of resistance and struggle *against* the trauma, they can recognize their skills of resistance and coping, as well as their knowledge of great pain and suffering. Resistance storytelling can generate collective strategies for coping and moving beyond suffering. Survivors can collectively build on the skills, talents, strengths, and knowledge gained through great acts of survival and resistance to oppression, and by persevering under great duress. These activities are counter to many dominant cultural practices, including therapeutic practices that encourage the retelling of stories of the most difficult experiences of violence. Without a purpose for the retelling of stories, it contributes to labeling trauma survivors in pathological illness-based terms and completely squanders the opportunity for both the victim and the professional helpers to understand how people survive great hardship and suffering.

Engagement in relationships with others via advocacy can also help to decrease shame, rebuild trust in others, and facilitate new relationships based on shared experience and goals. Advocacy also challenges survivors to take stock of their current self-capacities and provides avenues for learning and growing. They can learn about civil society institutions, travel to and from new locations, learn to communicate in new ways (e.g., direct vs. indirect communication, using the language of human rights), and learn how to stay safe and protect themselves. This engagement with their external environment develops a sense of environmental mastery and may highlight survivors' acts of resistance and uncover strengths.

For survivors of human trafficking, one prominent modern advocacy example is the creation of the US Advisory Council on Human Trafficking. Feeling frustrated that the US government did not take survivors' perspectives into consideration, a large group of survivors and allied NGOs campaigned to create an institutional structure for survivors to provide feedback and recommendations to US federal agencies. The US has seen a growth of survivor advocacy efforts since 2011, with the creation of the National Survivor Network (NSN). NSN is a membership-based group of self-identified survivors of human trafficking who primarily live in the

United States. Incorporated as part of a larger organization, the Coalition to Abolish Slavery and Trafficking (CAST), the NSN began to bring a collective survivor voice to national antitrafficking efforts (NSN n.d.). With a focus on policy advocacy, NSN helped shift common antitrafficking practices from ignoring and tokenizing survivors' voices to respecting and including survivor feedback. Another flagship survivor leadership program, the Survivor Leadership Institute (SLI) was launched in 2013 by Girls Educational and Mentoring Services (GEMS) and was designed to empower survivors of commercial sexual exploitation. Prior to SLI, GEMS supported youth survivors to advocate for policy change in New York (GEMS n.d.). There is still much progress that needs to be made regarding deeper integration of the lived experiences of survivors in policy and practice. However, NGOs, funders, and government bodies in the US are more regularly seeking meaningful inclusion and engagement with survivors as subject matter experts and consultants. Over the last decade, several independent survivor advocacy initiatives have developed (Smith 2018) in order to facilitate survivor engagement in antitrafficking efforts.

The key dimensions of advocacy for survivors of human trafficking mirror the elements of advocacy discussed in the previous section. At its core, survivor advocacy is trauma-informed and addresses psychological well-being. Table 17.1 outlines the core principles of the Legacy-Building Approach to Healing and recommends that these are adopted within post-trafficking interventions. The first

Table 17.1 Core principles of legacy-building approach to healing

Principle	Description	Related activities
1. Lived experience is a source of expertize.	Each person has gained insights from their lived experiences that can inform policy and practice.	Participating in advisory boards; leading direct service programs, consulting within the antitrafficking field; providing training to front-line staff.
2. Healing from trauma is an individual *and* collective practice.	Survivors are responsible for their own journey to address the impact of trauma, and they can positively contribute to the journeys of others impacted by trauma.	Pursuing personal healing practices; group conversations that support individual meaning-making; collective story telling; providing peer-support and mentoring; self-care to prevent burnout.
3. Community building resists oppressive practices and challenges structural inequity.	Survivors recognize that their lives are interconnected with each other and create spaces for groups to gather and challenge individualism and alienation. Survivors collaborate with, celebrate, and support one another in many dimensions of life.	Develop one-on-one relationships with fellow survivors; develop networks of survivors to harness social capital; create alternative institutions or structures of care (e.g., childcare collectives); organize collective direct actions.
4. Activities must create shifts in society that will improve the quality of life for survivors.	Individual and/or collective efforts are focused on action. Changes in material conditions and/or psychological experiences must be concrete.	Seeking legislative change and/or enforcement; distributing resources or improving access to existing ones; challenging or changing inappropriate public dialog.

principle is that lived experience of human trafficking provides expertize in survival. Although each survivor may need to work to unearth and articulate the invaluable insights about survival, the seeds of this knowledge are embedded in lived experience. In survivor advocacy, the life experiences of each person must be respected. Approaching survivors' lived experience as a form of expertize challenges and counters the negative self-beliefs of inadequacy, unworthiness, or that they have nothing good to contribute; these feelings are products of trauma. By working with survivors to help them articulate what they have learned through their lived experience, survivors can harness their own knowledge as expertize. This expertize can then be offered to other parties engaged in antitrafficking work, enabling survivors to use their expertize to create change. As mentioned earlier, any positive impact that these insights have on the actions or beliefs of others allows survivors to feel efficacious and to leave a new legacy.

The second principle is that healing from trauma is an individual and collective practice. This means that each person can define what healing looks like to them but does not heal within a vacuum. Trauma impacts the meaning-making systems, which are influenced by culture. For survivors to make meaning of their trauma, they will need to engage with the beliefs and practices around healing that are promoted by the cultures surrounding them. If the cultures within which survivors heal are inconsistent or different from previous cultural understandings, survivors will need the support of others to explore what elements of past and present culture they wish to incorporate into their lives. This is not an easy task. Therefore, peer support groups, creating space for survivors to pursue their healing journey, and collective discussions about healing are important. These discussions are central to advocacy, although they may appear more relevant to personal psychological functioning. Survivors' journey to healing may include their advocacy efforts; the two may be intertwined. Creating a place where survivors can channel healthy anger and focus their desire for justice allows for repurposing of life.

In order to create collective healing practices, principle three emphasizes the need to proactively build community because community building resists oppressive practices. Namely, community fights against alienation. "For one of the most vital ways we sustain ourselves is by building communities of resistance, places where we know we are not alone" (Hooks 2015, 215). Through building community with one another, survivors can create alternative mechanisms for their own well-being, decreasing situational dependence upon nonprofit and government support. Networks of survivors and peer support groups allow survivors to provide for their own care and interventions. It also allows for building a community identity, especially when the trafficking experience may have torn them away from previous communities of identity. Survivors of human trafficking often do not come out with a community intact and find it difficult to build relationships with people who do not share their human trafficking experience. Survivors must navigate living with their trafficking experiences in silence or sharing it with people who cannot relate. Building survivor communities resists the oppressive silencing tactics and allows survivors to self-define how they want to engage the broader world with their experiences of human trafficking.

The fourth and final core principle is that advocacy must create shifts in society that improve the quality of life for survivors. This principle is based in survivors' experiences of lots of "talk but no action." When people who do not have lived experience of human trafficking are responsible for changing policy and practice, the sense of urgency can be lost. Survivors seek changes that will directly benefit them, their loved ones, and their fellow survivors. This principle separates activities such as *sharing* personal testimonies, from *using* personal testimony to push for policy change. Personal testimonies, in and of themselves, do not necessarily change the material and psychological conditions for survivors in sustainable or structural ways. Survivor advocacy values lived experience from the standpoint that lived experience provides expert knowledge on key social issues. Personal testimonies used strategically to provide evidence or support for specific policy or practice recommendations *can* create lasting change. In this way, survivors can be heard for the parts of their stories they deem most relevant to create a shift in public policy. Labor rights campaigns are a successful example of liberation social psychology in action. Antitrafficking efforts that have utilized a labor exploitation framework have allowed the individual and collective to coexist. Remedies are sought with the understanding that human lives are impacted by labor exploitation; systemic change is led by the people who are impacted by labor exploitation that is rooted in capitalism's drive for cheap labor. Although these campaigns do not address the effects of psychological trauma, they change broader social conditions that can contribute to greater psychological well-being. Survivor advocacy challenges the pathological approach to psychological trauma, and promotes a trauma-informed, liberation approach. In survivor advocacy, psychological symptoms are not the focus. Advocating for the appropriate support to help deal with those symptoms, might be. Self-blame also begins to take a back seat, as survivors begin to link their personal experiences to historical and sociopolitical contexts.

17.3 Conclusion

Departing from the illness-based, pathology model of psychological well-being, the antitrafficking field can begin to imagine new psychological interventions. The focus can shift to human trafficking as a larger social issue – as the natural consequence to capitalism's drive for the cheapest labor, or as a consequence of the culture of colonialism which seeks dominion over equality of people. Survivors can become key leaders and stakeholders in addressing human trafficking and related root-social problems such as racism and poverty. Psychological treatment of survivors would then be focused on well-being – supporting survivors to develop a whole life with their entire personhood, instead of solely on managing distress symptoms.

Utilizing advocacy to address some of the effects of trauma minimizes victim blaming and pathologizing. Advocacy also addresses isolation, strengthens community networks, and increases internal and external resources available to a person. Advocacy as an intervention also benefits communities because there are more engaged citizens and residents participating in society. It is well understood that good relationships with fellow humans provide positive meaning to life. By providing survivors with the opportunity to move from a socially alienated position to a position of active citizenship, practitioners create a new type of psychological intervention – one that is trauma-informed and accepts the reality of trauma symptoms, but that also enables survivors to build meaning and hope in their lives and leave a positive legacy in society.

17.4 Recommendations

In order to shift psychological interventions for survivors from being illness and pathology centered to trauma-informed and well-being centered, researchers, practitioners, funders, and policy makers and practitioners can adopt the following practices.

1. *Invest in survivor leadership, education, training, and community-building* to ensure that: (1) survivors can inform, design, and implement innovative, community-based solutions; (2) survivors can build supportive communities as alternative institutions of care; and (3) survivors have the capacity to train and engage with allied professionals.
2. *Require that antitrafficking professionals in every sector receive sufficient education and training on the general effects of trauma*, including differences between the effects of interpersonal trauma, natural disaster trauma, and complex trauma.
3. *Address the systemic and structural forces that create victims of capitalism's drive for cheap and free labor, refugees of war and conflict, displaced citizens of climate change, and/or victims of housing shortages.*
4. *Create and invest time and financial resources to enable survivors to review and recommend changes to existing policies and practice.*
5. *Promote narrative-based interventions that place survivors' stories within a sociohistorical context.* This shifts the purpose from voyeurism to education for systemic change; the focus should be the context with the survivor story as a form of evidence.
6. *Integrate community building and/or development of social networks into treatment plans, care plans, and program outcome measures.* Practitioners can ask, "Who can you go to in case of an emergency? Who do you feel comfortable calling to socialize with? Who do you consider your community? What hopes do you have for them?"
7. *Prioritize funding for advocacy interventions that are led by survivors of human trafficking.* Include requirements for measuring the impact of the intervention on psychological well-being.

References

American Psychiatric Association. (2013). *Diagnostic and statistical manual of mental disorders* (5th ed.). Washington, DC: Author.

American Psychiatric Association. (n.d.). *DSM-5 frequently asked questions.* APA. https://www.psychiatry.org/psychiatrists/practice/dsm/feedback-and-questions/frequently-asked-questions

American Public Health Association. (2015). *Expanding and coordinating human trafficking-related public health research, evaluation, education, and prevention. Policy number 201516.* Available at: https://www.apha.org/policies-and-advocacy/public-health-policy-statements/policy-database/2016/01/26/14/28/expanding-and-coordinating-human-trafficking-related-public-health-activities

Anda, R. F., Felitti, V. J., Bremner, J. D., Walker, J. D., Whitfield, C., Perry, B. D., Dube, S. R., & Giles, W. H. (2006). The enduring effects of abuse and related adverse experiences in childhood. A convergence of evidence from neurobiology and epidemiology. *European Archives of Psychiatry and Clinical Neuroscience, 256,* 174–186. https://doi.org/10.1007/s00406-005-0624-4.

Bredström, A. (2019). Culture and context in mental health diagnosing: Scrutinizing the DSM-5 revision. *Journal of Medical Humanities, 40*(3), 347–363. https://doi.org/10.1007/s10912-017-9501-1.

Briere, J., & Runtz, M. (2002). The Inventory of Altered Self-Capacities (IASC): A standardized measure of identity, affect regulation, and relationship disturbance. *Assessment, 9*(3), 230–239.

Burton, M., & Kagan, C. (2004). Liberation social psychology: Learning from Latin America. *Journal of Community & Applied Social Psychology, 15,* 63–78.

Caldwell-Harris, C. L., & Ayçiçegi, A. (2006). When personality and culture clash: The psychological distress of allocentrics in an individualist culture and idiocentrics in a collectivist culture. *Transcultural Psychiatry, 43*(3), 331–361. https://doi.org/10.1177/1363461506066982.

Calhoun, L. G., & Tedeschi, R. G. (Eds.). (2006). *Handbook of posttraumatic growth: Research and practice.* New York: Psychology Press.

Charlton, J. (1998). *Nothing about us without us.* Berkeley: University of California Press.

Choi-Fitzpatrick, A. (2015). From rescue to representation: A human rights approach to the contemporary antislavery movement. *Journal of Human Rights, 14*(4), 486–503. https://doi.org/10.1080/14754835.2015.1032222.

Clifton, S., Fortune, N., Llewellyn, G., Stancliffe, R. J., & Williamson, P. (2020). Lived expertise and the development of a framework for tracking the social determinants, health, and wellbeing of Australians with disability. *Scandinavian Journal of Disability Research, 22*(1), 137–146. https://doi.org/10.16993/sjdr.688.

D'Amato, C. (2020). Collectivist capabilitarianism. *Journal of Human Development and Capabilities, 21*(2), 105–120. https://doi.org/10.1080/19452829.2020.1732887.

Dang, M., Bales, K., & Wright, N. (n.d.). *Wellbeing of survivors of slavery: A rapid literature review.* Manuscript submitted for publication.

DeGruy, J. (2005). *Post-traumatic slave syndrome.* Portland: Joy DeGruy Publications.

Diener, E. (2000). Subjective well-being: The science of happiness and a proposal for a national index. American Psychologist, 55(1), 34–43. https://doi.org/10.1037/0003-066X.55.1.34.

Ecks, S. (2016). The strange absence of things in the "culture" of the DSM-V. *CMAJ, 188*(2), 142–143. https://doi.org/10.1503/cmaj.150268.

Epston, D. (1990). *Narrative means to therapeutic ends.* New York: WW Norton & Company.

Finlay, J., Hardy, M., Morris, D., & Nagy, A. (2010). Mamow Ki-ken-da-ma-win: A partnership approach to child, youth, family and community wellbeing. *International Journal of Mental Health and Addiction, 8*(2), 245–257. https://doi.org/10.1007/s11469-009-9263-8.

Forstein, M. (2002). Overview of ethical and research issues in sexual orientation therapy. *Sexual Conversion Therapy: Ethical, Clinical and Research Perspectives, 7140,* 167–179. https://doi.org/10.1080/19359705.2001.9962290.

Freedom from Torture. (n.d.). *How we are run*. https://www.freedomfromtorture.org/what-we-do/how-we-are-run

Freedom Fund. (n.d.). *Our approach*. Accessed: https://freedomfund.org/programs/our-approach/

Gambrill, E. (2014). The diagnostic and statistical manual of mental disorders as a major form of dehumanization in the modern world. *Research on Social Work Practice, 24*(1), 13–36.

Girls Educational and Mentoring Services. (2013). *More than a survivor exhibit*. https://www.gems-girls.org/survivor-leadership

Girls Educational and Mentoring Services. (n.d.). *Survivor leadership*. Accessed: https://www.gems-girls.org/what-is-survivor-leadership

Halpin, M. (2016). The DSM and professional practice: Research, clinical, and institutional perspectives. *Journal of Health and Social Behavior, 57*(2), 153–167. https://doi.org/10.1177/0022146516645637.

Harvey, S. P. (2016). Ideas of race in early America. *Oxford Research Encyclopedias*. https://doi.org/10.1093/acrefore/9780199329175.013.262.

Hemmings, S., Jakobowitz, S., Abas, M., Bick, D., Howard, L. M., Stanley, N., Zimmerman, C., & Oram, S. (2016). Responding to the health needs of survivors of human trafficking: A systematic review. *BMC Health Services Research, 16*(1), 1–9. https://doi.org/10.1186/s12913-016-1538-8.

Herman, J. (1992). *Trauma and recovery*. New York: Basic Books.

Hinshaw, S. P. (2005). The stigmatization of mental illness in children and parents: Developmental issues, family concerns, and research needs. *Journal of Child Psychology and Psychiatry and Allied Disciplines, 46*(7), 714–734. https://doi.org/10.1111/j.1469-7610.2005.01456.x.

Hooks, B. (2015). *Yearning: Race, gender and cultural politics*. New York: Routledge.

Jensen, M. E., Pease, E. A., Lambert, K., Hickman, D. R., Robinson, O., McCoy, K. T., Barut, J. K., Musker, K. M., Olive, D., Noll, C., Ramirez, J., Cogliser, D., & King, J. K. (2013). Championing person-first language: A call to psychiatric mental health nurses. *Journal of the American Psychiatric Nurses Association, 19*(3), 146–151. https://doi.org/10.1177/1078390313489729.

Jones, K. & Okun, T. (2001). Dismantling racism: A workbook for social change groups. *ChangeWork*. Retrieved from: https://resourcegeneration.org/wp-content/uploads/2018/01/2016-dRworks-workbook.pdf

Katona, C., Robjant, K., Shapcott, R., & Witkin, R. (2015). *Addressing mental health needs in survivors of modern slavery: A critical review and research agenda*. London: Helen Bamber Foundation.

Kawa, S., & Giordano, J. (2012). A brief historicity of the diagnostic and statistical manual of mental disorders: Issues and implications for the future of psychiatric canon and practice. *Philosophy, Ethics, and Humanities in Medicine, 7*(1), 2. https://doi.org/10.1186/1747-5341-7-2.

Knifton, L. (2015). Collective wellbeing in public mental health. *Perspectives in Public Health, 135*(1), 24–26. https://doi.org/10.1177/1757913914563247.

Legacy. (n.d.). *In Oxford online dictionary*. Retrieved from: https://www.oed.com/view/Entry/107006?rskey=EvdKv1&result=1#eid

Levinson, D. R. (2011). *Overmedication of nursing home patients troubling*. Washington, DC: Inspector General, U. S. Department of Health and Human Services.

Loera-Gonzalez, J. J. (2014). The power of wellbeing discourses among indigenous and non-indigenous people in Mexico. *IDS Bulletin, 45*(2–3), 29–42. https://doi.org/10.1111/1759-5436.12081.

March for our Lives. (2020). *Mission and story*. https://marchforourlives.com/mission-story/

Martin-Baro, I. (1996). In A. Aon & S. Corne (Eds.), *Writings for a Liberation psychology*. Boston: Harvard University Press.

McDonnell, M., Robjant, K., & Katona, C. (2013). Complex posttraumatic stress disorder and survivors of human rights violations. *Current Opinion in Psychiatry, 25*(1), 1–6. https://doi.org/10.1097/YCO.0b013e32835aea9d.

McGoldrick, M., & Hardy, K. V. (2008). Introduction. In M. McGoldrick & K. V. Hardy (Eds.), *Re-visioning family therapy: Race, culture and gender in clinical practice* (2nd ed., pp. 3–24). New York: The Guilford Press.

McLean, A. (2003). Recovering consumers and a broken mental health system in the United States: Ongoing challenges for consumers/survivors and the New Freedom Commission on Mental Health. Part I: Legitimization of the consumer movement and obstacles to it. *International Journal of Psychosocial Rehabilitation, 8*, 47–57.

Mothers Against Drunk Driving. (2020). *Saving lives, serving people.* https://www.madd.org/history/

National Survivor Network. (n.d.). *About the National Survivor Network.* Accessed: https://nationalsurvivornetwork.org/about-us/

Office for Victims of Crime. (2020). *Human trafficking: Grants and funding.* U.S. Department of Justice. Accessed: https://ovc.ojp.gov/program/human-trafficking/grants-funding

Office on Trafficking in Persons. (2019). *Trafficking victim assistance program: Information and data.* U.S. Department of Health and Human Services. Accessed: https://www.acf.hhs.gov/otip/resource/tvap

Open Textbook Library. (2015). *Introduction to psychology.* Place of publication not identified: University of Minnesota Libraries Publishing.

Oram, S., Stockl, H., Busza, J., Howard, L. M., & Zimmerman, C. (2012). Prevalence and risk of violence and the physical. *Mental, and Sexual Health Problems Associated with Human Trafficking: Systematic Review, 9*(5), 1–13. https://doi.org/10.1371/journal.pmed.1001224.

Ottisova, L., Hemmings, S., Howard, L. M., Zimmerman, C., & Oram, S. (2016). Prevalence and risk of violence and the mental, physical and sexual health problems associated with human trafficking: An updated systematic review. *Epidemiology and Psychiatric Sciences, 25*(04), 317–341. https://doi.org/10.1017/S2045796016000135.

Pelka, F. (2012). *What we have done: An oral history of the disability rights movement.* Amherst: University of Massachusetts Press.

Perry, B. (1994). In M. M. Marburg (Ed.), *Neurobiological sequelae of childhood trauma: PTSD in children, in catecholamine function in posttraumatic stress disorder: Emerging concepts.* Washington, DC: American Psychiatric Press.

Pickersgill, M. D. (2014). Debating DSM-5: Diagnosis and the sociology of critique. *Journal of Medical Ethics, 40*(8), 521–525.

Pies, R. W. (2014). The bereavement exclusion and DSM-5: An update and commentary. *Innovations in Clinical Neuroscience, 11*(7–8), 19–22.

PLOS Medicine Editors. (2013). The paradox of mental health: Over-treatment and under-recognition. *PLoS Medicine, 10*(5), e1001456. https://doi.org/10.1371/journal.pmed.1001456.

Prout, S. (2012). Indigenous wellbeing frameworks in Australia and the quest for quantification. *Social Indicators Research, 109*(2), 317–336. https://doi.org/10.1007/s11205-011-9905-7.

Rise. (n.d.). *State-by-state legislative reform: Survivors' Bill of Rights.* https://www.risenow.us/campaigns/sexual-assault-survivors-bill-of-rights.

Rothman, E. F., Stoklosa, H., Baldwin, S. B., Chisolm-Straker, M., Kato Price, R., & Atkinson, H. G. (2017). Public health research priorities to address US Human Trafficking. *American Journal of Public Health, 107*(7), 1045–1047.

Ryff, C. (1995). Psychological well-being in adult life. *Current Directions in Psychological Science, 4*(4), 99–104.

Sanchez, R. V., & Pacquiao, D. F. (2018). An ecological approach toward prevention and care of victims of domestic minor sex trafficking. *Journal of Forensic Nursing, 14*(2), 98–105. https://doi.org/10.1097/JFN.0000000000000205.

Schrank, B., Bird, V., Tylee, A., Coggins, T., Rashid, T., & Slade, M. (2013). Conceptualising and measuring the well-being of people with psychosis: Systematic review and narrative synthesis. *Social Science & Medicine, 92*, 9–21.

Seligman, M., & Csikszentmihalyi, M. (2000). Positive psychology: An introduction. *American Psychologist, 55*(1), 5–14.

Shear, M. K., Simon, N., Wall, M., Zisook, S., Neimeyer, R., Duan, N., Reynolds, C., Lebowitz, B., Sung, S., & Ghesquiere, A. (2012). Complicated grief and related bereavement issues for DSM-5. *Depression and Anxiety, 28*(2), 103–117. https://doi.org/10.1002/da.20780. COMPLICATED.

Siegel, D. (2012). *The developing mind: How relationships and the brain interact to shape who we are* (2nd ed.). New York: The Guilford Press.

Slade, M. (2010). Mental illness and well-being: The central importance of positive psychology and recover approaches. *BMC Health Services Research, 10*(26). Retrieved from: http://www.biomedcentral.com/1472-6963/10/26.

Smith, M. (2018). *Human trafficking survivor leadership in the United States*. Freedom Network USA. https://freedomnetworkusa.org/app/uploads/2019/01/SurvivorWhitePaperDigitalFinalJan2019-1.pdf

Steele, L. G., & Lynch, S. M. (2013). The pursuit of happiness in China: Individualism, collectivism, and subjective well-being during China's economic and social transformation. *Social Indicators Research, 114*(2), 441–451. https://doi.org/10.1007/s11205-012-0154-1.

Swami, V., Stieger, S., Voracek, M., Dressler, S. G., Eisma, L., & Furnham, A. (2009). Psychometric evaluation of the tagalog and German subjective happiness scales and a cross-cultural comparison. *Social Indicators Research, 93*(2), 393–406. https://doi.org/10.1007/s11205-008-9331-7.

U.S. Department of State. (2016). *U.S. Advisory Council on Human Trafficking annual report 2016*. Washington, DC: U.S. Government Printing Office.

van der Kolk, B. (2005). Developmental trauma disorder: Toward a rational diagnosis for children with complex trauma histories. *Psychiatric Annals, 35*(5), 401–408.

van Heugten-van der Kloet, D., & van Heugten, T. (2015). The classification of psychiatric disorders according to DSM-5 deserves an internationally standardized psychological test battery on symptom level. *Frontiers in Psychology, 6*, 1108. https://doi.org/10.3389/fpsyg.2015.01108.

Weijers, D., & Jarden, A. (2017). Wellbeing policy: An overview. In M. Slade, L. Oades, & A. Jarden (Eds.), *Wellbeing, recovery and mental health* (pp. 35–45). Cambridge, UK: Cambridge University Press.

White, M. (1995). *Re-authoring lives*. Adelaide: Dulwich Centre Publications.

White, M. (2004). Working with people who are suffering the consequences of multiple trauma: A narrative perspective. *The International Journal of Narrative Therapy and Community Work, 2004*(1), 45–76.

Wilkerson, I. (2020). *Caste: The origins of our discontent*. New York: Random House.

Wolper, C. (2015). Joy DeGruy discusses post traumatic slave syndrome, historical omissions. *Daily Collegian*. Retrieved 23 October 2020 from https://www.collegian.psu.edu/news/campus/article_0286fad6-b33e-11e4-be9b-a75ceec12486.html

World Health Organization. (1948). *Summary report on proceedings minutes and final acts of the International Health Conference held in New York from 19 June to 22 July 1946,* Official Records of WHO No. 2, p16. New York: United Nations.

World Health Organization. (2009). *Changing cultural and social norms supportive of violent behavior*. Malta: World Health Organization Press.

Zimmerman, C., & Kiss, L. (2017). Human trafficking and exploitation: A global health concern. *PLoS Medicine, 14*(11), 1–11. https://doi.org/10.1371/journal.pmed.1002437.

Index

© Springer Nature Switzerland AG 2021
M. Chisolm-Straker, K. Chon (eds.), *The Historical Roots of Human Trafficking*,
https://doi.org/10.1007/978-3-030-70675-3